VIOLENCE AND RACISM IN FOOTBALL: POLITICS AND CULTURAL CONFLICT IN BRITISH SOCIETY, 1968–1998

Perspectives in Economic and Social History

Series Editors: *Robert E. Wright*
                    Andrew August

Titles in this Series

1 Migrants and Urban Change: Newcomers to Antwerp, 1760–1860
Anne Winter

2 Female Entrepreneurs in Nineteenth-Century Russia
Galina Ulianova

3 Barriers to Competition: The Evolution of the Debate
Ana Rosado Cubero

4 Rural Unwed Mothers: An American Experience, 1870–1950
Mazie Hough

5 English Catholics and the Education of the Poor, 1847–1902
Eric G. Tenbus

6 The World of Carolus Clusius: Natural History in the Making, 1550–1610
Florike Egmond

7 The Determinants of Entrepreneurship: Leadership, Culture, Institutions
José L. García-Ruiz and Pier Angelo Toninelli (eds)

8 London Clerical Workers, 1880–1914: Development of the Labour Market
Michael Heller

9 The Decline of Jute: Managing Industrial Change
Jim Tomlinson, Carlo Morelli and Valerie Wright

10 Mining and the State in Brazilian Development
Gail D. Triner

11 Global Trade and Commercial Networks: Eighteenth-Century Diamond Merchants
Tijl Vanneste

12 The Clothing Trade in Provincial England, 1800–1850
Alison Toplis

13 Sex in Japan's Globalization, 1870–1930: Prostitutes, Emigration and Nation Building
Bill Mihalopoulos

14 Financing India's Imperial Railways, 1875–1914
Stuart Sweeney

15 Energy, Trade and Finance in Asia: A Political and Economic Analysis
Justin Dargin and Tai Wei Lim

FORTHCOMING TITLES

Meat, Commerce and the City: The London Food Market, 1800–1855
Robyn S. Metcalfe

Welfare and Old Age in Europe and North America: The Development of Social Insurance
Bernard Harris (ed.)

The Economies of Latin America: New Cliometric Data
César Yáñez and Albert Carreras (eds)

Markets and Growth in Early Modern Europe
Victoria N. Bateman

Policing Prostitution, 1856–1886: Deviance, Surveillance and Morality
Catherine Lee

Respectability and the London Poor, 1780–1870: The Value of Virtue
Lynn MacKay

Narratives of Drunkenness: Belgium 1830–1914
An Vleugels

Crime and Community in Reformation Scotland:
Negotiating Power in a Burgh Society
Robert Falconer

Consuls and the Institutions of Global Capitalism
Ferry de Goey

VIOLENCE AND RACISM IN FOOTBALL: POLITICS AND CULTURAL CONFLICT IN BRITISH SOCIETY, 1968–1998

BY

Brett Bebber

Routledge
Taylor & Francis Group

LONDON AND NEW YORK

First published 2012 by Pickering & Chatto (Publishers) Limited

Published 2016 by Routledge
2 Park Square, Milton Park, Abingdon, Oxfordshire OX14 4RN
711 Third Avenue, New York, NY 10017, USA

First issued in paperback 2015

Routledge is an imprint of the Taylor & Francis Group, an informa business

© Taylor & Francis 2012
© Brett Bebber 2012

BRITISH LIBRARY CATALOGUING IN PUBLICATION DATA

Bebber, Brett.
Violence and racism in football: politics and cultural conflict in British society,
1968–98. – (Perspectives in economic and social history)
1. Soccer hooliganism – Great Britain – History – 20th century. 2. Soccer –
Political aspects – Great Britain – History – 20th century. 3. Racism in sports
– Great Britain – History – 20th century.
I. Title II. Series
302.3'3–dc22

ISBN-13: 978-1-138-66180-6 (pbk)
ISBN-13: 978-1-8489-3266-1 (hbk)
Typeset by Pickering & Chatto (Publishers) Limited

CONTENTS

Acknowledgements   ix
List of Figures   xi

Introduction: Sport, Politics and History in Post-War Britain   1

Part I: Violence and Politics in British Football
    1 An Introduction to Football Violence: Context, Community and
       Conflict   19
    2 Moral Anxieties, National Mythologies and Football Violence   39

Part II: The Total Policy of Containment
    3 Violent Environments: Physical Space, Discipline and Football Disorder   69
    4 Police and the State: Tactics, Networks and the Development of
       Football Policing   97
    5 Stretching Punishment: The State, Law and Order, and Threatening
       the Spectator   123

Part III: Racism and Cultural Conflict in British Football
    6 The Football Front: Neo-Fascist and Anti-Fascist Politics in Football,
       1977–85   147
    7 'Ten Years behind the Times': Racism and Anti-Racism in Football,
       1986–98.   175
    8 'A Different Set of Rules': Black Footballers, Anti-Racism and
       Whiteness   205
Conclusion: Legacies of Violence in British Football   231

Notes   237
Bibliography   269
Index   281

ACKNOWLEDGEMENTS

This book was written the help of many who offered their time and analysis. First and foremost, I would like to thank Laura Tabili, whose patient and wise guidance helped several of the better analyses in this book to flourish. David Ortiz and Susan Crane also helped shepherd early thoughts for the book and provided thoughtful suggestions for improvement. I would also like to thank Douglas Weiner and Kevin Gosner, who provided excellent training and inspiration across both geographical and conceptual boundaries. Elena Jackson-Albarrán, Julia Hudson-Richards, and Ziad Abi Chakra worked several drafts of chapters, offering both helpful writing tips and well-needed respite from the rigors of finishing the dissertation. Gracious financial support was given by the Social and Behavioral Sciences Research Institute at the University of Arizona, the Department of History, and the Barbara Payne Robinson, Edwin S. Turville, and Richard A. Cosgrove Funds.

I also benefitted from perspicacious counsel and collegial warmth at Presbyterian College, where many provided support while marshalling the final product. Rob Holyer and Anita Gustafson deserve thanks for their support of the project. I also received funding from the Faculty Development Committee to present early findings at a variety of conferences. Lastly, Dean Thompson was a kind editor and friend.

The generous people at Pickering & Chatto were both patient and helpful, including Daire Carr and Eleanor Hooker. I also benefited from the anonymous reviewers they commissioned, who helped the final product immensely. In the archives, Judy Vaknin at the Runnymede Collection was kind enough to provide lengthy access as well as all of the support necessary to find what I sought, and much more. Lucy Johnson, through her considerate graciousness, afforded me the opportunity to finish collecting documents at archives in London. Ben DeSpain and William Schanbacher offered the best comradeship in the world of ideas.

Finally, the most sweeping praise goes to my wife, Emily, and daughters, Elliot and Quinn, who provided time away from a wonderful family in order to finish.

LIST OF FIGURES

Figure 2.1: Cartoon by Ronald Carl Giles depicting Manchester United
Supporters' Club, *Daily Express*, 12 September 1974   58

Figure 3.1: Cartoon by Bernard Cookson depicting Denis Howell and
deterrents to pitch invasions, *Evening Standard*, 29 April 1974   86

Figure 3.2: Cartoon by Roy Ullyett depicting fan catapults, *Daily Express*,
24 May 1974   86

Figure 3.3: Drawing of pitch defence in Home Office files, undated   88

Figure 6.1: National Front advertisement on pamphlet, undated   157

Figure 7.1: West Ham Anti-Fascists logo   196

Figure 7.2: Chelsea Anti-Fascists logo   196

Figure 8.1: Paul 'Delroy' Ntende on cover of Roy of the *Rovers Monthly*,
2 (October 1993)   227

Figure 8.2: Photograph of Pelé and Bobby Moore, 7 June 1970   227

INTRODUCTION: SPORT, POLITICS AND HISTORY IN POST-WAR BRITAIN

Due to their public and publicized nature, sporting events have been recognized increasingly as venues in which broader social struggles have been reproduced and redefined.[1] Examining violence and racism in British football shows that from the late 1960s anxieties about race politics, class relations and state repression were represented and contested through violence and racist aggression at football matches. Class violence and racial abuse in football not only reflected broader cultural struggles and fractured social relationships in post-war Britain, but also produced new social anxieties and political questions. The state and leading political authorities responded to the presence of violence and racisms in one of the nation's central cultural institutions by re-examining policing and disciplinary policies for working-class citizens.

Rather than examining football per se, my principal aim is to investigate how this distinct cultural milieu became a site for the reproduction and performance of racial and class tensions, masculinity and racist violence. The environment of British football serves as an aperture through which to reassess the fundamental social and cultural processes within late modern British society, as well as the way politicians, lawmakers and grass-roots organizations approached them. Evidence will show that social conflict, allegedly eliminated by the post-war social democratic compromise, re-emerged in cultural contests over physical space and policing in football stadiums. Class discourses and practices resurfaced in football conflicts as global economic crises and retrenchment of social welfare apparently betrayed post-war social democratic promises. My research in recently released government documents shows that politicians and police authorities consistently met violence with their own repressive measures, escalating conflict and ignoring its relationship to larger social fissures. State authorities developed violent environments and exceedingly restrictive policing measures intended to discourage partisan activities by working-class youth and sanitize a growing leisure industry. Doing so involved the state, the press, football club administrations and fans in a battle of representation over football's meanings, jeopardizing the British national mythology of gentlemanly conduct and multi-cultural harmony.

Overt social discord from the 1970s onward coincided with the emergence of prominent black footballers, who became subject to racial abuse by spectators and discrimination within football clubs. From the late 1980s, racism against black players prompted anti-racist measures continuous with those used previously against football violence, again exacerbating rather than remedying the situation. Throughout the period, British football became a cultural location that several groups recognized as a venue for the contestation and manipulation of racial and class conflict: it captured the attention of the Home Office and high-ranking government officials, attracted neo-fascist nationalist parties, spawned several grass-roots anti-racist organizations, and garnered extensive national and international press coverage. In sum, the football milieu not only reflected social tensions occurring on local and national levels, but produced its own political conflicts, prompting widespread debates about social conflict, violence and racisms in post-colonial British society.

Historiography: Examining State Violence and Football Conflict

This research constitutes a divergence from existing approaches to state violence and football fan partisanship by sociologists, anthropologists and historians of post-war violence. Studies of state violence in the post-war era have concentrated on Britain's foreign interactions or decolonization. Caroline Elkins's recent study of the state's brutal oppression of the Mau Mau in Kenya provided one example of the state's willingness to engage in violence against its own subjects.[2] Analyses of the state's response to violence among its citizens, especially racial violence and the generation of moral panics, has received some analytical attention as well, concluding that the media and the state produced discourses which perpetuated social conflict on all levels.[3] This work builds on existing studies of moral anxiety and state violence by analysing the reciprocating violent formations within British football. Evidence will demonstrate that British government agencies and local police responded to expressions of social dissatisfaction by creating violent environments, instituting repressive police measures and extending sentencing measures. Rather than examining the social fractures which conditioned the emergence of violence in football, these agents demonized young working-class men and enacted violence against their own citizens, effectively renewing class conflicts through regulatory aggression. This episode in state violence will reveal where social democratic resolutions to conflict between working-class citizens and government failed and how state authorities violated their purported assurances to protect and provide for working-class British citizens.

Asking questions about football violence builds on but also departs from over three decades of study into the origins of social violence within this environment.[4] Commentators on football disorder have addressed the phenomenon of violence and aggression from different perspectives and through diverse theoretical approaches in what has become a massive body of literature.[5] Early researchers attempted to determine the causes of spectators' violence in an effort to minimize its incidence, and in certain cases, contributed to government policy discussions about the phenomenon. Sociologists used surveys, interviews with fans and newspaper reports to detail the long history of sports violence and its prevalence among 'rough' working-class men resisting the 'civilizing' imperative.[6] This 'figurational' approach addressed outbursts as a 'quest for excitement' within the constraining civilizing processes of modern society.[7] Social psychologists perceived football violence as a psychological reaction to boredom and a need to invigorate social relationships through the search for 'felt arousal' through violent interaction.[8] Sports anthropologists have entered the academic debate on violence and identity through participant observation.[9] Their ethnographies showed that specificities of cultural identity formation and sociological interaction among groups encouraged violence as an expression of social cohesion and community loyalty.[10] These researchers have effectively shown how football violence, because of its deep associations with group identity, partisan devotion, aggressive masculinity and resistance to authority, cannot be easily eradicated.[11]

This book represents a departure from previous studies of football violence in three ways. First, rather than further interrogating the origins of fan subjectivities or the group dynamics of social violence, this study looks at the ways in which the British state contributed to cycles of violence through directing policies against football spectators. As one historian phrased it, football violence 'remains important to any study of this period because it dominated the internal politics of football and brought the game more closely in contact than ever before with the government and the law'.[12] Analysing the role of politicians and state agencies in coordinating responses to football violence fills a gaping hole in previous research on the topic.[13] As the following chapters demonstrate, government and police authorities attempted a total policy of containment through a variety of institutional, legal and architectural means. Limiting spectators' mobility and increasing police powers reflected politicians' willingness to use violence against its working-class citizens. The first part of this study analyses how the state constructed normative discourses of class and gender which labelled working-class football spectators as deviant, brutish, belligerent and unmanly, and thus legitimated violent actions against them throughout the 1970s and 1980s. In the second part of the book I engage government and police records to reveal the critical role government ministers played in coordinating national police policies, architectural innovations and sentencing procedures for football spectators. While criminologists and sociologists have looked at the content of some official reports, none have analysed their political construction or their practical application and its outcomes.[14] My evidence demonstrates that Labour and Conservative politicians attempted to address larger, politically volatile social anxieties about law and order through consistency and efficiency in implementing policies against football spectators.

Second, analysing violent interactions between the state, police and football spectators requires contextualizing and historicizing the emergence of football violence within contemporaneous social and economic conditions of British society. Early Marxist interpretations attempted to explain spectators' violence through the lens of class and masculinity. Ian Taylor explained early manifestations of violence as a display of discontent among working-class men attempting to restore democratic control over a commercializing industry.[15] His later research also suggested that football disorder acted as release for working-class citizens alienated by the socio-economic and political dispossession experienced under Conservative regimes in the early 1980s.[16] John Clarke and Stuart Hall also suggested that violent subcultures in football reflected the need to reclaim community within fractured class relationships through activities such as group violence.[17] More recently, these ideas have been complemented by Alessandro Portelli, who attributed football violence, at least in part, to the development of a 'culture of poverty', brought on by a lack of participation in middle-class social institutions, an internalized sense of social marginalization and a generalized feeling of powerlessness and inferiority, especially in relation to the affluence of middle-class lives.[18]

Though some have challenged the idea that all violent offenders were from working-class backgrounds, police records analysed here and elsewhere support the fact that a majority of rowdy supporters during the 1960s and 1970s were young, white labourers.[19] As a review of arrest records shows in Chapter 5, nearly all arrested supporters were workers from various occupations, and were often fined according to what they could afford when sentenced by magistrates. In addition, most were under the age of twenty-five, and many were under the age of eighteen. Previous studies of Metropolitan Police records found that nearly 70 per cent of those charged with football-related offences were manual workers, 12 per cent were unemployed, and another 10 per cent were schoolboys.[20] Another study found that even as late as the 1980s, 91.5 per cent of employed offenders worked in manual occupations.[21] Though one group of ethnographic researchers working in the late 1980s and 1990s noted that many middle-class groups of supporters engaged in violence, as evidenced by the highly stylized and expensive outfits worn by Casuals during the period, these records revealed statistics in a much later period, nearly thirty years after football violence emerged from concrete social and economic circumstances in Britain.[22] Furthermore, most politicians and the public believed that most offenders were young working-class men, leading to moralizing discourses about the corrupting forces of degenerative youths, newfound working-class affluence and national decline explored in Chapter 2.

This book builds on the interpretations that stress the leading role of economic and cultural factors by providing concrete documentary evidence of the relationship between contemporary political and cultural anxieties, politicians and the state, and the football setting.[23] Rather than imagining a relationship between the interior football world and the exterior social and cultural context in which football acted as a microcosm of society, reflecting the problems and possibilities of the British nation, this work illuminates how meanings and cultural productions embodied in football also had effects on political decisions and social anxieties. Instead of treating events in football only as symptoms of broader social and cultural processes, it approaches the relevant historical actors as active agents shaping discourses about violence and racism. Surely, to some degree, debates within British football reflected broader social conversations about post-coloniality, nationhood and migration in British society. However, the representations of race, class and gender contested within football did not simply mirror extant meanings and discussions. The political and academic debates over football violence, and later football racism, became deeply enmeshed in actual political contests and 'the logics of particular political spaces'.[24] That is, discussions of the contemporary meanings of racism and anti-racism, violence and anti-violence, and the vulnerability and deterioration of Britain's youth culture, contributed to and produced new political and social tensions as much as they reflected them. The bulk of the first and second parts of this book explore the ways in which political authorities took notice of football's popularity in the post-war period and aimed to sanitize the sport as an activity representative of the purported genteel character of the nation itself.

Furthermore, in many of the documents and voices examined here, historical actors referenced wider conflicts within British society when explaining their participation in violence, racial abuse, and anti-racist movements. How these actors conceptualized this socio-political context, and the relationship between British society and events in football, reveals that they often understood problems in football to represent larger social and cultural patterns. These historical actors thought themselves to be participating in the manipulation of the British social landscape through their involvement in football. Spectators often attributed their actions to the failures of successive post-war administrations and the conflicts evident in late capitalist and post-colonial societies: economic depression, scarce housing and employment, race riots, immigration and social dislocation. Such articulations made football a particularly vivid lens through which to view difficulties of working and living in Britain since the late 1960s.

Third, this study attempts to show how the state contributed to conditions which made catastrophic football disasters probable through the extension of political control over private leisure and the sporting industry. Much of the academic attention paid to football violence has been catalysed by the intermittent occasion of large-scale disasters in football stadiums producing numerous fatalities. Disasters in Glasgow in 1971, in Heysel in 1985 and in Hillsborough in 1989 resulted in fatalities due to crushing, panic and asphyxiation in tightly packed spaces. Resultant public concerns about football violence, stadium management and the viability of the football industry in England forced the government to respond to each disaster with a full inquiry, a political tool aiming to ease fears and provide practical solutions.[25] Scholars have blamed poor stadium management, deficient design and the lack of government responsibility for working-class well-being for these horrific outcomes.[26] Chapters 3 and 4 will show that each disaster produced new governmental and police motivation to refine policing and management techniques and create new security networks. Therefore, each incident catalysed further discipline in the repetitive cycle of stricter restrictions on the activities and bodies of working-class spectators, paradoxically perpetuating the very physical environments producing such tragedies. In fact, the term 'disaster' proved entirely inappropriate upon close examination. As the evidence will show, government and police officials were aware of the potentially dangerous consequences of the piecemeal strategies they implemented and yet chose to enact them. Football disasters did not materialize from nowhere but proved to be the result of several factors – including fans' violence, the construction of restrictive and aggressive environments, and the poor state of football stadiums – many of which government officials failed to resolve although they knew about them.

Analysing Racism and Anti-Racism in the Post-War Era

In addition to contributing to studies of football and state violence, the third part of the project, which addresses the integration of black players into British football, also contributes to scholarly debates about racism and anti-racism in post-war society. Academic investigations of racism in post-war Britain can be categorized or divided along several axes, though any attempt to do so only provides an illusory organization to a wealth of intersecting studies.[27] Early sociological investigations responded to the growing number of black migrants and the emergence of racial conflict within British cities in the 1950s and 1960s. The creators of the 'race relations' debate often conceptualized the growing number of black migrants to Britain as a problem of assimilation. Early analyses suggested that time, acclimation and proximity would ameliorate prejudice by native white Britons and thus postulated the problem of 'race relations' as a problem of black presence.[28] Critics of this paradigm pointed out its failure to recognize the multifaceted constitution of social fractures and racial oppression within British society, especially as conditioned by imperial and post-colonial contexts, as well as ethnic mobilization against racial prejudice.[29] As the sociology and histories of race and racism developed, researchers engaged in theoretical and conceptual debates about racisms in Britain and the interconnections between analyses of race and class. Such debates tested the limits of neo-Weberian and neo-Marxist interpretations of data and the meaning of the notions of 'race' and 'racism' in contemporary political contexts.[30] The work of cultural studies enthusiasts engaged the ways in which 'race' and 'black' lives became sites of political and social struggle. They recognized that the contested conceptualizations of race could be the launching point for mobilization by groups of historical actors with drastically different political goals, such as the state, minority communities and nationalist political parties. How race and ethnicity came to be entwined in collective identities and political opposition through processes of social construction occupied groups like the Centre for Contemporary Cultural Studies in Birmingham.[31]

Like debates within sociology and cultural studies, my work seeks to decentre, destabilize and disrupt socially constructed categories while understanding their political contestation. However, it will pursue these goals while integrating concrete historical evidence of practices and activities that conditioned the language the historical actors used, and discuss how those practices and discourses changed over time. From the mid-1970s football provided a public arena for the discussion of racial issues. It is the central argument of this book that British football evolved into a contested cultural site where several social groups – including government ministers, Labour and Conservative politicians, police authorities, nationalist political parties, and grass-roots anti-racist movements – sought to manipulate the British social landscape through the sport. Discourses of violence and racism developed around British football which contributed to ongoing debates about essentialized 'Britishness', masculinity and propriety, and racism and anti-racism. These discourses played a vital role in educating the nation about the roles of violence, racial abuse and anti-racist political action in British society. Discussions of race in football acquired their particular content as social groups constructed definitions of 'racist' and 'anti-racist' that informed subsequent discourses about race politics in Britain outside the football environment.

The largest body of historical literature on post-war racism has focused on immigration policy and citizenship in post-war British politics, and the government's various efforts to balance labour demands with restrictions against entry.[32] These studies of high politics and policy-making added to our understanding of how official definitions of race in government rhetoric constricted immigrant livelihoods. This project aims to show how similar processes of aversion to black migrants occurred in specific cultural locations and social dialogues outside of high politics. It will complement these studies by demonstrating how political rhetoric was transferred and distorted in specific extra-political sites, particularly British football. Ideas of race, nation and masculinity derived from high politics were expressed through violence and racial abuse at football matches. Rather than evaluate language and discourse apart from social context, my project will explore how values informed, structured and grew out of concrete cultural practices. I propose to read social relationships back into discussions of discourse and imagine a wider field of practical and discursive tensions in football culture, uniting structural and discursive analysis through the practices of social and cultural history.

Another fruitful avenue of research has centred on the cultural production of 'Britishness' and belonging through the colony/metropole relationship. Though this binary was permeable and protean, it reflected the ways in which common-sense notions of British belonging and imperial culture saturated many Britons' lives and coloured their articulations of difference.[33] The evolution of legal nationality policy in the twentieth century reflected the state's divisive construction of racial difference in the metropole in response to colonial migrants and workers.[34] Colonial domestic lives also reflect the tension between nationality, race and gender.[35] In British football, the increasing number of black players challenged Britishness and provided opportunities for politicians and political interest groups to redefine and challenge existing ideas of nationalism and belonging in both England and Britain. But, as many historians have pointed out, 'Britishness' and national identities of the four nations were not always congruent.[36] Professional football reflected this axiom. For example, sports historians have revealed that football rivalries in Ireland and Scotland instigated racial and sectarian antipathies.[37] And yet state intervention into the football industry was largely carried out by English offices, though Scottish and Welsh police authorities and football clubs chimed in when asked. Admittedly, the evidence for this study is largely based in major cities in England, though conflicts at Welsh and Scottish clubs generated police and government documentation analysed here. However, nearly all of them discussed football as a *British* sport in *British* society. Therefore, this project analyses how discourses of violence and racism in football demonstrated government ministers' commitment to maintaining bourgeois British ideals, and how they capitalized on social movements in football to inculcate socially constructed British values. Assuredly, discourses of Britishness in football were dominated by English middle-class notions of belonging and propriety, as other studies of national and imperial identities have shown.[38] But British football, first through the problem of football violence in the 1970s, and again in discussions of football racism in the 1990s, provided spaces for historical actors to express and promote values of masculine decency, respect and discipline inherent to notions of Britishness experienced throughout the four nations. Understanding how different groups of supporters, the press and the state perceived these myths and how they functioned as forms of solidarity – and how they were challenged by violence and racism in football – will illuminate the links between British nationalism, popular racism and masculine values.

Finally, this study will reveal how football violence and football racism, usually depicted as two separate phenomena, were intimately linked.[39] First, racial abuse materialized out of a wide range of disruptive and violent practices at football matches. Evidence will show that spectators, both within and outside formal neo-fascist movements, practiced racial abuse as a response to concerns about thriving black footballers within the sport and prevalent social issues such as immigration and job competition outside of it. Racisms in football reflected the emotionality and competition embodied in violent interactions between rival groups of fans. Second, inasmuch as racisms in the sport developed from the same historical trajectory as football violence, anti-racism constituted an additional element of an expanded moral repertoire constructed to counteract football violence in the late 1960s and 1970s. As football violence emerged, state authorities instituted a variety of practical and rhetorical strategies to reclaim football as a site of order and harmony representative of the British nation itself. Later, as racism in the game overshadowed concerns about violence, similar normative processes of sanitization and repossession materialized from several branches of government and the public to protect Britain's image of harmonious multiculturalism. Football anti-racism became another form of institutionalized public order against customary expressions of social discontent, becoming representative of larger social fractures in British society and eliciting local political action and national political debate.

As the third part of this book will demonstrate, understanding the links between football anti-racism and anti-violence strategies implicated them in earlier historical manifestations of state violence and gendered standards perpetrated during the 1960s and 1970s. Though expressions of racism had been occurring at football matches since the 1970s, public awareness and political mobilization against the problem did not happen on a significant scale until the late 1980s. When they did appear, anti-racist organizations embodied practices and political ideologies present in state discourses about anti-violence decades earlier. Primarily, continuities of violence and gender exclusion marked the evolution of anti-racist action from anti-violence strategies. First, working-class spectators championed violence as a means to combat racism, advocating aggressive authority to combat unwanted behaviours. Both anti-fascist and anti-racist organizations' practices resembled the government's earlier utilization of intemperate policing and sought to revive the power of threatening violence to deter racial abuse. Second, the encouragement and continuation of community 'self-policing' as a suitable form of correction for the football environment emerged in anti-racist movements as it had previously in anti-violence campaigns.[40]

Football authorities and local police constables consistently encouraged community policing by individual members of spectating collectives, though these measures usually proved unsuccessful. Anti-racist spectators readily assumed the role of community policemen within stadiums, threatening punishment to perpetrators of racist activities. Third, just as violent environments made women's participation in football spectatorship subject to codes of masculine conduct, so too did the perpetuation of threatening violence within anti-racism movements. Women were almost always excluded from political participation against racism in football because violence perpetuated environments which discouraged women's involvement. Finally, while working-class violence endangered British national mythologies of peaceful class interaction and successful social welfare, racisms in football challenged prevalent ideas of multi-ethnic harmony and cultural integration. Both sets of myths required constant maintenance. Football, as the most publicized and popular British sport, came to represent these ideas of the nation. Politicians and sectors of the public capitalized on the opportunities violence and racism offered, imbuing football with new responsibilities to construct viable, normative sets of behaviour that reflected ideas of Britishness. These values clearly reflected gendered and racial understandings of what constituted proper masculine conduct in the setting of Britain's established working-class recreation, even as working-class men lost control over this site of leisure.

Rethinking Sports History

One of the primary purposes of this project is to complicate the existing narratives about the role of sport in society and its political utilization. Contemporary academic and popular understandings of football in Britain buttress ideas of its central role in British mythology and multicultural nation-building, from its role in education in schools and county pitches to the unfolding dramas between national sides. These latent associations always have a political trace, and the complex meanings infused in football in Britain need to be untangled and laid bare. The political investment in sport, where government agents have utilized sport to build favour and how sport figured in the complex webs of contemporary political and social relationships, needs to be recognized.[41] For instance, while the 'sanitization' of football aimed first at removing violence, it only did so through the creation of a wide web of violent punishments and the creation of restricted and oppressive public spaces. Rather than assuming football's natural role in anti-racist efforts as a means of social education without scrutiny, a better understanding of the historical and political development of anti-racism in football will reveal how various fan groups drew on previous state discourses of violence and aggression to construct an anti-racist platform. The assumption that football can be effectively used to publicize anti-racist discourses and implement new anti-violent mentalities will be challenged.

Though these assumptions may be utilizable in the short term, they also incorporated messages and meanings which went beyond a Manichaean scheme of antagonist/protagonist, violence/anti-violence and racist/anti-racist. This book attempts to demystify the complicated figurations in British football and its associations with violent social conduct and narratives of racism and anti-racism. This project is not a wholesale apology for working-class fans, but rather an exploration of the oppressive power disparities they faced and an analysis of the historical meanings state responses and fan movements generated. Spectators' adherence to violent codes of conduct rendered them culpable in creating environments of opposition and aggression.[42] Reading police reports and witness statements of these violent encounters revealed not only the practices police used, but the terror and fear instigated by spectator aggression and unwanted violence. And as the following pages will show, the state wanted to respond quickly to reinstitute security and safety in a very popular leisure arena, but found their responses ineffective, ill-informed and delayed by political expediency. But a coordinated policy to remove football violence ultimately stripped many football supporters of their civil liberties, whether or not they participated in violent conduct, to perpetuate a myth of security and propriety in British football.[43] In addition, the simplified and violent messages associated with football anti-racism movements betrayed the historical legacy imparted to them by government regimes that promoted violence and the creation of violent spaces as the means to solve problems of working-class aggression. Therefore, one must critically engage all angles and positions within the complex webs of power relationships constructed among football spectators and their governments. Inasmuch as sport will be interrogated, so too will assumptions about the purportedly beneficial roles of violence, anti-violence and anti-racism in British society.

Periodization and Sources

The book consists of three sections. The main evidence for Parts I and II is comprised of Home Office and Department of Environment documents composed from the late 1960s through the 1970s. Both agencies collected a wide variety of materials relating to football disorder, police activities, architectural changes and financial provision. These records have not been available to the public in the past due to the standard thirty-year embargo on British government records. My research period ended in 2007, allowing me to analyse recently released records from the mid-1960s to 1977. I also consulted records on earlier disasters and files composed by the Home Office in the 1940s and 1950s of isolated cases of football hooliganism. These materials reveal government ministers' activities and agendas on British football violence, as well as the politics behind the state's coordinated response.

The sources for Part III of the study come from a wide variety of document repositories and cover two key periods when neo-fascism, racism and anti-racism in football became politically prominent: the late 1970s and the late 1980s onward. For the most part, the analysis of these processes was culled from a collection of fanzines, newspaper and magazine articles, and organizational materials from *Kick It Out!* and *Football Unites, Racism Divides*. I also examined a wide variety of fascist and anti-fascist publications to illuminate the attitudes expressed by these social groups and the political practices they participated in, especially as they related to British football. Scrutiny of this diverse body of evidence has proven critical in grasping not only issues directly related to football, but enabling the much wider examination of how football figured in discussions of racism and violence in British society since the mid-1960s.

The standard binary between primary and secondary sources does not always prove fruitful in this episode of contemporary social study and recent history. Academics and journalists commented on the happenings within British football as the sequence of events continued to unfold, making the definitive separation of primary and secondary evidence untenable. Academics contributed to prevalent discourses about football violence and racism within the game, and in many cases worked with government commissions and fan-based associations to provide policy recommendations that directly affected political decisions.[44] In addition, football fans in representative associations also pursued academic research that contributed to ongoing discussions of the issues at hand.[45] Therefore, the multiple voices which created the evidentiary resources for this project cannot always be neatly categorized. The discourses and texts analysed here, be they created by academics or politicians, influenced the direction of social policy and public discussion of football-related issues. I treat all of these sources with care, providing background for each cache of evidence while recognizing the fickle distinction between secondary and primary texts in this topic of study.

I have adopted a critical analytic approach rather than a chronological evaluation or a total methodological project based on a predetermined research model. Chronology is important in understanding the development of historical trends and transitions within this specific story, as well as the larger surrounding contexts. I have attempted to provide chronological cues while maintaining an analytical approach that spans both space and time to indicate more widespread political and legislative developments as well as agency attitudes. Therefore, chapters have been organized topically, and use primary evidence created by a variety of social actors, from politicians to supporters' clubs to football authorities.

Exploring Race, Class and Power

Finally, any contemporary investigation into the historical and situational specificities of race and racism must recognize the relative autonomy of 'race' as an ideological and ontological concept while simultaneously appreciating its intersection with other categories of analysis in the complex constitution of power relations: class, gender, sex, age and religion, among others. That is, the concept of race cannot be blindly reduced to the dialogic struggles of material economics. Nor can it be separated from its involvement in the complicated and interconnected disparities of power which revolve around multiple conceptual axes.[46] Furthermore, attempts to use such contested terminology also must be continually undermined. The conceptual content of terms such as 'race', 'racism', 'class', 'gender' and 'immigrant' must not only be qualified but consistently questioned. The third part of this book, in large part, attempts to clarify how football provided an opportunity for different groups of social actors to give meaning to discussions of these terms.

The terminology 'black' and 'white' will be used carefully for several reasons, and these terms must be qualified. My use of the term 'black' includes anyone of Afro-Caribbean and Asian origin, though this general term should not obscure the variations in culture and identity under this umbrella. The term 'white' includes those not of Afro-Caribbean, African or Asian origin. The emphasis on origin proved the foundation for spectators and journalists' reformulated creation of an imagined black 'race'. The fans mapped this concept onto their grouping of Afro-Caribbean footballers by recognizing appearance cues that indicated non-British origins, such as variations in skin colour or accent, and discriminated accordingly. Mapping 'race' onto a group of individuals essentialized those individuals and assumed a homogenous concept of 'blackness', and its opposite, 'whiteness'. 'Race' as a differentiating factor has always been a figment of imagination, and despite many misconceived attempts, eludes any sound definition rooted in biology.[47] The changing conceptual terrain and constant reinvention of 'race' to fit that terrain allows a continuous genesis in any given society.[48] Therefore the distinctions made in this project follow those created by the subjects and actors themselves, and reflect the mental and ideological divisions they produced and reformulated constantly, though the analysis continuously questions the validity and stability of their usage.

Questions about the development of conceptualizations of race and racism within the public arena drive this investigation of the connections between racism and football. In particular, how and when does racism become an important political symbol and socially acceptable topic? For whom? In what linguistic and rhetorical frameworks are race and racism discussed in different pockets of society? What role do racist political ideologies and anti-racist organizations play in determining the saliency and content of conversations about racism in British society? Evidence will show that from the mid-1980s onward football became a central cultural and institutional site where ideas about racism and society could be enacted and debated. British football became an educative resource for anti-racist groups and central political bodies like the Commission for Racial Equality, and at the same time proved a fertile arena for neo-fascist recruiters. Analysis of the marriage of race and football offers compelling insights into the productive and discursive capacities of debates about race in the late twentieth century. Furthermore, the problem of racism in football, unlike political discussions of social policy, has been politicized publicly and discussed in astonishingly forthright terms. Critical analysis of the historical and ideological processes by which race came to be understood as a 'political symbol' or 'nodal point', a transition which some sociologists have labelled the 'racialization of political life and social relations', has been an increasingly fruitful area of social research.[49]

Paul Gilroy has argued that immigration, race riots and other episodes like the Salman Rushdie affair offer politicians and other social actors the opportunity to discuss race politics indirectly, without recourse to the language of race or conversations about racism.[50] In contrast, football's anti-racism campaigns became open public arenas where many could discuss racism and anti-racism without coded language. Chapter 6 will demonstrate that anti-racists gave particular content to the characterizations of 'racist' and 'anti-racist', assigning sets of behaviour which defined each label. They delineated regulated behavioural practices which could be easily defined as acceptable or unacceptable within contemporary expectations for public order at football matches. Analysis of how these terms became associated with this content will reveal that these characterizations oversimplified complex networks and fields of power relations among nationalist parties, non-fascist racists, and anti-racist supporters.

Finally, in the past sociologists have loosely utilized the term 'hooliganism' to encompass a wide range of ill-defined behaviours and practices, and used the label 'hooligan' to describe the actors who perpetrated them.[51] I avoid all use of the term here, except when describing the ways in which historical actors characterized spectators, to avoid perpetuating its negative connotations. Instead, I have used descriptive terms like 'disruptive', 'unruly' or 'rowdy' when discussing spectators whose behaviour challenged the regulating practices of others. In as many cases as possible, I describe their exact behaviours, including fighting, swaying, provoking the police and chanting, among others.

Outline of Chapters

The two chapters in Part I provide the background for later individualized analyses on violence and racism in the football setting. Chapter 1 explores the contexts and historical transitions that made an increase in football violence possible, while also delineating common forms of disorder. In the post-war period, football attendance provided a cheap, accessible form of leisure for working-class men and women, though women remained marginalized by prescribed forms of masculine conduct. From these communal experiences emerged increasing levels of organized social violence at football matches, a phenomenon known throughout the period of this study as 'football hooliganism'. In assessing both police reports and oral histories, the chapter explores the complex forms of disorder from several different perspectives. Rather than offer a single psychological or socio-economic cause for early football violence, I aim to provide local contextualization and historicization for the emergence of this peculiar phenomenon in the social and cultural struggles of post-war Britain.

The second chapter critically explores the moral anxieties constructed about and around football violence. I borrow the sociological concept of 'moral panics' to analyse the leading role played by political agents and police officers in sensationalizing football violence and demonizing those who perpetrated it. Government documents and correspondence reveal how national values of bourgeois propriety and classed paternalism imbued discourses about football violence. Several moral commentators, especially ministers in charge of sport, used various rhetorical strategies to harangue against the lawlessness, improper masculine conduct and moral degeneration they perceived in outbreaks of football disorder. These political and public expressions arranged a belittling discursive terrain where young working-class men were framed as criminal and animalistic while moral entrepreneurs offered the behavioural tonic to cure the 'hooligan' disease. These discourses justified the implementation of crowd control measures which paradoxically exacerbated rather than prevented violence. By breaking down the elements of the moral panic surrounding football violence, as well as investigating those who constructed such rhetoric, the complicated interstices within the construction of expressions of youth discrimination, implicit concepts of gender and class in national mythology, and the frameworks of moralizing oratory can be better understood.

Part II analyses the state's response to football violence. Each chapter looks at one of three component elements of the total policy of containment employed by politicians, police and football authorities to eradicate football violence. While much has been written about how commercialization and higher ticket prices constituted an attack on various fan groups, here I analyse how the practical implementation of spatial organization, policing strategies and threatening punishments directly targeted lively football spectatorship.[52] Using government files, Chapter 3 fleshes out the successive waves of political proposals meant to establish controlled and surveilled physical spaces within stadiums. The British government relentlessly endeavoured to institute disciplined and conditioned forms of football consumption through direct manipulation of the architectural environment. The chapter outlines the repressive manifestations of these policies as well as supporters' resistance to them.

In addition to physical divisions, the state also encouraged local police to apply combative and provoking regulation strategies that reinforced the aggressive characteristics of the football environment. Chapter 4 looks at how football provided a platform for both Labour and Conservative party members to extend violent and confrontational police tactics which aimed to demonstrate their commitment to law-and-order principles evident in both public and political discourses. Government inquiries shared information, considered new police approaches and arrest powers and developed sophisticated identification and communication systems that presaged the widespread implementation of closed-circuit television (CCTV) surveillance. Now subject to ever-increasing surveillance in highly disciplined and policed environments, spectators faced stringent punitive measures when apprehended. Chapter 5 analyses how government officials pressured magistrates' courts to consider new severe sentencing alternatives. As the state manipulated the mechanisms for punishment they continuously neglected the social and cultural background conditioning football violence, opting for expressions of authority rather than sustained efforts to address the origins of football violence.

In Part III, the focus shifts to the emergence of racisms and anti-racist movements in football. Chronologically, the scope of this section begins in the late 1970s and covers the next two decades. Topically, this section investigates the various responses to the emergence of successful black footballers. Chapter 6 examines how racial abuse and racial violence in the football environment was stimulated by fascist nationalist parties and their calculated demonstrations at football matches. The chapter locates fascist paper-selling and recruiting at local football stadiums within a wide range of political practices that proved somewhat effective for fringe nationalist parties in the key periods of the late 1970s and early 1990s. I also evaluate the materialization of anti-fascist fan groups which engaged in violent encounters with neo-fascists on a regular basis within contested football spaces. In the end, I attempt to come to some conclusions about the impact and legacy of fascist and anti-fascist groups on racisms and anti-racist social movements in football.

Chapter 7 looks at racism and anti-racism outside of fascist and nationalist influences. In some ways, this distinction between racial attitudes inside and outside the persuasion of fascism needs to be challenged. Previous studies have made the distinction in an attempt to discover the less overt forms of racial abuse in football which may have been obscured by the 'folk devil' of football fascism.[53] However, I aim to analyse prevalent forms of racial abuse and racial discrimination with an eye towards their significance in a post-colonial Britain riddled by controversies over immigration, race riots and competition for employment. Certainly, many fascists engaged in vitriolic commentary about these issues, and their influence on rhetorical and practical politics cannot be ignored. Some football specialists have disregarded fascist involvement as exceptional, but such outspoken opinions were always prevalent in discussions of racism in football. I also focus on the government and fans' reaction to racism and neo-fascism in football, noting the connections with previous efforts to sanitize football in the 1970s. In sum, early fan-based initiatives rekindled the threat of violence to address racism in an effort to purge football of its latest moral evil. National anti-racist movements also chose football as a highly publicized and usefully educative cultural institution through which to deploy widespread anti-racist messages. Both sets of actors oversimplified the structures and discourses of racism and anti-racism, providing an utilizable political success story that obfuscated indirect and inadvertent racisms.

The final chapter analyses the burden of multiple forms of racism and racial discrimination against black players. The development of 'whiteness' as the formation of imposed masculine behaviour within football imposed multiple normative expectations on black footballers. Analysing published interviews with black players reveal how they coped with pressures of propriety, loyalty and tempered aggression within the football environment. As racism became the primary moral concern within the football industry, anti-racist organizations advocated players as icons of gentility and acceptable anti-racist conduct. Such prescribed forms of behaviour recalled bourgeois standards of propriety, discipline and Britishness which precluded free modes of expression for black players in a challenging global market.

Overall, the evidence demonstrates that violent environments and state interventions into citizens' lives precipitated further acts of violence and racial abuse, occasioning conflicts that threatened to rupture the cultural fabric of local and national communities. Though football violence originated with fans' partisanships, the state's extension of control and discipline into football effectively exacerbated oppositional and aggressive environs within stadiums, and conditioned later grass-roots anti-racist movements. Just as football racisms grew out of football disorder generally, anti-racism developed from the impulse to maintain order and perpetuate national mythologies associated with British football. As the following analysis will show, the sport not only served as a window onto wider conflicts about morality, nationality, violence and racism, but also became a crucible of political and social anxieties which contributed to those contests and helped to define them.

PART I : VIOLENCE AND POLITICS IN BRITISH FOOTBALL

1 AN INTRODUCTION TO FOOTBALL VIOLENCE: CONTEXT, COMMUNITY AND CONFLICT

Throughout the 1950s and 1960s football attendance became a communal activity for working-class men and women, enriched by strong social networks and shared collective experiences. Football spectators gathered in multiple venues across Britain on the weekends to participate in customary activities that promoted specific values of locality, community and territoriality. Groups of violent youths that emerged from these informal social networks engaged in an increasingly large number of raucous and threatening activities throughout the late 1960s and 1970s. These disruptions ranged from cursing and taunting policemen to organized violent encounters between groups of opposing fans. Police reports afford the opportunity to examine not only the forms of disorder that spectators initiated, but also how the police framed their actions and responded to them. Using these sources, this chapter aims to contextualize British football violence and provide a background to the expansion of state control over this national sport. While providing a brief summary of broad historical transitions and social trends can be difficult, it will first provide social, economic and cultural contextual background. The second section recounts the forms of violence and disorder that British fans participated in, and the varied and conflicted responses towards their increasing incidence among many types of fans. This introduction to British football violence provides a background to the responses by the public, government agencies and local police authorities that will be examined in later chapters.

British Football Violence Contextualized

Several broad changes to British politics and society, and leisure culture specifically, gave way to the rise of football's popularity, as well as the violence that came to mark the sport from the mid-1960s. The relative affluence of British society in the 1950s and 1960s provided increased opportunities for sporting leisure and popular entertainment, and professional football became the mainstay of these weekend pursuits. Along with cinema attendance and seaside trips, football spectatorship developed into an accessible and widespread form of recreation.[1] Advances in British leisure received the full support of Clement Attlee's (1945–51) post-war administration. Attlee wanted to provide welfare and security for the British people that had been lacking since the interwar period. While this administration had no specific policy on sport, they did recognize the benefits of extending leisure and popular entertainment to British citizens. The proposed reconstruction of Britain's labour force and anticipation of full employment depended on balancing work with leisurely pursuits such as football spectatorship.[2]

Throughout the 1950s, programmes for physical education and participation proliferated, culminating in the establishment of the undersecretary position titled Minister for Sport in 1962 under the Conservatives, and the national Sports Council by Harold Wilson's Labour administration in 1966. Both major political parties promoted the extension of British sport to more participants, but also chartered research on perceived problems within British sporting culture.[3] Britain's second and more aggressive Minister for Sport, Denis Howell, oversaw the extension of state intervention into British football that will be discussed later. These developments resulted in skyrocketing interest in British sport, and football specifically, as a British tradition that provided not only opportunities for participation, but also for recreational and community-based football spectatorship. The marked interest that several post-war governments demonstrated in promoting grass-roots football participation linked directly to the widespread desire for the national team to succeed on the international stage. Throughout the post-war decades, with widespread media coverage and increased significance to the nation, 'football was probably more pervasive than ever before in British social and cultural life'.[4]

The intertwined interests of government and British football culminated in England's World Cup victory in 1966, arguably the world's greatest sporting achievement. The championship heralded Britain's return to the international stage after a period of decline. Defeats in sport throughout the 1950s mirrored Britain's international regression. In the first twenty years after the war, though post-war administrations had succeeded in returning affluence to British society for large segments of the population, they suffered international humiliation in the Suez Canal affair, the decolonization of Africa, and Europe's marginalization during the Cold War. England's victory in 1966 provided a symbolic but tangible sense of restoration of British superiority in both the sporting world and national politics.[5] Even the Labour Party capitalized on the victory, as Harold Wilson celebrated with the team on the balcony of the Royal Garden Hotel shortly after the match. This symbolic gesture was not only Wilson's attempt to garner political capital but also a projection of the change in fortunes for both British sport and British workers.[6]

Through the 1966 World Cup victory football became cemented as a primarily working-class bastion apart from other public school sports like cricket and rugby. England not only won the trophy, but also hosted the tournament, allowing more Britons exposure to football as a modern form of entertainment. It represented an improvement in fortunes for working-class spectators who closely identified with the team. The team itself had a particularly working-class feel to it: values of hard work and physical toil embodied in the English side won out over the flair and gusto of more talented global opposition. This construction of English playing 'style' as bullish and honest, constructed mostly by the media but reproduced elsewhere, represented values to which many working-class men related.[7] Football spectatorship at the local club level received a quick boost from the rise in national visibility and popularity of the sport. However, it became clear that some popular approaches to football spectatorship had changed from leisurely family recreation to stylized and fiercely loyal partisanships rooted in reinterpretations of working-class ideals. The marriage of working-class men and football continued, fuelled by new generations of supporters who grew up with the game.

Outside of sport, several shifts in the material and cultural realms of British life allowed for and perhaps encouraged increased levels of social violence by the mid-1960s, which often occurred within the sport by the end of the decade. Economic historians have claimed that prosperous national economies marked Europe for two decades from 1953, culminating in stagflation and fluctuating currency rates caused by the oil crisis of 1973.[8] Spurred by American investment and stable exchange rates managed by the European Payments Union and the International Monetary Fund, European economies neared full capacity.[9] Yet, the 'Age of Affluence' did not come to a full stop by 1973, but rather ground to a slow halt with consequences for most working- and middle-class Britons years earlier. Indeed, Britain's increase in social violence in football coincided with the beginnings of England's post-colonial economic decline.

Early successes in economic growth dovetailed with the post-war social democratic compromise. The Labour Party in Britain, like many European attempts at social democracy, fostered the management of a mixed-market economy, balancing private investment with state management of key resources and industries in a form of state-managed capitalism. Nationalization, centralized state planning and investment in industry pulled Britain's economy out of the post-war recession as both the Labour and the Conservative parties planned for full employment, living incomes, moderate wage raises, and the extension of social welfare services.[10] Health care, electricity, coal production and railway services all came under the development of the British state in a long period of state-supported economic growth. This prosperity also existed because successive government administrations effectively managed conflicts between labour representatives and the interests of capital until the mid-1960s, avoiding politically devastating strikes and crises of industrialization.

Yet, by this time, the side effects of constant economic growth gradually engulfed European nations, impelling Britain in particular towards decreasing government expenditure. Inflation afflicted working-class livelihoods in most of Western Europe as the money supply swelled beyond what was necessary for most national economies.[11] In November 1967, the devaluation of the pound pushed Harold Wilson's Labour administration to void the 'social contract' and decrease domestic spending by £716 million over the next two years.[12] Though the Labour Party had already removed Clause Four – the commitment of Labour representatives to nationalization of key industries for general welfare – in 1964, this retrenchment signalled a new era of social divestment. Roy Jenkins, Chancellor of the Exchequer at the time, imposed strict government expenditure restrictions and introduced several new taxes and levies as priority was given to balancing Britain's international deficit.[13] Labour effectively chose to maintain international capitalist relations rather than its promises of social democracy and public welfare. Because of these various impositions, British citizens, especially those in working-class households, began to feel the effects of intermittent periods of inflation and increasing costs of living since the mid-1960s. Britain's flagging economy created increased competition for jobs and estate housing, themes which, as will be shown, emerged in discussions about the origins of football violence. Concerns about economic opportunity coloured the political messages supporters espoused, which when coupled with increased local and territorial sentiments attached to football clubs, often conditioned increased levels of violence in football.

Concerns about economic competition also affected football supporters' approaches to the increasing number of both black Britons and black migrants in the professional ranks, producing social conflicts that often resulted in racisms and anti-immigration politics. As Part III of the book demonstrates, several interested parties used football in attempts to recreate the social landscape of Britain, with particular attentions to the racial homogeneity of sport and the wider society. These concerns must be contextualized within the broad range of emerging racial and anti-immigrant discourses of the post-colonial era. Enoch Powell's now infamous 'Rivers of Blood' speech in 1968 gave voice to a host of white concerns about the influx of migrants to British industrial cities. The Birmingham MP was responding to the ongoing debate about British immigration policy, a debate framed since 1945 in terms of national belonging, citizenship and legality.[14] Powell's linking of black people and criminality painted all migrants to

Britain as creatures of urban decay, a 'race apart' that threatened the very security of Britons' lives and the future development of the nation.[15] The speech capitalized on existing fears of migration and gave them an unstable political legitimacy, popularizing anxieties about integration and job competition. Powell became emblematic of a section of the British population that wanted to recreate a 'Little England', but felt powerless to defend themselves against the supposed coming socio-economic subordination to new commonwealth immigrants.[16]

The speech was also reflective of the expansion of white identity to include all working-class Britons, defined against colonized societies and commonwealth migrants first in the high imperial age, then again in the post-colonial period. As part of the 'changing symbolic constitution of racialized capitalism', white British identities expanded from bourgeois Victorians to include most working-class Britons through populist imperial and nationalist sentiments after 1945.[17] Just as the 'colonial frontier' came home to British cities, white working-Britons were also subject to base forms of imperial nationalism and the transition to welfare capitalism. Thus, immigration was not the only perceived threat to white, British identity from the mid-1960s: the contraction of empire, the coming European economic community, a declining national economy and even signs of American cultural dominance all encouraged conservative white racialized sensibilities.[18] Despite the fact that historians have repeatedly shown that migrants almost always filled jobs that most white labourers viewed as unskilled and therefore less desirable, Powell's speech both popularized the idea of the vulnerability of white-working class communities and became a significant moment in the post-war construction of racialized and anti-immigrant discourses.[19] As later chapters demonstrate, football supporters generated antipathies towards black footballers with many of these concerns in mind, both reflecting and contributing to broader debates about the cultural and social landscape of post-colonial Britain.

In addition to a declining national economy and the politics of race and nation, concerns about youth degeneration in an increasingly affluent and permissive society conditioned state agencies' and the public's responses to racism and violence in British football. From the 1960s forward, British governments also faced a number of challenges inspired by youth dissension. Cultural commentators and politicians became concerned about youth permissiveness, exemplified in drug use, pop music and generational rebelliousness.[20] The first development of youth subcultures had inspired new associations among working-class youth and perceived threats to security that became the subject of media and academic attention. Teddy boys and girls appeared in 1955 and spread from the inner-city to the suburbs, taking their unique blend of style and vandalism to the heart of the new, purportedly affluent Britain. The mods and rockers, the next wave of youthful threats to post-war British serenity, made headlines by vandalizing several seaside resorts in 1964. These style-conscious and increasingly violent subcultures became Britain's first post-war 'folk devils'.[21] To several commentators these subcultures represented the worst aspects of the rise of affluent consumer society, the outcome of a lingering social paradox in post-war Britain. While affluence and comfort were the aspirations of political and social interventions by post-war governments and the rise of the welfare state, many Britons resented the freedom that affluence produced. To many, the Teds, mods and rockers, and subsequent subcultural groups in later years, represented the replacement of production at the centre of social life with egregious leisure and consumption.[22] Post-war youths' penchant for expensive clothes and conspicuous consumption of drugs, clothes and alcohol supposedly indicated the unfortunate outcomes of new wealth and a more generalized moral decay in British society. These anxieties coincided with overstatements about the degeneration of British values within Labour's 'permissive society', where Roy Jenkins criticized puritanical restrictions on personal liberties as the party's Home Secretary.[23]

Academic studies revealed that the distress generated by youth subcultures was not merely a product of collective 'labels' but that these associations also had their origins in shifts in the structural and cultural make-up of British society. In the late 1960s skinhead groups constituted a collective attempt to reclaim working-class identity by emphasizing its masculine and aggressive character. Their symbolic representations of hostility and belligerence, epitomized by certain forms of dress and grooming, achieved social recognition inaccessible to them otherwise. The mods, in contrast, had dressed fashionably in an effort to express their figurative rise in social mobility, an attempt to mimic a livelihood not generally available to them.[24] Both subcultural movements became means by which working-class youths manipulated their immediate social environments and resisted class subordination through sometimes violent transgression. As reactions to modifications in the structural composition of class relationships, youth collective identities sought recognition of their public resistance. They achieved their goal. A series of media condemnations accompanied the rise in popularity of each youth subculture, and provided a framework for moral backlash by football spectators.[25] Youth subcultural movements also became linked with football, as skinheads and casuals participated in football violence and attracted the attention of police. These groups of rival fans also attracted widespread media attention that interpreted their violent transgressions as moral disobedience rather than expressions of class struggle or economic discontent.

The 1968 student uprisings constituted a transformational moment in public images of youth culture as well, giving legitimacy to many conservative Britons' fears about youth subcultures and dissent. Though far more threatening in Tokyo, Berlin and Paris, students mobilized in small scale in several parts of Britain. Specific university concerns about authoritarian university administrations and misgivings about academic research on behalf of the military soon blossomed into more formal critiques of the British social and capitalist system as a whole. The uprisings generated a series of theatrical and confrontational tactics calling for a hastened pace of government reform throughout Europe. Many British citizens and the state interpreted the events of 1968 as rejection of the tenets of modern liberalism and betrayal by its youth.[26]

Stuart Hall et al. argue that the 1968 events instigated reactions from the state that developed a definitive authoritarian impulse, in part as a response to anxieties about youth politics. The law-and-order theme defined the Tory election campaign in 1970, which succeeded by deepening fears of anarchic threats on local and state levels. Both political parties became sensitized to internal enemies, from immigrants to leftists to football 'hooligans'. In the same year, the Garden House Hotel trial made examples of disruptive students at Cambridge, six of whom received nine to eighteen month sentences for disrupting a private dinner meant to celebrate the success of military colonels. The Industrial Relations Act of 1971 subtly aimed at impeding labour strikes and preventing disorder from working insurgents. The Immigration Act of the same year concretized anti-immigrant attitudes and provided another tool through which law-and-order adherents could claim success against 'criminal' activity. The rupture between the daily lives of British citizens and the mechanizations of a state determined to react with a strong fist increased.[27]

Though it would be an overstatement to label these multiple challenges to authority a unified menace to ideas of sovereign government, challenges to authority from workers and youths provided a precedent for the extension of state power over areas of social conflict generally. As will be shown, the expansion of state control over the football environment, which also posed threats to gentrified moral codes and the mythology of Britain's national traditions, occurred during this period as well. The failed 1968 uprisings also intensified the polarization of British society, as the state and popular media quickly conflated the student movements with the destruction of British civil thought and morality from below. As demonstrated in the next chapter, one of the primary targets of politicians and moral entrepreneurs alike became raucous football hooligans, whose routine acts of violence and disruptive behaviour violated recent attempts at social regulation, and yet further encouraged discourses proclaiming the necessity of tough criminal action and moral regeneration. All of these images of defiant subcultures coalesced into a general condemnation of moral disintegration and youthful ignorance levelled by the media and much of British society. As Hall et al. noted, 'The themes of protest, conflict, permissiveness and crime begin to run together into one great, undifferentiated "threat".'[28] As a result, throughout the 1970s British administrations furthered their control over British social institutions, British professional football included. Youth activities like football spectatorship came under an increasingly watchful eye, bolstered by the development of television and the tabloid newspaper industry. Youth conduct generally, and working-class violence within British football specifically, became a focus of regulation and negotiation. As will be described below, the state legitimated its involvement in British football through discourses of increased criminal behaviour, accelerated social anxieties and the deterioration of the nation's juveniles.

By the 1970s, further economic woes overlapped with anxieties about youth dissent to create a generalized feeling of decline and lawlessness. Successive administrations from both parties failed to improve the standard of living and battle severe stagflation. Increases in retail prices – nearly 9 per cent on average from 1970–3 – and increased unemployment – nearly 900,000 without jobs – continued to present struggles.[29] The energy crisis of 1973 drastically effected both workers and the national economy, worsening a downward trend in living conditions begun in the late 1960s. Though administrations changed, the general failure to relieve pressure on the welfare state, or to address increasing employment and housing concerns, resulted in the intensified deterioration of inner cities throughout the 1970s. Despite the high hopes that accompanied the expansion of the welfare state immediately after the war, successive governments neglected to address the increasing severity of structural changes within working-class society. By the late 1970s, with the national economy in full decline and a second oil crisis looming, new economic promises seemed attractive. Disappointed by the Labour Party, and tired of mishandled industrial relationships over the winter of 1979, much of the electorate hoped for better outcomes through the Conservatives' new idealism and considerably different economic policies.

In the 1980s, Margaret Thatcher and the Conservative Party capitalized on widespread social and economic uncertainty by reinstituting neoliberal laissez-faire capitalism in Britain. Thatcher's free market principles, privatization of state industries, and uncompromising cutbacks in social welfare limited further the opportunities available to working-class people generally, and working-class youth specifically. Thatcher also relentlessly attacked trade union organization, reducing the collective influence of working-class men and women and curbing the efficacy of their political activity. Before Thatcher, both political parties agreed on a consensus Keynesian mixed-economy model that balanced private enterprise with the public ownership of key industries. Thatcherism's radical departure from mixed economies in favour of monetarism, privatization of national industries, and the deregulation of business moved away from seeking full employment and social welfare as worthwhile goals.

The Thatcher administration ushered in a unique blend of utopianism and law-and-order regulation. Its most vociferous critics articulated its distinctive ability to fluidly resolve its own internal paradoxes by uniting diverse threads of social discourse into a consistently contradictory programme.[30] Thatcher's brand of authoritarian populism promoted reductions in social welfare and the destruction of collective enterprise in favour of a renewed British individualism. An ordered, civil society was the goal. Extensions of state power secured an environment in which 'free markets' could thrive, regardless of the consequences for working-class men and women. This noticeable contradiction between processes of state expansion for social and economic regulation and the repeal of instituted welfare made working-class livelihoods increasingly difficult.[31] Consistent with this larger project, the football stadium became a central space of state expansion, as the Home Office called for special regulation of the football industry, and football spectators specifically, as a prime area in need of law-and-order upkeep.

Social exclusion also characterized Thatcherite policies. New Right discourse, from Powell in 1968 to Mrs Thatcher in the late 1980s, consistently articulated anti-immigrant and homophobic discourses to British citizens. Throughout her administration, Thatcher repeatedly manipulated popular fears and anxieties about distinct social groups within Britain to promote new political directions. Carnival violence in the 1970s and so-called 'race riots' in Brixton and Toxteth in the summer of 1981 exacerbated fears about migrant integration. Conservative white Britons perceived these incidents as opportunities to rethink harsher immigration policies, but also as intractable problems of law-and-order discipline among immigrant communities, especially young black men. Rhetoric demanding renewed moral codes became a consistent practice of the Thatcher government. The administration articulated a particularly conservative rendition of family values and bolstered British nationalism by linking this created ethos with individualism, hard work and economic renewal. Discourses of social exclusion for migrants, Britons of colour, and gay and lesbian communities became central to Thatcherite processes of moral revitalization. Identifying enemies who compromised British character and decency from within became a primary task as well, resulting in various forms of cultural racism and sexual discrimination. Overall, Thatcherism comprised a 'complex mixture of imagery, rhetoric and policies which was constantly re-defined in response to strategic circumstances'.[32] The Thatcher administration and its policies conditioned the football environment in several ways, as subsequent chapters will show. Conservatives identified violent football supporters as one of many 'enemies within', continuing a tradition of sensationalizing and ostracizing football supporters established by both parties in the 1960s and 1970s. Far-right policies also fostered an environment of racial exclusion that encouraged anti-immigrant and anti-black attitudes in society generally, but in football specifically.

From this wide context – the successive waves of fear about the emergence of youth subcultures, the changes in governmental approaches to British leisure and popular sporting entertainment, the convergence of working-class associations with football as Britain's national sport, the ever-present concern for the debasement of British youth and the failure to remedy worsening economic conditions – emerged the phenomenon of football-related violence and the moral panics associated with it.[33] The post-war union of football and the working-class became even stronger as the sport's popularity increased. It continuously offered a cheap and accessible means of entertainment, and local clubs built local and regional alliances with fan bases across the country. Football spectatorship provided not only a form of leisure on the weekend, but a social arena that provided opportunities for self-identification and community relationships. To attend football not only signified local loyalties, but national pride in the national sport.

How, then, did these historical realities affect football violence and racism, and the state's response to it? As explored in the introduction, scholars have attempted to explain the leap from generalized social anxieties and class exclusion to violent and aggressive forms of football spectatorship in various ways. Early commentators noted that the 'embourgeoisment of football' through processes of professionalization and internationalization prompted working-class fans to attempt to reclaim the intimacy of working-class communities through aggressive expressions of local solidarity, manifested frequently in affiliations with football clubs. The conflict between the watching 'styles' of generations resulted in a younger cohort incorporating violence into the weekend's entertainment.[34] Others have explained violence as intrinsic to processes of self-identification and masculine initiation in many communities of football spectators. Fans were socialized into quasi-violent cultures: cultures that accept moderated violence with variable determined limits depending on agreed social behaviours.[35] Violence was often an epiphenomenon of the social gatherings around football and the confirmation of masculine qualities.[36] The construction of rivalries also revolved around practices of identity formation: football fans affirmed who they were in conjunction with contrasting ideas of who they were not through the structure of oppositions in football rivalries.[37] Structural changes in the football industry, but also in the defining values of the working-class specifically, allowed for the expansion of violence among working-class youth. Processes of self-identification within a complex set of immediate and secondary contextual settings incorporated violence to bolster the masculine behaviours demanded by social incorporation into spectator groups. Of course, most expected the state to respond to protect the safety of sporting leisure, especially in football. But police and government authorities failed to understand the complex social and cultural dynamics of football violence, and eventually instituted changes to football spectatorship that haphazardly and unsuccessfully addressed the problem. Rather than ameliorating this conflict, the increasing presence of police and the development of violent environments, as I argue later, contributed to the escalation of violence at football matches as well.

Incidents of football violence and moral panics should be situated within these general transitions, but also recognized as productive of similar social conflicts. When outbreaks of youth violence, often highly organized and increasingly complex, threatened gentrified ideals on a regular basis, the framework for moral panics based on ideas of youthful exuberance and moral disintegration were already in place. When identifiable stylized groups, like skinheads and casuals became the recognizable face of classed football violence, condemnations of working-class subcultures were not only repeated but expanded. Thus, when the state responded, often in efforts to protect other fans and break ritual rowdiness, the perceived fractures in working-class communities justified the extension of state powers over the football industry and its working-class spectators, masked in the language of 'crowd safety', as simply another internal problem needing to be solved.

Forms of Disorder

Before analysing the state's activities in sanitizing football, investigative police documents, witness statements, oral histories and reports from constabularies reveal the dreadfully violent acts of many supporters. As working-class football attendance became increasingly popular, disruptive activities by a minority of spectators triggered the concern of local police forces and the Home Office from the mid-1960s onward. This section aims to elucidate the forms of disorder that proved threatening to the Home Office and local police authorities, as the Home Office's own documents and police reports they commissioned provide a window onto working-class spectators' weekly activities.

The mid-1960s marks a watershed in police and state concern about football violence. Though some analysts have traced rowdiness at football back to the nineteenth century to show continuity and the persistence of violence in the sport, an increased incidence emerged after 1966 in several large British cities, especially London.[38] Furthermore, the Home Office and national police authorities only seriously devoted resources towards alleviating the concern when it became a political conundrum at this point. During the 1950s and early 1960s only a few police records regarding disruptive football violence reached the Home Office, the government's body for securing domestic order and keeping the peace. These records reflect only minor violence at football matches prior to the late 1960s. Spectators regularly mailed complaints about cramming and the stretched capacity of certain terraces to police stations.[39] Others filed property damage claims when fans climbed on nearby rooftops or light poles to look in on a match at a nearby stadium.[40] Police duty agendas consistently listed monitoring turnstiles and the dissemination of crowds as top priorities.[41] For the most part, police concerns in the first decades after the war involved illegal entry, problems with dispersing crowds and the odd disruptive fan. Whereas police reports after the mid-1960s treated violence, vandalism and conflicts with the police as a matter of regular and routine behaviour at a match, limited reports from this period treat similar contraventions as extraordinary and relatively innocuous.

From the mid-1960s, the Home Office, the London Metropolitan Police and regional constabularies soon became aware of other, more violent developments among youth spectatorship. A wide variety of routine violent activities clearly provoked and demanded a reaction by politicians and local authorities. The Home Office, a protean agency within the national government in charge of securing domestic policy and affairs, requested reports from the highest regional police authorities, the constabularies. The police reports that the Home Office gathered, and the correspondence attached to them, show increased anxieties in the late 1960s and 1970s. They authorized greater police spending and focused their attention on violent altercations and the raucous activities of groups of football spectators. The documentary record makes it clear that by the late 1960s the nature of football spectatorship and youth involvement in it had changed drastically as the sport became increasingly associated with violence and disorder. It has been generally assumed that adolescent youths and males engaged in the majority of disruptive activities and organized football violence. Police records indicate that this is generally the case, although adults and women infrequently appear in arrest records. While the greater part of football-related violence stemmed from young working-class men, it is erroneous to assume that women and adults were never involved.[42]

Forms of disorder in the late 1960s ranged from missile and coin throwing to drunkenness and fights among fans. Police and state authorities expressed the greatest concern about pitch invasions, an early development in the array of disorderly activities. Fans would charge the field during or after a match for a number of reasons. Pitch invasions had traditionally been a way for spectators to connect with players and the club on special occasions. Young men also invaded the pitch to tease the stewards and police, and usually evaded punishment.[43] In one exceptional instance at the Tranmere club, near Liverpool, a spectator jumped onto the field and spanked the goalkeeper as he was preparing to kick the ball.[44] Though many state officials disregarded pitch invasions as a silly form of hero worship, organized spectators sometimes invaded the playing field with more violent intentions.[45] In anticipation of an unfavourable result, fans often invaded the pitch in order to have the game cancelled. On one occasion in Newcastle in June 1969, nearly 3,000 fans poured over the boundary walls, throwing bottles and trash onto the field, and refused to leave until the referee abandoned the game.[46] Other fans invaded the pitch to physically assault players of the opposing team. Nearly 1,000 Chelsea fans fought their way through police lines to attack players of Luton FC at a match in 1975.[47] Some spectators attempted to harm the referee in the event of unfavourable decisions for their team. At Leeds in 1971, several fans attacked a referee during a match, leading to three arrests.[48]

During the early 1970s, pitch invasions occurred nearly every weekend, and they became the most noticeable activity of disorderly football spectators. They constituted not only a disruption to the match, but also represented a breakdown in the ordered world of policing and crowd control. This collective act indicated that spectators no longer respected the delineations of physical space instituted by club authorities and transgressed the boundary between the field and the terraces. While earlier invasions had been good-humoured, frequent violent instances revealed more rebellious and aggressive intentions. The transgression of pitch invasions not only indicated violent or unruly conduct, but also violated the revered distinction between the private space of the playing field and the public space designated for fans.

In addition to the emergence of frequent pitch invasions, the press and public officials gathered a wide array of activities under the umbrella term 'hooliganism'. Academics, too, have perpetuated the use of this term by intermittently attempting to define its scope and give it a closed definition.[49] The term came to represent a variety of activities, both within the stadium and outside of it, which proved threatening to the semblance of order instituted by police, stewards and other official extensions of the state. On the terraces, surging and swaying among large groups of standing spectators became increasingly dangerous at some grounds. Swaying had been an acceptable form of fan behaviour, especially during the match when excitement peaked. One spectator described them: 'There were vast wave-like movements of supporters tippling down the terraces, so much so that I began to feel seasick in the stands'.[50] These movements coincided with the excitement of the match, a consequence of particular incidents within the game. But some fans would push violently from the back of the crowd, often in unison, moving the entire crowd forward unexpectedly and causing pressure to mount at walls and barriers on the edges of the terraces. This often occurred, as this fan recalled, when a group of fans pushed on a group of opposing spectators: 'There's, say, probably 40 or 50 of you, and you used to shout your team's name and you was behind them and you pushed forwards in the terrace and that was it'.[51] Excessive swaying and surging, especially in capacity crowds, often could cause difficulty for fans attempting to keep their balance, avoid getting stomped, and find necessary air. One man remembered 'a night when there was too many people in there ... If there had been pushing that night then what would happen was your chest would take it, the brunt of it if you was in front of a barrier. I wouldn't say I was frightened, but I was concerned.'[52] Belligerent fans often transformed good-natured swaying into aggressive and violent surges that not only caused physical harm, but caused a more general feeling of anxiety in the terraces.

Other conflicts on the terraces included recurring violent encounters between opposing groups of fans. In the early years of increased football disorder, between 1968 and the late 1970s, rival supporters planned on meeting and fighting one another inside and outside the grounds. These conflicts were deeply associated with territorial values and represented a localized form of territorial conflict. The most common form of territorial conflict within the stadiums was the infiltration of segregated areas. Eventually, as discussed later, police and club officials routinely segregated fans in order to prevent violence and keep rival supporters away from one another.[53] Breaking into the other spaces of the stadium became a rogue adventure that involved clandestine and patterned attacks. Fans would sneak into the areas designated for the opposing supporters and start a violent melee. One fan described the process:

> About 20 minutes before the game started, a hole appeared in this mass of red [Charlton's fans wore red] and it spread. It was like a stone being dropped into a pool and the ripples spreading out, and the ripples disappeared and it was all as it was before, but what came back was a mass of blue and then it was singing, 'Millwall, Millwall', and that was the first time that I had seen an end being taken.[54]

In such confined and tightly packed spaces, spontaneous conflicts could drag in people who had no violent intentions, and cause collateral damage to those caught up in the action. Invading fans meant to raise anxieties and promote an environment of hostility and violence, allowing for their group to exert its control over specific spaces in the terraces. These territorial battles could go back and forth throughout a match. Some fans even invaded the pitch, crossed the field of play, and jumped over the barriers to invade the other team's section en masse, as occurred in Bristol in 1973.[55]

One of the earliest researchers into football hooliganism evaluated endtaking as the foundation of territorial conflicts between rival supporter groups. Through ethnographic study Peter Marsh found many of these violent invasions were merely repetitive and theatrical, rarely resulting in aggressive violence. Many spectators 'bluffed' violence, he contended, through posture, empty threats, and blows intended not to harm, but to scare. Fans ran at each other but rarely intended to seriously hurt the opposition.[56] My research, in contrast, indicates that while certain social norms may have dictated acceptable and unacceptable forms of violence within the terraces, police and ambulance reports consistently revealed that violent conduct resulted in severe acts of physical harm. Though the conduct can often be characterized as ritual and repetitive, it also proved highly dangerous and physically threatening.[57] Several police reports indicate that conflicts between fans often involved various types of weapons. Bricks, pipes and other found materials escalated the nature of the violence in very hostile situations. Stabbings, though much less common, occurred on occasion.[58] An air gun, though never fired, was also confiscated at one particularly heated match at Liverpool in 1972.[59] On average, for every large group of arrests made by police, usually totalling between twenty and forty persons, one or two were charged with possession of weapons.[60] Other scholars have emphasized the importance of territorial conflict among groups of competing spectators. The spaces which groups of fans inhabited and defended routinely on the weekend took on an ancestral significance, one which could not be menaced by outsiders. The defence of this territorial turf became a priority when fans would visit, often leading to very aggressive pitch invasions and end-taking conflicts.[61]

These territorial conflicts attracted the attention of police patrolling the matches, charged with keeping order in an increasingly chaotic environment. While most police authorities wanted to get through the day without incident, part of the experience for spectators involved intermittent conflicts with the police authorities present at the match. Territorial conflicts between groups of fans extended to spatial conflicts between police and spectators. The City of Oxford police commented that spectators frequently taunted officers, noting that fans regarded the interaction as 'part of the afternoon's entertainment.'[62] When a 1967 government inquiry sent out questionnaires to regional police authorities, requesting information on the relationships between the crowd and police, many remarked that fans were unwilling to help procure their violent or disorderly companions. In fact, fans often impeded police in their pursuit or identification of specific rule-breakers.[63] Supporters also threw missiles, stones and coins at officers on duty at matches, repeatedly and consistently in certain cases.[64] While police officers usually stayed near the pitch or in gangways in an effort to maintain order, when they entered the territory of the crowd they found a hostile welcome. The Chief Constable at Newcastle upon Tyne City Police remarked, 'Police are fair game and are obstructed, abused and occasionally assaulted when taking action against a disorderly element'. He added that 'we have been the target. In past years this was mainly good humoured as when snowballs are thrown to fill in the waiting before a game commences'. Regrettably, he concluded that 'we are someone to vent feelings on.'[65]

As young men attempted to evade police prosecution, encounters could be exceedingly violent. One police report, from an incident inside the stadium at Swindon in 1976, provides an example of the regular hand-to-hand combat that policemen came to expect in the terraces:

> A youth at the front of the crowd was seen to throw his head back and spit in the face of a constable who had his hands full escorting a youth from the ground. A P.C. went into the crowd and managed to grab the youth who had spat but ten or twelve others prevented the Officer from making his arrest by pulling them apart and also by punching and kicking the P.C. until his hold on the youth was dislodged. One of the assailants then landed a violent blow with his fist full in the Officer's face, causing

his nose to bleed. The same man then kicked the officer in the back, the blow striking the lower part of the spine.[66]

Reports like this surfaced frequently, and officers came to regard such encounters as routine and unexceptional. The relationships between the fans and the police who regulated their behaviour deteriorated, and violence between the parties escalated and became a normal fixture at football matches across Britain.

Spectators also clashed with authorities and each other outside of the stadiums. Police reports often recall attempts to enter the matches without paying for admission. At Ibrox Park in Scotland visiting fans often charged the turnstiles in groups, gaining entry to the park through force and the use of large masses of people.[67] Fans would also climb walls and use scaffolding from local construction jobs to scale over stadium barriers. Visiting fans often tried to gain entrance without payment, as the price of admission and a train ticket to the stadium could prove costly. Conflicts between groups of fans also occurred outside the stadiums on a regular basis. Groups of rival fans appeared at the matches with the expectation of a 'punch-up' or territorial conflict as repetitive violence became a staple at many grounds across England by the mid-1970s.

Visiting fans triggered the most consternation from local police officials. Groups of loyal fans followed their teams to away matches, and often made their vacation into an invasion of another English or European city. Upon their arrival, away fans frequently stormed the city plazas and shopping centres of the cities they travelled to, announcing their presence not only to other fans, but to the rest of the area's inhabitants. One supporter remembered 'walking down the main road and suddenly a sea of youths came down the road ... They virtually took the whole street over and that was the first time I really saw the power of all these youngsters getting together and frightening people'.[68] These incidents were most likely to occur near railway depots, coach parks, or other areas where fans first exited their coaches or trains. One police report described the mayhem caused by a group of Manchester United supporters visiting Southampton for the day. After repeated unsuccessful attempts to charge the entrance gates, a group of 150 fans 'ran along three residential streets in the vicinity, jumped and danced on parked motor cars, kicked the panels and broke windscreens as well as throwing any moveable object they found ("no waiting" cones and the like) through the windows of the houses'.[69] These random acts of violence did not require a purpose. Wreaking havoc and eliciting anxious and intimidated responses from local citizens, police and other spectators provided its own reward. One fan remembered:

> It wasn't particularly an act of violence, it was a ludicrous, hysterical act. Throwing a toilet out of a train window was funny. It's a set of surreal actions, to take a toilet out of an old train and through a window. When you're in a group and when you see this person walking around with a toilet, it's funny, and the toilet goes whooshing out of

the window ... We could walk up and down the High Street and everyone would look at us and everyone would be frightened of us and we wouldn't have to do very much, just shout and swear a bit: 'You're gonna get your fucking heads kicked in'.[70]

Indeed, broken windows in city plazas and in stores near football grounds provided the justification for the majority of police reports. Vandalism, especially to any building or business associated with the local football club, became extremely common.

Local police units frequently recognized the changing conduct of fans and the escalation of their violence. Officers knew that spectators justified and carried out their violence because of club loyalties, and the reports and updates sent to the Home Office reflect local officials' disdain for the growing sense of team allegiance and organized violence. The constabulary from Dumfries and Galloway in Scotland remarked, 'It is significant that the members of groups indulging in hooliganism are invariably below normal intelligence'. Amid a short tirade on their behaviours, he added, 'They are dedicated in support of a team and become wholly and completely identified with it. What happens to the team happens to them ... if the team is beaten, they are also beaten and their ego is destroyed and consequently they seek revenge.' This close identification with the club's fortunes led, he alleged, to unrestrained emotive aggressiveness: 'They consequently let off steam gloating over the vanquished and vesting their high spirits on other people and property'.[71] Though police could be exceedingly denigrating towards young spectators, they also acknowledged that their conduct reflected the solidarity of social relationships forged through football spectatorship.

Police forces also recognized and followed the increasing organization of spectator groups, which grew along with other changes in football spectatorship. Several stations noted that leadership had emerged in specific groups, giving form and regularity to chanting, singing and dress at matches. The Stoke-on-Trent City Police observed that supporters 'attend football matches intent on provoking trouble or looking for excitement, and it appears to be a game of follow my "leader". There is a certain degree of organisation'.[72] These organized groups became more visible as football matches became places where youths engaged in violent conflicts that represented battles over club loyalties, class identification and regional affiliations. The police and press first identified skinheads as the cultural group linked to football violence, using their subcultural identity as an easy scapegoat for instigation. The newspapers and television news programmes publicized their activities as well, giving skinheads a visible arena through which to make their brand of working-class violence known.[73] Skinheads attended football matches weekly by the late 1960s, claiming the terraces as their home grounds, and defended them vigorously.[74] In Liverpool, police knew that groups of skinheads engaged in 'trophy hunts', where they would attack rival fans and steal their scarves, usually emblazoned with team colours and badges, and wear them on their belts to the match.[75] Police warned youth spectators trying to avoid violence to hide their scarves until inside the stadium in Manchester.[76] Police reports often mentioned local groups of skinheads specifically, blaming rival groups for initiating violence both inside and outside the stadiums.[77] Police perceived conflicts between and among skinheads to be of a different degree, decidedly more violent and capable of more damage to property and person.

Skinheads were not the only subcultural groups to engage in processes of group identification and territorial conflict at football grounds, but merely the first to be associated with it. Groups of football spectators and organized encounters, often noted by the press and academics as the central motivation behind football violence generally, became decidedly marked by the mid-1970s. As social conditions deteriorated with the British economic crisis of the early 1970s, football provided not only a weekly leisure but also increased excitement, release and socialization through organized youth gangs. Social interaction and the excitement of violence provided adventure, escape and community outside of typical relations within work or the family. 'Firms' of violent football spectators developed around working-class social institutions like the local pub, neighbourhood associations, and kinship networks – all of which were nurtured and sustained in the football environment.[78] Their activities encompassed a wide range of socially disruptive activities, from organized stormings of shops and city plazas to staged encounters with firms of other teams.[79] This new organization of football violence has been much studied, partly because it provided a recognizable face and sensational aspect to football violence which the media consistently publicized.

Football 'casuals' also received an inordinate amount of attention from press and public. Casuals represented a stylized and chic departure from other working-class associations, renewing aggressive relationships with other supporters and the police. Many casual movements emerged in the late 1970s in large cities in the North and parts of London.[80] Identified by the blatant display of the latest trends and high-dollar fashion, casuals expressed alternative claims on class identification. While skinhead subcultures could be interpreted as reclamations of working-class identity through an emphasis on violent expressions and gritty lifestyles, casuals have been read as the more fortunate beneficiaries of Thatcherite individualism. Lacking traditional opportunities for working-class cohesion, casuals sought to expose their mild successes within ruthless free market capitalism through costly outward signs of identification.[81] These groups became increasingly associated in the 1980s with racism and sexism, travelling extensively with their football teams as they played in Europe. They also provided a new form of self-identification through music, fashion and consumption, based on the latent acceptance of social hierarchies within the working classes generated by Thatcherite social policy.[82] These issues will be elaborated in later chapters. Suffice it to say that casuals and other football 'firms' represented the main thrust of organized football violence from the 1980s into the early 1990s.

Conclusions

This section has introduced the various forms of football violence, its organization, and contextual settings. Football violence emerged from an honoured working-class community activity, built on social networks and shared leisure. As social conditions deteriorated in the 1960s and British society faced pressing questions of social welfare and labour competition, British working-class men and women chose football as an outlet for community development and social cohesion. Dissatisfied with the social outcomes of incessant economic problems as working-class agendas received little attention in either political party, working-class men tested social formations within football spectatorship. From these social networks emerged increasingly organized and stylized violence, fuelled by local allegiances and constricted outlets for expressions of discontent. Football became cemented in working-class life from the 1960s, but became increasingly associated with the more hostile aspects of working-class violence, emergent subcultures and organized conflict as the post-war period proceeded.

2 MORAL ANXIETIES, NATIONAL MYTHOLOGIES AND FOOTBALL VIOLENCE

Several groups surrounding the football industry – including clubs, police officials, the press and the state – created a moral outcry about the increasing outbreaks of violence among working-class youths. Though some scholars have noted the development of a moral panic in football, especially as articulated within the popular press, this chapter aims to analyse the construction of this moral panic and contextualize it within the political and social context of the late 1960s and 1970s.[1] While press discourse certainly contributed to the sensationalization of football violence, this cultural crisis cannot be understood without attention to the leading role of political rhetoric from moral entrepreneurs and police agents who powerfully engaged the public and used football disorder to displace anxiety from the material to the cultural realm. Certainly, supporters instigated, organized and carried out violent activities, forcing political authorities to act. Public and political fears of football violence were not unfounded. Yet, given their inability to prevent the phenomenon or effect improvement in British society and the football industry in material terms, politicians instead used the occasion to address propriety and perceived national decline. The moral reactions against football disorder provided opportunities for British politicians from both parties to redefine and maintain ideas of nationhood, acceptable working-class conduct and suitable masculine behaviour. Their political arguments displaced responsibility for poverty and unemployment through the revival of Victorian discourses. Further, I suggest that the panic over football violence cannot be removed from the other cultural dynamics within British society, including concerns about lawlessness, moral degeneration, and the national ethos, in a time of economic struggle for working-class men and women.

Previous studies of moral discourses in football have mainly used newspaper sources, astutely analysing the processes of news production, language, accuracy and selectivity.[2] Academic interest has also often focused on the question of how the press affected the levels and styles of football violence in the late 1980s and 1990s, when researchers first approached the topic.[3] Other scholars focus on the period after 1985 and Margaret Thatcher's inquest of football violence as the apex of the moral panic.[4] In contrast, this chapter explores the rhetorical strategies used by responsible parties such as politicians, police and football authorities to demonize working-class spectators in an effort to address social and cultural anxieties about football violence as it emerged as a significant political embarrassment in the late 1960s and 1970s. I also explore the intersections between working-class football disorder, national mythology and paternalist discourses. The combination of voices from several different groups of social actors – governors in charge of sport, industry officials and police agents – combined with press depictions to make such rhetoric particularly powerful. Though they often spoke in unison with the press, political and police agents had the power to affect outcomes directly. The central role of politicians, especially Minister of Sport Denis Howell (1964–70 and 1974–9), cannot be understood without attention to the extant social and economic concerns within British society that moral commentators associated with football disorder.

The first section of this chapter will examine the moral apprehensions football disorder generated and the historical actors who contributed to their formation. While police authorities projected a need for law-and-order discipline, politicians used public declarations to generate political capital, and thus not only aggravated the moral concerns about football violence, but benefited from them. The second section discusses how football disasters and working-class football violence, especially the initial instances of English deviance abroad, proved a pointed threat to British national mythology in at least two ways. First, football violence challenged the image that working-class men and women existed peacefully within a stratified Britain. British political administrations continuously assumed that the tenuous harmony between labourers and the middle-classes could be maintained despite challenges from trade unions, immigration conflicts and high levels of unemployment throughout the post-war period. Working-class spectatorship and conflict within British football threatened this mythology of cohesiveness. Second, English football violence abroad, especially two high-profile instances in the 1970s, initiated prolonged debate about the image of Britons and the British nation on the Continent. Examining this arena of social conflict reveals how nationalist sentiments, gendered and class-based values, and working-class violence intersected in a well-publicized and globally visible British tradition.

Analysing the Moral Panic

Moral panics have been the subject of significant research by sociologists concerned with the interaction of systems of representation with social and cultural tensions, fuelled by sensationalized reporting and the intermittent perceptions of breakdowns in social order. The concept cannot be taken as self-evident.

Moral panics, loosely defined, take the form of persistent campaigning by several interested parties – in this case the press, concerned politicians, football authorities and police specialists – which appeal to sections of the public who appear alarmed at perceptions of social and cultural disorder. The moral boundaries, including which behaviours are considered immoral, and the prescriptions for more 'proper' conduct, always remain flexible, unclear and often negotiated. Politicians often capitalize on these overgeneralized public sentiments with legislative or punitive measures that aim to neutralize the perceived threat.[5]

These consistent cultural fears, especially those about 'yob' or 'hooligan' culture threatening British respectability and decency, have long historical roots dating back to the preindustrial and Victorian periods. Narratives of decency and stability within a Britain characterized by emergent moral deterioration and criminal violence prove consistently anachronistic and imaginary. In each successive time period the characteristics of respectability and civility that seemed 'common sense' to social elites were consistently challenged by successive waves of disruptive elements within the social fold. The present depicted in social discourse, whether during the Victorian concern with the moral outcomes of employing youth in industrial society, or the post-war concern with youth subcultures, repeatedly neglected Britain's cultural inheritance and threatened the 'British way of life'. In these declensionist storylines, the erosion of social discipline could only be resolved through recovering the mythological characteristics of Britain's previous 'peaceful' period. Social commentators ignored the historical consistencies of crime and social disruption in every period as they sought nostalgically to regenerate a moral and ordered society. The employed idioms of change could only be counteracted with vocabularies of continuity if Britain was to recover from the perceived resurgence and acceleration of hooliganism and crime.[6] With each prescription for renewing national moral health the moral repertoire of proper conduct increased.

Initial theoretical conceptions of moral panics emerged from the regular concentration on perceived affluence and moral deterioration among working-class youth. Early studies identified the media-fuelled moral disquiet with two competing youth subcultures, the mods and the rockers, in the mid-1960s. These works stressed the central role of a 'folk devil' – the very term used indicated a threat to civil righteousness – by the political right, journalists, or other socially accredited experts.[7] Marxist scholars have also examined the complex interactions between deviant youths and social elites acting as moral police, and how they are shaped by socio-economic pressures and press coverage.[8] These studies lent themselves well to analysing football violence. Hall astutely argued that press coverage of football disorder catalysed public opinion, and mobilized 'support for certain lines of preventive, remedial or controlling action'.[9] The national press succeeded in granting urgency to the problem by pushing sport to the forefront of the news production cycle through specific selections and sensationalized presentations of violent incidents. News reporters amplified the seriousness and scale of the problem they set out to remedy, and in the process ignored the social context and cultural struggles that produced violent negotiation.[10]

However, in addition to press discourses, the role of government and police perspectives in shaping the moral anxieties surrounding football violence must also be understood. While others have examined the editorializing aspects of the press, it must be recognized that the press often conveyed discourses initiated by government and football authorities. Government officials, football regulating bodies, and police agents dictated the themes of widespread cultural distress and moral degeneration. State actors' use of violent language and militaristic rhetoric in describing football spectators' behaviour legitimated threats of violence by the public and the state to counter these activities. In both the press and government debates, violent discourse could be appropriated against violent subjects within a constantly exacerbated economy of language as a response to increasing moral uncertainty. Government ministers and football authorities depicted football 'thugs' first as aggressive and threatening to civil society, and subsequently at war with the authorities and disciplinarians that policed them. In many cases, their assessment of violence and conflict was correct. Yet, politicians led the police, the public and the press in promoting a repertoire of disdainful labels that registered spectators as timelessly and inherently violent subjects, not actors engaging in political or social activities. Nearly all political discussions during the period failed to recognize the social agency of these activities and instead focused their discussions on the cultural and moral impact of their violence. Politicians' paternalist discourses focused on denigrating unruly football spectators as young, working-class and deviant, ignoring their purpose or the meaning of their actions. By positioning spectators as menaces to civil society and social respectability, government officials could position themselves on the side of discipline, order and control in a two-sided battle for the moral landscape of Britain. Rather than recognize the interplay of social tensions and new social formations within the football arena as a response to economic conditions, politicians battled against the perceived threat to British culture embodied in fans' behaviour. Exacerbating extant moral concerns with a new thematic element of football violence subtly disregarded the material hardship faced by working-class men and women, and instead demonized them as cultural deviants.

Of course, recognizing the disproportionality of elevated moral anxieties does not neglect that violence occurred repeatedly. Some have expressed concern that analysing the outbreak of the moral anxieties surrounding football violence neglects the severity and incidence of violent episodes.[11] Furthermore, labelling any phenomenon a 'moral panic', scholars argue, invites an emotional response that connotes anti-rationality and polemicism, and ultimately ignores the measure of deviant activity.[12] Rather, analysing the development of moral discourses within their local and national contexts reveals the multiple subjectivities involved in state discourse, political strategy and the construction of moral principles within bourgeois society. Examining the polemicism inherent in the policing of moral boundaries further elucidates how disruptions like football violence afforded opportunities for a variety of social actors to readdress notions of safety, civility and nationality. Attempts at establishing the frequency and degree of football violence must be accompanied by analysis of the social discourses that surround them.[13] Certainly the state needed to address this outbreak of violence, but their responses reveal how politicians used the situation to buttress British notions of propriety.

The Moral Panic in Social Context

Concerns about moral boundaries do not arise out of a social vacuum. They are conditioned by social relations and can be influenced by tangible changes in social composition and disordering events. These moments of rupture that instigate re-evaluation of contemporary moral standards usually draw on other extant social anxieties and reflect deeper fears about the more general onset of 'troubling times'.[14] In fact, the ensemble of moral alarms 'appear to draw upon, recirculate, and rearticulate cultural thematics and symbolic linkages that have earlier, recurring, and continuing incarnations'.[15] Episodes of moral panic should be analysed not as discrete events but as integral to ongoing historical processes of moral revision that periodically reveal new divisions and new concerns about multifaceted social relationships.[16] Thus, moral discourses must be analysed with an eye toward continuity and change, not as perpetual or timeless, but shaped by local configurations and new social fissures that indicate recent themes of concern.[17]

In the first decades after the war, concerns with subcultural groups overlapped with the proliferation of violent football-related activities and discourses of the moral deterioration of youth. As early as 1957, local newspapers blamed Teddy boys for thrown missiles and pitch invasions.[18] Decades later, the identification of 'skinheads' as principal instigators within groups of community-based fans and travelling ensembles concretized the associations between youth subcultures and violent activity. Football violence, both within and outside individual subcultural groups, helped to activate press concerns about community-based violence, not least because of England's imminent hosting of the World Cup in 1966. Several press outlets demanded strict control and proper behaviour from local communities of fans in the build-up to the international tournament. In 1964 the *Daily Mail* issued a warning: 'Eighteen months from now the widespread and curious world of Association Football will look at the game in the land where it was born. They will shudder to see how tired, worn, even wicked it is'.[19]

The media certainly played a large part in giving social meaning to football violence. In order to make sense of a series of chaotic and disruptive events, the press engaged in processes of identification and contextualization that situated specific events into groups of like social problems. This selective presentation of news organized patterns of discourses that conveyed recurrence and continuity of disruptive events within a common stock of social assumptions.[20] Thus football spectators became associated with 'hooligan' or 'yob' culture in general. The set of disruptions specific to the football setting were reported as consistent with other challenges to civil society and proper moral conduct like youth subcultural groups, especially when activities specifically involved 'skinhead' participants. A *Times* article revealed these methods of social identification and contextualization:

> The skinheads are young working class youths (they are normally aged about 15 to 17) who wear short hair – but not always cropped – jeans with braces, and heavy boots. They have been hanging around in gangs for about a year. They are often football supporters ... Their favourite recreation is 'aggro' (aggravation) which means fights – at football matches ... In London they tend to dislike Pakistanis and Indians.[21]

Such a vivid description not only labels and typifies the subcultural participant, but collapses him/her with other widespread social concerns, most notably the outbreak of football violence and persistent racial tensions in the late 1960s.

Though the media became the public outlet for moral fears about football violence, cultural and social debates about football violence originated from other social agents. Parliamentarians, police and football industry regulators mediated conversations about football violence and its place in British society. Football commissions, generated by the Home Office and the Department for the Environment after successive high-profile violent episodes, provided the catalyst for concentrated political action and the generation of the source material used in this chapter.

Government ministers, especially those at the Home Office in charge of domestic order, closely monitored any social disruptions, and considered causes for their common genesis. They situated football violence as one of several political and moral issues related to law and order. Home Office press summaries clearly reflect these contextual connections. Prepared as general memos to inform Home Office representatives of the latest and most persistent news topics, they indicate the matters that the state's watchdog agency followed. The summary from 26 September 1969 can serve as a representative example. Couched within a number of topics is a section with the heading 'Soccer Hooliganism'. Notes followed that stated the coverage of each paper, giving special attention to how police, court and government authorities were perceived in the press. It recounted that the '*Guardian* and others report that the football supporter who was sentenced to two and a half years' imprisonment for assaulting a police officer is to appeal the sentence'. It also recorded that the '*Times* and *Daily Telegraph* report yesterday's comment by the senior law lecturer at Watford College of Technology that "we have relaxed too readily and too quickly our legal sanctions and deterrents against violence". More important than the papers' focus on policing spectator conduct are the other headings that surrounded the summation of the days' news on football disorder. The structure of the press summary demonstrates that Home Office agents monitored football violence alongside other cultural dynamics. Under the heading 'Public Order', the Home Office reported that several papers were covering the disturbance caused by a 'hippy squat' at Clerkenwell. The summary also listed a quote from the *Daily Telegraph*'s interview with a judge of London Sessions: 'Show the birch to a hippy or skinhead and you show him the light and the way back to respect'. The selections revealed the Home Office recognized the punitive rhetorical responses to social discontent, but more importantly that they looked at each social anxiety ('soccer hooliganism', 'hippies', 'skinheads') as only a part of a more holistic framework of law and order concerns within domestic society. The Home Office, here and elsewhere, made both rhetorical connections and concrete associations between the different elements of a widespread context of moral anxieties.[22] Though each topic was treated independently, the recurrence of these and similar headings litter press summaries from the late 1960s, indicating that discourses of football violence were deeply embedded in other cultural themes.

Suggestions submitted to the Home Office in the early 1970s also reveal how the public experienced the moral panic over football violence. Office agents composed a laundry list of suggestions from the public that indicate the ways in which they too funnelled disparate social problems into a framework of collective civil decay. Several of their suggestions presaged the architectural changes that British football stadiums underwent in the following decades. In addition to changing the seating arrangements and increasing ticket prices, other suggestions, including vertical pens, electric fences and fan segregation, provided more direct means of defining political space within stadiums. One documented suggestion asked for a combination of 'moats, dye-sprays, fire hoses, and water cannons' to maintain order at matches. Others focused on forms of cultural practice associated with football spectatorship and working-class youth specifically. Some suggested the removal of alcohol from football, but also a ban on team colours, team scarves and other representative favours that expressed team loyalties and were seen to exacerbate community conflicts. One suggestion noted that the 'abolition of pop music (which depraves)' would aid in the elimination of football violence. Many called for heavier punishments, birching and longer detention sentences to deter such undesired behaviour.[23] Public submissions emphasized weeding out undesirable youth rebellions through harsh punishment and localized confinement.

For the public as well as the press, football violence became enmeshed in a larger, more ubiquitous framework of moral anxiety.

Football authorities, too, echoed these sentiments by lashing out against football violence as a social evil, and not merely a sports issue. Their reaction, primarily, served a practical purpose. Football disorder in the cheap terraces could discourage other fans from paying for the more expensive seats at matches, thus decreasing Football Association and club revenues. Football hooliganism also surely contributed to declining attendance in the 1970s. The clubs often fielded criticism from politicians, the public, and the press as the prime culprits in allowing football violence to continue unabated. Football violence threatened their longevity and prosperity as businesses, but also the public image of football generally. Clubs deflected these criticisms in different ways, most often by publicizing anti-violence warnings within club programmes and on loudspeakers at stadiums. At Celtic in Glasgow, the club's newspaper chided, 'If you think your violent acts or obscene songs somehow contribute to the advancement of Celtic – FORGET IT. Celtic want none of you – and we appeal to the thousands of decent fans to help us in our efforts to see that sanity prevails'.[24] Football figureheads also made more explicit calls for football violence to stop, again linking their specific complaints to larger moral discourses. Walter Winterbottom, former England national team manager and director of the national Sports Council, held a strong voice in the governance of British football, and served on government commissions to address the problem. After spotting a spectator carrying an axe at a match he attended, Winterbottom remarked,

> It pinpointed the fact that in a violent society people become violent. There is a feeling not only that something has got to happen to control these people but you have to decide on an important balance between what good comes from freedom in society and what evil comes from it. A violent section of the community is using football to express their violence. Football must inevitable suffer.[25]

Rhetorically, Winterbottom wanted to separate respectable football from disreputable violence, a lively national tradition from the ignominious aggression that tainted it. Though football authorities received pressure from other social groups invested in the moral panic, they also contributed to its escalation.

Interest Groups and the Articulation of British Morality

Traditionally, professional groups such as religious associations, social workers, teachers, and police authorities also fuel moral panics in an effort to maintain security and career longevity within their own professions.[26] A number of interest groups and bureaucratic agencies, each with their own complex of shifting and competing political agendas, also attempted to influence the social landscape by publicizing football violence as a moral dilemma.[27] The composition of such groups ranges from grass-roots movements to established political lobbyists.[28]

First, the strongest moral language came from organizations that developed in order to combat violence through sport. Like anti-racist groups in subsequent decades, many anti-violence organizations used sport as an entryway into moral education. The Home Office received several letters from the Association Internationale Contre La Violence Dans Le Sport, a Paris-based international organization, which formed in 1972 after several incidents of sporting violence in both France and England. Its self-described main initiative was 'to encourage and reward the spirit of fellowship and sportsmanship of the child' and to 'spare no effort in improving the child's attitude in his relationship towards others'. This could be achieved through 'a re-education of players and spectators, too often unable to keep their self-control'. The Association aimed at instilling moral education through lessons in violence available in the contemporary football environment. 'The very harmony of the family circle and everyday life is in the balance', director Charles Drago argued, because of the persistence of football violence.[29] To many anti-violence groups, the links between the moral education of Britain's youth and the development of football disorder could not be clearer.

Second, police organizations and police attitudes collapsed germane social concerns into a general milieu of youth insubordination. The cover of *Police* magazine promised an investigative report into 'Hippies and Hooligans' in a 1969 issue. The police reporter showed disdain for both social groups, and linked them under a common theme of cultural decay and defiance. The unnamed reporter first demonstrated the swift hand of authority with a brief account of the forced removal of hippy squatters from an abandoned Russell Square squat: 'It was a copybook example of decisive police work and showed the public that the law of the land can still be enforced – a fact which many people were beginning to doubt'. The reporter continued with a description of what the police found upon clearing out the building:

> When the hippies moved out, every room was ankle deep in filth, including human excreta; every lavatory was blocked, obscenities were scrawled on every wall, and dozens of hypodermic needles were found. A month after the occupation, the stench left behind by the beautiful people still contaminated the air.

The report called on classic strategies of defamation and deprecation to typify 'hippy' youths, associating them with drugs and unhygienic filthiness. It also divided the groups involved into Manichaean sectors of good and evil, wise police and misguided youth. Protesting sympathetic press coverage, the reporter quipped that 'the latter is not the victim of anything, except his own self-pity, arrogance, or inadequacy'. Finally, the police represented their moral position as self-evident and universal among British civil society: 'They must know that the vast majority of the British public does not give a damn about the hippies, except to wish that there was something that could be done to get rid of them'.[30]

The supplementary article on football 'hooligans', written by Ted Deighton, Secretary of the Leeds Joint Branch Board of Police, drew on similar cultural fears and rhetorical formations. Deighton vehemently recounted the social ills associated with football disorder:

> Week after week, season after season, the problem becomes worse ... Today in most towns and cities where there are reasonably successful football teams, violence, hooliganism, and vandalism are on the increase ... What is the mystic source of soccer hooliganism? Is it pot, pop, beer or what?

The writer only offered that some arrestees were drunk or high, but did include that 'the noise of the jungle beat going full blast has an effect on the crowd'. This odd inclusion of the influence of pop music again revealed that football violence could be associated with a broad array of social fears of youth insubordination and moral depravity. Noting that 'self-discipline [was] becoming less and less evident', Deighton blamed the press for amplifying the level of behaviour: 'One has only to see the publicity given, for commercial reasons, to sex, pop noises, and other so-called modern entertainment, to see that there is a line of association between this [football disorder] and vandalism'. Like hippies, unruly football spectators also constantly engaged too much of the police's time and attention, further encouraging crime in other social arenas. Thus, deviant youths not only engaged in criminal acts but encouraged them in other settings, perpetuating the need for a large police presence.[31] The impression of a pervasive social malaise permeated this police perspective, coalescing different elements of a repertoire of anxieties into a common thread of anti-authoritarianism.

Questionnaires returned to the Harrington commission, one of the first social research projects into football disorder supported by the Home Office, also reflected prevalent police attitudes.[32] Though many police reports to the central government maintained a fair objectivity in asking for greater resources or commenting on the increasing or decreasing levels of activity, others made explicit moral statements. One verbose chief constable in York laid out many of the contemporary moral and mythological themes present in other submissions. When asked about the 'seriousness' of the problem he replied: 'The problem of hooliganism is clearly a serious one and is obviously not unconnected with the modern trend of disregard for authority, a complete lack of thought for others and the result of the widespread lowering of moral standards'. When asked about the age of the offenders, he responded, 'I would not suggest the trouble makers are solely teenagers although they seem to form a majority but there is often included older persons who should know better and set a better example. What all have in common is a complete lack of discipline, self respect and sportsmanship.' Again, the constabulary situated the problem at hand within larger moral themes of disrespect for authority, relevant not only to youth but pervading 'society' generally. Like nearly all of the police submissions, he ultimately recommended stiffer punishments and encouraged the Home Office to ask magistrates' courts to impose them.[33]

Third, while both the press and the police surely shaped the moral discourses and social anxieties about football violence, politicians and administrators had a massive impact on the acceleration of fears as well. From the late 1960s onward, beginning with the construction of the Harrington commission, both Conservative and Labour factions remained deeply concerned with the outbreak of football violence. Several highly publicized incidents of football violence and football disasters occasioned opportunities for MPs to accuse the reigning administration of failure to act on the lasting issue of football violence. Politicians, especially those with responsibility for sport and culture in Britain, made sure that the topic was debated several times a year. These events ensured that the issue remained in the public discourse throughout the 1970s, receiving attention from press and the public intermittently.

Each party showed alarm at the prospect of losing voters who supported football and despised the recent changes within the football environment. Politicians issued disdainful public statements against football disorder and shared the moral apprehensions expressed by the public. Parliamentary debates and Home Office correspondence reveal politicians' attempts to capitalize on public sentiments throughout the late 1960s and 1970s. Beginning under the first Harold Wilson administration (1964–70), debates about football violence engaged Home Secretary Roy Jenkins, and many other MPs. Political discussions continued under Edward Heath (1970–4) and Wilson's second term as the Safety at Sports Ground Bill emerged. The Bill aimed at providing a safer entertainment environment through measures against crowd control and efforts towards stadium modernization.[34] Though the questions raised often attacked members of the opposite party, the elements of political rhetoric present shaped the moral panic surrounding football violence. Furthermore, discussions within the Labour Party revealed the widespread social anxieties that pressured local politicians.

MPs wanted the Home Office to recognize and address two interrelated concepts. First, violence had by the late 1960s become excessive and more widespread, and now politicians requested more vigorous governmental attention. Politicians consistently brought the issue of football violence before the House throughout the 1970s as the level of violence failed to abate, despite the formation of several special committees to address the issue. Second, violence among working-class spectators now impinged upon football as a leisure and weekend entertainment for British citizens, leading to decreased attendance at stadiums nationwide throughout the next decade.

To address public concern, politicians first wanted to acknowledge that sporting leisure for bourgeois attendees had become a dangerous and off-putting endeavour. In an early discussion in 1967, Labour MP William Price from Rugby asked Jenkins if he was

> aware that this is becoming a major social problem which needs urgent Government action? Will he do all he can to deter this small minority of thugs and hooligans who are bringing this game into disrepute and at the same time ruining the enjoyment of hundreds of thousands of people?[35]

Politicians wanted to make evident to the public that the government recognized the problem as a serious one and empathized with their annoyance at having their entertainment interrupted. Kenneth Lomas, Labour MP for Huddersfield West, hounded Dick Taverne, the Undersecretary for the State, asking the Home Office to recognize that the party had a serious issue to address. He bluntly stated, 'Thousands of people have their recreation at football matches ruined by hooliganism'.[36]

When the issue was raised again in 1977, Walter Johnson of Derby (Labour) commented, 'It is no good pussyfooting around. We must deal with the people involved as young thugs who are destroying the game, upsetting decent people and preventing ordinary people from enjoying an afternoon to which they have looked forward all week'.[37] Football stadiums had become contested political spaces, clearly labelled 'unsafe' and conducive to violence. While working-class spectators envisioned the stadium as a place to explore community loyalties and contest social policy, politicians wanted to clean up the football environment for respectable spectators. These transgressions of safety recognized by the government and consistently reported by the press, fuelled ubiquitous moral anxieties. Many members of Parliament were compelled to recognize the imposition on the football industry and treat the public's fears with serious political consideration. At certain times, the severity could be potentially overstated to make the point. Martin Flannery of Sheffield (Labour) claimed, 'It is a terrible and intractable problem. It is almost as difficult of solution as the problem of Northern Ireland'.[38]

Jenkins and the Home Office under Wilson initially demurred from engaging in serious discussion about football hooliganism, and generally ignored some of the earliest calls for action from other Labour and Conservative MPs. On several occasions Home Office representatives made it clear that the private football industry could not be invaded by state control, nor could they interfere with the punishments meted out by the magistrates' courts. Dick Taverne stressed twice in response to calls for action that, 'It may be a serious problem, but it remains a fact that the responsibility for public order is that of the management of the football club, which has the opportunity to hire as many policemen as it thinks necessary. I do not think that this matter calls for direct action by the Government'.[39] In

October of the same year he added that, 'I am aware that a lot of entertainment is being spoiled, but it would be quite improper for the Home Office to start instructing officers of police when to prosecute and when not to prosecute'.[40] This initial hesitancy by the Labour Party to engage football violence reflected the economic strains taking on the issue would create. By assuming responsibility for public order in football, the state would have to increase its spending on policing and local government, something the Home Office could not afford near the end of the Wilson administration. Therefore, Jenkins and his administrators consistently strove to make clubs more responsible for fans' conduct. The Home Office could also easily state that it had no jurisdiction or authority over the separate bodies of police administration and magistrate courts.

Moral Entrepreneur: Denis Howell

This position changed under the leadership of Denis Howell, MP from Birmingham and Undersecretary for Education and Science. Scholars have noted that ruptures in the moral certainty of civil society are often accompanied by moral entrepreneurs, social agents who attempt to concretize public opinion on crime to increase social control and moral regulation.[41] Entrepreneurs exploit social fears to further the goals of their interest group by attaching themselves to moral causes. In the late 1960s, Howell, more than any other politician or public figure, made football violence representative of other social anxieties in Britain. Howell's position in the DES took on all sport-specific responsibilities when Wilson made him the first Labour Minister for Sport in 1964. When Howell's undersecretary office was moved from DES to the Ministry of Housing and Local Government in 1969, and again to the Department of Environment in 1970, he assumed more responsibility for sport policy, especially as football disorder became a more hotly debated topic.[42] After several high-profile incidents during the 1970/71 season, Howell established a Working Party to address crowd safety and football violence from a legislative and political perspective. The Working Party gave him a specialized apparatus from which to explore the problem of football violence, and solidified his position within the government as the leading authority on the problem of law-and-order within football. His political strategies as Minister of Sport during the Wilson governments (1964–70, 1974–6) and Callaghan administration (1976–9), as well as Shadow Minister for Sport during the conservative Heath administration (1970–4), dictated government policy on football violence, the football leisure industry and government control of the football environment.

Howell entered the position of Minister for Sport as a highly regarded mind on sporting policy and the sporting industry, a colleague that Wilson trusted as more than a puppet advisor. A previous short-lived attempt at installing an agency in regards to sport politics under Conservative Quintin

Hogg during the Macmillan government had proven unsatisfying. The position needed an authority on sport, and Howell, having served as a Football Association referee, knew sporting values and the role of sport in Britain well. He fought throughout his tenure for increased funding for sport with the Sports Council, both for working-class participation and industrial and national sporting performances. He also represented Birmingham, an industrial West Midlands district. His capabilities as a down-to-earth politician steeped in sporting history and working-class conflict made him the perfect candidate for the government post and the leader of the Working Party on crowd disturbances and football violence.

Howell's early contributions to the Commons debates revealed that he too remained reserved about influencing magistrate or police protocol to address the practical problems of football disorder.[43] But he publicly addressed accusations that Labour had remained inert for too long by expressing his desire to begin pursuing the punishment and elimination of violent football activities through legislative means, a sentiment that was well-received by other MPs and the public. This punitive reaction became a concentrated rhetorical strategy meant to ease public fears through the promise of future peace. In the future, Howell wanted to restore football harmony through the removal of violent subjects through the threat of drastic punitive measures and new legislation. He often did so by promising to protect Britain's national sporting reputation.

Challenges to British National Mythology

In addition to contributing to narratives of British social decline, football violence, especially cases when British football violence erupted abroad, enabled several interest groups to re-evaluate Britain's sporting mythology and its importance to the national ethos. In the post-war period, Britishness continued to be a highly contested social and cultural concept.[44] British historical consciousness and Britons' sense of themselves could be drawn from a wide range of narratives and practices through which ideas of Britishness and British heritage could be constructed.[45] As in the nineteenth century, British cultural traditions evolved over time in ever-changing historical contexts, using available relationships, practices and symbols.[46] The creation and maintenance of national traditions often stemmed from ruling elites' desire to impose social prescriptions for behaviour and ritual.[47] Long-standing national ideas could also be embodied in myths, which functioned to express ideas of Britishness deriving from older, collective narratives about the origins of national community.[48] National mythology contributed to the definition of the historical community, its moral boundaries and acceptable forms of social life.[49] These national myths can be composed of cultural traditions such as football spectatorship, but can also be challenged by them.

Post-war British football violence allowed politicians to maintain ideas of respectability, bourgeois values, and notions of 'civilized' British society as they demonized violent spectators. British sportsmanship and sporting myths embodied ideas of propriety and gentlemanly conduct representative of distinct ideas of Britishness espoused in earlier eras. British politicians defended these national virtues, as they were both re-enacted in sport's public theatre, and repudiated by British subjects engaging in football violence. Football violence challenged national mythologies by tainting Britain's national sport and most cherished entertainment industry. England's victory in the 1966 World Cup cemented football not only as the working-class sport *par excellence*, but as the national sporting heritage to be enjoyed by all. From the late 1960s, football violence disturbed the articulation between sport and nation as the communal tradition became embroiled in violence and enmeshed in ubiquitous concerns about social civility.

Several groups of social actors seized the opportunity to reassert multiple sets of values that contributed to British national culture. First, politicians and football authorities used various rhetorical strategies, which intermittently amplified or diminished the scope of the problem, as one of several concrete and discursive tactics aimed at cleansing football of unwanted violence. Second, the first high-profile incidents of football violence overseas challenged the image of British civility in the Continent and forced politicians to respond. Their reactions afforded them the opportunity to express Britain's national values by protecting the virtue of its national sport, and ultimately escalated the perceived severity of football violence.

Rhetoric and the Nation: Protecting Football's Reputation

In a quick review of Parliamentary debates, Richard Giulianotti astutely noted that from 1968–70 political concerns over football violence significantly escalated as violence increased. Politicians first identified football violence as a political problem during this period, and perceived it as a threat to public and private property. They raised social unease about the emergent phenomenon and eventually promoted a 'problem-solving' approach to this new political question.[50] This increase in attention resulted in the first two formal government investigations into football violence, the 1968 Harrington report and the 1969 Lang inquiry, both of which reveal much about the early frames of political discourse regarding football spectator indiscipline.[51] After 1970, high-profile cases of football violence and intermittent football disasters kept the question of football violence in British society in the national consciousness throughout the next decade.

One can discern in political statements about football violence several discursive tactics that allowed politicians flexibility in addressing the problem as a blemish on the national image. First, the dichotomy between localized violence and national meaning was effectively used to generate concerns about football disorder on both local and national levels. On some occasions, local politicians categorized football disorder as a localized issue that could be easily contained and addressed. This strategy eased local fears about social disruptions within urban areas and de-emphasized the problem on a local level, displacing the perception of violence onto other localities. In successive debates about football violence, several MPs chimed in with a defence of their constituents. Lomas (Labour – Huddersfield West) assured the House that 'this kind of problem does not apply to Huddersfield Town Football Club'.[52] Leslie Spriggs (Labour) of St Helens was proud of his constituents' behaviour:

> My constituents have more sense than to behave badly at such fixtures ... It is a pleasure to hear the comments of my constituents when I speak to them on Saturday evenings following my parliamentary surgeries. They are most excited when giving accounts of first-class matches ... and they appreciate a game that is well and decently played.[53]

Like Spriggs, many noted that their areas did not suffer from what seemed to be a growing national problem. They typically cited disorder at Manchester and Liverpool, industrial cities where well-known groups of travelling spectators originated. Such defences minimized the impact of football disorder on local reputations while simultaneously affirming it as a national dilemma. The associations with the northern deindustrializing cities also drew on long-standing reputations of militancy, disorder and crime in those areas.[54] Ultimately, this interplay between the national and the local allowed flexibility in generating political and moral claims about football disorder. Spriggs could comment with disdain that 'I cannot understand why anybody should want to misbehave at sports fixtures and inflict bodily harm on anybody', without having to condemn his own voters. Further, politicians like Spriggs could be seen to be tough on crime while simultaneously championing the pious moral conduct of their constituents.

More often, football violence was articulated as a national problem composed of the aggregate incidents of violence in several different parts of England and Scotland. As mentioned above, when seen as a national crisis, football disorder could be easily linked to moral discourses about youth degeneration. Politicians and football authorities who portrayed the problem of football disorder as widespread and ubiquitous could easily make a causal relation between this growing phenomenon and national moral concerns about disorder among young Britons. Mythologically, this strategy of nationalizing the phenomenon deemed it less connected to football, and thus protected football's national reputation. That is, if football violence could be seen as the outcome of generalized moral degeneration and not constitutive of it, then football could be relieved of a violent reputation. As early as 1965 the Football Association wrote to the Home Office stating that they were 'becoming increasingly exercised at the disorders which take place at football league grounds. We appreciate that these disorders are symptomatic of the lowering of standards of behaviour in all walks of life, but we are anxious to preserve the good name of football'.[55] Discussing football disorder as a national *and* moral problem not only elevated the level of social concern but also relieved football of the mythological burden of violence. Over-all, in presenting the problem with a repertoire of local and national rhetoric, politicians could simultaneously protect the reputations of their constituents and the national sport while maintaining a firm posture against social violence enacted within the football environment.

In stark contrast to the first approach, the second major rhetorical strategy politicians employed aimed at separating working-class violence at football matches from society generally. Like nationalizing the phenomenon, this strat-egy also aimed at protecting the mythological sanctity of the national sport. Though football violence was clearly a national problem, some depicted it as a problem acted out among 'uncivilized' sectors of British civilians. Discerning 'the blot on society' as apart and separate from the majority of the social body became a key function of the moral panic. Most often, politicians articulated this separation by arguing that violent spectators had no real affinity for football but merely chose this social arena as the place to conduct violent business. Spriggs argued vehemently: 'These thugs go to different parts of the country and enter sports grounds without any intention of watching a good game of any sport'.[56] The Football League agreed with this sentiment: 'There is growing evidence that, from the moment these people go to football matches, they are making it quite evident that their only reason for being at the match is to "have a go" at the opposing supporters'.[57] Driving a wedge between the national sport and the spectators who tainted it served to protect the sport as the iconic heritage of the nation. Keeping British football as a civilized tradition within a civilized nation became a central theme of political discourse about football disorder.

Local politicians and police also advocated the position that a small disruptive minority used football as their playground for violence. This argument allowed them to protect the local experience as well as the national sport. If the minority could be weeded out, then the local atmosphere of amicable football entertain-ment in large cities and small towns alike could be restored. After an infamously large disruption in Newcastle in 1969, the local police noted that 'the trouble mainly stemmed from the desire of a large number of people who were out for a day's drinking and used the football match as an excuse to provide the opportu-nity to satisfy their wishes'.[58] They had apparently noticed such behaviour at several matches earlier in the season, but chose to prosecute only when local fans garnered national press coverage. Liberal MP Clement Freud (Isle of Ely) asked the rest of the House to recognize that 'there is a great deal of hooliganism around which is now being vested in soccer'. He added, 'If there were no soccer, it is possible that the hooliganism would spread to badminton and ping pong'.[59] Again, the sentiment that violent youths utilized the football setting to engage in violent conflicts painted British football as a location victimized by working-class disruptions, ignoring community and club-based loyalties that appealed to many spectators. The fact that post-war football had been concretized as working-class tradition and popular leisure was not considered important.

Politicians separated football and violence as two discrete spheres of activity, distinguishing between 'desirable' and 'undesirable' football spectators based on class distinctions. In order to separate football violence from football, they quickly established and disseminated distinctions between appropriate and inappropriate groups of spectators to the larger public body. The distinction would both allow and encourage the violent minority to be extracted from the football environment. Politicians, football clubs and fans alike created this problematic dichotomy and implied the elements of social class and 'respectability' inherent in it. 'Troublemakers' and 'thugs' comprised the undesirable groups of football spectators: painted as inherently violent and animalistic, they ignored all prescribed codes of respectable conduct. Almost surely young working-class males, they inhabited the terraces on most weekends and wreaked havoc on the surrounding urban environs. Desirable spectators, in contrast, followed bourgeois codes of conduct, acting according to civil expectations of respectability and gentlemanly Britishness, and could usually afford seated accommodation at football matches.

Nearly all government, police and club documents discuss fans according to this binary, making the terms recognizable, clear-cut and value-laden. Most often, the undesirable spectators' most deplorable transgression was that they were 'dumb youths'. The Chief Constable in Sheffield and Rotherham commented: 'In the main they look what they appear to be, normal young hooligans often possessing little or no intelligence'.[60] Other commentators assumed the youths could be easily influenced and prone to volatility. The Harrington questionnaire asked the police authorities for their opinion on whether these youths could be easily induced to violent action by the media or their companions. Harrington and his committee assumed that while such behaviour could be expected from previously delinquent juveniles, those with a clean record must be susceptible to 'over-excitement'.[61] Several police noted that while known deviants could manipulate any given football setting to accommodate their activities with guile, other working-class kids could be easily pressured. In matches of great importance with large crowds, wrote the Deputy Chief Constable at Liverpool, 'the high level of hooliganism and misconduct ... created circumstances in which the great majority of spectators were confused in strange surroundings, and local youths were prepared to take advantage of the unusual situation'.[62] The Cheshire Constabulary used even stronger language to indicate their impressionistic nature: 'The mob mentality encourages cowardly nonentities into actions which they would never consider in isolation'.[63] Nearly always regarded as overemotional and prone to peer pressure from their delinquent counterparts, working-class youths generally composed the group designated as 'hooligans' and 'undesirables'. Though correctly labelled as violent, the press, politicians and police also labelled them immoral, unintelligent, excitable, uncivil and barbaric.

These stereotypical designations of spectators as dim and obtuse, depraved and violent, emotional and insulting, constituted an implicitly classed and gendered discourse. The anatomy of stereotypes often involved a series of inter-connected associations derived from several different axes of power.[64] These implicit connections between degeneration and working-class traditions drew on long-standing discourses of intelligence and morality that constructed pater-nalistic relationships between working-class men and their superordinates. Reifying football spectators as impish subjects in need of moral education struc-tured a relationship where implicit notions of class provided the main division between politicians and their subjects. In addition, assumptions of inappropri-ate emotionality drew on socially contingent associations with the 'feminine', and therefore denigrated spectators' masculinity. Postulations of supporters' stupidity also structured the figurative relationship, wherein spectators failed to meet the high standards expected by well-educated politicians and self-styled intellectual superiors. While politicians, football authorities, police officials and the press almost never overtly discussed class difference or defined masculinity, their discourse implicitly constituted a paternalistically classed and gendered discussion of football spectators.

The dichotomy of fan designations also worked to preserve a second myth. If the first myth to be protected was one of propriety and non-violence in a civilized Britain, then the second intersecting national myth involved the peace-ful harmony between social classes. Though social fractures pervaded post-war relationships, both political parties worked tirelessly to ensure that workers and middle-class citizens existed cordially even as the social gap between rich and poor widened after 1967.[65] Politicians gathering votes across the social spec-trum laboured to maintain the semblance of national unity despite these social fractures. Football violence, carried out mostly by young working-class men, made evident the widening fissure between bourgeois values and everyday work-ing-class experience. Discussing fans in the collective language of 'desirable/ undesirable' or 'genuine/troublemaker' allowed politicians and others to discuss the conflict between fans of different social backgrounds without explicitly dis-cussing class. Working-class youths could be lumped together homogenously as inherently violent and overemotional by their 'civilized' middle-class counter-parts, but the explicit language of class conflict need not be used by politicians. The term 'riff raff' appeared frequently as a coded term in both political and public discourse, as in the political cartoon by Ronald Giles depicting the gap between 'genuine' supporters and violent fans at Manchester, where the Man-chester United Supporters' Club frequently chimed in on discussions castigating their raucous peers (See Figure 2.1).

"A nice hero's welcome from
the United Supporters' Club
this is!"

Daily Express, September 12th, 1974

Figure 2.1 Cartoon by Ronald Carl Giles depicting Manchester United Supporters'
Club, *Daily Express*, 12 September 1974 © Express Newspapers, image provided by
British Cartoon Archive, University of Kent. The sign top right reads: 'Manchester
United Don't Need Riff Raff'.

Distinctions among fans not only provided a means by which to extol virtues of
civility, but also a method of discussing disparity between working-class youth
behaviours and bourgeois moral ideals without overtly challenging the myth of
national social peace.

In addition to the clearly identifiable fan binary, the second rhetorical strategy also demanded that the undisciplined group be seen as a small minority
overwhelmingly outnumbered and surrounded by the more 'civilized' majority.
Though this was the state of things in many localities, emphasizing the rhetoric
often obscured the social nature of football-related disorder. Mr Lewis Carter-
Jones (Labour) from Manchester relayed many politicians' consistent fears that
'a minority group is being allowed to dominate the pleasure and enjoyment of
the majority'.[66] Representing violent youths as a small minority indicated that the
problem could be more easily handled. Small groups of violent deviants allegedly
could be taught how to behave by a more civilized and overwhelming majority.
Painting violent spectators as a weak and marginal body within the larger body
of football spectators as a whole also contributed to their position as separate.
Mr Follows of the Football Association promised that 'the clubs certainly did

not recognize the hooligan fringe as genuine supporters', a position that was echoed by club chairmen throughout Britain.[67] In a separate Home Office meeting other club authorities conveyed that 'they were worried that the sport should be identified with this kind of misconduct'. The Home Office and club representatives agreed that 'a football match provided the occasion for misbehaviour, but the persons involved were usually not genuine supporters and the football clubs wanted nothing to do with them'.[68] Both Home Office representatives and football clubs often emphasized that the minority could not be 'genuine' supporters. Their authentication could only be confirmed by proper conduct that eschewed violence in the football environment.

In a third rhetorical strategy, the regulation of football violence was removed from the level of leisure and entertainment and situated within problematic law-and-order discourses. Politicians and football officials recognized that football disorder was understood as similar and indeed connected to other social concerns about widespread violence, moral degeneration and disorderly youth. More than that, elevating the topic to a law-and-order problem allowed politicians to address this social concern at a legislative level in cooperation with local police and magistrates' courts. Most importantly, politicians addressed it as a 'law and order' topic rather than a 'sporting' problem, implying that it could be quickly remedied without challenging the integrity and popularity of the national sport.

Howell often indicted football as a law-and-order dilemma, leading the charge against football violence for the Labour Party. Eager to dispel ideas of British football as a national sport in decline, Howell consistently expressed his disdain for soccer malfeasance:

> It is important, however, to reiterate that it is a blot on our society. I find it deplorable, as does the Home Secretary, and we are determined, by every means in our power, to stamp it out. I am sure that ... all those concerned will support us in this endeavour. It is a Home Office matter, one of law and order, rather than a sporting matter.[69]

As seen in this representative quote, the aforementioned strategic manoeuvres pervaded Howell's discussion about football violence. First, football violence is taken from the level of localized conflict and situated as a challenge to national society. Second, Howell assumed that a minority group of violent spectators can be identified and excised from the football environment. Third, the behaviour was condemned as a moral and civil evil, located within the government's purview of law-and-order, and removed from the sporting industry. Finally, the promise of quick retribution through future government action promised to ease social fears about the recurrence of such violence in the future.

Howell and other politicians often emphasized the threat that football violence posed to national values of civility and respectability as well. After calling for a fresh round of government meetings to discuss the problem with his Working Party in 1975, Howell called football hooligans 'pathological thugs. They are rejecting society and all its civilised values. We have got to show them that we are not giving in to these irresponsible lawbreakers.' Not to be outdone, the Conservative voice on sporting issues, shadow minister Hector Monro, commented: 'The thoughtless thugs have to be brought to their senses severely if football is to survive'.[70] According to these political threats, the apparent lack of civility and proper conduct could be counteracted with warnings of harsh punishment. Ensuring that inherently violent subjects would be punished for uncivilized acts served to represent politicians as tough on crime and protective of the nation's proposed values.

Protecting the reputation of football itself became synonymous with the idea of protecting the nation's respectable values. Members of Parliament, and Howell specifically, could not allow such a challenge to Britain's sporting tradition to go unpunished. After each incident of football violence was publicized widely in the press, politicians reiterated their desire to protect the national sport from a violent reputation. Ivor Clemitson (Labour) of Luton cried out in a Commons debate that 'we need to do far more thinking about how we can control the hooliganism which is blighting and ruining what to me is the greatest game that man has ever invented'.[71] If football as a sport mythologically represented the esteemed values of the nation – hard work, respectability, toughness and fair play – then a blight on the game could be interpreted as a blight on the nation itself. Eldon Griffiths, a leading voice on sporting issues for the Conservative Party and the Minister for Sport under Heath, explicitly connected the image of the nation to the appearance of sport as a British tradition: 'What has been happening on our football grounds is an affront to the sporting ideal, a disgrace to the game of football and a blot on the reputation of this country in the world'.[72]

In all of these political statements, articulated in public debate and through the press, concerned politicians worried most about the presentation of the sport to the nation. Practically, it provided an available and cheap form of leisure and entertainment for Britons. Mythologically, football signified a national heritage and custom deeply connected to the national values championed within British civil society. Politicians, especially Denis Howell as the leading voice on sport in Britain, used this opportunity not only to reaffirm their position within their Parties, but also to rearticulate the importance of football within society and Britain's sporting reputation within the global community.

British Violence Abroad: The First Incidents

Ideas of Britishness embodied in sport received their harshest challenges from the first incidents of British football deviancy exported abroad. The most successful British clubs also participated in several European competitions, and loyal fans followed their teams to the continent. Spectators' values of community, territoriality and loyalty often led to violent conflict among groups of British fans and continental spectators. Not simply domestic problems, these events forced the Home Office, and later the Foreign and Commonwealth Office (FCO), to deal with criminal acts of violence carried out by British football spectators in cities abroad. Two incidents in particular – in Mexico in 1970, and in Rotterdam in 1974 – forced the FCO and the Home Office to generate diplomatic strategies to safeguard Britain's international reputation. While exporting British football violence eventually became more frequent and again consumed the defenders of moral and national virtue in the 1980s, these first incidents reveal how the state dealt with initial challenges to the sometimes violent image of British citizens overseas.

The English looked eagerly to the 1970 World Cup, held in Mexico, to see if the British national football team could repeat a world championship. The Foreign and Commonwealth Office also scrutinized the team and its travelling fans. Haunted by fears of an international press conflict and growing levels of domestic football violence, English involvement in the 1970 competition heightened government anxieties about the image of British football abroad. The FCO hoped for an uneventful tournament and watched British travelling fans closely. But the FCO also anticipated that using football to facilitate subtle diplomatic tactics would allow the agency to address the contest over Britain's sporting image in Latin America. Commonwealth Office agents showed particular concern over the bad press the national team received after England beat both Mexico and Argentina in the 1966 competition. Mexican public scorn for the British team peaked when several British press outlets and the Football Association objected to holding the competition in Mexico, citing problems with altitude and underdeveloped infrastructure and stadiums. They also criticized Mexico's role as host of the Olympic Games in 1968.[73] One FCO officer remarked, 'The UK received such a bad press in the Argentine (and in the rest of Latin America for that matter) that relations at a working level cooled decidedly in Argentina for an embarrassingly long period. It was all sour grapes.' British Commonwealth officials, in an effort to re-establish their working relationships at the government level 'thereafter did go to considerable lengths to try to redress the balance and to defend our sporting ability and integrity'.[74]

The FCO, in conjunction with Howell, also tightly controlled the exposure Mexican journalists had to the British team, and sent a representative along with the squad to supervise their interaction.[75] Both the Home Office and the British Embassy in Mexico shared their concern that bad media relationships could hinder international relations, blaming 'an unduly one-sided attitude by British Press commentators' along with 'Mexican chauvinism', and 'the refusal of Mexican media to come to terms with the ground rules for contact between themselves and our Team Manager and players'. Noting that 'the Mexican press has been childish, ignorant and sometimes vicious', the Embassy concluded that 'the sooner the Mexicans teach their public to grow up the better'.[76] Despite their obvious paternalist condescension, all three British agencies ensured that both the Mexican and British press did not continue to badger or bait one another, and attempted to remove any political overtones from the football tournament.

The Embassy also proactively attempted to improve Britain's footballing image by encouraging Mexican football authorities to award English captain Bobby Charlton, the darling of English soccer, an honorary award. The governor of Jalisco presented Charlton with the Jalisco Sportsman of the Year honour during the tournament, the first time the medal was given to a foreigner. The Embassy telegraphed Howell and the FCO, stating that 'the governor's gesture was made in part to diminish unfair criticism of the England team'. They encouraged the domestic offices to promote the story within the British press, inviting both the BBC and ITV to film the event, and noted that the Embassy would be 'grateful for anything the news department can do to give prominence to the story as demonstration that basic British-Mexican friendships are unaffected by current polemic of sporting journalists'.[77] The public display was meant to convey messages of public reconciliation and promote objective press perspectives within a volatile environment. More importantly, the event revealed that maintaining Britain's sporting image proved imperative to international political relations.

Though, in the end, only a few isolated incidents of British spectator violence occurred in Mexico, the embassy wrote that 'England's elimination in the quarter final was disappointing but a relief'.[78] The American Department of the Foreign and Commonwealth Office echoed the sentiment:

> We were indeed disturbed at the hammering which our relations with Mexico were receiving and must admit to sharing your sense of guilty relief when England went out – if only because there is now some hope that for the next four years at least we can continue to conduct our relations with Latin America without burning resentment.[79]

Both Home Office and FCO officials realized that Britain's elimination from the tournament would lead to no further opportunities for fan violence. In the end, only a few publicized scandals regarding unpaid hotel bills really reflected poorly on British fans.[80] But both offices' concern about the impact of disruptive episodes abroad intensified after football assumed its place within national mythology through debates over football violence and working-class spectators at home.

Apart from the World Cup, European competitions provided opportunities for British fans to follow their club teams, often providing pretexts for violent conduct on the Continent. The first few incidents of violence in Europe forced Howell and the FCO to assume responsibility for political or financial damage incurred by European neighbours. In May 1974 several Tottenham Hotspur FC fans followed their squad from London to Rotterdam, and violence involving both sides' supporters marred the match. British fans arrived in Rotterdam early, and many drank heavily on the trip over. Though the first leg of the match in London saw no spectator violence, the proceedings began with 750 spectators tearing up the British Rail Ferry 'Avalon', resulting in the cancellation of their return tickets.[81] Throughout the afternoon police were inundated with complaints about the 4,000 Spurs fans who made the trip over. The final consular report read like a riot commentary:

> There were many cases of petty pilferage in shops, unpleasant arguments, occasional fights between the English themselves and also one or two with some Dutch supporters, and some stone throwing at shop windows. One Furniture shop had its contents taken out on to the pavement and a clothes shop was ransacked, clothes stolen, and till box taken away.[82]

By the time the actual match began, several fights involving weapons ensued within the terraces. Police reporting to the scene engaged in violent encounters with the fans while attempting to quell the fights and disarm the Dutch and British spectators. British fans broke down the rails and wooden chairs adjoining the terraces and threw them at their Dutch counterparts. In the end, the local Red Cross treated 120 people, eighty were hospitalized, and damage to the Feyenoord ground totalled nearly 20,000 guilders (over £3,000).[83]

Despite warnings from the Home Office to pay attention to fans' behaviour, the British Consulate-General in Rotterdam, W. F. B. Price, remarked that colleagues from the Consulate and the Embassy 'allowed their own belief in British standards of fair play to cloud their judgement and they underestimated the potential danger of unchecked hooligans'.[84] Price, after interviewing the police involved, admitted that the situation became severely violent and life-threatening: 'The situation was no doubt a dangerous one with a distinct threat of danger to life'. Yet, he downplayed the political ramifications of football violence on the Continent, stating that 'the matter should not be exaggerated ... Every nation has its hooligans and fighters. The honour of the British nation has not been dragged through the mud by the behaviour of the Spurs' fans. Soccer is not that important.' Price repeatedly noted that Dutch police authorities and government representatives agreed with British ambassadors about the incident and encouraged all parties to 'forget the sorry story'.[85]

In London, British domestic representatives disagreed. Though Price may have been correct in assuming the Dutch wanted to ignore the incident, he drastically underestimated the challenge that European public awareness of British football violence presented to the British themselves. In London, the public and state representatives alike were furious at fans for their conduct and at foreign ambassadors for their negligence. The national press presented the violent episode as a dangerous extension of domestic football affairs. The *Times* blew the story out of proportion, asserting that 'Rotterdam had not been visited by such scenes of violence since before the war'.[86] *Guardian* reporter Peter Cole quoted an unidentified Red Cross spokesman: 'They were like animals, these drunken English kids. We've never seen anything like it before and we never want to see it again.'[87] Both reports emphasized violent engagements between spectators and the damage to property that the Dutch club and Dutch citizens incurred.

Howell, away on vacation, issued a statement through the Department of the Environment: 'The behaviour of some football supporters is intolerable. These Spurs fans were not only representing the Tottenham club, which has a fine record in Europe, but they were representing the British people'. Like the national team itself, British spectators assumed the responsibility of British representation while abroad. Labour MP Tom Torney of South Bradford echoed Howell's reaction: 'These fans are regarded as ambassadors for Britain when they are abroad. I am utterly disgusted with them'.[88] Price too expressed consternation over the damage to perceptions of British propriety. In private correspondence to the Consular Office in London he wrote, 'We on our side have important morals to draw – not least the danger of sending young supporters abroad in floating pubs to arrive at the football venue with plenty of extra drinking hours in hand'.[89] Though football violence may have had little actual influence on inter-European relationships, British politicians from several different agencies condemned football violence and its reflection upon British values. Such assumptions effectively accorded football fans power over foreign policy.

The public also responded to the Rotterdam fiasco, revealing that many British citizens felt the ordeal possessed political and mythological ramifications as well. Using language drawn from emergent law-and-order discourses, several Britons expressed their dismay to their local MPs and the Foreign and Commonwealth Office. One man wrote the Netherlands Ambassador in London:

> I feel sure many of my fellow countrymen share my shame and disgust and would like it placed on record that my feelings are typical and trust your countrymen will understand that this behaviour is not representative of the British public in general and know that a warm and deep regard exists between the people of both nations. I am confident that you will receive many letters in a similar vein from others of my countrymen, and can only express my own personal deep regret for this incident.[90]

The letter was forwarded to the FCO as evidence of the British public's disappointment with British spectators. Another man wrote his MP, Margaret Thatcher:

> I am sure that you share with the rest of us a feeling of outrage at the disgraceful happenings of yesterday in Rotterdam. I am writing to ask you to press the Government to send an official apology to the Dutch Government for the behaviour of thugs and vandals who should never have been allowed to visit a foreign country.[91]

Thatcher forwarded the letter immediately to the FCO, asking that the Embassy indeed issue a formal apology.[92] Both letters affirmed the fears of Howell and the FCO that the public also regarded the incident as a blow to Britain's sporting image.

All parties expressed the need to protect the role of football in Britain's national mythology because it bolstered Britons' ideas of themselves. Football violence reflected poorly on constructed representations of civility and propriety. More importantly, the first incidents of British violence exported abroad inhibited the projection of those national values to the Continent. Football violence abroad engaged European counterparts in an ongoing process of maintaining Britain's national values, but only inasmuch as they provided an audience for behaviour that transgressed appropriate British demeanour. These contraventions also provided opportunities for British authorities to engage a second and more important audience: the British public. Domestic football violence created a pretext to discuss moral regulations of working-class young men, while international football violence revealed how enmeshed those moral discourses had become with the imagined national ethos.

An important aspect of the events in Rotterdam is that the FCO suppressed several complaints of brutality and unnecessary force by Dutch police. The day after the incident, a consular official telegraphed FCO headquarters, noting, 'Members of the Embassy who were present say that feelings were running high on both sides and there may well have been some provocation' of British fans by Dutch officers.[93] Price spent the first few days after the incident interviewing both English and Dutch fans, as well as the local police. He wrote to the British Consulate that, 'I suppose that a lot of the complaints and questions you may have to answer will be about alleged police brutality ... When they did wade in (as they then had to do) they may have over-reacted'.[94] In his final report Price recounted that after British spectators attacked eight officers in an initial clash, the Chief Inspector at the stadium returned to the Spurs' section with fifty uniformed, baton-wielding officers with batons midway through the first half. 'His orders to his men were to go in and hit hard', Price declared. 'His men had to force their way up the staircase against a rush of spectators trying to get away from the scene. The Dutch [police] themselves admit that some of the British injured in the baton charge were probably innocent bystanders'.[95] The Dutch police 'have accepted the situation philosophically', noted Price, 'and feel that the least said the sooner mended'.[96] Clearly, the Dutch police minimized the claims of alleged brutality by capitalizing on the British ambassador's desires to avoid reconciling financial and political damages.

At least one MP confirmed that several of his constituents testified to severe police brutality and asked that the FCO and the Home Secretary look into these claims.[97] Errol Rasin, a Spurs fan who broke a leg in the melee, also told the

Guardian, 'I blame the Dutch police for the whole thing. I was at the bottom of the stand, which was very full. Suddenly the police attacked and everybody fell on top of one another'.[98] Jenkins asked the FCO to handle the request. Conservative Roy Hattersley, Minister of State at the time, gave a diplomatic but unsatisfying response. Noting that 'we have had a number of letters expressing regret at what occurred', he told Graham to inform his constituents that 'the unfortunate yet inevitable point is that on such occasions innocent bystanders do get hurt'.[99] Both state ministries preferred to move past the incident without disturbing the Dutch government any further. They purposefully neglected to investigate several claims of police brutality, instead opting to resolve the incident through a formal apology to the Dutch. The FCO and the Home Office sidestepped questions about who instigated the violence and how the police exacerbated the conflict. Instead the tested narrative of British working-class spectators, drunk and disorderly, disrupting the purity of the game and misrepresenting British citizens' ideas of themselves, proved more readily believable.

Later that summer, disturbances among Manchester United fans in Ostend, Belgium, gave Howell the opportunity to chastise improper spectator conduct publicly. Howell raised the oft-suggested threat of ticketing controls, a subtle means of restricting access to matches. He stated later in 1974 'We have to make sure that tickets for these games go to people who can conduct themselves properly'. He added that 'what we want is for bona fide supporters to go to these matches – people who can be a credit to the club and the country. I am not surprised that people abroad are getting fed up with the action of these hooligans'.[100] These high-profile foreign incidents clearly embarrassed the British government, and in each case the resident consulate issued several apologies while Howell and other moralists in Britain chastised working-class men for their behaviour. Howell expressed frustration with foreign violence to the House after an incident with Leeds United fans in Paris the following summer: 'The time has come when we must stop that practice ... It is a disgrace, which must be brought to an end ... No one was more humiliated than I was at having to apologise to the French Prime Minister for the behaviour of so-called football supporters. They were behaving like louts.'[101] Howell not only communicated his embarrassment to his colleagues, but again concentrated on behaviour and conduct of working-class spectators, condemning it on moral grounds. The extension of domestic football violence to the Continent allowed Howell to elevate the issue in public consciousness, promoting further means of working-class exclusion such as ticket controls. British football disorder not only reflected poorly on local communities and challenged the limits of civil conduct; it also forced state and citizen alike to re-evaluate the national mythology of British class harmony and the beneficial international image of sport.

Conclusions

British football violence, both within and outside Britain, challenged ideas of national respectability and national cohesiveness. British ideas of civility and gentlemanly conduct, articulated by various moral and political agents, were challenged by violent behaviour among both players and spectators. Moral anxieties about football violence did not arise in a social void, but were articulated through a variety of cultural themes that expressed fears of working-class youth dissidence, moral deterioration in society generally and perceptions of a growing breakdown in law-and-order. Politicians and press agents, including Denis Howell in particular, exploited these social apprehensions to generate political capital by articulating their toughness on criminal issues and appearing to be integral to regenerating national values. By advocating discursive strategies to limit, define and sensationalize the problem, the British state contributed to making the conflict over British football violence one of the major moral issues of the 1970s. When political attention and press coverage amplified the social significance of football violence, the rhetoric proved extremely powerful. The development of these political attitudes and the elevated position of football violence in British public consciousness allowed the state to promote and execute new policies of punishment, exclusion and segregation. These policies are explored in Part II of the book.

PART II: THE TOTAL POLICY OF CONTAINMENT

3 VIOLENT ENVIRONMENTS: PHYSICAL SPACE, DISCIPLINE AND FOOTBALL DISORDER

Throughout the 1970s the Home Office, the Department of the Environment and local police authorities in areas across Britain sought to control fans' behaviour through a variety of institutional, environmental and legal measures. While the present chapter focuses on the creation of spectating environments that aimed at restricting violence, Chapters 4 and 5 evaluate the multiple policing and juridical changes ushered in by the state. Together the three chapters reconstruct the integrated approach the state and British police advocated to discipline the growing number of unruly spectators. In many ways, these policies reflected the discursive construction of unruly spectators that challenged the sporting mythology of British nationalism. The creation of football 'hooligans' as animalistic and brutish allowed severe and violent physical measures to be taken against spectators without significant public outcry. As I argue in this chapter, governmental authorities developed architectural policies of dividing physical space and restricting spectators' movement that created stadium environments which invited instability and threatened rulebreakers with increasingly violent outcomes.

Successive Labour and Conservative governments gradually increased control over spectators throughout the 1970s. Manipulations to the physical environment in this arena had been ongoing since the post-war period, as sizes of crowds increased and football disorder accompanied the game's increasing popularity. The long processes of physical manipulation culminated in the 1989 Taylor Report, produced after the lethal Hillsborough disaster, where ninety-six travelling Liverpool supporters died on 15 April 1989 at an FA Cup semi-final with Sheffield Wednesday. Most of those who died were crushed to death or suffocated within the enclosed confines of an overcrowded pen in the Leppings Lane end of the stadium. Lord Justice Taylor chaired the inquiry into the disaster, and the ensuing Taylor Report resulted in the widespread commercialization of football, the end of terrace spectating through the introduction of all-seat stadiums, and a significant decrease in the levels of football violence. While most sociologists have focused on the drastic changes to the football environment after the publication of Taylor's recommendations, this chapter will focus on earlier manipulations of physical space that made disasters like Hillsborough possible in the first place.[1] Though all-seated stadiums eventually provided an answer to immediate fears about crowd safety, the framework for architectural manipulation and spatial division had been in place for many decades. By the 1970s, through policies of fan containment, supporter segregation and restrictive physical barriers, football authorities followed the state's chief suggestions by manipulating the architectural settings in which football violence took place. Encouraged by the state and British police forces, clubs across Britain facilitated the construction of violent environments that aimed, paradoxically, at preventing violence.

Scholars have conceptualized the typical stadium in the post-war era diversely as a prison, a theatre and an embodiment of Jeremy Bentham's panopticon.[2] Segmentation of spectating and playing eras has ushered in the delineation of enclosed spaces, constantly monitored by police, which closely resemble other contested spaces of power such as prisons, hospitals and schools.[3] Such comparisons have enabled scholars to compare the modern stadium to Michel Foucault's history of the prison and his reading of Bentham's panoptical schema as well.[4] Just as Foucault's history of punishment traced the evolution of public discipline into private, segmented prisons, the modern stadium has evolved from an open and free arena of spectating into a highly disciplined and controlled environment.[5]

This chapter builds on these perspectives by tracing the development of the controlled environment before the Taylor Report. Rather than assuming that all-seated stadiums provided a necessary answer to football violence once and for all, evidence shows that the seated stadiums were the last of a long series of developments in architectural and environmental control of football spaces that occurred at government behest. The modern stadium was not created out of a social and political vacuum, but rather over time and through significant contests for power and social control. Rather than merely conceptualizing the stadium as a Foucauldian space, this chapter will make clear the multiple physical divisions within the stadium that the British government and British police attempted to institute throughout the 1970s, revealing an evolution in disciplinary spatial practices. This evidence is culled from private government files – correspondence, meeting minutes, memos, briefs, press clippings – collected by the Home Office and the Department of the Environment as they contemplated remedies to the social problem of football violence. Furthermore, police reports and oral testimonies also reveal the negotiation of meaning and contestation over physical spaces both within and outside the stadiums during the late

1960s and 1970s. In much of Foucault's work, power, in its various devilish and capillary manifestations, often goes uncontested. This chapter will also address the adverse social reactions, among football supporters and clubs, to the government implementation of physical discipline.

In hindsight, the policies of immobility and containment which emerged reflected the state's increasingly regimented yet unsuccessful response to a complex and intractable social phenomenon. Football violence surely was the work of its participants, but the policies and practices developed to prevent it often worsened the problem. Government authorities clearly wanted to ensure the safety of all spectators, but often approached the violent supporters with disdain, and regularly showed less regard for their security. The resulting changes to stadiums reflected the difficulty of attempting to protect all spectators, clubs' financial interests and the British Home Office's reputation. Governing authorities attempted to identify and discipline the violent minority through new schemes for spatial organization that affected all supporters, resulting in methods that paradoxically endangered everyone while providing security for none.

Treating all supporters as subjects of spatial discipline not only proved ineffective but also attempted to control risk by assuming all supporters in terraces could be violent. This approach emphasized anonymity in the application of spatial constraints in attempts to provide security for all. As others have noted, targeting groups instead of individuals, based solely on their potential for disorderly conduct, was a type of risk management that diminished civil liberties. Treating supporters universally as potential delinquents jeopardized the principles of legality and personal liability that constitute democratic legal frameworks.[6] These measures thus constituted a breach of post-war social democratic promises in this particular arena of leisure. And as mechanisms for social control they blurred the lines between acceptable and punishable behaviour by promoting anonymity, thus often encouraging the very behaviours they hoped to prevent. Furthermore, they worked to build a reciprocal cycle of distrust between social control agents and supporters. Attempts to manage risk through spatial organization, as well as policing and legal punishment, were also hindered by difficulties in the structure of British government: local and national offices faced problems of mediation and competition as all worked to present the image of security and order.[7] As the following chapters show, government agencies and police, even when working in concert, could not effectively eliminate football violence, and often exacerbated social conflicts in the sport.

This chapter first outlines the divisions of physical space employed in stadiums during the emergence of football disorder, from the late 1960s to 1970s. The strategies of spatial division better assisted police work and aimed at keeping fans controlled within specific spaces. The second section evaluates the government's drive for architectural changes as a key element of their total policy against football violence. Denis Howell's leadership figured heavily in creating a mentality of social discipline and concretized policies of containment in development since the 1960s. The third section evaluates the various resistances to the state's implementation of its spatial policies in British football. Spectators who inhabited these areas intermittently invested them with various social meanings as they did in previous eras: belonging, territoriality and community, among others. These values contrasted with many of the divisive implementations that aimed at breaking apart physical spaces and divesting them of social meaning. Overall, the chapter traces the changes in physical environments of stadiums that resulted in a highly disciplined sports setting where spatial divisions facilitated a total policy of containment.

The Development of Physical Space Divisions in Football

Government officials, especially those at the Home Office and Department of Environment in charge of sport, gradually created policies of spatial division to aid police. Architectural manipulation became a key component in fighting football violence and separating rowdy fans from 'genuine' supporters. The divisions of physical space progressed over time from impromptu and makeshift developments at local clubs to national Home Office mandates. In order to understand how these policies developed, one can look at the evolution of physical policies by government agencies during the period. From the late 1960s through the 1970s several government commissions, including the Wheatley licensing scheme (1969–72), the committees that constructed the Safety at Sports Grounds Act (1973–5) and Howell's Working Party on Football Hooliganism (1973–7) generated multiple sets of architectural policies. Each set of recommendations built upon its predecessors and contributed to the ongoing expansion of architectural means of behaviour control. By the mid-1970s a total policy of containment emerged that effectively integrated perimeter fences, penning, crush barriers, gangways, and an overall policy of fan segregation and division.

The final result of these inquiries, and the definitive articulation of the total policy of containment, was the Safety at Sports Grounds Bill enacted in 1975. The Bill followed the recommendations of the Wheatley report, which though published in 1972, never became law until Labour reclaimed a majority. Though couched in the language of 'crowd safety', the Bill addressed both popular fears about football disasters in unsafe, decrepit stadiums and the threat to the enjoyment of football leisure by disruptive, violent fans. 'Crowd safety' became a euphemism for the total clean-up of the football industry, from stadium provisions such as toilets and concessions to the architectural imposition of physical discipline. Through updating stadiums into modern, 'safe' spaces for regulated entertainment, clubs and government officials could also battle disorderly fans by creating tightly controlled and divided terrace areas. As Richard Lane at the Home Office noted, 'The line between measures for crowd safety and those for combating hooliganism can be very thin'.[8] Broadly, the Bill constituted a strong central government intervention into the football industry and a major imposition into private, commercial leisure provided by football clubs. It created a licensing scheme that mandated updates to terrace structures, crush barriers, stairways, egress and ingress provisions and other architectural considerations for crowd mobility and crowd control.

The Bill was long delayed in the debate stage, stemming from the lack of financial provision for clubs, especially the smallest ones, to implement the mandated changes quickly. Though the Bill was first introduced in 1972 shortly after the publication of the Wheatley report, it was not enacted until Howell solved the financial paradox. The state could not recommend drastic architectural changes to private stadiums without providing at least partial provision for the construction costs. Howell devised a solution by creating the Football Trust, an independent body in charge of distributing money for the changes. The Trust was funded by the 'Spot the Ball' competition, a nationwide lottery based on determining the position of an absent ball in a sports photograph.[9] In addition to the lack of financial provision, football clubs also worried about immediate problems with new statutes. Thus, the Bill's demands were not made completely mandatory right away, but rather certain changes were implemented over time for clubs of different sizes and levels of financial stability.

In constituencies like Manchester and London, both Labour and Conservative politicians milked the Bill for political capital and capitalized on public opinion against football violence, as the Bill promised changes to stadium landscapes that would further deter raucous behaviour. As Denis Howell noted:

> It is not just a question of how we can control large numbers of people gathered together in a sports ground. Considerations of safety for the public have become much wider than that. They involve questions of discipline – perhaps 'indiscipline' is the right word – of the followers of sport.[10]

Clearly, government officials and police intimately linked crowd safety and behavioural control as congruent problems to be addressed by architectural manipulation. By tracing the development of the Bill, government correspondence and political debates generated by it, its preceding reports and Howell's follow-up Working Party, one can begin to trace a narrative of the gradual implementation of environmental discipline.

Before football violence became recognized as a national problem in need of government intervention, attempts to manipulate the physical environment of football stadiums had been mostly instituted by clubs at the behest of local police. Usually, police formed barriers by positioning officers between the field of play and the terraces, and often between groups of rival fans. Using policemen as barriers took considerable manpower, however, and police often recommended that more permanent barricades be instituted. Police also frequently asked for cleared 'gangways' within the terraces: pathways that police could travel to gain entry into crowded areas to keep order. Gangways also provided entry points for ambulance services in case of an emergency.[11]

The 1967 Harrington Commission, the first government-sponsored investigation of football disorder, considered architectural manipulation briefly and attempted to address the concerns of police.[12] Police submissions to Harrington's research committee and the final report itself reveal the earliest suggestions for physical space divisions. The Chief Constable in York stated plainly what he wished to see at all stadiums:

> The proper definition of gangways, particularly in the popular and standing parts of the ground. In this respect I feel that more thought should be given to the provision of gangways as 'firebreaks' and indeed on some grounds where behaviour is particularly bad these areas could be split up and sealed off into 'pens' so as to prevent undue movement and to segregate the unruly. This would help overcome the difficulty the police face in sorting out the few trouble makers in a large group of people.

When asked to consider further what physical barriers might be helpful, he replied: 'Perhaps if it was possible to segregate the two sections and "contain the enemy", in the form of the hooligans, more active support might be forthcoming'.[13] Not only did the constable recommend physical confinement for rival fans, but he also supported penning as a way of keeping violent terrace fans away from their seated counterparts and the field of play in general. Recommended throughout the period, pens served two functions: they kept fans within the confines of the terraces and kept violence away from the rest of the stadium. Pens worked alongside the policy of fan segregation, which aimed at separating home and away fans in an effort to minimize violent encounters between the two groups. The quote also suggests that public and political support could be created by showing that local police would not tolerate lawlessness within stadiums. The constriction of movement was the key element in this proposal for physical discipline: decreased mobility purportedly precluded activities such as fighting, swaying and surging. His sentiments were representative of many of the police reports submitted for Harrington's review.

Another submission from Glasgow's chief constable, called for means of control for 'packing' the pens as fans entered the terraces. He complained that 'when cash payment is being made there is no way of limiting the admissions to any part of the ground. This results in bad packing and reduced freedom of movement for police'. He recommended turnstile counters and radio control towers that could determine when to close the pens based on crowd density.[14] Police, by the 1960s, were experienced in controlling crowd densities among terraces, but the advent of penning policies made filling the pens to a proper density a more detailed endeavour. Preferably, officers allowed fans entrance to the pens to an ideal mass where fan mobility was sufficiently restricted, but gangways were kept clear for police intervention. Minimizing the possibility of spectators' physical movement while simultaneously allowing police to enter the crowd and make arrests or ejections became a constant question for football police.

In the same submission, Constable Robertson also suggested that English and Scottish stadiums borrow the continental practice of fencing off the perimeter of the field to prevent pitch invasions and other disruptions to the most protected and sacred space in the stadium: the playing field.[15] He bluntly stated his opinion of pitch invasions: 'This is controlled in other countries by ditches and wire netting. Assuming the crowd is to be abandoned to its own furies, these are excellent.' Otherwise '[crowds] prevent the police from taking prisoners down to the track and from sending reinforcements from the track on to the terracing'. The constable's comments confirm that police attitudes could be extremely hostile to fans. The association between vicious animals in cages and rowdy fans in pens is perceptible in the constable's comments as well. Penning became not only a means of control but also a punishment for fans in some police districts. Inasmuch as penning helped distribute crowds throughout the terrace areas and kept disorderly fans off of the field of play, the pens also resembled cages where raucous spectators could enact their violent theatre without disturbing the rest of the attendees. The constable also suggested that some police preferred not to interfere or uphold the preference for order during terrace conflicts, preferring not to bother with fan conflict. Others hoped to maintain tranquil behaviour through intermittent interventions into the pen.

In the final report in 1968, Harrington followed the constables' directions and recommended an integrated series of architectural innovations that would work together to control fan violence. The report concluded that any kind of perimeter barrier could be particularly useful in light of the Glasgow constable's observation of European success experimenting with wire fences and ditches. The report added, though, that 'wire fencing interferes with vision and may inflame the crowd, and ditches filled with water may be preferable'.[16] The commission also recommended that these concrete ditches be bridged in certain areas for police access. Such barriers would be difficult to climb and 'considerably reduce the number of police required to patrol the perimeter as only a few would be required to control the bridges'. Other gangways and tunnels connected to pens needed to remain unblocked or were useless. The commission also suggested that clubs and police make the most of existing barriers in stadiums where the playing field was surrounded by a running track, as at Wembley in North London and Ibrox and Hampden Park in Glasgow, the three largest stadiums in Britain.

'Where such a track is impossible a steel barrier in the form of an arc behind the goal pushing the spectators well back has been shown to reduce considerably the throwing of articles at the goalposts'.[17] Such barriers also increased the space between the field and the terraces, thus allowing police more time to impede possible pitch invaders. The final recommendations – namely the policies of enclosed penning, fan segregation, and gangway provision – established a foundation on which subsequent government officials could build the architectural component of the solution to football disorder and fan violence. In essence, the research committee gathered a wide assortment of impromptu physical space implementations which aimed at solving immediate problems.

A year later, Sir John Lang chaired the first Working Party on Crowd Behaviour at Football Matches, requested by Denis Howell and the Labour party to investigate crowd disturbances in a more formal and authoritative fashion than Harrington's experimental survey. Under Lang, a party of technicians, football authorities, Home Office representatives and police directors visited clubs, held discussions with local police forces, and reported back to the Minister for Sport throughout the 1968/69 season.[18] While the report addressed many of the same questions about violence prevention, player discipline, police organization and crowd safety as the Harrington report, during its preparation members engaged in long debates over perimeter fencing and police access. The debates, conducted in meetings with constables and club leadership, revealed the multiple suggestions and complications introducing perimeter fences and crowd enclosures engendered.

The most prominent topic during the investigations became the usefulness of perimeter fencing and its possible dangers to terrace supporters. At Newcastle in May 1969 a pitch invasion threatened to cancel the results of a nearly completed match between Newcastle FC and Glasgow Rangers. It was evident from the fans' behaviour that the invasion, carried out by nearly 500 spectators, was meant not only to disrupt the match but to encourage the referee and football officials to call for a replay. While visiting St James Park in Newcastle, Lang's Working Party engaged in a lengthy discussion with local police over the difficulties caused by perimeter fencing and enclosed fan terraces. Police at Newcastle argued that although a few meant to have the game cancelled, policemen on the spot acted quickly to pull spectators over the low barrier and onto the pitch to avoid crushing at the front of the enclosure. They reacted negatively to the Working Party's suggestion of raising the barrier from four feet to eight feet tall. The police noted that

> the invasion of the pitch acted as a safety valve, it provided an outlet for the tension which had gradually built up to subside. A very high fence would have prevented spectators getting to safety from the 'centre of trouble' and made it difficult for ambulancemen to have got into the crowd to attend to or even reach spectators in need of attention.[19]

They recommended that if the Working Party wished to recommend higher fences at all grounds, perimeter fences should be equipped with gates to relieve pressure at the front or bottom of the enclosures where people could be crushed against the barriers, and 'escape spaces' be provided between the field and the perimeter.

In preparing the final draft of the Lang Report, members of the committee debated over the stringency with which to suggest higher, tougher perimeter fencing and barriers. Early drafts included extra paragraphs which addressed the 'safety valve' approach to perimeter fences and warned clubs planning on installing high barriers of the dangers of tight enclosures:

> The question of erecting barriers designed to prevent spectators from invading the pitch and thus interfering with play can present difficulties. In theory, it would be possible to say that it is essential wherever serious encroachment on the playing area is to be apprehended – and this would apply to any ground likely to be used often for very important matches – such barriers should be erected. We are thinking in terms of an 'unclimbable' fence to a height of not less than six feet above the playing surface which while permitting spectators to view the game would effectively prevent any serious invasion of the pitch. Barriers of this kind are frequently seen at the more important stadia overseas. But escape on to the pitch is sometimes the only way in which spectators who are uncomfortably close to fighting and other dangerous incidents developing in the middle of a crowd can remove themselves to safety ... if such a barrier would lead to the elimination of an escape route from a dangerous situation, it should not be erected but in lieu additional police, who should face the crowd at moments of excitement, should be stationed in parts of the ground at which trouble is thought possible.[20]

The paragraph would have warned clubs clearly that enclosures could become dangerous as spectators could not avoid fights, swaying, crushing or riots if they occurred within the enclosed pens without an escape outlet through the fence barrier nearest the pitch. Lang intended to include the paragraph in the section on perimeter policing but faced strong opposition from other members of the Party.

Though the Working Party meant to provide counsel on ideal architectural conditions, they also remained responsible for presenting a message to the public of total control and future safety at football matches through the absolute elimination of football violence. Thus, several members opposed any spectators on the pitch whatsoever, regardless of the circumstances. Many members seemed willing to compromise spectators' safety for the purposes of political theatre. Walter Winterbottom, former England national team manager and director of the national Sports Council, objected to the paragraph's inclusion because he felt that spectators should seek the exits and the top of the terraces, where they entered the enclosure. He argued to the other members in his draft comments, 'I am not at all keen about the proposed alteration ... I think it is an exaggeration to say that when a disturbance occurs on the terraces the first thought of the spectator who is not involved is to rush on to the football field.'[21]

However, close packing of the enclosures aimed at restricting mobility of the crowd entirely, especially during large derby matches where crowd disturbances were more likely. It would take great effort and much time for an individual to move through the forcefully packed crowd and up the terraces, especially during moments of panic. Achieving exit through the upper entrances rather than over or through the front barriers would be nearly impossible during large disturbances, small riots or group fighting within the enclosures.

Mr Denis Follows, representative to the Party from the Football Association, objected strongly as well, fearing the caveat revealed the lack of authority and control within the stadium environment. 'In the first place may I say that I do not agree in principle with the philosophy that a football pitch should be used as a kind of escape route for spectators involved in disorder on the terrace', he argued. 'I think this is a philosophy of defeatism. Certain grounds must have bigger barriers between the spectators and the playing pitch ... This is ridiculous.' He further protested that using police instead of six-foot tall barriers prevented them from being among the crowd and attending to the disturbances themselves when they arose.[22] Though the final resolution to the debate is unclear, chairman Lang dropped the warning paragraphs from the final copy of the report. Such debates revealed that members of the 1969 Working Party knew of the potential dangers of enclosing fans without proper outlets for their safety, were warned by police of the potential for disaster on several occasions and still neglected to include these warnings in their endorsement of stronger and taller perimeter barriers.

Instead, the section on physical space division in the Lang report proposed a multifaceted model that comprehensively accounted for crowd mobility and crowd disorder through a variety of stadium modifications. Like the Harrington report, the Lang report envisioned a model architectural environment that elevated contemporary stadium standards to facilitate more invasive police practices. Gangways and barriers within the terraces aimed at building small enclosures to prevent crowd mobility and facilitate policing. New measures such as funnelling systems of ingress, effective controls on total admission and police-regulated crowd packing were also recommended. A laundry list of possible field barriers was also included, with suggestions for wooden fences, iron railings, brick or concrete walls, sunken terrace depressions and dry moats topping the list. The report contained few warnings against the possibilities of 'crushing' within enclosures, and only proposed that crowds should be packed tighter to prevent any movement at all.

The third and final government commission of this period, the Wheatley inquiry, resulted in a licensing scheme to regulate stadium safety, and ultimately prepared the way for the Safety at Sports Ground Bill. The Wheatley commission proceeded in the aftermath of the Ibrox stadium disaster on 2 January 1971. As spectators left the match during its conclusion, the home team Glasgow Rangers scored to tie the match. Several spectators on an old stairwell leading to the top of the terraces quickly reversed their direction to return to the terraces, and a build up of pressure occurred resulting in the collapse of the stairwell's barriers and sixty-six fatalities. The newly appointed Conservative administration quickly called for an investigation into stadium crowd safety and stadium modernization, chaired by Lord Wheatley, a former Solicitor General for Scotland and Labour MP. Even though the fatalities were not due to violence per se, the commission's charge included a wide-ranging investigation of stadium security provisions and the means by which further changes to stadium architecture could aid in the crackdown on football violence. The Wheatley investigation, like the Lang report, involved interviewing clubs, police liaisons and fielding public suggestions for new approaches.

Because earlier suggestions for spatial discipline had not prevented football violence, the commission adopted a more traditional scientific and experimental approach to physical space and the human body than its predecessors. Their penchant for modernist approaches to social problems can be seen in the methodical approach to football violence during the inquiry. The Home Office certainly encouraged this new agenda for social research into the problem, appointing a technical director and a committee of architectural officers to the party, while football and political representatives had composed the previous committees. The Conservative administration, and Eldon Griffiths, Minister of the newly minted Department of the Environment, expected concrete advances in deterrents to football violence through the proposed licensing scheme aimed at 'crowd safety'. The Wheatley commission also drew on several technical reports and experiments carried out by Home Office scientists and independent architectural firms to build a cache of evidence before determining the proper recommendations for football clubs. These reports often tested the physical limits of the body in tight, immobile enclosures in order to determine suitable conditions for spectating in terraces. In addition, shortly after the Ibrox disaster, Sports Council director Walter Winterbottom had begun his own investigation into stadium environments during the latter half of the 1970/71 season, and turned over his research and recommendations to Wheatley's group. Winterbottom's report and evidence, though never published, proved a significant complement to Wheatley's own research, and included several technical reports as well.[23]

Shortly after the disaster, Home Office scientists drafted a brief report for cabinet-level ministers, including Eldon Griffiths and Henry Munro at the DOE, the point men charged with sports governance under the Conservatives. The report amassed research from local councils and professional architects. The Home Office's Chief Scientist and author of the report, C. J. Stephens, recognized the possible dangers encountered within terrace enclosures and aimed at determining their threat to safety. The report called for future technical experiments to ascertain, the precise causes of injury or death in these situations. Both the construction or simulation models and the nature of preventive measures would differ according to the proportions in which it is found to be necessary to counter massive crushing forces causing collapse of the chest cage, traumatic asphyxiation, suffocation, trampling injury, pressure of the soft tissues against hard objects so as to cause internal injuries, or limb fractures. It would also be helpful to know whether these injuries are due to forces directly downwards on to the ground or sideways against firm structures, or between persons.[24]

In this report, the body became the central focus of technical research and proposed experimentation. As several cases of crushing and physical injury had been reported both in the press and to government officials, the technical party focused their research on injury tolerance and the direct causes of physical damage within the terraces. By the mid-1970s, the government's insistence on containment and spatial organization led to experimental research on bodily injury and the possible violent outcomes of government-recommended spectator controls.

The stairwell incident at Ibrox directly reflected the possibility of a major accident within the terraces, as the two physical spaces, the terraces and a large stairwell, directly resembled one another. It became clear in the report that the possibility of a similar disaster in the standing accommodations alarmed the Home Office and the Department of the Environment, as well as the technical advisors. Thus, Stephens's report also recommended specialized scientific investigations into three main problems evident at Ibrox and other sites of physical injury at football matches: crush barrier placement, crowd movement and terrace slope incline. Crush barriers, common among terraces, aimed at preventing 'surging' and excessive movement within the terraces. Placed both perpendicular and parallel to the field, crush barriers were steel or wood beams raised three to four feet high that prevented surges within the crowd. Steep inclines and untested barriers could lead to serious injury when 'domino-like movement' forced spectators into contact with barriers and the boundaries of physical enclosures.[25] Thus, further experimentation needed to determine possible injury zones:

> A thorough investigation of the statics of the pile-up: – what is the extent and shape of the lethal zone and of the non-lethal injury zone – how are these affected by such factors as the steepness of the slope, the height, width and depth of the steps, the presence of level landings, the nature and position of retaining barriers or hand-rails, crowd density, and so on.[26]

Again, technical advisors deemed scientific analysis necessary to determine possible bodily injuries within delineated spaces. Further, the quote implied that non-lethal injury might be an acceptable outcome of enclosed spaces if lethal injuries could be avoided. Presumably, experimentation to determine the exact physics of pressure and motion against crush barriers on steep slopes would reveal the acceptable limits for bodily damage. As evidenced in this report, the Home Office adopted a policy of scientific experimentation that would provide precise technical answers to questions raised by dangerous stadium environments. In general, the proposed experimentation and early conclusions do not show great concern for the well-being of spectators but, rather, a rugged determination to define the limits for acceptable bodily injury. The modern, methodological approach focused on the body and the implications of corporeal damage within the punitive physical environments created to limit the mobility of spectators. The platform for social research into football violence now incorporated research onto the bodies of suspected perpetrators.

In addition, Winterbottom's research focused on defining divisions of space that demarcated acceptable physical dimensions per person within terraced areas of the stadium. The endless search for technical precision characterized Winterbottom's investigation as he attempted to create the ideal physical conditions to recommend to football clubs. After surveying nearly sixty stadiums, Winterbottom concluded that when packed to maximum densities, some terraces only provided 1 foot width of space to each spectator. He recommended 1 foot 9 inches minimum, and a mere 2.25 square feet of occupied space per person. Slope inclines at some stadiums also could be at a ratio of 1:2 with 8–9 inch rises per 14 inch flat step.[27] While this provided excellent sight lines for spectators, 'we are of the opinion that this is too steep a slope for big terraces making it necessary to have more transverse barriers, separated by fewer steps of terrace', he stated.[28] These small spaces and dangerous slopes could easily produce serious injury during times of swaying or in panic situations within enclosures.

Winterbottom also oversaw laboratory testing on crush barriers at several grounds that produced 'chest pressure tolerance thresholds' to be considered when clubs determined the construction of new steel rails. After witnessing engineering tests at Crystal Palace and Sheffield United's grounds he concluded that 206 pounds per foot was the maximum physical pressure the human body could withstand. He added that 'the size of the barrier will no doubt affect the tolerable chest pressure and hence both barrier spacing and design load'.[29] In essence, Winterbottom wanted to determine the limits of pressure on the body in order to establish where to place physical dividers such as crush barriers and terrace gangways so as to maintain limited crowd mobility without major injury.

The creation of an imaginary stable environment with minimal physical threats enabled Winterbottom to continue to recommend disciplined structural spaces that aimed at minimizing football violence. Such an ideal space could not be constructed without technical experimentation of the limits of the average human body under extreme pressures. While such experiments were not done on actual persons, simulations allowed the technical advisors to recreate the conditions and dynamics of swaying and surging within enclosed terraces. In sum, the physical limits of the human body determined the spacing and strength of physical barriers implemented into the architectural skeleton of any given sports ground. As one Winterbottom commission document summarized: 'Human injury tolerance is a further important factor closely related to the design and planning of barriers, staircases, etc'.[30] Adopting the language of modern engineering and architecture made scientific experimentation an acceptable practice for government-sanctioned social research into football violence. The Wheatley and Winterbottom reports pursued this direction, formulating acceptable limits to physical enclosure and bodily pressure thresholds with pseudoscientific precision.

Denis Howell and the Total Policy of Containment

Denis Howell, as in his righteous castigation of rowdy football spectators, played a significant role in the development of physical space policies. As Minister for Sport from 1964–70 and 1974–9, Howell served the Labour Party by being at the forefront of the battle against football violence in English, Scottish and Welsh stadiums. Howell oversaw the Harrington and Lang reports, two independently commissioned investigations into football hooliganism, during his first term. While the Conservatives held the Parliament during the early 1970s, Howell closely followed his counterpart, Minister for Sport Henry Munro (1970–4) and pushed the Parliament to debate the Safety at Sports Grounds Bill. By the time the Conservatives lost control of Parliament, Howell reassumed his position, quickly created a Working Party to stamp out the growing incidence of football violence, and claimed credit for himself and Labour in finally passing the Sports Grounds Bill into law.

After reassuming a more dominant role in ministerial politics, Howell aimed at finalizing a total policy of containment in order to discipline the spectating of football fans. He consistently sought to limit spectators' overall mobility and design architectural standards for modern stadiums that threatened fans with built-in consequences for football violence. Howell, more than any other political figure or football authority, aspired to stamp out what he defined as morally corrupt football violence through the menace of compensatory violence.

By the 1974–5 season, when Howell's Working Party travelled to nearly every large sports ground within Britain, his office advocated stronger political language, making more adamant recommendations about segregation and terrace divisions. Troubles with English fans abroad during the season spurred tougher restrictions on European matches as well.[31] The Party's primary tactic of restricting spectators' mobility extended to environments inside and outside the stadium. As one Home Office official stated:

> The Working Party's basic strategy is now to improve the effectiveness of the policy of containment, while considering the scope for more positive action such as fundamental research into the motivation of hooliganism. The containment strategy can be sub-divided into behaviour inside the stadia, transport to and from matches, and control of crowds between bus and coach stations and football grounds.[32]

The fundamental division between inside and outside the stadium had long been in discussion among government authorities, mainly because it determined whether clubs or the state paid the policing costs at each match. After problems with travelling spectators on trains, ferries and coaches in both domestic and foreign matches, Howell also increased efforts to police spectators' behaviour outside of the stadium as well.

Generally, the Working Party's approach to policing behaviour outside stadiums was to keep spectators enclosed in divided terraces within the stadium in the first place. Fans' violence could be more effectively policed and perpetrators apprehended when physical boundaries diminished the likelihood of spectators' flight. Keeping spectators inside also reduced the amount of criminal damage done to local shops and plazas when spectators stormed the area, as well as to unmanned railway stations. As one Scotland Yard commissioner stated, 'There is no doubt that as supervision is increased progressively through these phases so the disorder is retarded and this ultimately results in damage to trains and railway stations where, because of circumstances, they are temporarily without effective supervision by police'.[33] The displacement of fan violence onto the streets, pubs and rail stations outside the stadiums occurred during a time when police demands within the stadium already taxed available police officers and local police resources.[34] Police and government officials feared what violent activities spectators would engage in without physical impediments to flight, especially when open city spaces often had fewer police patrols than normal. This concern, in some areas, led to police advocating fewer ejections when fans caused disruptions. When police ejected fans they removed them from a confined, regulated and surveilled space into open settings where more space and idle time could lead to staged fights or group ambushes during or after matches.[35] Howell's Working Party, in consultation with police authorities in several different areas of Britain, accordingly attempted to keep disorderly fans within closely supervised terrace enclosures with limited mobility.

Once within the stadium, spectators in the mid-1970s encountered well-ordered and stricter constraints on their mobility under the Working Party's governance. The Party pressured clubs into converting all terrace spaces into tightly packed pens to prevent their ability to move. 'Crowds have movement available. We must stop that by dividing up these large areas in some way. I am in favour of doing it by isolating parts of the crowds with specific entrances and exits', Howell noted shortly after assuming leadership of the Working Party.[36] Segregation also became a more regimented element within the arsenal of physical discipline in the mid-1970s. Segregation provided the most direct means by which opposing groups of fans could be separated, especially during matches where rivalries between groups could be heated. Howell retrospectively admitted, 'I had to segregate fans because we'd got these terrible fights going on. I thought the only way I could deal with it at that moment was to make sure that the two sets of rival supporters were kept apart.'[37] Howell's desperation led him to promote segregation as a resolution to the problem of football violence, when practically the strategy actually increased hostilities between fans. One fan remembered that 'a lot of it wasn't about the fights. The police made it a confrontational situation by keeping us apart.'[38] Dividing fans into separate enclosures often encouraged territorial meanings that fans could engender with specific spaces within the stadiums. Territorialities often bred spectator violence as rival groups sought to defend terrace areas from one another. Segregation also clearly defined the opposition: rival fans knew where other fans spent the majority of the game, where they gathered, and often how they could be attacked. Furthermore, these segregated enclosures usually bordered one another, allowing defined groups to be within inches of each other, facilitating missile throwing and verbal abuse. In one particular situation at Ayresome Park in Middlesbrough, police erected the tarps used to cover goal areas during rainstorms in order to prevent the segregated groups from seeing one another. The impromptu measure worked to prevent rival spectators from aiming tossed stones and bottles at one another.[39] Though it certainly prevented some violence, spectator segregation, in many cases, worked against police as it encouraged the definition of opposition and implicitly promoted confrontation.

Penning supporters also raised questions about civil rights, especially when doing so constituted unlawful imprisonment. According to a former manager, Arsenal football club experimented with a separate cage to corral spectators temporarily who had been apprehended by the police. Terry Neill remembered,

> At Highbury we tried to surmount this problem [fan disorder] by having a caged-in area where we could detain troublemakers until they could be dealt with later. But a roving TV camera at one of our matches spotted the 'cage' and it was quite properly pointed out that to detain people in this manner was illegal, so we had to get rid of our cage.[40]

This apparatus resembled a holding room or prison cell where police could temporarily detain arrested persons while they were being processed, or prevent them from participating in conflicts for the rest of the day. Holding rooms became a fixture of police requests to clubs at many grounds, and were consistently recommended by the Working Party as well.[41] However, Neill correctly discerned that unlawful detention constituted a breach in civil rights. The incident also disclosed that clubs and police considered the possible public backlash against the ever-increasing severity of discipline.

The sources suggest, however, that most clubs followed the Party's recommendations without fuss, but Howell still feared the prospect of crowd disasters and fatalities.[42] He consistently maintained the necessity of police intervention, both to prevent criminal assaults within the enclosures and to ensure officers could aid in emptying the areas in case of emergency. Police intervention could only be facilitated by gateways in the perimeter barriers.[43] In a public address to the Commons, Howell surmised that European police did not enter the crowd 'because in Europe they do not want to. They have a different approach from ours. They put all the spectators together, pen them up and say, in effect, "It is up to you. We are not coming in." That is not our approach. We attach great importance to the ability of the police to get in and out of the terraces when they want to.'[44] Howell therefore emphasized the importance of gangways, walkways and dry moats where police could roam freely and monitor the crowd. The quote also reflects an overall concern for the prevention of disasters, though an unfinished and unsuccessful approach to achieving safety.

In an effort to perfect spatial discipline, Howell also fielded a wide range of commercial barrier products that reveal the multiple problems spatial divisions generated. For the most part, Howell only passed on these private engineering plans to the major clubs, who would have been responsible for payment and installation. One engineering firm devised a series of collapsible fences that withheld more pressure than standard chain-link fences, interfered less with sight lines, and collapsed at the push of a button in a central control tower. Thus, if the need to avert a crisis arose, the fence could collapse and allow fans to avoid danger.[45] Another commercial firm marketed a sprinkler system, which when embedded in the grass around the pitch, would spray coloured dye on transgressors. The spectators could then be later identified by police for prosecution. The firm advertised their barrier as a more humane alternative than penning and enclosures:

> The measures taken must not insult the good nature of most fans, the object of the game being to entertain them, not to 'impound' them. It therefore seems to be quite unacceptable to fence in the crowd. Treat a human like an animal and he might well react with the law of the jungle. But most important of all, the action taken must work – work by deterring rather than imprisoning.[46]

The firm, McDonnell and Hughes Architects, openly challenged the fundamental premise of crowd enclosure and suggested that enclosing fans might paradoxically lead to further acts of violence. The language also suggested that incarceration presented fans as animals, an image all football and government authorities wished to avoid. Physical space divisions needed to be handled delicately in order not to inflame the public. Government and club authorities intended to employ spatial implements that enacted physical discipline and warned against possible transgressions without seeming overly aggressive and draconian.

Constables at Merseyside Police recommended against the sprinkler system's performance. Their recommendations to the Working Party indicate how police and the state struggled to balance discipline with embarrassment. Chief Constable Haughton specified that the dye would be difficult to control on windy days, leading to possible misidentifications as well as possible injury to police, stewards and referees, as well as spectators. His most astute observation, however, was that 'in these days the dye would probably be carried as a "badge of honour" by the hooligan'. He also added that 'the proposition sounds at least as "barbaric" as the simple proposition of fencing in and is likely to provoke reaction'.[47] Police, like government officials, paid close attention to public opinion about the consequences, dangers and perceptions of spatial divisions.

Press reactions to Howell's proposals reveal that journalists also recognized that such measures could be dangerous and intimidating, and wanted to pass on similar messages to their readership. While most press commentators supported the crackdown on disruptive fan behaviour, some mocked the physical divisions Howell recommended as too extreme. The *Evening Standard* recognized that the implementation of perimeter fencing at England's national Wembley stadium, resembled an animal 'cage'.[48] A wide range of political cartoonists found Howell's recommendations laughable. In a cartoon published in the *Evening News*, Bernard Cookson facetiously suggested that Howell might fill the dividing moats with piranhas to further deter pitch invaders (see Figure 3.1).[49] Another by renowned cartoonist Roy Ullyett intimated that fans would respond by building catapults to launch young spectators onto the field of play (see Figure 3.2).[50] Still others depicted alligators roaming sideline moats, razor wire around pitch barriers, and a chained gorilla frightening a terrace full of supporters.[51] These cartoons appeared intermittently after Howell commented publicly on the need for perimeter fencing and segregation, and the first caricature specifically villainized Howell. Such expressions show that commentators recognized the rapidly escalating measures Howell meant to institute, as well as the accusations of overwrought governance on security and public displeasure, especially among football fans, that they generated.

Figure 3.1: Cartoon by Bernard Cookson depicting Denis Howell and deterrents to pitch invasions, *Evening Standard*, 29 April 1974 © Bernard Cookson, Cookson Cartoons. The caption reads: 'Wade across? They could try, but it is full of Piranha fish!'

Figure 3.2: Cartoon by Roy Ullyett depicting fan catapults, *Daily Express*, 24 May 1974 © Express Newspapers. The text reads: 'You're about to make history. The first hooligan to invade a pitch by catapult across the moat.'

Public charges of brutality against spectators concerned Denis Howell and other police and government authorities. They consistently attempted to find a balance between architectural tools of discipline and the adverse public reactions against them. Implementing further changes and harsher disciplinary language against rowdy spectators became a constant process throughout 1974–6. But, maintaining the moral high ground through exerting discipline could not be compromised: government officials could not demonize spectators as inhuman and undisciplined if they failed to show equal restraint in their reactions to fans' violence. Howell understood this tension better than other members of the Working Party. Winterbottom blatantly ignored the possible ramifications of corralling fans, as well as the public perceptions of these measures. In reference to his strong support of segregative enclosures Winterbottom 'considered that the "concentration camps" aspects of such a practice were largely misleading'.

Further evidence reveals that Howell imagined even more drastic measures against football spectators. Though Howell and the Working Party intermittently expressed some sensitivities to the fatal dangers of penning and enclosures, confidential files suggest he exhibited little regard for the safety of lively spectators. A hand-drawn image, found tucked within the DOE files on the Working Party, supported the conclusion that Howell, and perhaps other government officials, envisioned sports grounds as war zones. I have concluded that Howell drew the image as well as the legend, since the handwriting surrounding the image matched the script of notes in his personal files. The image depicted a barrier to a football ground guarded by machine guns on 'fixed lines' which aim along the four linear boundaries of the pitch. Behind the goals, a strip of land mines ensured that no pitch invasions occurred from the more raucous terraced areas behind the goals (see Figure 3.3).[52] Howell envisioned direct and targeted hostility towards spectators, and working-class terrace fans specifically, carried out through warlike preparations which included constant surveillance and the use of extreme force. Such an imagined environment is predicated on a disciplined division of spatial boundaries within stadium confines, and reflected the policies already instituted by the Working Party. It expanded upon accepted forms of spatial division by adding the direct threat of violent, militaristic intervention should any transgressions occur.

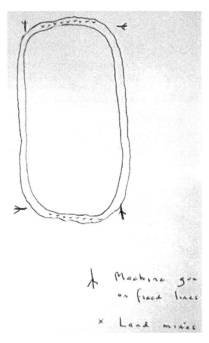

Figure 3.3: Drawing of pitch defence in Home Office files, undated
© National Archives (UK).

While such an image cannot be seen to be directly representative of Howell's public statements about spatial division, nor an illustration of the Working Party's attitude as a whole, it did betray the mentality of punishment and violence present which could underlie state efforts at spatial discipline. In fact, the image also revealed that Howell tenuously weighed his perceptions of possible public reactions against his own desires to enact harsh tactics. Though this diagram would not be acceptable to the public as either indicative of state policy or even as a laughable demonstration of bureaucratic imagination, its intentional secrecy did indicate that Howell knew the boundaries between acceptable and unacceptable forms of state intervention. Nonetheless, his disregard for spectators' well-being, and even his disdain for working-class terrace spectators, can be inferred from the special attention he directed to the area behind the goals in his drawing. Howell felt comfortable responding to fan violence with the threat of violence from the state. Envisioning the grounds as a war zone, complete with military weaponry, likened the spectators to tolerable casualties in the battle against spectator behaviour and the moral security of British society.

Resistance to Physical Space Divisions

The divisions of space within football stadiums, as in other public spaces, came to hold different meanings for the various groups of social actors that inhabited them on a weekly basis. These limited spaces, defined by both physical and imagined boundaries, became increasingly surveilled and controlled by the state as football violence increased throughout the 1970s. Disorderly fan activities often aimed at breaking down these physical boundaries and testing their resiliency, and the police and state responded by hardening the boundaries and policing them rigorously. As these spaces were manipulated and changed over time, older meanings were destroyed and new meanings subsequently created.

Some existing spatial boundaries became increasingly contested as football disorder increased in the late 1960s. Most prominently, the division between the field of play and spaces for spectating came into question because of the frequency of pitch invasions by exuberant supporters. The pitch invasion not only indicated a blatant transgression of the space reserved for players, but also represented a larger breakdown in the total authority and control of the football environment. On one level, invading the pitch disrupts the game and contravenes known regulations of the spectating area. On another level, the invasion also indicates a breakdown in the policing of that spectating area, and represents a larger mishandling in the control of the entire environment. No other transgression of physical boundaries more powerfully suggested that the ordering of the stadium was under stress, and that police efforts to control fans had failed.

After local clubs and police implemented the government's policies on spatial division, pitch invasions also signalled that these barriers too had proven ineffective. In 1967, one police liaison mentioned that moats only mildly deterred invasions. He commented, 'It is not unknown for spectators to wade through the ditches ... and water may not be a sufficient deterrent'.[53] Indeed, it is easy to imagine that barriers aimed at preventing invasions could generate a challenge for spectators. When a fan returned wet to the stands, it could be seen as esteemable among one's fellow spectators. Barriers could, in certain cases, encourage pitch invasions by providing another obstacle to overcome. Their transgression could also serve as an additional way to annoy the police.

End-taking, where a group of fans invaded the terrace area designated for the other team's supporters, also constituted a practical form of resistance to physical boundaries. End-taking aimed at contravening fans' segregation as a policy within stadiums. Though end-taking surely comprised an element in territorial contestation between rival groups of fans, it also rendered the police's segregative strategies useless. Segregation and penning no doubt encouraged territorial meanings for various groups of spectators, especially when these spaces were contested by rival groups. Police and government officials aimed to divest these spaces of the territorial bonds fans created with specific terrace areas by determining their boundaries and who could inhabit them during the match. However, end-taking regenerated the opportunity for territorialisms in the stadium by contesting the neutrality given to segregated spaces by police. Fans reclaimed the ends as ill-defined and negotiable through violence, challenging the physical barriers instituted by the state.

Terrace spectators also continued to challenge the economic and spatial boundaries between seated and standing attendees. Terrace fans often evaded police and attacked seated areas. In 1975, at a match in Nottinghamshire, travelling Manchester United fans 'invaded the Members Stand, damaging the seats, breaking windows of the stand and press and public announcement boxes, and also damaging wooden fencing at one end of the stand'.[54] In this particular example two symbols of social control became the object of the supporters' destruction: the seats and the wooden fence barrier. Though spectators damaged nearly every area they could get to, here the police noted that the fans specifically targeted seats, an expression of resistance to economically defined class divisions within the stadium. They also attacked the fences enclosing the seated stand, the barrier which maintained the spaces of financial privilege and cultural difference.

Fans at the match also broke down the physical barriers in their own terraces and endeavoured to remove other architectural dividers like crush barriers. Shortly after the disorder began 'Manchester United supporters were seen to be breaking down parts of a timber and corrugated iron "crush" barrier which ran the length of the enclosure … Long lengths of timber and broken pieces of corrugated iron were tossed in the air and again the Police entered the crowd to restore order'. Once within the crowd, 'Police were subjected to a barrage of stones, beer containers and pieces of the broken crush barrier'.[55] In another incident at a Merseyside derby, police reported that away fans brought tools with them to remove crush barriers with less effort, showing that they premeditated such attacks on the terrace environment. As they hoisted the barriers in the air Liverpool supporters jeered 'Goodison Park is falling down!'[56] The chant indicated territorial rivalries carried out through attacks on the opponents' stadium as a sacred space. But spectators also directed their destructive efforts at crush barriers, because like other physical divisions, they represented the implements of spatial control and police efforts to curb crowds' mobility that spectators rejected. Directing their aggression at the boundaries themselves, rather than at other fans or the police, indicated dissatisfaction with the presence of physical means of social control.

Though responsible for inciting much of the violence, supporters also complained verbally about the brutality they experienced during the government's programme of physical enclosures and segregation. Many non-violent spectators objected to the treatment of football patrons as an undifferentiated population of thugs. In 1967, Howard Kaye wrote to the Arsenal FC club chairman to object to the idea that 'Arsenal management have decided to cage-up their supporters on the terraces'. Though he admitted that young spectators often interrupted the match with pitch invasions, he added that 'this has occurred from time immemorial and surely does not warrant such drastic action'. In this case, new policies infringed upon older activities that expressed close bonds between club loyalties, terrace spectators and sacred spaces. Kaye also protested against the new measures:

> Mr. Chairman, the supporters that you see gathered before you on the terraces are not dogs, nor are they the cloth-cap workers of the 20s or 30s, whose lives revolved around the factory floor and the Saturday afternoon football match; they are intelligent human beings who are just as likely to patronise the opera after the football match as they are the greyhounds.

Unlike several of the moral commentators and government officials who espoused rhetoric against 'hooligan thugs' without remorse, this fan distinguished between the more violent elements of the crowd and the majority of fans seeking a non-confrontational weekend entertainment. The strict programme of physical intimidation endangered their enjoyment by assuming all fans needed to be disciplined. The quote also indicated that fans sometimes paid less attention to class distinctions than government officials. Kaye also recognized that penning and enclosures could paradoxically encourage violent activities rather than eliminate them. 'I firmly believe that until a different attitude is taken to the man on the terrace, violence will increase. The man on the terrace should be welcomed at a football match and not merely tolerated'.[57]

Some fans expressed similar resentment that police and government officials perceived fans' disposition as universally violent and unruly. After a series of run-ins with local police at a match in Sheffield, one woman witness issued a lengthy statement complaining of police treatment and physical arrangements upon their arrival at the match. She noted that 'the general attitude to football supporters is "guilty until proven innocent"'. She added, 'We the supporters would like to have a say in the preventative measures against hooliganism ... We feel that only by engendering a mutual rapport between fans and police will hooliganism be removed from football and at the moment we go in fear of our lives'.[58] Physical discipline carried out against all non-seated fans lumped them into a single, undifferentiated mass deserving of cavalier treatment. In a letter of complaint to the constable, she added that 'we are sick and tired of being treated as second-class citizens just because we go to football matches. We are respectable girls and we should be treated as Human Beings'.[59] Authorities presumed all spectators to be culpable and subjected non-violent spectators to potential abuse. In response, spectators voiced their objections to the physical environments and policing accompanying the government's crackdown on fan disorder in the 1970s.

Other spectators also made sure that the minister's office understood that 'genuine' supporters also rejected the embarrassing conditions of terrace control enacted upon them. Howell's office received several letters from supporters' clubs, formed not only to protect the traditions and heritage of football-supporting in local areas, but also to separate fans interested in the sport and its traditions from violent spectators. The Manchester United Supporters' Club frequently wrote Howell, especially after incidents involving supporters with allegiance to the club. Supporters' clubs wanted to ensure that Howell was aware of the benefit of non-violent fans among the terraces, especially when such fans could not gain access to seated stands at away matches. Like the women above, they did not want to be subject to the same harsh physical restraints as their disorderly counterparts. The club's chairman, C. D. Smith, wrote to the Department of the Environment:

> I fully appreciate the concern that a few hundred unruly fans can cause, in terms of damage and safety both to players and the reputation of the game and under no circumstances do I even attempt to condone their actions. I do, however, honestly believe that any action that may be taken should, in all fairness, take into account the non-involvement of in excess of 55,000 spectators, who made absolutely no attempt to encroach on the pitch.

After the match, both local and national television stations suggested that Old Trafford, Manchester United's home ground, would be closed while changes to the terraces could be installed to prevent further incidents. Smith pleaded: 'the whole point of this letter is to request, on behalf of the genuine and well-behaved supporters, that the punishment to be meted out be confined to those supporters'.[60] These pleas indicate that fans, along with police and clubs, recognized the distinction between violent and non-violent fans in the same way as physical barriers helped to define these fan groups. Assemblies of non-violent fans feared that new changes to stadiums' physical environment would impose on their entertainment, and might even result in temporary expulsion from the stadium altogether. These spectators repudiated their violent counterparts in order to convince the government that physical discipline did not suit the entire spectating populace.

In addition to spectators, clubs also expressed distaste for the government's architectural proposals. Most prominently, clubs worried about the large construction costs of implementing the recommendations. This concern was evident in several sections of the Winterbottom and Wheatley reports. Winterbottom's investigation revealed that clubs had differing opinions on whether terraces should be divided. Celtic FC wanted to protect their own liability, countering the prevailing policy of restricting crowd mobility. The club 'felt that crowds should be allowed as much freedom of movement as possible in order to be able to escape from nuisance or danger'.[61] Several clubs expressed alarm not only at the financial sums needed to manipulate existing terraces and stands, but also at the possible dangers physical barriers could create.

The installation of segregated stands also created several new problems for clubs. The government consistently recommended that tickets be issued to all spectators in an effort to increase the efficiency of police in segregating fans. Ushers and police could distribute fans according to their team allegiance. All-ticket policies also aimed to reduce overcrowding in certain areas of the stadium and mitigate the accumulation of fans at paying turnstiles just before the match began. Before all-ticket matches became accepted as the norm, most fans, especially terrace spectators, paid for general admission upon arriving at the ground. Clubs objected to the segregation tactic partly because it meant that tickets needed to be printed and distributed, sometimes weeks in advance, again increasing the costs to finance-minded clubs. Nottingham County FC complained that the club spent an extra £350 on ticket printing and distribution in anticipation of an upcoming match when admission to the stadium cost only 60p.[62] Such procedures proved a financial and administrative annoyance that challenged working standards within club management. The club also spent thousands of pounds to install new barriers and employ more police and stewards when the largest clubs visited. While fans' behaviour in smaller locales rarely necessitated stricter measures, Howell and football authorities mandated changes to small stadiums as well in anticipation of conflicts.[63] These changes often forced new financial and administrative problems upon clubs.

Police also faced new challenges in ensuring that segregated fans entered the proper enclosure in the first place. At Middlesbrough police ran into unanticipated obstacles separating home and away supporters: 'The police sometimes had difficulty in carrying this [out] when both teams wore the same colours, but were usually able to go by accent'.[64] External markers provided police with imprecise means of segregating crowds as carrying out new policies created practical problems. Segregation also caused accretions of spectators at turnstiles waiting to gain entry into their designated enclosures, providing police with yet another difficulty. Before the installation of enclosures, fans often proceeded to the turnstile entry which contained the shortest queue. Now, fans faced longer lines and extended waits to gain entry. At Upton Park police found that home fans frequently entered the visitors' enclosure not to instigate violence but to avoid protracted delays. The situation caused further problems when visiting fans arrived late to find little or no room in the enclosures to accommodate them.[65] Police became particularly concerned about visiting fans who could not gain entrance: they became a massive security threat to surrounding pubs, shops and city plazas. Yet, police and stewards could not admit them to home spectators' enclosures because they feared away fans would provoke the home crowd.

In many cases, segregation could aggravate existing administrative problems leading to more conflict within and outside the stadium.

Due to difficulties with administration and police, as well as their intermittent sensitivity to supporters' complaints, clubs resisted executing government spatial division policies. One of the Winterbottom commission's main directives involved investigating whether or not clubs had implemented the Lang Report's recommendations. The group found that most clubs found segregation to be excessive, especially when enclosures aimed at corralling young men away from other spectators. 'Segregating young people into pens is no longer thought to be essential. Indeed, some grounds have done away with separate penning because boys prefer to be with parents or older youths and they seem to cause less nuisance when they are not herded together.'[66] Appendix A to the report documented that as of 1971 fifteen of thirty clubs in the first and second division implemented only partial or no segregation among the terraces. In Scotland, only two of fourteen clubs had complete segregation. Many clubs resisted putting into operation segregative policies until Howell returned to office and increased the pressure on clubs and police.

Overall, the state faced significant struggles in implementing its spatial policies as clubs, police and fans protested government recommendations. Spectators objected to being cordoned off within tightly packed and heavily surveilled enclosures. They often objected to being treated as an undifferentiated mass of violent and animalistic subjects. In several instances, violent fans expressed their displeasure by directing destructive efforts at the representations and symbols of physical division. Clubs and police also recognized that segregation and enclosures created dangerous and potentially violent situations unanticipated by government ministers. The financial and administrative burden of architectural policy weighed heavy on fiscally strained clubs as well. Since the movement toward the policy of total containment was enacted piecemeal, police, fans and clubs consistently articulated their discontent with the ongoing implementation of these principles through various forms of resistance.

Conclusions

In addition to understanding the mandate for all-seated stadiums as the beginning of a new era of commercial football, we can also see this later directive as the final step in a long transition from unregulated football entertainment to disciplined and attentive sports consumption. The 1989 Taylor Report built upon existing policies which regulated physical space through tactics of division, segregation and enclosure. These policies, constructed in the 1960s and 1970s, provided better police facilitation and aimed at containing and controlling fan behaviour both within and outside stadiums. Throughout, government officials and police management of physical space reflected their multiple prejudices against violent spectators as working-class, young and male. The body, as a scientific and technical concept, became increasingly subject to government research that attempted to define the boundaries of acceptable injury. Because these mechanisms constituted a hostile reaction to spectators and a financial burden to clubs, they faced opposition from both groups of social actors. Divisions of physical space and segregation threatened the physical well-being of spectators by creating an environment that defined opposition, created possibilities for injury through crowd immobility and attempted to treat the problem of crowd violence through the creation of a setting where violent reactions were both threatening and plausible.

4 POLICE AND THE STATE: TACTICS, NETWORKS AND THE DEVELOPMENT OF FOOTBALL POLICING

Contemporary academic commentators have suggested that, in a general sense, the football arena reflected the axiom that increased social control often leads to increased social deviance.[1] More specifically, and through the use of documentary evidence in this chapter, I will show that increased police interventions into the social arena of football produced mutual antagonisms between spectators and police which resulted in a greater incidence of police brutality. Police officials, through the organization of the sports ministry in London, tested new tactics which produced reciprocal enmity between the two social groups in progressively more harsh and violent environments within and around stadiums. Police constables and spectators negotiated new social spaces as they emerged, most often through interactions between police and fans that became fiercely hostile. This chapter shows how in the late 1960s and 1970s these contentious relationships developed over time and were contingent upon directives from government inquiries. Controversial police practices since the 1990s, which have been the focus of other studies, drew on long-standing approaches which developed through fragmentary and unsystematic trials in previous decades.[2]

Previous academic inquiries into policing football have been almost entirely ethnographic, and therefore focused on the period after the late 1980s, when anthropological and sociological interest in police involvement in football peaked. These studies provide useful models for understanding police behaviour and interpersonal interaction between fans and police over the last twenty years.[3] Though insightful into police and legal practices at specific locales, these academic inquests have often been anecdotal and descriptive, rather than analytical or historical.[4] This chapter relies on police reports, records from Home Office meetings with police officials, and other government correspondence and documents to elucidate the government's role in shaping police policy on a national level in regards to football violence. These reports disclose the expansion of new tactics, shared information, and the historical development of policing football violence as it emerged in the late 1960s and 1970s.

Though the government did not test specific policing strategies, they certainly aimed to project an image of public security and governmental authority by increased policing of football violence. Government and police officials wanted to cultivate an aura of toughness within a cultural context where the public valued law-and-order discipline. Like architectural changes and threats of greater punishment through magistrates' courts, heavier police intervention signalled a response to social fears of youth degeneration and violence. These strategies performed a political function as well as a practical one. While others have commented on how police used conflicts with spectators as opportunities to improve constables' authoritative image, I argue here that the British government advocated a similar logic.[5] Government officials used a strong police presence to capitalize on the public's fears about football violence, rendering government ministries intimidating and inflexible to 'hooligan' criminals while displacing blame for social problems.

Finally, the areas of social control on which scholars have concentrated their attention reflect contemporary political concerns with civil rights and invasions of privacy, especially undercover police infiltrating football gangs and closed-circuit television (CCTV).[6] Existing academic analyses of CCTV and police brutality often neglect the relationality, negotiation and historical evolution of police tactics and implements of social control. Processes of identification, communication and arrest in football policing developed over time, contingent upon immediate circumstances and the contest between different groups of social actors. In essence, CCTV and ID cards for spectators did not arise out of nowhere in the mid-1980s. These provocative instruments were the outcomes of longer transitions within policing mentalities, developmental processes that emphasized the need for better criminal identification, and early attempts to negotiate police strategies that prevented football violence. Evidence shows that processes of identification and verbal communication networks predated CCTV as the state and police officials attempted to develop more precise intervention and control tactics. In order to understand the emergence of these invasive practices, one must also understand police tactical development within the football world as well as the historical context in which they surfaced.

Police Actors and the Rise of Police Presence

As football violence emerged as both a practical and political conundrum in the late 1960s, Home Office ministers and police officials discussed possible solutions at the highest level. Through the government-commissioned inquiries into football violence, Home Office and Department of Environment authorities debated police tactics, analysed what worked in different situations and shared ideas about police conduct. These discussions involved police figures on several different levels. The Home Office consistently met with the Association of Chief Police Officers (ACPO) and the chief constables of each borough in England and Scotland. In addition to these national meetings, ministers from the different commissions and Denis Howell's Working Party often met with local police officers and station managers while touring each club's stadium. Therefore, the national government discussed ideas on all levels both in an effort to build a homogenous national police policy against football violence and to measure its practical implementation in stadiums. Though these commissions settled on final recommendations that they intermittently distributed to football clubs, police practices were the product of high-level professional discussions, clubs' direct circumstances, the nuances of individual stadiums and local police routines.

Several different groups of police actors could be involved in the supervision of any given match. British transport police monitored spectators' travel to and from the match on railcars and train stations. Traffic police maintained the flow of vehicles in and around stadiums, but also monitored the spectators within eye's view outside the ground. Local police officers could occupy any number of predetermined positions in or around the stadiums, and many of them volunteered for overtime duty or were forced to work during bigger matches. Police spotters and plain clothes policemen patrolled the streets and the terraces, monitoring spectators' behaviours. They often called on uniformed police for assistance in regulating problems. Stewards received pay for their surveillance of in-stadium activities: they monitored what happened in the terraces and asked for police assistance for any suspicious conduct. Rather than treating police as an undifferentiated body, understanding their interaction with supporters necessitates distinguishing their direct responsibilities in any given situation.

Generally, police constables became the means of implementing the policies of containment and crowd regulation debated on the national level. Their interaction with sports ministers and government officials can be described as presentational and authoritative. Police officials wanted to expound their competency in directing the events around football matches.[7] Like police reports, police interviews with Denis Howell and others never admitted defeat and attempted to convey the semblance of trustworthiness and fortitude. In addition, they consistently downplayed the gravity of any given incident, and frequently saw the media's sensationalization of events as counterproductive.[8] Police officials wanted to be seen as level-headed, in control of events, and preventing escalation. Police reports of actual incidents present a similar posture. They conveyed their organization, preparedness and authority over any given episode by telling the story, noting which officers dispelled the riotous spectators and how they conducted themselves. Many of them gave details of the game, including what events might have caused changes in fans' behaviour.[9] In most of their interactions, police officials communicated their competency and diligence, especially when taking their local ideas to national government representatives.

One frequent topic of discussion among the government and police officials was the rising cost of regulating matches as the numbers of police rose. As noted earlier, police costs drastically increased as police presence multiplied. Generally speaking, the Home Office made it clear that any police forces used inside the stadium should be compensated by the clubs, and police resources used outside were paid by the state. Clubs, however, were often reluctant to pay for rising police costs. As one New Scotland Yard official lamented, 'There's no profit in security'.[10] Comparing the number of police staffed for matches before and after the outbreak of football violence reveals the extreme escalation of policing costs. In the 1950s and early 1960s clubs used minimal security and rarely paid exorbitant police fees. As one police superintendent in Millwall mentioned, 'The rough and generally accepted yard-stick of 1 P.C. [police constable] per 1,000 spectators has always been used as a basis'.[11] Even matches where police expected trouble or club officials worried about security outside of grounds drew ratios such as 1:500 or 1:600.[12] Before the late 1960s, clubs usually employed one Chief Inspector, one Police Sergeant, and fifteen to twenty Police Constables for duty inside grounds, with twenty to forty extra officers for traffic duty outside the grounds. Police expected few problems and therefore rarely needed to employ extra officers during matches.[13]

Provoked by the increased incidence of football violence, police ratios changed to approximately 1:100, or even lower, as clubs and the state requested additional officers. By the mid-1970s, routine league matches had gradually increased the number of officers to about 200–300 officers per match.[14] When clubs expected larger attendance, they kept police on call and managed the match by a rough estimate of one officer per hundred fans.[15] Smaller clubs also reinforced police regulation when larger club followings visited their grounds. Halifax Town FC employed 65 police to monitor 5,849 spectators (1:89) when they expected trainloads of visiting Aston Villa fans.[16] In some rare cases, where both sides had large followings, clubs could employ over 600 officers for a single match.[17] Clubs also supplied stewards to supplement official police, most of whom 'have no powers except to ask or encourage spectators to move away from gangways, or to identify troublemakers'. Arsenal and Manchester United used 100 stewards at each match, and the Football Association employed 1,000 for each game played at Wembley stadium.[18] In response to the rising prevalence of football violence, clubs and the Home Office drastically increased the number of police and stewards present.

Relations between fans and police ranged from amicable to abusive. Obviously, contact between the two groups could be cordial when the terraces proved less violent. Police chiefs often assigned officers to fixed posts week after week to encourage police and fans becoming familiar with one another, much like the foot patrols later recommended in conflict-ridden neighbourhoods after the 1981 race riots. PC Alan Smith remembered, 'You'd get to know the fans, that was the idea of it'.[19] The assignment could foster harmonious relationships between the two groups, but was meant to give the police the advantage of identifying individual troublemakers should any problems arise. In some stadiums, this policy ensured cordial rapport was built before football violence increased in the mid-1960s. One PC at Arsenal FC in London recollected the mood in the early 1960s: 'It was lovely. They used to really look after you, the supporters. You weren't a copper, really. You were just there.' The afternoon could be completely pleasurable for police, who got paid handsomely to watch a match. The same officer commented, '1958, 59, into the 60s, it was sheer enjoyment. We came here, we watched the football and we got paid for it. We got paid overtime! And never any trouble.'[20]

At many grounds, harmonious relationships between home supporters and the police extended into the 1970s as fans and police became familiar with one another. Police officers often defended fans from their locale, and attributed all of the trouble to visiting supporters who raided an otherwise peaceful environment. Several reports include special notes that express the police's praise for the home supporters.[21] In one witness statement, a Middlesbrough fan complained that the local police were apathetic to protecting them from home fans and perceived away supporters' presence to be the catalyst for violence. The police denied the witness's group an escort after a bloody incident occurred seconds earlier, and one officer said, 'It's you lot from Middlesbrough that's causing all the trouble'.[22] Fans also praised police, albeit infrequently, when they did provide security within violent fracases. One travelling fan wrote to Halifax police after a match: 'May I take the opportunity to applaud and congratulate your force and yourself on a truly magnificent plan and operation last Saturday in getting M.U.F.C. supporters safely to their coaches. It goes without saying, that [there] would have been a "bloodbath" otherwise.'[23] Indeed, relations between police and supporters could be good-natured, especially when mutual interests of safety and security prevailed.

However, police reports more frequently indicated violent and hostile relationships between the two groups in the majority of matches. Certainly, police officers usually documented transgressions and not celebrations of good conduct. Nonetheless, their reports suggested the prevalence of antagonistic relations with spectators. In addition to listing the approximate numbers of those arrested and ejected, many police reports also listed injuries and included narratives of conflicts with fans. One representative report at White Hart Lane, Tottenham Hotspur FC's home ground, listed seven arrests and three police injuries: one officer got a bruised cheek while fighting with a fan, another received bruised ribs while fighting with the crowd, and the last had his skull membrane broken after being kicked in the head while wading into the crowd to stop a disturbance.[24] Police also took abuse when manning the divisions of physical space, usually from missiles thrown from the terraces. One superintendent reported that after several youths threatened to invade the pitch in Leeds, 'I therefore formed a line of officers between that Stand and the goal line to prevent any further interference. These men were subjected to missiles in the form of coins, bottles, beer cans, stones and in one case, an open knife, from spectators in the North Stand'. No serious injuries were sustained but the superintendent feared for his officers' safety in future episodes.[25] Police reported hundreds of episodes similar to these, reporting fans' hostility when police enforced policies of containment and when they entered the terraces to stop transgressive behaviour. While peaceful relationships between fans and police prevailed in some areas, most notably in smaller clubs and where large groups of travelling supporters failed to materialize, interaction generally became more polarized and oppositional. In response, police consistently tested new tactics which aimed at better identifying suspects and more effective intervention.

The Development of Tactics and Strategies

Throughout the period, police at both the local and national levels experimented with new techniques that fostered stricter control of spectators' behaviour. These ideas were shared at national meetings of police organizations, through government inquiries into police strategies at large matches and through government ministers' visits to local grounds. Many of these strategies evoked new anxieties among spectators within the stadiums, intensifying tensions between the police and supporters. New police strategies made the distinction between spectator and police highly identifiable as traditional agreeable relations broke down. The antagonistic and confrontational nature of police relations with spectators helped to define opposition not only between groups of rival fans but also between police and spectators generally. Yet, these tactics discussed at the national level were only intermittently and inconsistently implemented.

One scholar typologized five basic police practices by observing Aston Villa FC in Birmingham in the late 1970s. Police used their presence, verbal warnings, physical searches, ejection and arrest as their fundamental strategies in deterring unwanted behaviour.[26] In my review of police reports, I have found that police certainly used all of these practices, but in diverse ways in different grounds. Police constables only used tactics that succeeded within direct circumstances and according to immediate demands for order within their districts. When some tactics failed to provide the necessary control, local police changed them on-the-fly, leading to the piecemeal development of football police practices across Britain. As in any contest for social power, intermittent conflicts constituted the negotiation of power on the ground level, and both spectators and police contributed to the materialization of new forms of social control.

As football violence emerged as a severe problem, the government thought that proliferating police presence would intimidate rowdy spectators into normative behaviours. Police in Glasgow felt that when crowd troubles began to surface during the 1968/69 season, a temporary increase in police at league games for a few months would ward off any further disturbances. Police representatives suggested to the Lang commission that 'a temporary increase in the number of policemen be utilised, until such times as the situation returned to more normal conditions'.[27] Government ministers also wanted to present numerous police officers strategically at different spaces inside and outside stadiums to project their authority. They assumed that if spectators witnessed long lines of police they would be less likely to commit transgressions in the first place. Frank Williamson, Her Majesty's Chief Inspector of Crime, wrote to the Home Office: 'Obviously the police strength around the ground and on the ground must be of such a nature as to indicate a real certainty of detection to those who are inclined to commit any offense'.[28] He added in another Home Office briefing that these police should be placed in calculated locations where crime could be effectively deterred through the threat of detection.[29] The desire to represent police authority through a show of numerous officers aimed to maintain peaceful conduct as visiting spectators passed through the city.

Police officials also experimented with other strategic displays of power. In Stoke, local police stations agreed to crack down on disorder and violence early on in the season to alert those involved of the competency of resident constables. They wanted to notify the local press about their early exploits and thus publicize their regulation of behaviour early, setting a tone for the rest of the season.[30] Williamson also felt that sending particularly competent police along with clubs' travelling supporters would diminish the amount of criminal activity in other grounds. He recommended that police place their most competent and threatening officers at the main sites of trouble at away matches.[31] This practice would breed familiarity between travelling fans and daunting police who began to catalogue their behaviours.

In the main, increased police presence failed to prevent or deter football violence. Further, greater numbers of police officers caused other problems. Harrington's group, who read reports from every major constabulary office and conducted fieldwork at several matches throughout 1967, found that police presence produced paradoxical results. 'At times the mere sight of police officers in strength seems to antagonize and inflame the crowd', they reported. Furthermore, 'large numbers of police on the perimeter can obstruct vision. We have seen this inflame spectators whose views were obstructed'.[32] Harrington's group interpreted these findings as further evidence of the need for moats to free police from patrolling the boundaries of the field. More importantly, the efforts of police officials to show their force in numbers infuriated and annoyed the crowd, exacerbating hostility between the two groups and often leading to increased conflict between them. Resentment stemmed from all different types of fans who disliked being overpowered and constantly monitored. 'Abuse comes not only from the section of the crowd from which the offender is being removed' in the case of an arrest, Harrington noted, 'but also from persons who are presumably responsible citizens'.[33] Increased police presence made spectators exceedingly uncomfortable, and often intensified existing tensions within stadium grounds.

In addition to displaying their considerable authority, local police forces also tried out new tactics for entering in the terrace areas. As shown above, police constables were injured when they went into the terraces to make arrests, break up fights, and stop other disturbances. Spectators often attacked them or inhibited them as they moved toward the centre of disorder. Police developed tactics that provided greater protection in numbers when they found it necessary to wade into the terraces. 'Snatch squads' enabled police to dive into the crowd and make arrests or quell disturbances while other officers fended off attacks from spectators. In practice, the police usually snatched everyone within arm's reach and ejected them when a fracas ensued. David Smith, Chairman of the National Federation of Football Supporters' Clubs recalled: 'Constables jump into the massed spectators in an attempt to quell the so-called trouble and, as a result of the tightly packed crowd and therefore the inability to reach the designated location, proceed to evict many innocent supporters'. He further complained, 'There is no doubt in the minds of a great many supporters that the majority of arrests made within the confines of a football ground involve innocent supporters', which moved supporters towards 'a policy of non-co-operation'.[34] Arrests and violence which targeted random supporters, rather than those culpable for disorder, alienated innocent spectators.

Police constables at Manchester often charged the crowd to prevent swaying and surging within the enclosures. Manchester United supporters' well-earned reputation for violence was met with innovative and dangerous police tactics. One of Howell's constituents protested police tactics in one confrontation, noting that he hated to see 'a group surging forward and then witness a line of Policemen with arms linked having to charge the crowd like a bull dozer'.[35] Such charges certainly endangered both police and spectators, and betrayed that the police were willing, and sometimes eager, to engage in violence with raucous fans.

The use of police dogs and mounted police also endangered fans but provided police with a protective companion and innovative ways of directing and threatening crowds of spectators. Mounted police afforded constables a larger physical presence while directing traffic. Horses worked like moveable walls: they closed off streets, directed crowds through walkways between the rail station and the stadium, and closed off throughways for traffic. Officers frequently used horses to escort crowds on the long walk from the train station to the stadium, closing off side streets and ensuring that spectators followed a guided path.[36] Most major grounds employed mounted police by 1971, not only for traffic direction, but also for crowd control.[37] As segregation emerged as a routine policy at most major clubs, horses could also provide separation between rival groups before officials could install permanent barriers.[38] Police horses also became a symbolic threat to potentially rowdy fans. Like a police baton or other weaponry, police horses were tools at the disposal of the officers which could be used to cause panic, intimidate groups of fans, and extend police officers' individual power. In essence, mounted police offered both a flexible and portable barrier but also a menacing presence in theatrical displays of police power.[39]

The introduction of police dogs became hotly contested among police officials and the Home Office in the late 1960s. Like horses, police dogs exacerbated spectator anxieties and could be extremely dangerous when mishandled. Therefore, public officials reluctantly initiated dog patrols in very defined situations. As early as 1965, the ACPO considered police dogs as effective tools in preventing violence and controlling crowds during the upcoming World Cup. Early trials of dog patrols at Derby had proven successful, and the ACPO found that the use of police dogs at continental stadiums suggested that they might help constables control activities at the grounds.[40] However, both historical precedent and Home Office orders prevented the use of dogs specifically for crowd management. When Dennis Fellows at the Football Association raised the notion to the police superintendent at Catford police station, in charge of patrolling Millwall's home ground in central London, station managers and the club reasoned that the Home Office would never allow it. The superintendent commented that 'it would not be favourably received in many quarters ... The inherent dangers were all too obvious'.[41] Early on, officers recognized that dogs could be threatening, but also hazardous if uncontrolled or attacked in riotous situations.

A confidential document prepared for the World Cup disclosed police knowledge about the potential for violence with dog patrols around football crowds. The Metropolitan Police Commissioner's Office prepared a brief on police dogs to be distributed to stations using them during the 1966 proceedings. It began by stating their utility: 'Dogs are a very effective deterrent against rowdyism and when used to patrol areas where this may occur often prevent it from developing'. The commissioner added, 'Experience shows that a handler and his dog can safely deal with a small compact group of people, of a dozen or so, and the dog controls them by showing aggressive intentions whilst on a short lead'. The threat of aggression and the potential for violence made the dog a valuable weapon against a small group of disorderly fans. However, interaction with crowds could be chaotic and ill-defined, and in many cases 'the dog becomes confused and cannot be under the strict control of the handler. If it is accidentally trodden upon or if the handler is jostled, pushed or assaulted, the dog will tend to bite indiscriminately.' Clearly, police officials knew the risks of introducing dog patrols, especially in the melees which commonly occurred at football grounds, yet nonetheless established them as a resource in the battle against football violence. Most importantly, the document noted that 'dogs must not be present or used at demonstrations or at political or industrial meetings'.[42] Metropolitan Police recognized the Home Office mandate against using dog patrols for crowd management, yet designated football matches as non-political events, and therefore outside of standard 'crowd control' regulations, in order to be able to use them in this specific setting.

Police authorities clearly understood the dangers of using potentially dangerous dogs, especially in tight and chaotic environments, and therefore wanted to manage the public fallout regarding their use. After also noting that dogs could indeed 'bite indiscriminately', the ACPO commented: 'Further, and this is quite important, the use of dog patrols may have an adverse effect on police/public relations'.[43] Rather than serving the public, the use of dogs at football matches concretized polar opposition between the public and police. Nonetheless, police officials accepted the faulty premise that the use of violence against football spectators would reduce violence altogether. Dog patrols constituted a menacing threat to spectator safety, but proved a risk police officials willingly accepted.

Members of Parliament relished the idea of dog patrols keeping crowds in order and intimidating fans, and urged that it become part of the government's suggestions to clubs. James Johnson (Labour, Hull) remarked, 'There has been marked efficiency, on the pavements, by the police, much of which is due to the use of dogs. We in Hull believe that bullies and thugs fear police dogs.' Even Denis Howell admitted that dogs could be inexact in their identification of defenders: 'There is some evidence that it is difficult to control spectators with dogs actually near them, because dogs cannot pick out offenders'.[44] Police reports indicated that dogs did indeed cause severe alarm among spectators. One match investigation report noted that after the introduction of police dogs, pitch invasions ceased immediately: ' their effect on the crowd was dramatic. A large number of them who previously had appeared to be affected by mass hysteria immediately changed mood to one of apprehension and near panic and rapidly retreated.'[45] Clearly, police dogs and police horses imparted terror in confrontations with football fans. As police officers, clubs, and the Home Office became more comfortable with their use at football matches, they became an increasingly effective tactic that used the threat of violence to ward off potential violence.

Police authorities and government officials also advocated the development of various strategies in which spectators policed each other. Many police officers complained that fans failed to offer any kind of support to the police in their efforts to arrest or eject other spectators. Police in Edinburgh lamented that 'the general public are in the main apathetic towards the difficulties confronting the police and are seldom prepared to give physical support'.[46] Spectators also rarely came forward as witnesses in court.[47] Police believed that fans failed to help the police because they feared retaliation: 'Some hooligans are so vicious that members of the public are afraid to identify them to the police'.[48] Other police officials told members of the Lang inquiry that asking 'genuine' spectators to identify culprits for ejection or arrest worked very well. The Lang inquiry hoped to further such strategies by asking supporters' clubs to keep their own blacklists, denying transgressors special travel privileges or ticket allocations.[49] Both tactics used spectators to help police identify perpetrators of violence, but proved imperfect and subjective.

Stadium stewards also became a mechanism for control. Culled from the home team's supporters, stewards provided a mediating role between spectators and police. Stadium stewards performed many of the tasks which constables did not want to become involved in: removing alcohol, stopping foul or threatening language, stopping underage drinking, packing pens and breaking up dense crowds. Stewards acted as intermediaries between police and supporters. In the 1950s and early 1960s, before football violence emerged as a serious problem, stewards provided the essential functions of maintaining safety for supporters, often by building relationships with them. One steward at Arsenal described his role:

> I quickly learnt that I would have to put up with a good deal of banter from the crowd ... The only method of gaining the confidence of the people is by addressing them personally, and it was surprising how quickly they responded. When they found one was pointing to them as an individual and was anxious to place them in a spot which was vacant, they moved with alacrity ... The two years I have spent on this task have proved to be very enjoyable. I have made many friends with the spectators and look forward to the many individual chats I have each week.[50]

Such affable relations continued as football violence increased, though now police and club officials redefined the stewards' role.

Government officials, club authorities and police constables used the genial interaction between stewards and spectators as a strategic means to better facilitate police work. In addition to their accepted responsibilities, 'stewards could also be trained in the projection of the "family entertainment image", and thereafter could be the social contact and link man in each crowd compartment'. Within a few weeks, 'because spectators usually foregather in the same places week by week – each compartment would become a social entity, common to the regular supporters, their families, friends and associates'. Stadium managers too found the development of community relations an effective mechanism for crowd control, especially the relationships between stewards and their surrounding spectators.[51] Stewards could direct fans in pens and monitor spectators' mobility through friendly interaction. Clubs also wanted to use spectators' congenial associations with fans to restore football's wholesome image in light of outbreaks of violence.

Yet, as the bifurcated opposition between spectators and authorities became clearly defined, stewards became perceived as agents of the police and were disrespected by spectators. Police often co-opted stewards to help identify culprits within a crowd. Early on, police could refrain from ejecting spectators, allowing stewards to choose the most disruptive elements of a crowd for eviction.[52] Stewards were also expected to keep an eye on known 'troublemakers', prevent crowding in police gangways, and offer the police assistance in a supervisory role.[53] Their role as eyewitnesses and in identification could be valuable to police who were often involved in other tasks. Spectators despised stewards who aided the police in making arrests. Many stewards were drawn from the same spectators' clubs which lobbed sneering and scornful criticism at 'hooligans' and 'thugs', and therefore easily transitioned into a role that policed 'proper' spectator conduct and behaviour. Yet many stewards disliked the liability of policing the crowd. Supporters' clubs in Scotland only reluctantly accepted the idea because 'stewards receive little, if any, respect'.[54] Scottish police officials also doubted that their new authority would be respected, and argued that spectators would only reluctantly accept stewards' direction with greater training and over time.[55] Stadium stewards became a key element in the development of police strategies but came to be resented as they adopted powers that aided officers in conflict with spectators.

As other tactical mechanisms developed, police and club authorities also considered how to conduct interventions into spectators' activities. Police initially adopted a very defensive and reluctant stance toward intervention: precedents drawn from the first post-war decades stipulated that police generally maintained order through service-oriented supervision. In essence, early police orders allowed police employed by clubs to keep stairways clear, prevent unauthorized entry, and comply with club officials' requests.[56] Most often, these interventions took the form of immediate removal from stadium grounds. However, police officials quickly wanted to expand police powers of arrest and detention during crowd disturbances, especially when urged by the Home Office and members of Parliament. In late 1969 police department legal officials promoted more arrests rather than ejections, noting that charging the offender provided immediate intervention and prolonged detention. 'The most effective way of combating hooliganism was quick, effective justice', noted J. F. Claxton, Director of Public Prosecutions. He added that 'if it became known that a hooligan was likely to be taken into custody as soon as an offence had been committed this, he would have thought, would act as a strong deterrent'. So too would the conference's recommendation to detain offenders through the weekend until they could be arraigned at magistrates' courts on Monday morning. Most importantly, 'the person would in any event be likely to be prevented or at least deterred from committing further acts of hooliganism'.[57] Ejections merely removed the potential for disorder from within the stadium to outside it. Arresting fans eliminated both dangers and increased the perceptions of police authority.

The Home Office also discussed powers of arrest at length, including the possibility of arrests en masse when proper identification of criminal subjects could not be obtained. In 1969, Chancellor of the Exchequer Roy Jenkins, urged 'that the solution is to arrest all the hooligans apparently concerned (without identifying the actual individuals responsible for the actual damage) for causing an affray or some similar offence. This will pose problems for the police, but the Home Secretary [James Callaghan] feels that public opinion would be behind them.'[58] Home Office officials told Claxton that such collective arrests would be particularly useful in the football setting and in incidents of railcar damage.[59] Both the Director of Public Prosecutions and Her Majesty's Inspector of Crime, two nationally authoritative police officials, warned that such arrests would produce civil rights violations and the possibility of negative legal recourse.[60] Yet, in the case of more serious weapons charges or police assaults, the Director's office recommended arresting as many subjects as possible, noting that 'I have little doubt that Magistrates, in the present climate of opinion, would deal severely with those [cases]'.[61] The Home Office consistently urged police authorities to extend their powers of arrest, use the most generally adaptive police charges, and detain arrestees for long periods in order to maintain their tough stance against law-and-order transgressions. Such instructions paid attention to violations of civil law only inasmuch as they reflected poorly on the Home Office and the police's public relations.

Local police stations also asked central authorities in London for permission to conduct group arrests, regardless of evidence or other justification. The Chief Constable at Liverpool wrote to the ACPO: 'It has been proved that the law is inadequate to deal with a situation where a large group of hooligans are on the rampage'.[62] In a brief prepared for Scotland Yard and other police authorities, district officials issued their complaints: 'Many serious offences such as theft and robbery are carried out under the protection of the group and it is difficult to mount a successful prosecution against the individual concerned because of the lack of direct evidence'. They listed several concrete examples where magistrates either dismissed the case or discharged offenders with a reduced fine. 'This brings to light the difficulties which the police have in dealing with gangs', they concluded. 'When viewed in the cool atmosphere of a court of law, [it] takes on a different complexion'.[63] Looking to sidestep due process, police consistently begged for a more expedient legal or legislative apparatus by which to arrest and convict spectators in groups.

Arrests, as opposed to ejections, also provided evidence of successful police crackdowns on deviant behaviour and became a display of potential consequences for rowdy spectators. The Home Office feared that low arrests numbers reflected poorly on their ability to control crowds at matches. Home Office representatives concluded: 'If there had been violence at a particular match and police activity to curb it, it looked odd if the next day only a very small number of people were charged because the police had concentrated on ejecting rather than arresting'.[64] In a few cases, police felt compelled to defend their low arrest numbers to the Home Office. One supervising officer wrote, 'The small number of arrests was not due to inactivity by police but rather that incidents simply do not arise when police are present'.[65] While ejection afforded a quick and easy solution for immediate predicaments, arrests addressed the larger political concerns about apparently incorrigible football disorder on a national level. Arrests could be recorded, while ejections usually went without note, allowing the Home Office to calculate the statistical incidence of violence and disorder.

But increasing the number of arrests at matches exhausted police resources and presented other unanticipated problems. One supervising officer noted, 'Several arrests were made but, unfortunately, each arrest invariably meant that a police officer left the pitch and as [such] this process was a severe drain on police strength'.[66] A Glasgow officer commented that 'if 150 arrests are made, no police are left to deal with further disorder'.[67] While the addition of police dogs helped, at many grounds sergeants also began deploying constables in patrols of ten, with a supervisor and detective assigned to each group.[68] Arrests could then be made without significantly depleting the practical capacity of the police or their carefully presented visual authority. One police briefing indicated that officers took their encounters with fans to be representative of their ability to deal with direct conflict: 'If incidents occur it is important that only sufficient officers as are necessary move to deal with the incident and not the whole serial otherwise we are quickly faced with a deteriorating situation'.[69] The Home Office's request for greater arrest numbers at matches where violence commenced thus lead to tactical changes in police intervention and arrests.

Police also developed the controversial tactic of detention to alleviate the lengthy burden of formalizing arrests. Instead of finalizing the process of an arrest, which could remove an officer from duty for the balance of a match, police began asking clubs for detention facilities to be installed on the premises. State officials and police officials concurred that such facilities would be critical in facilitating arrests.[70] Some local police forces also employed vans which could detain more spectators during exceptionally contentious matches.[71] Frank Williamson, Her Majesty's Inspector of Crime and consultant to the Home Office, suggested that detention rooms be used to facilitate arrests, but was 'emphatic about the value of arresting and charging rather than merely attempting to detain'. Home Office officials quickly noted, though, that police had no official power to detain without making an immediate arrest.[72] Here again, police officials sought loopholes in police processes and the legal infrastructure in efforts to create effective tactics that served their immediate interests.

Like the development of other police strategies, balancing arrests and ejections developed out of state officials' desires to display their authority and competency in a law-and-order context. State-initiated police activities aimed at representing the weight of their significant social power, backed through the use of force and menacing violence. Police practices accelerated tensions among spectators and between fans and police, provoking opposition as older, service-oriented tactics became less effective and were ignored. When community relations between police, stewards and spectators were recognized, police and clubs exploited them in efforts to identify potential offenders. In sum, state-mediated police responses to increased football violence ensured an antagonistic, confrontational and threatening environment in the terraces.

Police Brutality and the State

Police brutality became another component of the materialization of aggressive and oppositional relations between football spectators and police. In many situations, police constables adopted an antagonistic stance towards spectators, replacing erstwhile approaches based on service and protection. While these new attitudes could become aggressive and eventuate in bodily injury, they also often led to officers' refusal to engage with spectators at all. Negotiation for control of new social spaces between the two groups resulted in the creation of increased tensions and potentially vindictive police actions.

Many of the complaints issued against officers noted their apathy towards citizen protection and their unwillingness to help any spectator, regardless of their conduct or stature. After being attacked in the streets outside the stadium, two members of the Middlesbrough FC Supporters' Club asked for police protection until they entered the stadium. One sergeant replied, 'You don't demand anything here', and then ignored both men. The two men were later attacked again by fans supporting the other team.[73] Some stewards criticized police for being 'unwilling to get among the trouble makers and sort them out'.[74] In a number of cases, police expressed their disdain for spectators by failing to prevent violence on the ground level. Refusal to protect citizens and prevent aggression exacerbated hostile police and spectator interaction and led to outright police negligence. In one atypical case, police refused to grant an escort to coaches bringing spectators to a match. The bus came under attack by a group of fans on the street, and a brick was thrown through a window, striking a fourteen-year old boy in the face, causing severe damage to his cheek and eye. In the official police report, both the driver and the trip organizer complained that such injury could have been avoided but police refused to shield them from attacks.[75]

More commonly, however, spectators complained about severe brutality when police did engage with spectators. One exceptional case revealed in detail the oppositional relations generated by the excessive use of police force. Several young women from Leeds protested against their particularly harsh treatment one Saturday afternoon, and placed their experiences within a larger framework of repeated and publicly accepted police brutality against football spectators. While waiting in line to enter the premises 'they tried to crush us with their horses and came at us with Police dogs. If you didn't get out of the way you got hit, whether you were a lad or a lass we were all treated the same.' They continued by recalling other acts of brutality against their companions: 'In the ground we saw 3 Policemen dragging a Leeds fan out by his hair, they threw him over a barrier and onto a spiked fence ripping his shirt to shreds. Before you start thinking he deserved it, he didn't.' Other pieces of the statement complained about unwarranted arrests and police negligence. They concluded: 'It is always said that hooligans cause trouble but this proves that Police will pick on anybody even if they don't do anything'.[76]

In separate letters, the women also complained about tactics intended to cause panic among spectators. After having her foot trampled by a police surge using mounted horses, one woman reported, 'I do not consider it a responsible thing to do, to ride horses at crowds and cause this kind of panic. There were small children queuing with us who could easily have been knocked to the floor and trampled.' Later, while she was pushed against a barrier outside the stadium queuing for entry, a policeman kicked her in the shin because she could not move forward.[77] A mounted police officer told one of the women that he 'would like to see the whole lot of you get done', hinting that police used horses not only to induce fear but potentially for physical aggression against spectators.[78] In each case spectators resented police provoking anxiety and terror among crowds, noting that police practices caused more disorder rather than maintaining order. In the ensuing Yorkshire police investigation into accusations of brutality, one mounted police constable admitted, 'In crowds, such as which was present that day ... it is inevitable that at sometime, someone is bound to be trod on. It is a hazard over which, in scenes like this, the rider of the horse has little or no control.'[79] Much like physical space divisions, attempts to control crowd behaviour and prevent violence actually created an increasingly hostile and violent environment where opposition and mutually reinforced antagonisms became clearly defined.

Police brutality also treated spectators as a homogenous group, failing to differentiate between fans engaged in violent activities and those trying to avoid participation in them. Reifying spectators as a single, inherently violent assembly engendered violent attitudes towards the entire crowd. One fan remembered fearing the entrance of police into the terraces: 'They'd just get in there and whack people ... If it was persistent they'd go in there and break it up by matching aggression with aggression really. That was like an unwritten law up there.'[80] Such statements indicated that unwarranted and indiscriminate police violence proved consistent in some grounds, especially when young spectators were targeted. 'The police just come pushing through the crowd and on many occasions punching their way through, grabbing youngsters for nothing', wrote one fan. He declared, 'Don't treat us as the thugs from behind the goal, treat us as supporters'.[81] Clearly, many spectators did not want to be typically recognized as part of the social problem, but as social subjects deserving of the basic social services of police. Further, treating them as a homogenous mass of vicious subjects denied their very calculated and passionate club loyalties. Such aggressive attitudes failed to enhance police authority and instead produced increased hostilities among all parties involved.

Unsurprisingly, the government defended excessive police force as warranted by the violence of the fans and the gravity of this ongoing social disturbance. Desperate to seem stringent against increased football violence, politicians' discourse on police violence reinforced the authority of the police by whatever means necessary. Denis Howell's comments consistently emphasized police tolerance, avoiding direct discussion about police brutality while tacitly endorsing their forceful authority. In the wake of a series of spectator complaints about brutality, Howell addressed Parliament:

> This nation has good cause to be thankful for its police force. When I go abroad and see how the police forces elsewhere deal with these troubles I realize that the self-discipline and tolerance of the British policeman is unmatched anywhere in the world. Some of our worst offenders have good cause to thank the tolerance of the British policeman, even though it is running a bit short these days, and they might stop to consider that aspect of the matter.[82]

Howell defused the complaints on a national level by focusing the conversation on the benefits of police intervention and championing their leniency and forbearance. While he implicitly acknowledged that occasionally constables applied excessive force, he simultaneously inferred spectators' culpability. Notably, Howell emphasized the police's self-discipline, a quality which he elsewhere praised frequently and denigrated spectators for lacking. Though Labour Home Secretary James Callaghan admitted in a Commons debate, 'That is not to say that the occasional policeman does not lose his temper. He would be less than human if he did not.'[83] In many instances, police presence deterred violence as they hoped. But ignoring criticisms of police behaviour allowed the government to continue to use strong police tactics against spectators in the public battle over football violence.

Like divisions of physical space discussed in the previous chapter, the rising frequency of police brutality and indiscriminate police aggression further alienated football spectators from the football environment. Government sports ministers strongly supported the police's position as defenders of order and discipline in a chaotic social environment, yet they frequently contributed to and escalated aggression and antagonisms.

The Development of Verbal Networks, Police Identification and CCTV

Previous sociological investigations provide essential understandings of police conduct, but neglect to understand that police strategies developed over time and were contingent upon immediate circumstances and police and spectator experiences in individual grounds. Gary Armstrong, the most prominent ethnographer on football policing, has focused much of his work on undercover police investigations and CCTV from the mid-1980s onward, elevating concern for violations of privacy and the unwarranted surveillance of spectators.[84] The Home Office, though, developed earlier forms of these strategies in the late 1960s and 1970s, revealing the historical contingency of football policing. Rather than assuming the perfection of power and panoptical surveillance manifest in recent CCTV advancements, one must recognize that spectators' aversion to surveillance and technological setbacks shaped the evolution of power relations in football policing. The evidence presented here builds on recent scholarship which questioned the exactness of power manifest in video surveillance by revealing impediments to surveillance and identification processes in one of the earliest experimental sites for this equipment.[85] Though CCTV would later be championed as a key element in the crackdown on football violence during the late 1980s, it became only the most recognized outcome of a series of trial practices that sought to increase individual attention on individual crowd members. Processes of criminal identification and the institution of CCTV, like other police tactics, incurred serious setbacks and developed over time. In sum, the demand for individual detection, arrests and punishment led to the gradual development of invasive police practices which proved only mildly successful.

As soon as police confronted greater challenges policing football spectators in and around stadiums, they attempted to develop verbal networks of communication to facilitate contact between officers, the club and rail authorities. Such contact aimed at reducing the levels of football violence and criminal interests outside stadiums by delivering information about spectators' activities over vast spaces. These systems developed on the fly in the late 1960s and early 1970s, and

became the foundation for recent attempts at centralized intelligence and communication in football grounds. Initially discussing 'intelligence arrangements',
Home Office officials and chief constables wanted to ensure that the most fruitful
information came into the hands of as many police officers and railway managers
as possible.[86] Both the Harrington and Lang commissions insisted on the necessity of radio communication for better police work. Home Office administrator
D. J. Trevelyan, a key figure in handling the Home Office's facilitation of football
policing, and Frank Williamson, the HMI for Crime, invited police constables
throughout Britain to discuss intelligence arrangements and information networking. Constables at the conference reported that clubs initially cooperated
with government requests for police radio antennae to be established at stadiums
to better assist police in establishing functioning networks.[87] Williamson also
visited several clubs to obtain a working knowledge of local intelligence arrangements. The Chief Constable of Staffordshire and Stoke invited Williamson to
show him the capabilities of radio networking. 'Wireless communication with
personnel is also adequate and a sergeant is appointed to take charge of the radio
control', noted Williamson, who added that the club and police officers enjoyed
excellent communication about potential disturbances.[88] In the late 1960s, as a
first order of business in the struggle with football violence, government officials
ensured that local police stations installed effective verbal communication networks to facilitate information sharing among the policing bodies.

Radio communication generally proved successful, allowing police and clubs
to share information about events in disparate parts of the football environment. Metropolitan Police superintendent Commander Mitchell reported to
the Home Office, 'The general availability of personal radios has been of extreme
benefit in enabling senior officers in control to be kept informed of conditions
and to institute early remedial action'.[89] Mitchell also reported that thirty-seven
of the forty biggest clubs used radio communication to aid in police facilitation
and crowd control. Such communications better assisted direct intervention by
police and helped to distribute police resources according to need.

In Coventry, community members also used telephone hotlines, mimicking
police forces' establishment of means of communication to avoid problems with
football spectators. This exceptional case revealed that other members of the
community infrequently contributed to developing verbal networks. In 1975,
local storeowners and citizens formed an association which rotated public 'spotters', who advised local shopkeepers of oncoming rushes of spectators. This early
warning system enabled stores to lock up and avoid theft and damage, including
keeping customers in the shops until trouble passed. The Coventry Chamber
of Commerce stated, 'We are certain that customers won't mind being locked
inside the stores should any trouble arise. After all it will be in their own interests
as well as ours'.[90] While in the main police and clubs paid for and experimented

with radio networks, in specific cases community members also benefited from introducing verbal systems.

Several grounds experienced problems implementing the systems, providing further evidence that such networks, though strongly encouraged by Home Office directors, could only be established partially in some areas. As late as the mid-1970s, high costs and police frugality prevented every officer from having a personal radio at most grounds. In some cases, only a small percentage of constables used the sets, and police used loud hailers to transfer information across city blocks and between sectioned terraces.[91] Winterbottom's investigative crew noted their findings: 'In some instances the site of the ground tends to interfere with reception from divisional channels'. They recommended police experiment with new radio communication devices.[92] At one match in Luton, police experienced severe technological difficulties which hindered their ability to monitor the entire area. 'Problems in Police control were experienced after the Match because of the break-down of the special personal radio network', noted the supervising officer.

> Considerable difficulty was experienced in contacting supervising officers in an effort to move men quickly to trouble spots and to obtain situation reports. This was partly due to a break-down in the sets or batteries themselves and partly due to the noise and violence in which the Officers were working which prevented them hearing their radios clearly.[93]

Such problems meant that local organizers needed to adapt their systems to the on-the-ground circumstances, and only through experimentation and negotiation did effective verbal systems of communication develop in and around football stadiums.

In addition to piecemeal development of verbal networking, government and police officials also considered several police tactics aimed at fostering better identification of individual spectators targeted for arrest. Without a significant precedent, local police stations could endeavour to develop such systems with little legal interference, and often with great encouragement from their superordinates at the Home Office. Communication networks expanded from radio-based contact to prematch consultations between clubs and police from different areas of the UK. Police officials shared information about known violent offenders and instigators, including photographic profiles, which allowed organizers to prepare for key matches and oncoming hordes of travelling fans. At several junctures, the Home Office facilitated these meetings and conversations. In 1970, the Home Office, football representatives and the highest police authorities in London concurred, 'Identification of troublemakers, either individually if possible, or as groups, was of crucial importance. The clubs and their servants often had information which was very valuable and liaison with the police should be as close as possible.'[94] The number of prearranged cooperative meetings increased as government officials nurtured the improvement of inter-action and consultation not only between clubs and police in individual cities, but with the Home Office as well.

The idea of sending known police officers with away fans not only provided an example of recognized authority for travelling spectators, but also allowed police from different cities to share information on disorderly supporters. In 1969, Frank Williamson revealed that the Metropolitan Police had recently instituted the practice of sending constables familiar with groups of rowdy fans to away matches. The travelling police could inform local supervisors of particularly trou-blesome individuals. Williamson recommended to other district supervisors that they adopt the practice. Assistant Chief Constable P. D. Knights of Birmingham responded that 'this had been done at one stage though there were difficulties about sending policemen outside a force's area'. Presumably, jurisdictional red tape prevented a seamless process of arrest and conviction when officers oper-ated outside their district. Nonetheless, the constables agreed to use the practice in special situations and during high-risk matches.[95] At a subsequent meeting, Home Office officials also discussed the problem of identifying those responsible for damage on train cars. In similar fashion, they recommended posting police familiar with groups of spectators at rail stations during train boardings, stops and departures.[96] Such tactics aimed not only to actually identify culprits and prosecute illegal activities, but also used the perceived threat of identification to deter misconduct. These practices were built upon pre-established information collected by local police officers and passed between constables within stations, indicating their advocacy of informal profiling measures.

The use of photography, largely unregulated and legally unjustified, was also advocated to foster better individual identification and personal conviction. Like other police ideas, it also faced problems of implementation. In Coventry, police immediately photographed offenders with the arresting officer, ejected them and avoided the problem of time-consuming arrests. Using the photos of offenders and their arresting officers, constables could pursue individual convictions on their own timetable.[97] Photographic profiles proved only mildly successful at London-based Queens Park Rangers FC. Commander Jackomann complained that 'identification of hooligans was made extremely difficult by the very limited provision of photographic equipment in London police stations. It was only possible to photograph convicted offenders' as well. Indeed, photographic equip-ment could be expensive and troublesome. Further, new perpetrators could not be photographed without a prior conviction. In many areas, police reported that they rarely arrested the same offender twice in a single season, rendering photog-raphy only marginally practical.[98] Without informally ignoring police regulations, photography only proved worthwhile in a limited number of cases.

By the mid-1970s, several police stations kept full photographic dossiers of notorious spectators in their areas, and willingly shared the information with other police districts. I have found evidence that police photographed and profiled offenders in at least six different locales – including Coventry, Manchester, Middlesbrough, Newcastle, Stoke and Scotland Yard in London – and that the Home Office encouraged and practically facilitated this practice.[99] At Scotland Yard offices they began to build photographic profiles of the most serious offenders, which were destroyed if the arrests did not lead to a court conviction.[100] 'Close liaison was maintained with other Police Forces', reported Stoke City police officials, 'and an exchange of photographs and other intelligence took place'. Howell's Working Party investigators thoroughly approved.[101] At Manchester United's Old Trafford ground, notorious for spectator misbehaviour, local police adhered to similar practices. In a 1976 meeting with Home Secretary Merlyn Rees, supervisors reported, 'Known trouble makers were barred when recognized: the force had a photograph library of the worst offenders with which officers could familiarize themselves'.[102] The implementation of photography allowed officers to maintain regulation of football spectators across district boundaries. It also facilitated the early development of profiling culprits, maintaining informal visual records of the most serious offenders at the largest clubs in England. These dossiers prefigured later developments in football intelligence collection and undercover policing from the mid-1980s forward, including the creation of the National Football Intelligence Unit.[103]

Government and police officials also considered formalizing identification profiles in the form of identification cards, though the idea never materialized due to several setbacks. It is well known that Margaret Thatcher strongly advocated a nationally organized ID card scheme in the late 1980s, but was rebuffed by the Taylor inquiry.[104] Less well known, however, is the fact that Denis Howell and the Department of the Environment sought to implement multiple identification schemes in the mid-1970s. Encouraged by the successful implementation of ID schemes at local clubs and in supporters' organizations, Howell explored the possibility of coordinated schemes which would help to exclude disorderly spectators. Like other police tactics, the ID card scheme met with both fervent approval and negotiated resistance by various social bodies.

Many segments of the public found the proposal for a nationally organized scheme to be the solution to the problem. Howell received several letters from members of the public begging for the scheme to be implemented, especially after he leaked the idea to the press.[105] Several architectural firms submitted formal proposals for nationally coordinated schemes that drew on the latest computer technology available.[106] Howell balked initially, but asked the Football League to investigate the feasibility of such a scheme on a national level and approved of an identity card trial scheme for young fans at Coventry City.[107]

Clubs in Cardiff, Blackburn and Everton also implemented similar trials on a short-term basis, and mostly for away matches.[108] British Rail also considered them for all travelling passengers at several points in the development of their pricing and crowd control policies.[109]

The fundamental support for identity cards, though, came from football supporters' groups, who often implemented their own schemes. The National Union of Football Supporters, an offshoot of the larger National Federation of Football Supporters, attempted to convince Howell to employ them on a national level. Their chairman, A. Johnson, berated Howell:

> The solution to all these problems is photo-type identity cards, and you know it ... Yet this scheme is not introduced, we feel, because these people would rather let spectators get hurt for the next month or two, than bow to public demand, which would not satisfy their own egotism ... Identity cards would solve all aspects of hooliganism throughout the world, and for all four divisions of the football league, with no club in a position to offer lack of finance, or shortage of materials as an excuse for non-compliance ... Your only chance is by way of being subtle, for these hooligans have no mind of their own, and intelligence would baffle them. Give them an identity card and let them figure that one out.[110]

Such statements drew on well-established distinctions between 'respectable' fans and 'hooligans', furthering the denigration of working-class men and youths. Johnson also implied that the technological element of ID card scanning would inhibit disorderly working-class supporters from attending the matches due to their alleged lack of competency. Supporters' clubs added a new dimension to the identity card scheme as well by threatening the privilege of admission. As one of Howell's constituents wrote to him, 'this might help to sort the chaff from the wheat'.[111]

In the end, Howell wavered on a nationally organized scheme, though, because he anticipated it might prove to be politically infeasible. Howell used the *idea* of the scheme to seem tough on football violence, but it never materialized. In addition to lacking the necessary funds, he also received several warnings about foreseeable problems with these systems. Most significantly, clubs became concerned that identity cards would reduce 'through-the-gate' traffic and therefore decrease revenue. In 1989, this became a major stumbling block in their consideration as well. Rejecting admission based on identification also led to policing problems similar to those raised by ejections: fans outside stadiums caused more problems than when enclosed in controlled environments. In consultation with Howell's Working Party, Stoke officials 'unanimously agreed that such a system was impracticable. It was considered that the need to refuse entry to non-card holders would create an impossible situation for Police, Stewards and Turnstile Operators.'[112] Department of the Environment and Home Office bureaucrats also considered 'whether the issue of these cards affects the liberty of the subject'. After consultation from other legal authorities in the British government, they concluded that football clubs retained the right to refuse admission to private property at any time.[113] However, it is doubtful, knowing the police and government's previous proclivity for dossier-building, that such a scheme would have been used only to refuse admission. Nonetheless, though Howell enjoyed the public attention which identification card schemes generated, their development beyond the local club level never became a realistic possibility until 1989, when the Taylor Report recommended their use.

Police also infrequently experimented with closed-circuit television in stadiums in efforts to incorporate a visual element into their networks of communication. CCTV developed from other successful visual surveillance techniques employed by the police in the late 1960s and 1970s. As early as 1967 police districts reported that they experimented with binocular surveillance from raised points above the stadium, where police could observe crowd behaviour from a distance.[114] Combined with radio communication, such visual surveillance could better facilitate police interventions into crowds and improve police deployment to various parts of the grounds. At Leeds, they incorporated spotters into a more widespread field of surveillance inside and outside stadiums. 'Observation points were available from a special box and from a seat reserved in the Director's Box', they reported. 'Spotters equipped with binoculars and personal radios were used'.[115] In this system, criminal activity could not only be reported verbally, but observed and witnessed visually, providing stronger evidence in a court of law. Police developed these practices on their own, and government ministers never utilized them or passed them on to other clubs.

Government officials, did, however, discuss the implementation of CCTV on several occasions. Throughout the period trials of CCTV proved unsuccessful in several different stadiums as the technology lacked sophistication and failed to function in a new environment. The Harrington Report indicated that 'some reports were received on the use of closed-circuit television, but the indications are that it has not yet been used very successfully in helping to overcome the problem of identification and apprehension'. The commission hoped for a better future for the technology: 'It is quite possible that its uses have not yet been fully explored and a knowledge that a secret camera is watching spectators could have a deterrent effect on misbehaviour, at least for a time'.[116] The Lang commission also mentioned it as a prospective practice to be used in tandem with physical space divisions and better verbal communications.[117] Most authorities wanted improved visual surveillance to deliver the threat of detection and identification, in addition to supporting evidence for convictions. Early Metropolitan Police trials of CCTV in 1968–9 also failed, but provided another intimidating surveillance practice. Commander J. H. Gerrard reported to the Home Office and other leading police executives, 'Closed circuit television had been tried experimentally but so far was not a success. High-powered binoculars, on the other hand, had already led to seven convictions and were having a deterrent effect on those who knew they were under this kind of observation.'[118] Though CCTV failed, expanded visual surveillance effected the desired response from spectators.

Howell gave special attention to the possibility of installing CCTV in 1974–5 during the second reading of the Safety at Sports Grounds Act. Interested MPs such as Neil Macfarlane (Conservative, Sutton and Cheam) wanted Howell to seriously consider federal funding for developing visual communication networks into full-scale CCTV systems. Macfarlane noted: 'It is something which has not generally been developed in this country and it would remove the problem which the police have at the large grounds in winkling out the troublemakers swiftly'. He added that binocular stations worked for commissioners in the metropolitan areas, and that government provision for CCTV could only support the police in deterrence and identification.[119] Howell responded:

> During the period September–December 1974 six experiments were carried out by police in the West Midlands area, but useful results depended on the natural light being adequate ... Especially if special equipment were necessary to overcome the problem of inadequate light, the installation of CCTV would be expensive.[120]

Indeed, visibility and clarity proved the greatest obstacles to advocating new systems, whose cost needed to be justified to clubs and local police stations alike. Though Howell and other government officials considered CCTV an effective resource for detection, identification and police deployment, its high costs and uncertainty about its effectiveness kept the systems out of football stadiums until the mid-1980s.

Aided by the Football Trust, established to help clubs make architectural changes to stadiums, most major football clubs installed CCTV only after 1986.[121] Several scholars have argued that CCTV, along with stadium seating, provided the most effective solution to football violence.[122] However, the transition to the contemporary surveilled environment did not occur seamlessly. Rather, other visual surveillance techniques predated CCTV and early systems failed to provide usable visual evidence. Clearly, while the extension of video surveillance became a functional police practice in several different police districts, CCTV could not be transferred into the football stadium with precision. Its early trials reveal that while government officials desired to use technology to improve processes of identification, deterrence and visual networks, their efforts were subsumed by simpler forms of visual surveillance that delivered evidence and improved deployment to police on the ground.

Conclusions

This chapter explored the development of police tactics as constables, the government and spectators negotiated the social settings of football and its policing. Like divisions of physical space, policing tactics developed over time and aimed to present authority through displays of strength, numbers and intimidation. The development of police tactics helped to define opposition between police and spectators, establishing polarized positions within tactical struggles for social power. Increasingly brutal police strategies created a mutually antagonistic environment where mentalities of opposition and territoriality were encouraged. The government, in support of police, advocated increased police presence and invasive measures in order to project an image of national security and intolerance to criminal activity. Such practices promised enhanced deterrence and identification but often failed to deliver. While many of these tactics proved successful, they always faced challenges from spectators, problems of financial restrictions and issues of practical implementation. In a focused and spatially confined struggle for power, government officials, police and spectators determined the outcomes and effectiveness of police practices.

The development of police strategies coincided with physical space divisions and sentencing revisions to constitute the government's enactment of tough law-and-order principles against British working-class deviants. However, most police strategies proved counterproductive in the 1970s and 1980s and further exacerbated relations between the state and supporters. Police tactics proved especially disadvantageous when they treated spectators as a homogenous group of violent subjects, arresting or enacting violence against innocent bystanders and often denying individual legal rights. The state's propensity to use violence, here through the development of intimidating strategies, again demonstrated their willingness to demonize, discipline and castigate working-class citizens who challenged their authority.

5 STRETCHING PUNISHMENT: THE STATE, LAW AND ORDER, AND THREATENING THE SPECTATOR

The previous two chapters examined coordinated police tactics and physical space divisions, emphasizing the state's use of aggressive tactics to prevent football violence. Throughout government discussions, authorities failed to consider social research into the background of football violence, instead opting for increased punishment as its most effective disincentive. In this chapter, evidence will show that football governors also explored ways of manipulating the legal system in order to enact extreme punitive measures against rowdy football supporters, arguably exacerbating and provoking the behaviour they sought to control. In the late 1960s and 1970s, Home Office and Department of Environment officials explored how to maximize legal punishment by pressuring the magistrates' courts, working to change available arrest charges and exploring new sentencing options. Under pressure from MPs, police authorities and the public, sports governors attempted to appease calls for swift justice and harsh penalization. As moral anxieties about football violence developed, government officials responded by endorsing law-and-order principles and attempted to deter violence through disproportionate punishment. As football violence escalated and became a political embarrassment, government officials carefully inquired into ways of manipulating the process of conviction and sentencing for football spectators. Several government parties explored punitive measures like steeper fines, extended custodial sentences, juvenile detention, exclusion from matches and even corporal punishment, which were met with varying levels of success. In doing so, successive governments again focused on cultural expressions of authority and social rectification rather than the debilitating material circumstances which contributed to outbreaks of social unrest. Sports authorities, and the Department of Environment in particular, attempted to institute unprecedented curbs on civil liberties and transgress the boundaries of the legal system. Ultimately, manipulating the mechanisms of punishment proved counterproductive as changes escalated violence and failed to prevent further criminality.

Previous academic research into the legal consequences of football violence focused on the period since the 1980s, reflecting the paucity of investigations into the historical development of punishment as football violence emerged.[1] Though a few early studies suggested that football spectators received harsher punishments than other arrestees who committed similar transgressions, the research here reveals how high-level government ministers influenced police discretion on arrests and magistrates' sentencing procedures.[2] Contemporary research focused on how undercover police operations in the mid-1980s led to the use of excessive charges of conspiracy and affray in a few highly publicized, symbolic trials.[3] The evidence analysed in this chapter, however, illuminates how magistrates and police officials established novel arrest and sentencing practices replicated across Britain as football violence continued through four decades. Inasmuch as government officials provided outlines for police work and coordinated between different districts across Britain, they also influenced magistrates' decisions about acceptable punishment both directly and indirectly. Enacting punishment became an important element in the 'processual social drama' government officials and police authorities created through criminalizing spectators' behaviour.[4] Police and government authorities influenced cultural interactions in football by attempting to present the illusion of control by escalating punishment for offending supporters. While physical space divisions and police tactics worked to prevent violence in an immediate sense, sports governors presented magistrates' punitive decisions as authoritative and preventative. Though hearings and court cases received less press attention during the 1960s and 1970s than in the late 1980s, they still proved important to government officials to display authority and illustrate the potential consequences of football disorder. Authorities and sports governors, analysis will show, wanted to ensure that the legal system was seen to punish unruly spectator behaviour as it emerged, presenting excessive punishment as necessary to justice and the maintenance of social order.

In addition, the emphasis on punitive justice ideology indicated in the legal history of football violence reveals that penal reform, championed by the Labour Party in the 1970s, was contested and negotiated through youth criminality in British football. Though Labour officials passed the 1969 Children and Young Persons Act (CYPA) in the hopes of instituting youth rehabilitation and reform in the penal system, episodes in the history of football violence challenged the exigency of reformers and revealed fractures within the Labour Party over how to treat youth transgression and breakdowns in social authority. In the end, social democratic promises of welfare and penal reform were challenged by the political attractiveness of law-and-order discourses in a period of massive social and economic change.

This chapter first explores problems in the legal process, from arrest to trial, which the state faced in attempting to ensure that spectators faced conviction and heavy sentences. Ministry correspondence, Home Office briefs and parliamentary debates reveal that government ministers considered several forms of punishment, explored in the second section. The final section will show how the state moved from a policy of non-interference with judicial affairs to pressuring magistrates, deliberating legislation to intensify criminal charges against football spectators and investigating alternative punishments outside the boundaries of British law. In the end, the sources reveal that the Home Office, the Department of the Environment, Denis Howell and other moral entrepreneurs faced limits to their law-and-order campaigns, as many of their attempts failed to sway magistrates' decisions or transcend the confines of the legal system. Nonetheless, by attempting to enact strict discipline and heavy punishment against those they considered a threat to Britain's moral and social fabric, government officials sought to assuage fears about lawlessness and disorder as young working-class men disrupted the nation's revered pastime.

Legal Punishment for Transgressive Spectators: Problems and Process

Police arrests of unruly spectators revealed several weak links in the juridical chain, especially as they arrested offenders, attempted to process charges and brought the transgressors to court. First, since nearly all of the arrests were made on the day of the match, usually on Saturdays, police faced delays in bringing spectators to a formal hearing. Unless the local station was willing to hold multiple arrestees until Monday, when the magistrates' court reopened, they could not always present transgressive spectators before magistrates. Consider police decisions at a Bristol-Cardiff City match in 1974, where groups of partisan fans clashed before the game outside the entryway to the stadium. Local officers 'were able to corner the gang concerned and consequently a much higher percentage of the youths concerned were arrested than was normally the case'. Police reported to Denis Howell's Working Party that they detained 137 young Cardiff fans between the ages of twelve and twenty and processed only twenty arrests. Constables phoned the parents of the others, requesting that they travel to Bristol to collect their children and receive a verbal reprimand from the local police. 'It was felt by all concerned that it was essential for parents to be made to understand their responsibility for their children's actions', noted one officer. Parents of fifteen children refused to come, and the officers released them that evening. The twenty arrested spectators created a massive workload for the local police to process before Monday's court opening. 'In this instance the police worked all night to ensure that the arrested youths appeared before the magistrates', as soon as possible. Paperwork, interviews and filing formal charges on twenty cases tied up several members of the local police staff for the entire weekend.[5] In addition to problems of workload, police faced a second problem. They did not always prefer to hold arrestees from outside the town overnight, especially juveniles. In this case, police opted to contact parents of the youngest and least serious offenders as an alternative to formal arrest and court sentencing. They created substitute punishments which attempted to shame juveniles and punish parents as well, through the cost of a return trip from Cardiff to Bristol to collect their children.

Third, police could not always procure a quick hearing. If magistrates' schedules proved busy or police resources stretched, police could face delays in bringing arrestees to trial. The Bristol police worked through the night because, as the report noted, during the summer, court cases could be delayed two to three weeks on average. If two weeks elapsed before court hearings could be scheduled, police could not guarantee that offenders would return for the court date. Returning to the local magistrates cost away supporters money and time, and they often failed to appear.[6] Fourth, if much time elapsed between the arrest and the hearing, the arresting officer often declined to bear witness, due to scheduling conflicts or lack of concern. In autumn 1970, shortly after the Conservative administration took office, new Home Secretary Reginald Maudling insisted that police officers give their full cooperation to football clubs who prosecuted offenders, noting that officers needed to appear in court on charges against arrestees to ensure conviction.[7] In addition to difficulties with police resources and administration, problems with court scheduling and testimonies contributed to difficulties convicting spectators arrested at matches.

Facilitating arrests and sentencing also depended on the charges police selected. Police could choose from several ill-defined charges to best suit the nature of spectators' transgressions, but preferred minor charges which ensured easy conviction. Until the passing of the Public Order Act of 1986, overlapping legislation allowed for certain behaviours to be charged under several different broad directives. Section 5 of the 1936 Public Order Act allowed police to charge violent spectators with 'use of threatening or abusive or insulting words or behaviour', a charge which could be widely interpreted and broadly applicable to many types of conduct. Other charges of criminal damage, public drunkenness, obstructing or assaulting police and possessing an offensive weapon applied in a variety of situations, though police chose these charges less often.[8] In London, police could also select between national and local prosecution in addressing threatening or insulting behaviour under the Metropolitan Police Act of 1839.

More serious common law offences, such as unlawful assembly, affray or riot charges could also be levelled at spectators, though police only issued these charges in extreme cases. Instead of charging spectators with 'summary' charges in magistrates' courts without a jury, police could also bring more serious 'indictable' offences to the Crown Courts to be tried before a jury. Not surprisingly, police preferred sending the cases to magistrates' courts for several reasons. Indictment trials could be drawn out, costly and delayed. Convictions could also be more difficult to ensure in a jury trial, where evidence and police testimonies were not only necessary but scrutinized, whereas a magistrate could quickly issue a sentence. In addition, if suspects were convicted, any claims for damages involved with the case were transferred to the state, which became responsible for reimbursement of damages under the Riot Damages Act of 1886. Furthermore, the results of magistrates' decisions could never be appealed. Because of these deterrents, though police had discretion in which charges to use, they most frequently used the umbrella charge of threatening and insulting behaviour, which could be easily applied to many different activities.[9]

Reviewing police statistics collected in Home Office and DOE records revealed much about common police practices. Both departments regularly requested arrest schedules, police diaries and charge sheets from local stations across Britain. Though records are not complete, police in Tottenham, Shepherds Bush, Bristol, Scotland Yard and other areas diligently sent documents to Whitehall between 1969 and 77, even when they were not requested. These statistics roughly match earlier criminological research on sentencing.[10] Police most often used 'threatening behaviour', but also charged arrestees with 'criminal damage', 'assault on police' or 'use of an offensive weapon' in slightly more complicated cases. In the case of summary convictions, threatening or insulting behaviour could be met with a maximum of three months' imprisonment or up to £100 fine. Magistrates often used these maximum guidelines, but developed different sentencing standards in each district. Though most magistrates across the nation issued fines ranging from £20 to £100 for threatening behaviour, magistrates in Tottenham routinely issued the maximum £100 fine by the 1976/77 season.[11] They most often chose fines rather than detention, with other charges carrying slightly different sentences: £75–100 for insulting words, £100–150 for offensive weapon charges and, in one rare case, twelve months' detention for theft.[12] In Bristol, though standard fines ranged from £20–50, magistrates grew fond of charging restitution claims in criminal damage cases where club or private property was injured. All told, restitution and fines could total nearly £200 in many damage cases. Both of these districts proved substantially more punitive than other districts. Magistrates in Fulham proved much more lenient, especially in 1976–7, when only rare cases brought fines in excess of £50 for any charge. Charges of drunk and disorderly conduct or threatening behaviour usually resulted in fines of £10–25. In roughly 10 per cent of the threatening behaviour charges, Fulham magistrates sentenced spectators to a mere twelve hours at a local attendance centre.[13] Magistrates used personal discretion in sentencing transgressive spectators, and responded to public panic differently, but usually followed informal standards established at each district. Therefore, depending on the location of the match, spectators faced widely varying police charges and sentences across Britain.

In the early 1970s police rarely levelled more serious indictable offenses in Crown Courts, but they became more widespread as media coverage of undercover police operations and football spectator conspiracies blossomed in the late 1980s. In fall 1971, the High Court in Dudley heard the first charges of affray and riot brought against football spectators. After a match between Wolverhampton and Nottingham Forest in September 1971, West Midlands police charged seven men, aged sixteen to twenty-five, with charges of riot, affray and using an offensive weapon. At the trial in February 1972, five civilian and eight police witnesses testified that the men had attacked a coach carrying opposing fans away from the stadium after the match, and a jury convicted five of the seven men on affray and weapons charges. The judge dismissed the riot charges on the grounds that the spectators had not gathered with 'unlawful intent'. The younger offenders were sent to juvenile detention centres for three months while two adult men received twelve and fifteen months' imprisonment.[14] However, this case was exceptionally rare.[15] These steep charges proved more difficult to convict, costly to marshal and time intensive. The evidence reveals, however, that the Department of the Environment, in charge of sports governance, followed these rare cases, interested in the effect of their outcomes for further Crown Court trials of football spectators. Indictable charges became more popular in the late 1980s under Thatcher when charges of affray and conspiracy could be levelled in high-profile media trials.[16]

A review of the charge sheets and arrest schedules from several police stations across Britain also demonstrated the social composition of most arrested spectators. Several previous studies have established that most offenders from this period were young, white labourers, and evaluation of records in Home Office files confirm this assessment.[17] Because most police records were sent to the Home Office upon request, no full assessment of any local office's arrest records for an extended period was possible. Nonetheless, the sampling of records collected by the Home Office was extensive, including police diaries from nearly every major city, with an emphasis on clubs in and around London. In particular, the Home Office also requested records from high-profile matches and dates when violence captured press headlines. For example, charge sheets from Tottenham and St Anns Road from late February 1977 show the following occupations for offenders: 'lathe setter', 'trainee welder', 'cook', 'tool-maker', 'print finisher', 'sheet-metal worker', 'machinist', 'miner', 'electrician', 'driller', 'postman'.[18] General terms like 'juvenile', 'schoolboy', 'labourer' and 'unemployed' were also frequently used. Other routine filings with the Home Office reflect similar representative working-class backgrounds for most violent offenders in major British cities.[19] As demonstrated below, magistrates often considered offenders social backgrounds when using fines as sentences, placing another obstacle in the path to harsh punishment.

In sum, redundant and ill-defined government legislation allowed police officers discretionary use of a wide variety of charges to prosecute unruly spectators. Police preferred to use wide-ranging charges such as threatening behaviour or criminal damage, which only required bringing the arrestees before a magistrate rather than a drawn-out criminal trial. Nonetheless, police still faced several obstacles to conviction, including lack of evidence and testimony, hearing scheduling, and timing. Police faced pressure to bring arrests through to conviction, but doing so often required extra hours on the job and fighting through administrative difficulties.

Forms of Punishment

Despite the increasing number of arrests, a wide range of social actors complained about magistrates' failure to deter violent spectators' conduct through punishment in the courts. MPs and police officials consistently asked for fines and the maximum punishment allowed by legislative guidelines. Government officials hoped that excessive punishment would deter unwanted behaviour. Many suggested punishments outside the boundaries of contemporary law, meant to deter football disorder through violent threats and cruel retribution. Sentencing and arrests also became key elements in law-and-order policy, which allowed MPs to gain public favour by supporting excessive punishment for criminalized football supporters.

Government officials and local police often disagreed about arresting offenders. Unsurprisingly, police often preferred to eject or warn spectators rather than arrest them and issue charges. As discussed earlier, problems of individual identification among group activities often inhibited police from recognizing which spectators were responsible for specific transgressions. Identification proved problematic in areas like train cars, queues, terraces and other crowded areas inside and outside of stadiums. Furthermore, as mentioned earlier, arrests were often resisted not only by the arrestee, but by those around him/her, especially when the arrests occurred within the terraces. Home Office officials and members of Working Parties on football violence, however, pressed police to make arrests as often as possible. As discussed in Chapter 4, they perceived that higher arrest numbers indicated to the public that government and police authorities had effectively addressed the issue of football violence with quick action and practical justice. Arrest statistics could be distributed to the public through the media to reveal how diligently the Home Office and local police prosecuted violent spectators.

When they did make formal arrests, however, police wanted magistrates to quickly wrap up the cases and issue severe penalties to discourage others from participating in football violence. Frank Williamson, Her Majesty's Chief Inspector of Crime, suggested to the Home Office that 'the correct thing to do with such persons is to charge them with a specific offence or take them before the magistrates at the earliest opportunity and cause them to be bound over to keep the peace'. 'Binding over' was a legal power exercised by local magistrates to hold accused offenders for a limited period in effort to prevent the prospect of future disruptive acts. If a prosecuted individual agreed, charges could be dropped in exchange for time spent in holding. Technically, it was not a punishment for past acts, but an exercise of magistrates' authority to presumably keep the peace. It was preferred when no witnesses were available for conviction, and often to promote expediency in specific cases. Binding over ensured that the offender had the incident recorded but bypassed the potentially lengthy prosecution and sentencing process. No less an authority than Williamson, the Home Office's chief police consultant, advocated such measures to promote quick processing of arrest charges and swift resolutions to weekend disorders, often in cases where other football supporters failed to testify as witnesses and no conviction could be ensured. He added, 'This would act as a deterrent in the future and protect police officers who had physically ejected disorderly people from a football ground from the danger of complaints about the use of excessive force or police powers'.[20] The idea not only reflects the problems police faced in securing convictions and in presenting arrestees to magistrates with concrete charges, but also that many police feared accusations of rough treatment when they ejected fans or detained away spectators. Police from several districts echoed the sentiment. In Stoke, police wanted to bring offenders to the courts on matchday to present the judges with arrestees 'dressed as they would be for the match and in the same frame of mind'.[21] Howell's Working Party agreed that displaying spectators' emotionality and provocative game-day garb to the magistrates would result in steeper punishment and praised police in Newcastle for attempting the same process.[22]

Police were also aware of the ways in which spectators skirted fines and hoped that magistrates could imagine new possibilities for punishment. Police superintendents in Bristol 'felt that punishments should be realistic. A fine was often met by a "whip-round" amongst the friends of an arrested youth.' Such complaints referred to supporters who collected money from groups of fans to pay for individual fines. As alternatives, they suggested detention on matchdays or fines and prison sentences for the majority of juvenile offenders.[23] The complaint reveals that spectators often circumvented direct punishment through collective action. Such activities essentially made fines neither costly nor punitive, but rather furthered the reciprocal process of encouraging stronger punishment. Local police recognized that monetary fines often did not always lead to deterrence and advocated more extreme removals of personal freedoms.

While police dealt with the practical problems of arrests and punishment, MPs intermittently debated the matter in Westminster. A strong consensus emerged from both parties: spectators should be punished to the full extent of the law, and magistrates should be encouraged to sentence them accordingly. As early as 1967 several MPs asked Home Office Minister Dick Taverne to impose tougher penalties on those found guilty of football disturbances.[24] When train damage emerged as a costly government problem, authorities urged concrete action. Conservative Teddy Taylor (Glasgow) asked Minister for Transport Richard Marsh if he was aware 'that in a recent case vandals responsible for 800 pounds' worth of damage were fined only 5 pounds each?' He suggested 'that the Government would have the general support of the public if they provided for more effective penalties to deal with recent orgies of vandalism'.[25] Emphasizing the moral as well as physical challenge football violence posed to government, the statement implied the sexualization of violence and intimated the excitability and animalism of working-class spectators. Frustrated with the costly problems local police, transport authorities and football clubs faced, MPs consistently harangued Cabinet leadership for their failure to deter further violence.

The matter enraged members so much that parliamentary debates on adolescent crime or national sports financing frequently digressed into workshops in which representatives brainstormed cruel punishment in desperate bids to curb football violence. Such discussions testified to the depth and breadth of the problem, as well as the general confusion of politicians in how to ameliorate it. MPs frequently suggested new forms of punishment including habitual delinquents' exclusion from matches, detention sentences and a return to corporal punishment for adolescent offenders. Many of these suggestions strayed beyond the recommended sentences for juveniles and the maximum guidelines for punishment under the 1936 Public Order Act. Both Labour and Conservative ministers fielded suggestions for mandatory attendance centre orders, where young fans would be required to appear at local correctional stations on matchdays, to be supervised by police. Under the existing guidelines, however, the centre issued the schedule of appearances, not the magistrate, so neither police nor judges could order that spectators be prevented from attending the next game.[26] One Home Office brief also warned that 'it would be wrong in principle to associate the police with punishment; but added to that is the fact that the police would be thus troubled at a time when they were under particularly heavy pressure in any case'.[27] Some Home Office officials worried that attendance centres required extensive resources, including overtime pay for the constables that manned them, and Saturday attendance could not always be practically or financially assured.

Other members suggested compulsory civil service and hard labour as compensation for harm done to British society. In one particularly heated debate, after a series of football disturbances in spring 1977, Walter Johnson (Labour: Derby South) noted, 'I was interested in the suggestion that thugs should be dealt with by a type of military service'. He proposed the establishment of a special branch of military service, under the supervision of the Army, and recommended that offenders complete three to four month tours. 'Some would call it conscription, but I do not mind what it is called. Let such people be subjected to a discipline that they do not get in school or at home', he argued. He asked Home Office officials to convey the idea to the Secretary of Defence.[28] Later that spring, Leslie Spriggs (Labour: St Helens) asked for a drastic increase in penalty under the current laws and advocated that police use criminal prosecution rather than summary charges or fines: 'We should pass the maximum possible sentences on the thugs so that they can be put away for long enough'. His final suggestion was the most severe: 'Instead of being allowed to watch football they should be made to work with a shovel on match days', presumably in some form of civic labour programme.[29] Both suggestions intimated that football disturbances not only reflected the deterioration of Britain's cultural core, but also contributed to it. Young working-class support-ers epitomized the deterioration of youth, who apparently lacked core British values of hard work, discipline and temperance. In both proposals, guilty supporters should be made to restore the nation through manual labour and compulsory service, which would remedy the flaws of their personal charac-ter as well as of young working-class men collectively. MPs here attempted to devise plans for convicted spectators to repay a perceived debt to British society, imagining punishment that not only excluded fans from the realm of football but also provided practical forms of obligatory service which could be more punitive than current correctional options.

While many proposals for exclusion emerged in political discussions, manipulating ticket prices and fines found the most favour among government members and police, revealing that government officials associated football vio-lence with poverty. Suggesting heavier fines or prohibitive ticket prices revealed that regulators aimed at excluding disruptive spectators from consuming the sport and participating in its rituals. 'Would it not make sense', Ivor Clemitson argued (Labour: Luton East), 'to devise a punishment to prevent the offenders from attending football matches for a considerable period of time?' Neil Mac-farlane, later Conservative Minister of Sport under Prime Minister Margaret Thatcher, replied that the average fine should be £400 rather than £40. 'There must be scope for hitting the persistent hooligan very sharply through his wallet', Macfarlane added.[30] The simplest way to deter football disturbances, government officials argued, was to increase fines and make attending matches more difficult. This tactic revealed that politicians viewed the problem as firmly rooted in young working-class communities where increased fines would have a serious impact. This implied association of poverty and punishment, which emerged in nearly every political discussion about football violence, exposed the class dynamics of a government attempting to control the behaviour of working-class youths.

Heavier fines and costly youth ticket prices targeted several different dimensions of working-class football consumption, and reveal the assumptions government officials made regarding punishment. Clearly, the inconvenience of paying a significant fine proved annoying, if not extremely difficult, for arrested supporters. Some of the above suggestions insinuated that some offenders should be indebted to the state for significant periods of time. With less disposable income, government officials assumed offenders would have less to spend on football attendance. In addition, sports governors connected post-war fears of working-class affluence expressed during the Teddy, mod and rockers scares, with the need for punishment. [31] Under these classed assumptions, the simplest approach aimed at limiting opportunities for football consumption for poorer offenders. Encumbering disposable income through monetary punishment would rectify the entire social problem.

Finally, regulators assumed that increasing fines would force parents to be more responsible for the actions of their children, especially when away from home. Police at Middlesbrough and Sunderland routinely insisted parents retrieve their children, and occasionally pay their fines, when local magistrates sentenced younger offenders. [32] Travelling to pick up adolescent supporters, especially on short notice, could be very expensive for working parents. In this case, parents of the accused became the targets of punishment as much as juvenile offenders. Such imaginative punishments attempted to discipline working-class families and not merely individuals. Consider similar assumptions about working-class families and the indiscipline of working-class mothers in Denis Howell's comments on the origins of football violence. Labour's leading sports governor speculated: 'We all have our pet theories ... I have my own prejudice. In most working-class homes the mother is the disciplinarian. A lot of this trouble can be traced back to the time when mothers began regularly to go out to work.' After sympathizing with mothers who have to hold down three jobs and seem exhausted, he noted that 'the easy way to get the children away from under their feet is to give them 50p to go out'. Mothers preferred to relax and watch television, Howell noted, and therefore contributed to a lack of communication and discipline within working-class families. [33] Howell's rare attempt to explain the origins of football violence laid blame on working-class mothers and the fragmentation of working-class families. Though Howell also mentioned secondary issues of social deprivation, boredom and education, his explanation subtly accused working-class women of laziness, indiscipline and improper parenting. Regardless of his supposed sympathies for women in work, Howell censured supporters' mothers for failing to control the emergence of working-class affluence and football violence among their teenagers. Howell never mentioned the role of fathers, presumed to be absent or uninvolved in family relationships. Fines or requests for pickups by local police, encouraged by the central authorities and assumptions of working-class affluence, thus attempted to discipline working-class families as well as individual spectators.

In addition to heavier fines and family discipline, another series of punitive suggestions called for reinstating corporal punishment for young offenders. Here supporters' discourse began to reflect media attention to football disorder, which repeatedly included calls for birching, thrashing and hosing down offenders as moral anxieties about football violence blossomed.[34] The Football Association and football supporters' clubs across the UK also championed the use of birching and the implementation of stocks at stadiums.[35] Supporters' clubs, often composed of more traditional football supporters, proved to be the most fervent advocates of corporal punishment, especially reviving use of the birch. As mentioned in the second chapter, supporters' clubs helped to define the distinction between 'genuine' fans and 'troublemakers'. Supporters' clubs often envisioned themselves as the protectors of forms of gentlemanly consumption against more physical, collective forms of spectatorship. Members of the supporters' clubs petitioned the government to use the full complement of available punishments to prevent disorder, but emphasized the need for physical castigation. The Manchester United Fan Club, proudly proclaimed as Manchester's oldest supporters' organization, wrote to sports governor Denis Howell, 'They are not true supporters of Manchester United but troublemakers. They want sorting out and giving the birch. That would stop them. Talking to them won't neither will fines. They have too much money. £5 means nothing to them these days.'[36] Fears about working-class youth affluence encouraged a constant escalation in the severity of punishment. The club's comments reveal that sections of the public sought to escalate punishment and reintroduce physical castigation because they perceived the transgressors to be more than able to pay for fines. These forms of punishment also reinvigorated discourses of young working-class men as infantile and bestial, assumed to be teachable only by the birch or the belt. Gentlemen spectators considered working-class supporters not amenable to social rehabilitation and implied their irrationality. These class discourses rendered young working men incapable of change, denied their status as rational subjects and completely ignored any consideration of their political or personal motives.

Despite extreme calls for corporal punishment by the public, the national government never reinstituted physical castigation. Government officials and police authorities settled for flexible fines and minimal detention as the harshest options for penalizing supporters and their families. Though they could not force magistrates to utilize any particular option or maximize sentences, they imagined punitive alternatives that reinforced the false assumption that excessive punishment unequivocally deterred further transgression. In the period under study, there is little if any evidence to support this assumption. From the period of its emergence in the mid-1960s, football violence proliferated quickly despite manipulations to fines and punishment. The social and political roots of football hooliganism, often ignored by government officials, were not well understood and the popularity of the phenomenon could not be stymied by mere punishment.

Changing Legal Standards? From Non-Interference to State Involvement

Nonetheless, to appease calls for swift justice and heavy punishment, several branches of the national government as well as MPs attempted to exert pressure on judicial authorities. Though some state officials initially defended the right of magistrates and the judiciary to choose sentences and levy penalties as they saw fit, others soon tampered with legal process. Denis Howell, the leading voice of law-and-order against football rowdyism, attempted to circumvent legal and political restrictions through several political avenues. He repeatedly initiated cabinet-level discussions that tested the limits of the Department of Environment's autonomy and attempted to extend the authority of one of its undersecretarial agencies, the office of the Minister of Sport. As part of his crusade against working-class football supporters, Howell explored several avenues with Home Office legal officials and other government experts. Between 1974 and 1977, in his second term as Minister of Sport, Howell attempted to ascertain how his agency could adjust arresting and sentencing procedures without inciting allegations of operating outside the law. Persisting in his belief that stricter punishment deterred further transgressions, Howell aimed to ensure that the third arm of his campaign against spectators would incorporate an intimidating display of authority to disorderly working-class spectators.

Howell, though, was not the first to attempt to sway magistrates' sentencing decisions, although he proved the most persistent in establishing his own political theatre. Howell built on punitive policies constituted during the early emergence of football violence in the late 1960s. John Lang's initial 1969 inquiry responded to police demands that magistrates impose steeper fines and pursue more serious charges. Glasgow police and local club Rangers FC officials pleaded 'that when apprehended first offenders should receive stiffer fines than at present imposed by the magistrates'. Repeat offenders 'should be remitted to the Sheriff's Court for the wider discretion and bigger penalties such Courts could inflict'. Local police also protested that fines were paid in instalments, which allowed less affluent spectators to pay off high fines over time, thus diminishing their deterrent value.[37] Alan Hardaker, chair of the Football League and member of the inquiry committee, seconded the protest, noting that only magistrates' maximum guidelines would produce the necessary discipline: 'The Football League clubs believe that what is happening in football is symptomatic of the growing indiscipline of certain elements in the country, and until the police are supported by stronger action by magistrates, there is little that can be done to deal with the problem'.[38] Implied class discourse again marks Hardaker's remarks, tacitly endorsing strict punishment as the only remedy for outbursts by troublesome working-class spectators. The committee debated at length the inclusion of recommendations to pressure magistrates to take further action.

Chairman John Lang, like other Home Office officials before and after him, recognized that compelling magistrates or Crown Court prosecutors to pursue steeper sentences and criminal charges could not be achieved easily. Making suggestions to any court without legislative mandate violated the boundaries established between the judiciary and Parliament. In a memo to other inquiry members, Lang noted:

> I am aware that when we were considering the working of our report, we felt that any seeming interference with magistrates was a 'hot potato' but I have swung round to the view that a guarded reference to standard of punishment might be possible. The absence of any such reference might be criticised.[39]

The inquiry feared that the general public and political opposition would attack their final recommendations as soft on criminal football activity. Lang's committee included a veiled recommendation that magistrates make the maximum sentencing limits standard. 'It would be wrong for us to seek to interfere with the discretion of the courts ... but we are bound to express the hope that magistrates will ... award punishments that match the seriousness of the offence and are likely to serve as an effective deterrent'.[40] Lang's committee, the first state-sanctioned inquiry into football violence, wanted to project an image of state authority, manifest in architectural changes, improved police procedures and stiff punitive deterrents. Since they could not directly control the third element of their law-and-order programme, they attempted to sway magistrates to support their objectives.

Home Office and DOE agents recognized that influencing magistrates' decisions could provoke a public or political backlash. As police officials, government representatives and the Lang inquiry exerted pressure on the Home Office and Department of the Environment to compel magistrates to issue tough sentences to football offenders, other government officials initially defended the judiciary's right to act without external interference. In 1967 Dick Taverne of the Home Office defended the magistrates' sole jurisdiction over punishment, and in 1969 Home Secretary James Callaghan upheld this separation.[41] Callaghan's Conservative successor, Reginald Maudling, maintained the position and declared 'that he shared the view that offences of violence of this kind had to be treated very seriously, but he had no powers to give instructions to the courts'. Instead, he suggested that 'public opinion was a powerful influence here', intimating that the Home Office could build public favour to persuade magistrates to impose harsher penalties.[42] Though ministers and MPs could not formally pressure the lower courts, they could build the perception that the public also demanded steeper penalties. Callaghan also informed Lord Chancellor Quintin Hogg of the displeasure recorded by Home Office ministers and the governors of sport 'in case he has an opportunity for bringing the public concern on these issues to the notice of the magistracy'.[43] Without direct influence on the judiciary, Cabinet-level ministers used the public to build support for inflexible standards of punishment against lawlessness in football. Since the media usually supported the Conservatives' castigation of football supporters generally, calling on the public for support proved a worthwhile political tactic. As with the moral arguments they constructed in public discourse against rowdy football spectators, political officials forwarded calls for punishment with the support of media networks and social reformers. Such subtle political manipulation proved only the first step in promoting punishment as the political answer to the conundrum of football violence.

Magistrates varied in their response to public and government pressure, but continuously defended their right to determine the standards for punishment. In Newcastle, magistrates levelled lower fines because, with high levels of unemployment, they wanted to ensure that supporters could actually pay the fine. Though several police constables complained that their authority was weakened by lower fines: 'it was recognised that in an area of high unemployment, there was little point in imposing heavy fines'.[44] Here, the possibility of collecting the fine or recovering money for damages determined the level of punishment, not political pressure. After 1973, this policy was standardized under the Powers of Criminal Courts Act, which required that magistrates consider the means of the offender in assigning a fine, and many also allowed payments in instalments.

However, in 1975, The Magistrates' Association, the representative body of local magistrates, asked the Home Office to pursue legislation to expand the punitive standards available in summary sentencing.

> A meeting of our Council today endorsed the recommendation ... that we should urge Her Majesty's Government to consider extending the age range and expanding Senior Attendance Centre facilities to a level that will enable the Courts to deal promptly and effectively with football and other hooligans.

The centrepiece of the consortium's recommendations was the extension of the use of attendance centres for young offenders, which they found more threatening than the less stringent juvenile sentencing standards or fines. When scheduled for matchdays, twelve-hour attendance centre sentences could prevent fans from attending matches. The magistrates' assembly thought such sentences 'would be particularly useful as suitable reporting centres for football hooligans, providing punishment without loss of job and also prevention of further trouble-making on succeeding Saturdays'. They added that the use of attendance centres on Saturdays would have wide public acceptance and therefore be a politically viable sentencing alternative. Cognizant of the constraints on police resources, the magistrates recommended that centres hire staff to monitor the centres on Saturdays. Attendance centres could also be used, they noted, as punishment for groups, especially when magistrates avoided pursuing time-consuming individual sentences.[45] The letter revealed that the magistrates' association faced similar challenges of dealing with public pressure and the practicalities of the judicial system and responded by asking Parliament to extend juvenile punishment, not through heavier fines or stronger custodial sentences, but through alternative sentencing procedures such as attendance centres. Throughout, they defended their right to choose the sentencing within the boundaries determined by the law, yet responded to growing pressure to sharply punish transgressors.

Despite the clear line drawn between legislative and judicial authority, Denis Howell's response to pressure from other MPs and the public broke earlier Home Office promises to avoid direct interference with juridical outcomes. When Labour reassumed power in 1974 and Howell launched his public campaign against football violence, he also attempted to extend the power of his office to influence juridical procedures against spectators. Under Howell's leadership, Labour immediately attempted to pass the Safety at Sports Ground Act, which eventually extended government authority in licensing and architectural regulation. At the same time, Howell and his Working Party on Crowd Behaviour worked to circumvent legal and political restrictions through several political avenues to ensure the authority of the legal process. They consistently sought out ways of manipulating the legal process and extending punitive standards against persistent offenders. Howell repeatedly initiated cabinet-level discussions that tested the limits of the Department of Environment's autonomy and attempted to extend its purview of sports governance. Between 1974 and 1977, in his second term as Minister of Sport, Howell attempted to ascertain how his agency could adjust arresting and sentencing procedures without inciting allegations of operating outside the law. Persisting in his belief that stricter punishment deterred further transgressions, Howell aimed to ensure that his campaign against spectators would incorporate an intimidating display of authority to disorderly working-class spectators.

In particular, three political episodes demonstrate Howell's eagerness to convert moral campaigns against football supporters into political capital by stretching the limits of acceptable punishment against offenders. The first occurred in August 1974 when Howell pressured the Home Office and other Labour ministers to support his law-and-order struggle against football supporters. Autumn 1974 saw several high-profile cases of violence, including the

Tottenham Hotspur incident in Holland and a murder in Blackpool.[46] Howell responded with a well-publicized tirade in which he promised that his Working Party would root out football violence by advocating the full repertoire of available punishments. Howell complained that 'detention centres' were merely 'half full' and that magistrates should be encouraged to sentence offenders to custodial detention: 'Once they were able to go to matches again they would think twice about misbehaving'.[47] Howell made a key mistake in confusing detention centres and attendance centres, for which several Home Office officials reprimanded him. Considered a very serious custodial sentence, magistrates could only order detention centre sentences for three to six months, and usually refrained from the sentence as the three centres in southern England proved perpetually full.[48] Attendance centre sentences could be ordered for a single Saturday, but not even the Home Office could order the centres to be open over the weekend if resources proved limited. Furthermore, they could not be used for offenders over the age of seventeen.[49] Despite the blunder, Howell requested a meeting with Roy Jenkins to urge the Home Office to support his insistence on stricter punishments.

Shortly after Howell's tirade, he and the Home Secretary convened to 'discuss the relationship between his interests as Minister of Sport and your [Jenkins's] overall responsibility for problems of law and order', but the meeting resulted in Jenkins asking for diplomatic cooperation from Howell in the best interests of the Labour Party.[50] Home Office officials had shown some reservations about Howell's campaign against spectators, especially his insistence on forcing magistrates' sentences.[51] As Home Secretary, Jenkins also considered football disorder a severe social problem, but resented Howell's attempts to force the Home Office to make legislative changes so that the Department of the Environment's sport office could carry out its punitive agenda. Howell argued that he 'had acted on the assumption that there was a need for someone in the Government to appear concerned and active'. Howell's recommendations to the Home Office included changing the 1969 Child and Young Persons Act (CYPA) to include steeper punishments for juvenile offenders. He noted that 'a common complaint was that first offenders could not be adequately dealt with and could not be sent to detention centres'. Furthermore, 'while fines of £100 ... seemed large, they could easily be met by a whip-round among associates'. Howell also recommended that community service be considered if the Home Office pursued revising the CYPA, which provided the legal framework for adjudicating juvenile crime. He also cited support from several magistrates and juvenile social work groups which advocated the extension of detention and attendance centres.[52]

The episode reveals fractures in social democratic approaches to welfare and social reform. Jenkins's response indicated the ambivalence of the CYPA and the much-debated penal reforms it attempted to institute in an effort to address political concerns about the increase in criminality in Britain, both within and outside of football. In the 1966 election, the Labour Party heavily campaigned on a law and order platform, and for the first time matched the Conservatives ambition for penal reform. [53] Because of the perceived increase in youth criminality, the Labour Party used the 1969 CYPA to fulfil many campaign promises regarding juvenile crime. The CYPA allowed Labour to acquiesce to public demands for stiff penalties while also allowing for rehabilitative reform. The Act proved incredibly flexible, addressing longstanding concerns about social rehabilitation without removing the possibilities of retributive justice legal models. James Callaghan instituted the bill as a welfare-based approach that united care and control. However, without unanimity of penal philosophy of magistrates, and any consensus on the non-implementation of the reforming provisions, welfare-based reform made only moderate strides. [54]

Ambivalence within the justice system and Labour Party officials allowed Howell to attempt to exploit the loopholes in legal process for football offenders. Despite the warning from a Home Office Research Study that 'it seems unlikely that institutions will make any serious impact on the reduction of juvenile delinquency [because] their present theoretical orientation and practice cause them to pay insufficient attention either ... to factors in the offender's environment', Howell persistently advocated various forms of detention that neglected environmental or rehabilitative factors. [55] Instead, Howell promoted the use of attendance centres, which 'were originally proposed in 1938 as short sharp shocks involving hard physical exercise and strong discipline', and whose emphasis on physical retribution remained strong. [56] All of Howell's attempts at extending legal punishment promoted a punitive approach based on the assumption that retribution – through fines, detention or deprivation of liberties – forced offenders to realize the damaging effects of their criminality on themselves. [57] This penal justice model, here advocated by Howell, failed to recognize the social deprivations and environments from which youth violence emerged, the political or personal messages conveyed in partisanship violence in football and the reciprocal effect of positioning the police and the state as the opposition or object of further violent acts. The legal context which helped constitute Howell and others' responses to football violence allowed for a return to punitive retribution despite calls for welfare reform in the juvenile judicial system.

Jenkins responded to Howell's request not because of any love for welfare-based penal reform, but by protecting the interests of the Labour Party's political initiatives rather than succumbing to the Department of Environment's concerns about football disorder. Jenkins disliked the idea of changing the CYPA because Labour had gained much political capital by appearing tough on crime when they passed the Act during their last administration. [58] Jenkins said 'he was aware of a certain amount of criticism of the 1969 Act, some of which was probably justified. There was a need, however, to handle such criticisms carefully, as the Act had been Labour Party legislation.' He added, 'There was no advantage in stirring up discussion of the existing Act until the Government had worked out clear proposals for legislation to take its place'. On community service, Home Office legal advisors reminded Howell that offenders had to consent to the sentence and be willing to participate, and that civil service rarely worked as a punitive measure. The Home Office's head legal official 'had reservations about presenting community service as a negative way of keeping people out of trouble. This could damage its image and alienate those on who one had to rely to make it work, in particular probation officers.' The Home Office denied Howell's request for expansive community service but did agree to look into a legislative amendment that would allow magistrates to assign and schedule attendance centre appearances.[59]

Despite consistent pressure from Howell and the Department of the Environment, the Home Office found it disadvantageous to privilege the fight against football hooliganism over the entire political image of the Labour Party. Jenkins clearly agreed with Howell about the gravity of football disorder and its impact on the image of Great Britain. However, the Home Secretary recognized that in seeking to appear inflexible on juvenile football disorder they could not compromise Labour's other legislative and political goals. He acknowledged that football disorder contributed to the growing sense of social disorder and youth crime, but in order to pursue revisions of legislation against juveniles, the Home Office could not betray that their existing measures had already failed them.[60] Howell's initial attempt to expand punishment against juvenile football offenders fell short not because of any outspoken voices against the alternative punishments he proposed, but because of practical and political obstacles.

With little help from the Home Office in securing detention sentences, Howell turned to local government to pursue other modes of exclusion. Howell asked his own legal advisors and Home Office legal officials if police or the Department of Environment could ban consistent troublemakers from attending matches indefinitely, perhaps through local authorities. To his dismay, the law disallowed any government or police branch from banning anyone from commercial industry. Such a suspension could only be initiated by the football clubs as the owners of the private land the stadiums rested on. The legal advisers remarked, 'If a court punishes an offender for misbehaviour at a ground, that is as far as its control of the offender could go, and subject to his complying with whatever disposal the court makes, he is free to re-offend if he wishes'.[61] Howell then investigated the possibility of a county injunction against groups of persistent offenders, which would also exclude offenders from matches. Howell and DOE officials complained, 'In the case of an offender under 21 years of age, the imposition of imprisonment is of course hedged around with "safeguards" which make it a penalty rarely imposed'.

An injunction from a county court would not allow imprisonment or detention, but could be useful if Howell could show that, 'none of the sanctions open to the criminal courts appear to have any deterrent effect'.[62] However, local police would have to gather evidence of criminal activity on several occasions before an individual injunction could be filed and approved. Again, Howell faced the practical difficulty of the immense resources required to prosecute individuals, and eventually stopped pursuing local government avenues.

The second notable incident occurred when Howell attempted to circumvent the magistrates' decisions altogether by promoting the use of heavier criminal charges tried in the Crown Courts. By summer 1975, Howell again requested that the Home Office consider supporting his campaign for tough punishment. In the midst of attempting to pass the Safety at Sports Grounds Act, Howell proposed another bill which would extend the punitive standards for magistrates' sentences. In a private meeting with Jenkins and other Home Office officials, Howell asked the Home Secretary to forward a concurrent bill on punitive criteria. Jenkins immediately denied the request.[63] Two months later, with the support of Conservative and Labour MPs, Howell threatened publicly to pursue charges of affray and riot.[64] Howell forced a meeting with Jenkins by making his case through the newspapers, calling for more serious attention to the ongoing problem. Howell came to this meeting prepared with a list of grievances about the legal constraints on his campaign against football offenders. In addition to clamouring for raising maximum sentences for summary offences, Howell asked the Home Office to encourage police to charge fans with indictable Crown Court charges. He also requested that Jenkins review 'whether magistrates make sufficient use of their power to remit offenders for sentencing in their home area'.[65] Jenkins appeased the Minister of Sport by listening to his complaints, but took no formal action. Nonetheless, the incident again reveals efforts by Howell and the Department of the Environment to maximize the punitive measures available within the legal system, and to stretch the law when they thought current measures insufficient for castigating young offenders.

The third and final episode unfolded as Howell sought reauthorization for corporal punishment after attempts to manipulate other legal and judicial processes failed. In 1977, Home Secretary Merlyn Rees acquiesced to several calls for corporal punishment for violent football offenders and met with Howell to discuss the matter. Rees prepared a series of briefs that specified maximum sentences for various summary and indictable offenses and the existing powers of both magistrates' and Crown courts. Howell and Rees discussed the possibility of physical punishment, but Rees made it clear that no corporal practices could be instituted under current law. Reinstating corporal punishment would require new legislation, as the practice had been abolished in 1948. Rees stressed to Howell that the 'Advisory Council on the Treatment of Offenders considered the matter again in 1960 and concluded that, contrary to popular belief, there was no evidence that corporal punishment was a particularly effective deterrent, and they did not recommend its restoration'. Subsequent attempts to make such practices available to judges for sentencing had also failed.[66] Despite the abundance of government voices asking for physical punishment as an alternative sentencing option for football offenders, Rees blocked any attempt to circumvent the law. He also became the first government voice to investigate and challenge the assumption that physical castigation could deter unwanted behaviour in football.

These episodes in ministerial dialogue reveal the state could be disunited in its approaches to juvenile crime and football disorder. Howell considered a wide variety of punishments and used the threat of further experimentation with alternative punitive measures to generate an image of Labour's steadfast approach to law-and-order discipline. Howell reached the limits of his crusade within the confines of his own party, who, according to Roy Jenkins and the Home Office, did not want to discredit their own law-and-order legislation in order to create new juvenile legal standards. Jenkins valued the general image of the party, especially its reputation for working-class discipline, above serious attempts at penal reform. However, he set aside Howell's specific concerns with football violence to protect the idea that Labour legislated effectively over time. Importantly, Howell received no public opposition to his constant clamouring for increased punishment. Public and political opinion firmly supported Howell's legal pursuit of criminalized, young working-class men. Nonetheless, practical and political roadblocks prevented sports governors from manipulating the legal system beyond informal recommendations and public pressure on magistrates.

Conclusions

During the 1970s, though government authorities failed to promote any concrete changes to football legislation or the legal apparatus, they exerted informal political pressure against magistrates and police constables. By encouraging magistrates to make maximum punishments standard and supporting indictable charges instituted by police, government officials helped to shape policies on football regulation and punishment which continued to be advocated for the next forty years. Though the 1980s saw several symbolic changes to the law, such as the removal of alcohol from football grounds in 1985, the standards for criminal penalty surrounding the sport emerged during the late 1960s and 1970s through contests for political favour and in efforts to appease the public's desire to end lawlessness within football.

Punishment formed a key role in the social drama of law-and-order as it consummated criminal prosecution and contributed to a sense of potency against working-class crime. Punishment promised that the transgressive individual would pay, often literally, for his or her disobedience. In particular, government officials hoped to punish working-class supporters through heavy fines, enacting classed assumptions about football violence and issuing a symbolic strike against post-war affluence. Completing this cycle with strict castigation represented the strong presence of law and the inflexibility of successive government administrations against working-class youth crime. As violence worsened within and outside stadiums, political authorities sought to escalate punishment, and considered several new alternatives, in efforts to deter further offences. These actions reinforced the criminalization of communal forms of football spectatorship and aggression. Many of the proposed penalties included violent or laborious elements which would task the body, reinstituting corporal punishment. Although never enacted, these suggestions again demonstrate the government's readiness to advocate violence to prevent violence, especially against unruly working-class spectators.

Finally, the promotion of physical punishment against young working-class men and financial retribution for parents exposed the assumptions Home Office and DOE officials perpetuated about poorer citizens. Working-class men and women supposedly lacked discipline, especially in urban areas where football violence frequently occurred, because working women failed as mothers. Not only did work deny them the time to instruct their children on temperance and the values of discipline and hard work, they also provided them with excess wealth which contributed to the deterioration of appropriate forms of consumption. Class discourses about corporal punishment rendered young men not only incapable of proper social conduct, defined by bourgeois values of propriety and gentlemanly consumption of leisure, but also animalistic and puerile. Subjects without reason like disorderly football spectators could only be rehabilitated through threats to the body. In sum, discourses redolent of working-class rehabilitation emerged in discussions of punishment for football violence, which acted to punish not only young working-class men, but also their families.

These actions clearly contradicted and even undermined the Labour Party's commitment to working-class social initiatives in the 1970s. Football violence often forced supposedly labour-friendly governments to the limits of social democracy. Successive Labour administrations could not operate democratically and achieve their goals of reinstituting law-and-order principles. By attempting to manipulate public opinion and suggesting compromises to judicial independence, Denis Howell and others exposed fractures within Labour's approach to working-class communities. Football violence clearly became a political embarrassment and unsolved problem, bringing perceptions of the working-class family to the fore and revealing classed assumptions about lawlessness and affluence that pervaded British society.

Incorporating excessive legal punishment into arrest and sentencing procedures supplemented changes to physical environments and police tactics in state authorities' total effort to deter football violence. However, as successful black players emerged in the late 1970s, and became subject to racial abuse and political demonstrations, those concerned about the fate of British football contended with a new moral problem.

PART III : RACISM AND CULTURAL CONFLICT IN BRITISH FOOTBALL

6 THE FOOTBALL FRONT: NEO-FASCIST AND ANTI-FASCIST POLITICS IN FOOTBALL, 1977–85

Though their participation had a much longer history, successful black players began to appear frequently for some of England and Scotland's largest clubs in the mid-1970s. By the early 1980s, black players were a fixture at most clubs and began to be widely integrated into the sport. Several neo-nationalist groups – often labelled or self-identified as neo-fascists – responded with vitriol to their expanded involvement, contributing to the creation of a wide range of racist discourses and activities. In response, football clubs, grass-roots organizations and the British government expanded their programme for the sanitization of football to include a new problem. In addition to the growing violence of supporters, a wide range of authorities and a growing proportion of the public worried about racism within football. Football racism not only questioned peaceful integration in post-colonial Britain, but also built on existing anxieties about lawlessness and disorder within the nation's most popular sport. Much of this unfolded during the Conservative administration of Margaret Thatcher, when anti-immigrant ideologies were concretized within an increasingly conservative political landscape. Though Thatcher often lambasted rowdy football supporters for their failure to comply with law-and-order, the most significant battles for control of the football environment occurred among several smaller grass-roots organizations. As the final part of this book will demonstrate, race and football intersected in multiple ways, providing opportunities for politicking for a wide range of neo-nationalist and anti-racist groups.

This chapter will analyse neo-fascist and anti-fascist activities in British football from the mid-1970s, investigate how they influenced debates over race and working-class politics in this vivid cultural and social sphere and examine the intersections of sport with social, political and economic concerns brewing outside the stadiums. In the late 1970s and 1980s, neo-nationalist groups attempted to utilize the public environment of football to promote their ideological and political agenda by exploiting controversy over black players. Neo-fascist factions like the National Front deliberately capitalized on unease about successful black players in England's most popular and emblematic sport to attract new rank-and-file members through forms of street politics such as marching, rallies and publicity stunts. To combat the successes of neo-fascist recruiting and their gains in public recognition, anti-fascist political factions protested their presence within football and aggressively challenged their growing popularity with violent practices of their own. As a result, both racial violence and concerns that neo-fascists articulated about late twentieth century social problems – such as immigration conflicts, an unstable economy and high unemployment rates – attained heightened exposure in both public and political spheres. As a result, neo-fascist and anti-fascist groups conditioned and often determined the discourses of race, class and violence which materialized within the nation's most popular sport. The production of racial difference and the politics used to combat it not only reflected British social conflicts and unresolved political disputes, but became productive of cultural discord and social controversy. In sum, as evidence will show in the next three chapters, football became implicated in the making of multiracial Britain.

Unlike football violence, most football racism went largely unrecognized by large government agencies. Review of the available files in the Home Office and the Department of the Environment revealed hardly any discussions of racism in the sport. Much of the public and political debate about neo-fascism and racisms in football did not emerge until the late 1980s, when grass-roots political organizations and football fanzine editors began to challenge the pervasiveness of racial abuse and racial discrimination in professional matches. While these organizations and their objectives are the subject of Chapter 7, this chapter looks at the emergence of neo-fascist politics and the racial meanings they created in football during the previous decade. Understanding how neo-fascist involvement in football conditioned discussions of racism and anti-racism in later periods is crucial to tracing the evolution of racist attitudes and the historical construction of political messages meant to oppose them.

As racist and neo-fascist expressions surfaced within football, those who worked to sanitize British football and protect its harmonious and refined image adopted concerns about race into their moral repertoire. That is, distress about violence within football was now supplemented by growing anxieties about the presence of racism within the sport. As politicians and the public continued to imbue sport with representations of the nation, new myths about what sport should epitomize appeared. Whereas previous anti-violence campaigns targeted working-class youth for tainting the symbolic demonstrations of appropriate masculinity, deference to authority and gentlemanly Britishness, racism within

British football challenged the mythology of a peaceful multicultural Britain in the post-colonial era. While all of the emblematic pressures for harmony and mannered cultivation remained in British football, the social rifts and cultural questions raised by its working-class spectator base widened to include constructions of race and expressions of racism. These challenges emerged as football faced its most crippling commercial period in the modern era, where ongoing violence and the emergence of commercial television contracts contributed to declining attendance.[1]

Analysing neo-fascism in football has been recently derided as replicating the public's search for a 'folk devil' to blame for a complex and multifaceted series of racist behaviours.[2] As will be discussed below, this criticism is valid when levelled at anti-racist and anti-fascist initiatives which unfolded during the late 1980s and 1990s. Many of these programmes, supported by media perspectives which promoted neo-fascism as a hot news topic, championed battling neo-fascism rather than racisms within Britain, and especially within British sport. While these movements will be contextualized and analysed later in the next chapter, it is important to recognize that many academic studies promoted a fictive separation between neo-fascism in football and racism in football. They did so in an attempt to locate and identify the constantly changing discourses of racism outside of neo-fascism, a project which they carried out with analytical precision.[3] They concluded that a focus on neo-fascism precluded the more politically useful investigations into non-fascist articulations of racism and racial abuse. On the contrary, evidence will show that analysing the convoluted interaction between racism and neo-fascism, and anti-racism and anti-fascism, reveals their interconnections and the historical construction of dominant discourses about race and racisms within the football arena.

Rather than denying the influence of neo-fascism's discourses within the world of sport, this chapter attempts to position the role of neo-fascist ideas and anti-fascist political movements as they contributed to non-fascist forms of racism and anti-racism. In doing so, the separation of fascism/racism and anti-racism/anti-fascism will be challenged as the links between each are made plain. The messages and language used by neo-nationalist political parties certainly conditioned, and often determined, the discourses of race, class and violence which materialized within British football, drawing on concerns about late twentieth century social problems such as immigration conflicts, an unstable economy and high unemployment rates. No matter the level of their involvement, they certainly helped constitute political demonstrations and dialogues about racism, determined the shape of anti-racist activities and helped to catalyse and shape a variety of racial abuses within the sport. At the very least, the National Front's presence helped to aggravate a social venue already fraught with racial tensions, and again positioned black players within larger post-colonial frames of reference. Without doubt, the National Front's activity during this period fostered the image of football as a white bastion of British identity, with unanimous black immigrant exclusion.

Studies of neo-nationalism and neo-fascism in Britain have also concentrated on two main bodies of study: voting patterns and political ideology.[4] These academic studies clearly reflected concerns about neo-nationalists winning local and national government elections and the appearance of simplified anti-immigration doctrine during two key periods of neo-fascist popularity: the late 1970s and the early 1990s. While such studies disclosed much about neo-fascist politics, other works addressed the relative successes of neo-conservative politics and the far right in post-war European history. These analyses reformulated how historians calculate political 'success' by reassessing how the deployment of disruptive social messages and the creation of cultural conflicts succeed while efforts at the ballot box fail. Some scholars now believe that the impact of neo-fascist and neo-nationalist groups has been underestimated and that these factions have successfully responded to gaps in democratic representation.[5] While dominant political parties and academics relegated these factions to the margins, others have measured their political impact discursively, analysing how their messages and spectacle altered the behaviour of major political parties, affected local and national policy initiatives, and helped to constitute the terms of debate for contentious issues like immigration and racial violence.[6] Rather than reifying neo-fascism as tangential to sport or external to it, this chapter supplements this work by exploring how particular social dialogues about race in football were organized around neo-nationalist concepts, politicians' fear of their public impact, and the anti-fascist groups which challenged them.

The first section of the chapter suggests that neo-fascist groups effectively utilized the football arena to convey broader political messages about the British social landscape and that their impact extended beyond rank-and-file members of neo-nationalist groups. The second section contextualizes neo-fascist football recruiting within a wider range of peripheral political practices in urban areas, noting that paper-selling 'pitches' outside football stadiums became fundamental to the social success of both neo-fascist and anti-fascist groups. Using anti-fascist literature and memoirs, the third section evaluates the efforts of anti-fascist groups to disrupt neo-fascist practices. Their attempts to challenge neo-fascism adopted oversimplified articulations of racism and fascism, and relied heavily on reciprocating violent political action which intensified earlier government trends in promoting violent community policing.

Neo-Fascist Politics and the Football Environment

The on-field success of several black footballers within Britain's professional ranks inspired varied responses from fans, players and the state across Britain. Although the first professional black footballer, Arthur Wharton, joined Rotherham Town in 1889, the exposure of black players and racist opposition to their participation significantly amplified as several black men succeeded as footballers in the transformed political context of the late 1970s.[7] Though their achievements have been valorized by contemporary anti-racist movements, very few black players succeeded in early twentieth century Britain and thus received little attention: their heightened exposure and continued success began in the mid-1970s and transgressed a culturally homogenous labour market and increasingly commercialized entertainment arena. Only four professional black footballers made a total of seventy-seven first team appearances for British clubs in 1974, and thirty-seven of ninety-two clubs had no black players. By 1993, those numbers gradually increased to ninety-eight players making over 2,000 appearances. From 1989 to the present, every club fielded at least one black player throughout the season. Spectators formed racial attitudes in response to black players' increased participation, both of acceptance and intolerance. Both players' accomplishments and supporters' responses attracted a sizeable degree of public attention and reflected lingering social unease stimulated by perceptions of interracial job and housing competition.

Cyclical global depression in the mid-1970s, partially attributable to increases in oil prices, continued to present difficulties for poorer sections of society under the Conservative administration of the 1980s. High unemployment rates and the retrenchment of social provision hit working-class men and women the hardest. Present from the 1950s forward, debates over competition in labour markets and council housing reflected white Britons' anxieties about black migrant labourers. In actuality, competition for work between native and immigrant labourers was far less intense than many perceived: migrants often filled the least desirable jobs in low-status sectors such as textiles and transport.[8] Nonetheless, debates about job and housing competition emerged in debates over the suitability of black footballers, foreign or British-born, and often resulted in expressions of racism and racial abuse inside stadiums as white spectators objected to the presence of highly skilled black labourers in the football industry. Studies of the emergence of black players and the variety of racial abuse they faced have been catalogued elsewhere, and the effect of this abuse is analysed in Chapter 8.[9] This section elucidates how neo-nationalist political groups responded to black players who challenged the white homogeneity of football labour, came to represent interracial conflicts over jobs and housing in tough economic circumstances and threatened understandings of Britishness embodied in the sport.

The frequent and public demonstrations of violent conduct solidified the National Front's infamous reputation within football. The National Front (NF), the country's most popular neo-nationalist faction in the 1970s, emerged from an alliance of far right political factions in 1967, with the express purpose of stemming foreign migration to Britain and challenging the idealization of multiracial societies. An oligarchy of ultraconservative intellectuals and dictatorial leaders steered the party's anti-immigrant and anti-Semitic policies, and eventually perceived football as a cultural site where such policies could be disseminated and promoted. Many rank-and-file members of the NF had strong connections to local football and readily used existing social networks to promote party interests. The NF also sought to challenge press accounts of black players in which sympathetic journalists gushed over their rise to distinction, creating their own press coverage of matchday activities and black players. Even positive press accounts fed stereotypes of the separateness of black players, emphasizing their creativity, flair and speed against the workmanlike and bullish style of traditional white British players.[10] Neo-fascist violence and racial abuse within football not only registered objections to the emergence of successful black footballers, and their supposedly uniform style, but also became a form of political practice which drew on the violent conventions of working-class spectatorship developed in the 1960s.

The NF's main outlet for distributing information among working-class football supporters was *Bulldog: The Official Paper of the Young National Front*. Edited by young party intellectuals like Joe Pearce, *Bulldog* functioned in at least two ways. First, the paper delivered the news, ideological messages and political propaganda the NF wanted to distribute to young rank-and-file members, often sold outside of football stadiums. Second, it published accounts of racial violence and football conflicts meant to inspire young neo-fascists to further demonstrations of violence as exhibitions of party loyalty. A column entitled 'On the Football Front', dispersed heroic tales of young neo-nationalists in violent action against unwanted immigrants or leftist sympathizers. Analysis of these incidents, as well as the ways in which the narratives were framed, reveals how football violence figured in the political repertoire of neo-fascism and became integral to their political strategy.

Many of the stories recalled in *Bulldog* gave detailed accounts of intrepid members engaging in violence with black spectators or harassing black footballers both within and outside football stadiums. In an article entitled 'Blacks Are Superior?' the writer complains about black players in British professional football and the high level of ability mainstream newspaper sportswriters attributed to them: 'So Britain's Black footballers think that Blacks have "more flair and speed" and that Whites are "skinny" and "pale"'. The author countered, 'If Blacks and newspaper journalists think that Blacks are superior, then most football fans don't agree! In particular, the newspapers condemned the supporters for throwing bananas onto the pitch.' Incensed by the negative coverage, the author boasted, 'Earlier this season Portsmouth fans went even further at Fratton Park. During a second division match a Black player who had been very offensive towards the home fans was pelted not just with bananas but with a large coconut which was thrown from Fratton End!' The writer concluded: 'Football fans believe in White Power'.[11]

This editorial is fairly typical of NF responses to black players. Most prominently, the division between 'Whites' and 'Blacks' was not only a political necessity for the creation of anti-immigration ideology, but also emphasized the cultural divisions neo-fascists wanted to promote between the two groups. The writer felt threatened by the connotations of pale skin with frailty and lack of vigour. In addition, throwing bananas and banana skins became the most popular way of protesting black presence in football. The symbolism of the banana recalled Britain's colonial past, recalling the subordination of colonial subjects and white British superiority, which was challenged by newspapers which affirmed black success. The act also repudiated the presence of black footballers, even those who were born in Britain, by symbolically asserting their colonial 'otherness' within the football environment. Fruit-tossing also representatively grouped black players as migrants and announced their exclusion from the drama and solidarity of white working-class football. The action also implied the animalism and savagery of black players, by identifying them as monkeys in need of food, opposing them to the purportedly civilized white spectators. Such imagery degraded the accomplishment of black players, emphasizing their supposed alterity and dehumanizing the players. Tossing tropical fruit also indicated the imagined re-creation of traditional colonial relationships and was meant to remind black players of their place within an implicit social hierarchy in past colonial relationships, and now the post-colonial world. Evoking objects that signified the past subordination of colonial labour reflected white Britons' anxieties about job competition and communicated their desire for white privilege within existing job markets, including professional football.[12] Furthermore, the writer assumed all supporters to be white and like-minded in their support for the National Front. This self-promotion colours nearly all of the *Bulldog* materials, where violence and racial abuse not only indicate their disapproval but constitute the climactic apex in the narrative drama. Such articles aimed to educate as much as they did to recall specific actions on particular Saturdays.

Banana-throwing became a frequently repeated response to black players by both NF members and others. Newspapers and journalists frequently cited it as evidence of the growing incidence of racism at matches. Remembering a match at West Ham in February 1981, Garry Thompson and Danny Thomas, two black players for Coventry, commented that the banana throwing and verbal abuse had become almost mandatory.[13] Grunting and mimicking ape noises usually accompanied the bananas, no matter the venue.[14] Other spectators ritually cried at the black players '"Ooh, ooh, ooh", the noise that a gorilla makes'.[15] Colonial and animal references attempted to establish the alterity and bestial baseness of black players, calling on stereotypes of black physical appearance and colonial labour relationships which emphasized whites' superiority in historical social hierarchies. The paper also encouraged and widely publicized other activities which promoted an extremely unwelcoming environment to black players. One letter to the editor boasts:

> Sunderland has had racists at the football matches for years, even though there can't be more than 100 Blacks in the area. But Sunderland is getting ready before they get here and every estate has NF graffiti. Every Black footballer or Black supporter who comes to Roker Park will think twice about coming back again.[16]

Other similar abuses abounded to create intimidating and violent terrace environments. In spring 1983, Birmingham NF members boasted of throwing beer cans at newcomer Noel Blake, who came near the terraces at St Andrew's Park to applaud the loyalty of the fans. Another supporter wrote, 'Manager Ron Saunders may have signed two Blacks, but this will not prevent BCFC NF supporters from following our team ... and we'll support them long after they've [black players] gone back home!'[17] Such objections indicate the increased level of racial abuse carried out by NF contingents within football.

In addition to abusing black players, NF members consistently engaged in racially motivated violence in the areas directly outside stadiums. One of the earliest stories posted in *Bulldog* involved football supporters attacking a nearby rally held by the Communist Party of England and the Indian Workers Movement. 'The United and Spurs fans sang "Rule Britannia" and some actually managed to get at the Reds, despite the police protection'. The writer added, 'One thing's for sure, the Communists will think twice before marching through Ilford and Barking again, especially if West Ham and Tottenham are playing at home'.[18] The incident, like many others, indicated the territorial dimensions of NF violence. Their attacks on other political rallies showed their aspirations to control local neighbourhoods and street corners as much as their ideological opposition to communism.

One of the most repeated narratives in *Bulldog* is the 'race riot', which included a description of racial violence where the opposing factions were supposedly divided by race alone. These discourses concretized the separateness and opposition of black and white identities in football violence. *Bulldog*'s editors included narratives of these encounters at home stadiums, away games and at English international matches abroad. In an article entitled 'YNF Organiser in Football Race Riot', the writer retold how one regional representative 'paid the price for defending himself against vicious Asian attackers ... Mark was caught up in a race riot when twenty Pakistanis, brandishing knives and other weapons, attacked a group of Whites.' The article conveyed the massive injuries Mark Plaza maintained and positioned him as a suffering victim of immigrant brutality, police negligence, and a corrupt judicial hearing which sentenced him to prison.[19] The narrative stressed the member's victimization and the illegality of the attackers' weaponry, in addition to their aggression and brutality. More importantly, the division between rival groups of fans was constructed along lines of race and not partisan supportership: white Britons versus Asian immigrants. Rather than focusing on the difference in team affiliation, the writer infused the article with racial and political content which formed the fundamental meanings within this educative description of racial violence. *Bulldog* editors consistently recast football violence as race riots, despite local club attachments, especially in hotly contested urban territories like north London or the Isle of Dogs.[20]

When neo-fascist supporters followed their team to the continent, narratives of racial difference were privileged over nationalist values, revealing the contradictory and unstable nature of neo-fascist ideology. Rather than adopting their team as the centre of their fanship, neo-fascists split the environment into white and immigrant spectators, even in foreign countries. Though they followed and supported their English team, they viewed the oppositional divisions within foreign environments as white versus black, not Tottenham versus Rotterdam, as the case may be. Despite their allegiance to England and its clubs, and the party's consistent expression of neo-nationalist views, nationalism faded as anti-immigrant racial policies stressed the inherent differences and violent antagonisms between imagined black and white groups of social actors. These narratives could be created when neo-fascists initiated attacks. At international matches NF members often infiltrated neighbourhoods known to be havens for migrant workers and nearby to stadiums. In 1981, violent clashes occurred in the Zeedyk quarter of Amsterdam, which 'is controlled by Black gangs of Surinamese immigrants. It is a "no go" area for local White youths. However, the Spurs supporters showed Dutch whites how it should be done.'[21] Defending national pride or an English club team only entered the report when neo-fascists claimed to be educating continental white men on how to deal with immigrants. Rather, the emphasis on inherent racial difference and violent antagonisms with immigrants allowed NF members to be simultaneously persecuted and heroic. Club allegiance became secondary to the constitution of racial antagonisms in 'race riot' narratives of football violence.

In addition to violent tactics and race riot narratives, the NF also continuously attempted to demonstrate their viability and popularity at football grounds. Demonstrations of NF's solidarity not only portrayed their imposing physical presence but also their political viability. One writer recalled, 'At Millwall, during the 1977 season, out of a home gate of 3,500, some two hundred young men were sighted standing shoulder to shoulder in para-military uniform, displaying the insignia of the National Front'.[22] Chants also emphasized commonality and political cohesion, and were adopted by NF members as ways of establishing their presence within the terraces. The club-specific chants which welcomed John Barnes to Liverpool in 1987 were well-known: 'Everton are White! Everton are White!' and 'Niggerpool, Niggerpool, Niggerpool!' echoed throughout the stadium at his debut.[23] So too were the classic appeals to white Britishness: 'There Ain't No Black in the Union Jack, Send the Niggers Back!'[24] Richard Turner, a sympathetic apologist for football culture in the 1980s, wrote, 'Racist chanting occurs at most, if not all, soccer grounds in the League'.[25] Chanting not only emphasized the unity of rank-and-file NF members, but also invited non-fascists to anonymously participate in threatening demonstrations against black supporters and players.

While many of the above examples provide evidence of the symbolic and representative demonstrations of the NF's anti-immigrant ideology carried out at football grounds, working-class people who supported football clubs on a regular basis provided a healthy recruiting ground for the NF as well. The distribution of newspapers and leafleting became the primary means of inviting new members into the NF fold. The newspapers, which required a small fee for purchase, also provided local branches with an indication of their popularity. Articles in *Bulldog* frequently used paper sales at football matches as the main gauge of community esteem and their impact on local politics. 'The new football season has started. Hundreds of thousands of youths are going to see their local teams play every Saturday. It is up to every YNF football fan to get his mates to sell *Bulldog* outside these matches.'[26] Newspaper-selling evolved into a contest, supported by the editors, to encourage active recruitment and the dissemination of party messages. One article stated, 'Leeds fans bought more than 200 *Bulldogs* every month at home games. Which team will be the best Front team this season?'[27] In the next issue, members responded by declaring their sales numbers and submitting photos for paper publication, several of which proudly displayed young recruits selling the paper directly in front of stadiums' main gates or nearby corners. Chelsea fan Nicholas Barrett reported sales topping 450 copies of *Bulldog* and *NF News* outside matches at Stamford Bridge.[28] Later contests were reported in tables on the *Bulldog* pages.[29] In sum, paper-selling not only served to educate or attract novices, but also provided a gauge of the popular support for the movement within local football clubs.

Other recruiting tactics drew on the NF's ability to transgress subcultural divisions among young working-class men in urban areas. Though the 'skinhead' identity and the stereotypes associated with it are usually associated with the movement, the NF also called for a unified anti-immigrant stance to be shared by several alienated youth subcultures in Britain. One letter to the editor from a North London member implored, 'The Whites must unite. Skins, punks, herberts, mods and casuals must all stick together against the Race Invasion of Blacks, Asians and Pakis.' A petition signed by football supporters of each subcultural movement accompanied the letter, which agreed to protest non-white players and spectators in stadiums in northern London, presumably through increased racial abuse and threats.[30] International matches at Wembley stadium also allowed NF supporters from several different parts of the nation to unite, neglecting the partisan loyalties which divided most violent supporters.[31] Recruiting new members at football meant spanning the divisions between subcultural and supporter groups, which if the article was credible, allowed for neo-fascists to be somewhat successful in unifying different working-class identity groups. Neo-fascists again transcended cultural and local identities by appealing to a dichotomized perspective of racial difference, in which black players threatened white homogeneity.

Figure 6.1: National Front advertisement on pamphlet, undated. The caption reads: 'It's For Sale! No, not the girl, but the t-shirt!' The T-shirt is emblazoned with a 'Chelsea National Front' logo.

Finally, *Bulldog* editors frequently employed a variety of gendered and sexualized images to entice football supporters to join the National Front. In these images, the attraction was not ideology or empathy, but the enticement of sexual interaction and masculine exploits. Popular NF strongholds like West Ham and Chelsea advertised T-shirts adorned with hybrid logos composed of club symbols and NF slogans. The advertisements displayed young women wearing nothing but the T-shirts, standing or sitting in sexually suggestive poses (See Figure 6.1).[32] Editors later combined many of these suggestive photos with an ongoing column called 'RAC [Rock Against Communism] Bird of the Month' photos. The RAC movement, the musical counterpart to the football front, suggested that NF members would have access to 'chatting up' young women at NF events.[33] Both series of photos suggested the sexual promiscuity of young female members and their accessibility to NF men. In contrast, corresponding images of men as hypermasculine, aggressive and capable of violence presented readers with the epitome of successful fringe political activists. A T-shirt ad for West Ham NF with a burly skinhead figure sold the idea of power and virility for men willing to participate in football violence.[34] Clearly, NF writers utilized understandings of gender and sexuality to bolster their appeal to men.

Like their recruiting tactics elsewhere, the NF underscored their ability to empathize with the plight of young working-class men, promising to exert political pressure towards bettering their livelihoods. These political promises often took the form of promoting expatriation for immigrants who many white Britons perceived as contributing to high unemployment rates, housing competition and increased levels of social violence. While extremist groups often articulated their disdain for diaspora Jews, Irish independence and major political parties, they fundamentally concentrated on the supposed perils of incorporating migrants into a multicultural Britain. The following quote exhibited the ways in which neo-fascists interconnected football leisure with their contempt for multiracial integration:

> To us whites football is a one day in the week outlet ... But for the other six days a week, our youth have to work and live with the coloured immigrants in their area. In those six days white youth have to endure a race-mixing nightmare. A race-mixing Hell where blacks rule the roost at youth clubs, discos, schools and football pitches on council estates ... Through the NF selling its papers at football grounds ... white youth can buy *NF News* and *Bulldog* and are filled with hope for the future. The football front is one of the most important developments of the YNF so far, because finally the white youth have a chance to show loyalty not only to their team, but also their Race and Nation.[35]

The writer exhibited the sensationalization of conflict within multicultural Britain customary to neo-fascist ideology, and blamed such disturbances on the influence of migrant workers. The segment also positioned football as an escape from contentious, racially divided urban environments. Again, the territoriality of public spaces figured in the discussion of immigrant infiltration, with more controlled environments near stadiums as the polar opposite to chaotic inner-city job competition, indicated by the ability to sell neo-fascist papers safely. Finally, overlapping partisan loyalties in football with loyalties to 'Race and

Nation' imbued NF membership with masculine ideals of loyalty and national solidarity in the face of imagined racial invasions. Such rhetoric clearly imbued football with a variety of representational meanings about job competition, housing and racial violence. Football, and the contests over the acceptance of black players, came to represent the multiple social fractures and political contests over multiculturalism extant outside the sport.

An empirical measure of either formal NF recruits or the participation of non-members in these activities was not possible with the present sources. However, early ethnographic work and journalistic investigations reveal the ways in which NF discourses and football practices influenced non-sanctioned supporters. One thirteen-year old remarked, 'It's all right some of 'em up the North Bank shouting out "National Front", but what they don't remember is that there's coloureds in the football grounds themselves ... they don't do no harm to nobody'.[36] Such sentiments revealed that while many NF practices such as chanting and saluting could be accepted by other spectators, they did not adopt them without scrutiny. In 1977, in responses to questions about football violence, another fan commented, 'I been inside a few times. Last one was for brickin' this Paki. I'm not 100 per cent for the NF. But you help out, like. You gotta think, "We're all here, everyone works, got 'omes here." Then you see these Asian families just come off the banana boat'.[37] Such ambivalence lent support to NF activities, and latent racist attitudes which supporters expressed adopted similar anti-immigrant tones, concerns about housing and employment, and colonial references espoused by NF members. Monolithic stereotypes were labelled onto the unwanted immigrant population, who apparently threatened labour security and the perceived homogeneity of non-black communities. Later anti-racist movements would approach these gaps in allegiance as evidence of neo-fascism's instability and weakness. 'For most of them, their racism is not clearly articulated or methodical', wrote one anti-racist writer. 'Many of them don't think they are racists at all but they will allow themselves to be drawn so easily into blind, ignorant prejudice by those fascist groups looking to recruit new members.'[38]

Though fans and players alike distinguished between those involved in the National Front and others, many stood somewhere between alliance and neutrality. One fan remembered his involvement in international football violence by saying, 'You've got to show some pride in your team. It's fucking pride. I know two blokes who are in Combat 18 because they believe in the English, no black in the Union Jack and all that. I mean, I'm really there for the football, but I do agree with them.'[39] Clearly, the NF did much to inculcate racist values by promoting anti-immigrant and anti-black discourses which non-fascists adopted into their own racial attitudes. The football terraces not only became a site of racial expression but of racial instruction. A teenage boy told Dave Hill, a prominent journalist, that 'I am in a racist organization. From going to Liverpool matches I have come to hate black people.'[40]

Contextualizing Neo-Fascism in Football: The Centrality of Non-Traditional Political Practice

Neo-fascist practices in football were only a few of several non-traditional political tactics which extremist parties used to compensate for their lack of overall success and party funding. Many popular and academic opinions have dismissed the presence of neo-fascism in football as tangential and unsuccessful: neo-fascists cannot be considered central to the social environment of the sport because they cared little about football itself. Instead, neo-fascists merely used football to achieve political ends, and proved unsuccessful in their formal recruiting efforts.[41] Police and government officials also deny their viability as it validates their work against the neo-fascist impulse in Britain.[42] On the contrary, football became a fundamental focus of neo-fascist organizers because most working-class people had at least some interest in football. Furthermore, while their recruiting success cannot be measured empirically, through the medium of football they significantly conditioned the frames of social debate and the terms of conversations about the British social landscape. Football became infused with anti-immigrant and racist propaganda because neo-fascists used forceful means of disseminating their messages and because many young working-class men listened to and rearticulated their dogmatic positions. By contextualizing neo-fascist political practices in football and comparing them with other informal means of fringe political campaigning, the centrality of football to neo-fascist goals becomes clear.

In general, without the wider political base and campaigning moneys available to traditional political parties, organizers oriented recruiting around the exploitation of social relationships and neighbourhood networks. Beyond these networks, neo-fascism relied heavily on cheaper forms of political recruiting, free publicity, and attention-getting tactics to build its support. While formal recruits who agreed to vote the party line were certainly welcomed, the latent ideological framework of neo-fascism relied on building a groundswell of cooperation and agreement from white working-class Britons. Only through the unity of working-class sentiment could fascists' larger goals of expatriation and social exclusion move forward. Neo-fascism also relied heavily on the negation of a variety of 'others' which threatened their viability and around which neo-fascism could build oppositional support: larger political parties, immigrants, police and the monolithic British state.[43] Football figured strongly into this ideological framework by providing a platform for negation and demonstration. The emergence of black players offered the opportunity to develop ground-level political networks through existing associations and social groups within football supportership.

Outside of football, the NF advocated a host of other informal political practices which allowed them to campaign in a cheap and purposefully controversial manner. All of these tactics – including marches, street violence and pamphleting – involved violence and territoriality. Most prominently, the NF became known for its marches and rallies, which often provoked anti-fascist responses and frequently devolved into riots. The march at Lewisham on 13 August 1977 marked the height of the NF's popularity and thrust them into the media spotlight as violent provocateurs. The NF chose Lewisham specifically to emphasize their territorial dispersion. Knowing that New Cross and the surrounding areas in London had become home to many immigrants and foreign workers, NF organizers sought to reclaim the streets of a formerly white working-class enclave.[44] Anti-fascist and black protesters fought with NF members, despite a heavy police presence, and the fracas cast both the extreme right and the extreme left as cheap instigators.

Street violence and leafleting were never random and had territorial and racial significance for NF members. Attacks by young men on migrants frequently occurred in contested public spaces and, in the case of attacks on Pakistani populations, at local corner markets. For example, in a Wolverhampton court hearing NF member John Spencer told the judge he committed attacks on local Pakistani teenagers and broke windows in Pakistani-owned corner shops: 'Wolverhampton is my town. It is sickening to hear it is being invaded by wogs ... The Pakis are the worst. They own the shops while the niggers roam the streets.'[45] NF recruitment campaigns also utilized flyers and pamphlets as means of disseminating political messages to a wider public. NF members targeted the dole lines, job centres and council housing estates as crucial sites for the deployment of propaganda literature.[46] Most flyers or pamphlets espoused neo-fascist fundamentals like the party's supposedly unique ability to cure unemployment, but others targeted adolescents and children through comics. Members distributed one particularly hateful comic called *Stormer* to local school districts in 1980 and 1981. The comic included an ongoing boy character named 'Sambo the Chocolate-coloured Coon' who continually became the subject of violence, and in one instance was roasted alive on a bonfire by his white playmates.[47]

These forms of political practice, especially marches and rallies, had a wide range of benefits for the fringe party. First, they invited press attention which furthered the public profile of the NF as threatening, intimidating and ready for aggression. Second, they often provided an opportunity to confront immigrants, anti-fascists and black protestors directly in violent encounters, a practice which became central to neo-fascist politics. In many cases, this violence could be both anonymous and without juridical consequences. Third, marches and pamphleting served as a demonstration of their strength in numbers, which could be encouraging to potential voters and new recruits. NF voters also turned out in greater numbers where they marched, and the NF gauged their success through examining attendance at neighbourhood rallies.[48] Marches became a standard practice of neo-fascists, and allowed the NF to achieve notoriety and exhibit its vehement distaste for its territorial and ideological enemies.

As neo-fascism gained popularity in the late 1970s, and the British economy worsened with no end in sight, newspaper-selling became the fundamental ingredient of recruiting, including the distribution campaign deployed around stadium sites. One *NF News* editor wrote on the importance of newspaper distribution: 'If we are to be taken seriously in our own communities, we must be able to instruct people of their diminishing rights and answer their questions'. *NF News* also launched a programme to encourage members to buy surplus papers and distribute them to others in their social networks. They reformulated their papers to further appeal to novices and indoctrinated members. 'We hope that you have all carefully read and thought about the outline of our new structure', pleaded NF editors. '*National Front News* and the NF sincerely hope and expect that the vast majority of our subscribers will become NF News Supporters. The National Front is now organized around the newspaper and increasing our circulation and influence is now more important than ever'. The column concluded that 'the 5 copies of NFN that you will receive each issue can either be sold or left in libraries, buses, etc'.[49] With the importance of the newspaper elevated within the party, the ability to sell outside of football stadiums became crucial. Neo-fascists in football not only used football as a place for demonstrating their control and strength through salutes, chants and abuses against black players; football and neo-fascism also became linked through the centrality of the newspaper and newspaper-selling as a political practice.

Many of the retold stories on leafleting or paper-selling also hint at the threats of physical confrontation between neo-fascist and anti-fascist political groups. In fact, the ability to sell newspapers on specific corners outside stadiums indicated the control over these physical spaces. Gary Mumford, NF Ealing Branch, wrote, 'Every time we sell we get rid of between three and four hundred papers, and we give out hundreds of leaflets. We may have an advantage at Chelsea because the Reds just don't have the bottle to come up and oppose us, so we sell in groups of two or three usually'.[50] Though Mumford clearly meant to convey his own accomplishments, his comments also suggested that physical confrontations often occurred when selling papers outside of matches. The right to sell newspapers in specific territories close to the football environment was often violently challenged by anti-fascist groups who operated within the same informal political arenas on the ground. Thus, selling political propaganda became not only a means of recruiting and ideological indoctrination but also evidence of violent, negotiated interaction between neo-nationalist and anti-fascist political organizations. Territorial wars for key corners outside of stadiums developed into a main site of violence between anti-fascists and NF members. Although football's defenders often depict racism as extraneous to the game, neo-fascists saw football as central to their racist political practices.

Inasmuch as selling newspapers at football games compares with the other standard fringe political strategies, football matches also provided another means of participating in publicity stunts and conflicts with mainstream media outlets over party legitimacy. Demonstrations of strength in numbers and collective racist abuse, often organized through rallying calls in *Bulldog*, served to build public attention for their activities and gain reputation within mainstream newspapers.[51] The most prominent public activity which capitalized on mainstream media interest in the movement was the 'League of Louts'. As part of an anti-NF campaign, the *Daily Star* established the 'league' to display the dangerous accumulation of NF members in football.[52] *Bulldog* editors capitalized on the opportunity, establishing the league as an ongoing competition for supporter groups participating in high levels of racial abuse and displays of party paraphernalia. Later known as the 'Racist League', it continued for at least four seasons. On one occasion, Newcastle NF members vaulted to the top of the league by chanting 'National Front, National Front', and 'Geordies Are White'. The chants forced a condemning public statement by Hari Shukla, an irritated Asian community relations officer, which paradoxically broadened the public effectiveness of the demonstration in London and Newcastle. In the same issue, editors lauded local Newcastle supporters for distributing leaflets for an away match at Chelsea. The leaflets issued a rallying cry for more NF and racist activity to prove 'that Newcastle are the top NF team. The *Bulldog* always has Chelsea top of the "League of Louts" but now is our chance to put ourselves at the top of the league'. The editors encouraged Chelsea supporters by noting they 'are still the most racist fans in London'.[53] Such antics encouraged letters to the editor which boasted of NF activities at different grounds, and pleaded for recognition of their defence of local territories.[54] More importantly, the editors at *Bulldog* exploited the publicity that other major news organs granted them, developing recognized competitive assemblies that engaged in frequent, repetitive demonstrations of racial abuse.

Within party circles, football also played a central role in the education and training of NF youth. John Tyndall, head of the National Front, promoted the development of white members' physicality and discipline through football. The YNF established their own youth leagues and five-a-side tournaments to encourage young NF members to participate. Tyndall even attended some matches to lend his support to adolescent recruits and hand out the trophy named in his honour for the champions of the London league.[55] Tyndall commented, 'I am very glad to see that the YNF is not all cold politics. Social and recreational activities are very important in capturing the interest of the young, and it is most refreshing to see that the YNF shows so much initiative in these fields.'[56] Older adolescents also established NF squads which competed in local leagues, with attention-grabbing team names like 'Rule Britannia.'[57] 'Good local publicity was received in West Bromwich when YNF football team "New Federation" entered the League', *Bulldog* boasted. 'Once again there were screams of protest from local Reds'.[58] Such teams not only built virile young members but also became a promotional act on the local level. NF local squads even fought with other ethnically based teams, and boasted of engaging in another 'race riot', this time at local amateur football.[59] Until the mid-1980s, the NF elite supported these activities as they did the widespread campaign to win recruits at professional matches. Local football played a central role, not only in its ability to attract young working-class men, but also to develop their physical discipline and develop social ties with other NF teens.

Mobilizing young supporters to travel abroad allowed NF members to use international matches as platforms for displaying their hypernationalism and loyalty to white Britain and white English players. In particular, the media found these international incidents the most disturbing, not only for their gravity and embarrassment but also for the sensationalization of the 'hooligan' type wreaking havoc on peaceful continental environments.[60] NF football supporters prided themselves on their international exhibitions of racist conduct and frequently boasted of the coverage their activities received in national papers.[61] Though they embraced the publicity, NF organizers challenged media representations or conclusions which they felt falsified their positions or compromised their esteem. In 1985, as investigations into the Heysel stadium disaster involving Liverpool fans in Brussels unfolded, ties to NF members who participated in the violence leading to thirty-nine deaths emerged. The National Front filed a complaint with the national Press Council to object to the connection between the NF and the tragedy made by the *Sunday Mirror*.[62] In 1982, they filed a similar grievance against BBC programming which also identified NF members as somewhat guilty for increasing levels of street violence.[63] Neither complaint forced a correction, but they revealed the NF's desire to counter negative publicity. As the NF came under public scrutiny for excessive violence, they increased their attempts to protect their reputation as a legitimate political force, though most publicity proved good publicity for a political group without the financial means to create their own.

In part because of the Heysel tragedy, but also because of the success of media and anti-fascist watchdog campaigns like *Searchlight*, the NF elite and other neo-nationalist fringe leadership groups moved towards abandoning their ties to sport from the mid-1980s forward.[64] Both the National Front and its successor, the British National Party (BNP), moved away from the compounding negative publicity inspired by football violence and overt racial abuse. After brief successes at the ballot box in the late 1970s, formal challenges to established political parties through parliamentary and local council elections failed miserably throughout Conservative administrations (1979–97). Several key neo-fascist factions turned away from the violent political practices which served them well in their rise to prominence, opting for a formal political strategy that catered not to youth, but to established voters. This turn required divesting themselves of responsibility for football violence, especially after constant media attention made football 'hooliganism' a nationally disparaged phenomenon. The 1985 Heysel stadium disaster, lamented by the press as the most fateful outcome of continuous football violence to date, became a key turning-point in neo-fascists' approach to football and football recruiting. John Tyndall had already turned on *Bulldog* after he left the NF to begin the British National Party in 1981. Tyndall called the 'Racist League' 'a juvenile pursuit that is wholly counter-productive to the cause of racial nationalism' and derided the *Bulldog* paper he once valorized as a 'moronic kindergarten magazine'.

In response to accusations of NF and BNP involvement in the Brussels tragedy, Tyndall wrote an editorial that first denied the accusations, then belittled aggressive football violence and called on young nationalists to rechannel their energies. He denied 'the idea that either the NF or the BNP could have whipped up the violence in Brussels, or indeed had any profit in doing so ... The healthy red-blooded young male has, as he has always had, a great fund of aggressive energy.' Tyndall continued by criticizing British government leadership: 'A disciplined society, inspired by the correct goals, will find a useful outlet for that aggressive energy'. He also noted that

> it is perhaps to be expected that the upholders of the old system of society, when confronted with the consequences of their own misrule, should seek to lay the blame, not on themselves and the institutions and values which they have defended across the decades, but on those who challenge them and who advocate an alternative system of society.[65]

In the face of public allegations, Tyndall not only used the Heysel incident to solidify his dissociation from violent political practices in football, but also to reassert neo-nationalist support for principles of discipline, social order and adolescent masculine virility. In a transparent twist of phrase, Tyndall also criticized the government for failing to provide outlets for supposedly inherent masculine aggressions. Nonetheless, Tyndall failed to address the basic concerns about NF or BNP involvement at Heysel, instead condemning the state.

After Tyndall's departure, a concerted effort to remove associations with fascism also inspired the National Front to divest itself of ties to football violence.

In the party's official political magazine, an unnamed editor remembered the events of the 1980s: 'The British people started to associate the National Front with trouble, with hooliganism and with neo-Nazism'. On the possible appeal to a wider audience without football politics, they added:

> While they like our policies they would not support a violent, unpleasant and incompetent organization which also contained a small but significant number of neo-Nazis. The membership of the National Front learned its lesson: we got rid of the hooligans, we became competent and efficient.[66]

Clearly, harmful publicity about football violence and its neo-fascist associations encouraged the far right to publicly abandon confrontational politics and overt racial abuse at football. While these same groups forged their early popularity through a variety of street political practices, including a widespread football recruiting campaign aimed at young working-class men, football violence eventually tarnished their formal political recognition and hampered their electoral success. As one *Searchlight* writer concluded, the public denunciations of football activity allowed far right movements to appear blameless while still reaping the benefits of ongoing neo-fascist and neo-nationalist practices in football well into the 1990s.[67]

The Response of Anti-Fascist Political Groups

Grass-roots political movements organized around a challenge to neo-fascism frequently mirrored their forms of practice and suffered from similar internal fractures. The Anti-Nazi League (ANL) became the best-known anti-fascist organization, with a popular political magazine, *Searchlight*, which circulated not only within the group but also reached a small public readership as well. ANL linked closely with the Socialist Workers' Party from 1977–81, a larger Trotskyist group frustrated by the reforms of Labour, until the SWP cast ANL off for their violent political practices. Another influential anti-fascist body, the Campaign Against Racism and Fascism (CARF) prided themselves on fighting racism as well as neo-fascism and split from the ANL over some leaders' perceptions that the battle against racism within Britain could not be limited to fighting neo-fascist politics. Other smaller socialist factions and cooperative campaigns like Anti-Fascist Action (AFA), Red Action, Workers Power and the anarchist group Direct Action Movement contributed to the multiplicity of anti-fascist viewpoints in Britain's fringe political environment.

The efforts of anti-fascist groups, and in particular the *Searchlight* publication, created much of the neo-fascist demand for a public denunciation of football violence and terrace abuse. *Searchlight* established itself as the leading anti-fascist watchdog magazine. It consistently exposed far-right movements attempting to operate in secrecy and laid plain their factional turmoil and racist ideologies. Their chief aim was to fight neo-fascist propaganda with exposure, rhetoric and informed arguments. The editors also frequently republished inflammatory articles by the Far Right or conservative press, and often requested that the mainstream media downplay neo-fascist activity. Above all, the magazine emphasized violent crime, retelling narratives of black victimization and neo-fascist criminality. It became the main venue of anti-fascist propaganda, and in the early 1980s, consistently began to monitor neo-fascist activities in football.

Early international episodes troubled *Searchlight* editors and demanded that they address the growing media frenzy surrounding football violence and its neo-fascist associations. After the Heysel disaster, the magazine published a special issue entitled 'Terror on the Terraces: The National Front Thugs Who Foul Up Football', which published a series of findings on their investigation into the topic. 'All over Britain, gangs of NF thugs have latched onto the more aggressive groups of supporters ... Their aim is to recruit members and supporters', noted the introductory column. 'They promote the nauseating racist chants and Nazi salutes which are now commonplace at our grounds and which give such deep offence to genuine sports fans'. The issue exposed several individual cases of neo-fascist football violence, and criticized the 'League of Louts' which encouraged racial abuse of black players. The editors also reprinted *Bulldog* articles which boasted of international demonstrations at England's matches abroad. *Searchlight* noted, 'Away internationals have a special fascination for the Front. Fighting on English terraces may pass the time, but for NF yobs putting the boot in on "inferior" foreigners combines violence with flying the flag'. Throughout the issue, violent photographs of the NF in action accompany the articles, most of which aimed both to deplore and expose the NF's activities in football.[68]

Outside of the propaganda and media wars, anti-fascists challenged neo-fascism on the streets as well, mirroring the centrality of violent confrontation and aggressive political and territorial negotiation in neo-fascist circles. Anti-fascist sympathizers opposed NF marches and paper-selling because they represented influence over the physical geography of local neighbourhoods and football clubs. Anti-fascists also extolled the bloody march at Lewisham as a pioneering moment in their own aggressive campaigns against the NF. The day's events became part of the oral tradition of anti-fascism, and several anti-fascist memoirs instil the riots with heroic characters and momentum-building fervour.[69] Anti-fascists also emphasized confrontations on the street. *Red Action*, the newspaper of the movement by the same name, remarked, 'Nazis need to control the streets. If they can do this they can not only influence people faced with mass unemployment, but they can attack ethnic minorities and create a nest of racial tension that can tear a community to pieces'.[70] Many anti-fascists worried about the perpetuation of violence neo-nationalists instigated by dominating corners within contentious neighbourhoods.

The NF's growing influence in football troubled anti-fascists not only because of the territorial implications, but also because it challenged football as a unified working-class tradition. After discussing how the sport became a working-class staple in the 1950s and 1960s, a 1982 editorial called on anti-fascists to reclaim football from neo-fascist infiltrators because it provided a locale for safe and admirable youth rebellion among working-class adolescents. On football in the 1970s: 'It became the natural arena for young working class kids to achieve the success and admiration from friends denied to them by soul destroying work and life style'. Whereas leftist groups had 'condemned young football fans as mind-less, moronic hooligans', the author lamented that neo-fascists embraced the insubordination of young working-class rebels towards the state. He concluded: 'No one would try to pretend that the football terraces are full of committed revolutionary socialists. There are cowards, braggards and bullies, and racism and sexism abound'. But, 'Football fans, skinheads, punk rockers, all will be the older working class of tomorrow. They will not be the only people needed to build a working class movement, but they will certainly be a most significant and enthusiastic part of it'.[71] Some anti-fascists bemoaned lost opportunities to engage in similar recruiting tactics, while reasserting the cultural significance of football supportership to working-class men. Like neo-fascists, anti-fascists saw football as central to their political goals.

Many anti-fascists opted for aggressive retaliation against their political rivals. Though some expressed concerns that violent politics emulated their adversar-ies, many anti-fascists saw violence as an essential characteristic of leftist fringe politics that stressed immediate action. 'We are proud of the image of being able to back up our words with actions, but we have been accused of being no better than the fascists, a squad of "macho boot-boys"', wrote one member.[72] Despite these reservations, the use of violence to combat neo-fascism triumphed. K. Bullstreet contemplated the use of political violence in his memoirs, remember-ing his service as essential to the protection of local communities. 'By crushing the fascists at an early stage I think it is reasonable to assume that Anti-Fascist Action has prevented numerous racist attacks and even saved lives', he wrote. 'For if the fascists were given the chance to freely march, sell their papers, and appear as a respectable political force they would just grow and grow'. The man also confessed his aversion to the use of violence: 'I am not a violent person by nature. I do not enjoy the idea of walking up to strangers and punching them, even if they are fascists. It's just something that needs to be done'. The memoirs frequently mention bust-ups at football matches, where even a verbal lashing could prove effective: 'I really admire those people who stand up to them alone at places like football grounds ... These verbal put-downs, often with passers-by looking on, are just as humiliating to a fascist as a kick in the bollocks'.[73] The constant verbal and physical confrontations were perceived not only as necessary, but as educative to a wider public who supposedly viewed the outcomes of such conflicts as representative of their political validity. Both neo-fascists and anti-fascists perceived violent victories as political ones.

Other anti-fascists echoed Bullstreet's ambivalent sentiments on football and political violence. 'The political violence we were forced to employ was not enjoyable. It was viewed as a necessary evil. Its role was to demoralize the enemy and to create a space for socialists and anti-racists to work in', remembered one anti-fascist.[74] Contrary to popular perceptions that both groups engaged in violence for violence's sake, anti-fascists expressed distaste for their participation in violence. Despite his aversion to engaging in violence, Bullstreet and others felt that unchecked neo-fascist provocation would lead to more attacks in the community. He wrote, 'If they go unchallenged they soon feel that they "own" the local streets, ie that it is their manor, and that mentality encourages them into more attacks'.[75]

Anti-fascists also perceived that aggressive street conflicts at paper-selling sites outside football grounds or at marches could be as appealing to young men as the opportunities for violence neo-fascism offered. One anti-fascist recalled that in the late 1970s, 'The image of aggressive, confrontational street politics which the SWP leadership encouraged led to a massive influx of young working class males and females'. The movement's emphasis on direct action presented a militant alternative to 'the arrogance and political snobbery of these self-proclaimed professional revolutionaries', referring to the SWP and Labour reformists.[76] Many frequently showed disdain for pacifist anti-fascism. Bullstreet confirmed that the Direct Action Movement sought to separate itself from the idea of liberal reform. 'It is also satisfying to be doing something really useful instead of arguing about political theory or dreaming about utopia'.[77] At times, anti-fascist literature reflected as much contempt for the broken promises of post-war socialism as the threatening alternatives of neo-fascist movements. Like neo-fascism, they capitalized on young men and women willing to participate in violent politics, offering working-class youth an alternative to neo-fascist participation in football.

While many of their attacks on neo-fascism involved infiltrating meetings or combat at marches and rallies, contesting the sites of paper-selling and leafleting at football matches also illustrated anti-fascists' territoriality. As neo-fascist leafleting at football began to emerge in 1977, the ANL responded with a campaign to counter the NF's message. Peter Hain, an ANL organizer, commented: 'We are involved at the moment in an instant rearguard battle to project a counterview at the grass-roots level, through leafletting at Millwall and other places'. He hoped to expand the campaign to other locales as it was 'an important issue for football with young black players coming through in the game'. The ANL also convinced prominent managers Brian Clough of Nottingham Forest and Jack Charlton of Sheffield Wednesday to lend their support to the short-lived campaign in hopes of bettering its public profile.[78] Importantly, the emphasis on leafleting at football matches revealed the perception that the NF's message could be negated or rendered innocuous because of the ANL's opposite efforts. Like violent confrontations, leafleting was a direct action, quick and cheap, which could address the weekly activities of the Front.

Searchlight also emphasized the paper battles that unfolded in the football arena. The magazine offset the football victories that *Bulldog* claimed with stories of arrests and convictions that ensued. 'Grounds where the NF are active are particular targets of NF paper sellers, who peddle the inflammatory poison which provokes so much of the racist abuse later heard on the terraces', wrote one editor. Other articles lamented the intimidating NF paper-sellers outside of specific stadiums like Stamford Bridge, and extended one club's threat to pursue charges against NF crews which superimposed their insignias onto club logos for T-shirts and stickers.[79] The ANL also emphasized the connection between violence and the presence of NF papers and leaflets, promoting the idea that where papers could be sold the NF could have free reign.

> Leaders of the National Front would have the public believe that the presence of nazi leafletters and newspaper sellers at football matches is in no way connected to the violence and hooliganism which takes place at soccer grounds. It is an argument they find impossible to back up when those very leafletters are brought before the courts.

The article mentioned several NF members brought to trial under the Public Order Act in both England and Scotland for breaching the peace and instigating fights with others.[80] The ANL accentuated the NF's violence, noting that papers gave evidence of territorial control which could lead to more attacks on community members and supporters walking the streets before a match. They lamented that paper-selling often went uncontested, not only because NF ideas made it into young men's hands, but also because anti-fascists had failed to challenge them. Like neo-fascists, anti-fascists developed the idea of paper-selling and contests for paper-selling at football sites as central to the negotiation of local geography.

Despite all of these attempts to challenge the growing incidence of NF demonstrations and assert their own territorial claims, most anti-fascist movements failed to develop a capable *anti-racist* agenda through football. Most anti-fascist movements emphasized that neo-fascists divided the working-class rather than stressing how they threatened the livelihood and prosperity of black or Asian Britons. The numerous anti-fascist serials and memoirs valorized their own aggressive challenges to neo-fascists instead of professing strong desires to battle racism or protect black lives. Violent politics dominated, where black and Asian families could be protected in the abstract through the paradoxical challenge of meeting violence with more violence. In addition, the anti-fascist ideological platform was extremely limited in scope. Incensed by the rhetoric against Jews, Asians and blacks in Britain, anti-fascists focused on the fascist associations within neo-fascism, illuminating the connections between British neo-fascists and other continental fascist movements. Doing so recalled the negative political legacy of German fascism from World War II. Targeting recent derivations of fascism proved easier than exploring the racisms inherent in British imperial ideology. Anti-fascists could mobilize against a familiar British enemy without confronting other constructions of racial difference in post-war British society. In sum, by underscoring both violence and fascism, anti-fascists failed to recognize or protect the multiple, diverse experiences of non-white lives in 1970s Britain.

The left's determination to win back football supporters from the influence of neo-fascism reflects their emphasis on class unity over eliminating racisms. It has already been noted that anti-fascist movements brooded over the lost opportunities to capitalize on the growing estrangement of young working-class men. Labour sympathizers too worried about the composition of terrace environments. One Labour publication commented on football grounds: 'Increasingly they have become concentrations of frustration and socially disaffected feeling. As such they offer ripe recruiting opportunities for the far right.' The writer added that

> If we are to combat it I would suggest the terrace areas a good place to start. It is at these grounds that working class kids are to be found along with Nazis in increasing numbers. And it is at these sort of places that we in the labour movement must be seen to be providing the alternatives. We are in danger of breeding a very violent and ultimately disaffected generation.[81]

Members of the labour movement expressed anxieties about the divisions that neo-fascism caused, impeding the success of working-class politics. Not only did neo-fascism create a threatening alternative to the left; it also jeopardized the supposed harmony brought about by Labour's post-war social democratic promises. By exposing the ongoing alienation of working-class supporters and the social divisions violent conduct reflected, the battle between neo-fascism and anti-fascism menaced attempts at working-class solidarity. These divisions troubled many factions on the left, from the official Labour party to factional anti-fascist movements.

Such an emphasis on unifying working-class men obfuscated the harmful experiences and racial abuses that non-white men and women faced on a daily basis. Focusing on violent politics and rectifying class divisions betrayed the anti-racist promises of the anti-fascist factions. This was as true within the football environment as it was in other arenas. Anti-fascist publications focused on the racial abuses perpetrated at football matches only inasmuch as they reiterated the baseness of their political rivals. Demonstrations like throwing bananas or chanting served as evidence of their adversaries' commitment to fascist principles, not as experiences which should be challenged because of their racial and post-colonial significance. The fact that black players and black citizens alike faced lived experiences of abuse and violence proved only a peripheral cause of political action. Approaching neo-fascism through aggressive anti-fascist agendas concealed and ignored the ongoing experiences of racism, both within and outside of football.

Advocating street-level violence and aggressive confrontations with neo-fascists also stressed that violent activities could be alleviated through the use of more violence. This conclusion reflected the state's approach to rowdy football spectatorship and partisan violence in the late 1960s and 1970s, and fed the machoism of gendered debates and challenges to racism. Like the Home Office and Department of the Environment, anti-fascist political movements adopted aggression as the status quo. The mutual antagonisms between neo-fascists and anti-fascists engendered a reciprocating violent environment, and failed to ameliorate hostility and polarization within fragmented social communities. Instead, violence from both sides encouraged the media and the public to view football and fringe politics as an unwanted marriage, marred by the excitability and immaturity of working-class youth from both poles of the political spectrum. Not only did this emphasis obscure the experiences of black lives, but it also promoted the illogical and impossible assumption that the cure for violent social interaction could be achieved through the endorsement of hostile street conflict.

Conclusions

Neo-fascist discourse about wider social concerns with immigration, struggles for jobs and housing, and race riots conditioned the social debates occurring within football. Neo-fascist organizations utilized the football environment to disseminate their ideological messages through a variety of political practices like chanting, leafleting and selling newspapers, changing football stadiums into sites of racist instruction. These practices overlapped with territorial concerns about black and immigrant infiltration into public spaces and city centres, especially football stadiums. The football milieu also provided a platform for recruiting and publicity stunts, which became fundamental practices, along with marches and rallies, that attempted to demonstrate party strength and provided opportunities for enacting racial abuse and provoking territorial violence. Football stadiums presented neo-fascists with a working-class constituency already versed in violent conduct and often alienated by British society and politics. Anti-fascists lamented their appeal and responded with their own propaganda campaigns. Both neo-fascist and anti-fascist racial rhetorics received public attention, demonstrating that football became an incubator for prevalent cultural tropes.

The battles over paper-selling at locations outside stadiums became a chief point of conflict between neo-fascists and anti-fascists, and must be recognized as a fundamental form of fringe political practice in the 1970s. Anti-fascists accepted aggression and territorial violence as a necessary evil, promoting mutually reciprocating violent environments around football stadiums. Their negation of neo-fascist political messages served not to reject their claims but to bolster them by accepting the standard forms of political practice: violence, aggression and territoriality. Though they met neo-fascists with direct action, anti-fascists failed to understand the nuances of neo-fascists' racial and post-colonial meanings, instead simplifying their political focus on their enemies' fascist associations. Above all, anti-fascists worried about neo-fascist infiltration and appropriation of the working-class sport par excellence, as well as how their appeal could divide workers. Leftist movements expressed apprehension about the future of the movement when predominantly white young working-class men attacked each other and their black counterparts. Their focus on violence also echoed earlier state programmes to eliminate social violence in the football realm by increasing the oppressive actions meant to deter it.

The anti-fascist concentration on fighting fascism explains the long delay in establishing a more focused anti-racist campaign in football. While racial abuse and neo-fascist demonstrations emerged more frequently in the mid-1970s, a consistent anti-racist campaign in football did not gain traction until the late 1980s. For nearly two decades, most football clubs, state agencies, spectators and the public ignored the growing incidence of racial abuse directed at black players and spectators. The next chapter will explore how and why the football anti-racist movement emerged, as well as its connections to its anti-fascist predecessors.

7 'TEN YEARS BEHIND THE TIMES': RACISM AND ANTI-RACISM IN FOOTBALL, 1986–98.

In 1994, at the height of the anti-racist campaign in British football, one fanzine editorial read as follows:

> The logos and slogans denouncing racism at matches look and sound great, but are ten years behind the times. The time to really stand up and shout was in the seventies/ early eighties ... The majority of those who verbally abused black players have changed their tune with the emergence of black players throughout the country.

The author concluded, 'Acceptance comes with integration and there can be no denying there is a totally different mood to that of ten years ago, and before.'[1] The quote revealed that despite the ongoing efforts of anti-fascist militants, overt expressions of racial abuse within the football environment did not subside until the early 1990s, as widespread public, grass-roots and institutional movements rose to challenge the phenomena. Many felt the activist consensus lagged at least a decade behind the emergence of football racism. As analysis in this chapter will show, fan groups and agencies of the British government capitalized on the opportunity to tackle racism in football by creating a broadly educative and aggressive campaign against overt racisms at football matches. As peaceful multicultural integration became the goal of many British politicians in the 1990s, the development of anti-racism in football became vital to the promotion of harmonious race relations. Though successful in reducing the immediate incidence of neo-fascist demonstrations and explicit racist conduct, many of the grass-roots political organizations targeting football racism established continuities with aggressive violence and community policing tactics the British state advocated against football violence decades earlier. Following the lead of their anti-fascist predecessors, many anti-racist movements in the late 1980s and early 1990s oversimplified articulations of racial integration and anti-racial messages, developing anti-racism in football into another struggle for the sanitization of football and the permeation of public order. Reinventing football consumption with little reference to spectators' political and social attachments to the sport or black players' lived experiences of racism, they obscured how fans integrated local, national and racial meanings into football spectatorship.

Inasmuch as the public's ongoing anxieties about football violence expanded to include racisms within football, the state's promotion of anti-violence grew in the last twenty years to cover anti-racism. After a groundswell of support for anti-racist initiatives from fanzines and grass-roots supporters' groups, the Commission for Racial Equality (CRE), the government agency charged with maintaining peaceful multiculturalism and eliminating discrimination, matched their ambition with a state-supported anti-racist campaign in football. The massive publicity blitz succeeded in bringing attention to the problem and making discourses about racism in British society more visible and accessible. Despite its lack of a recognized moral entrepreneur like Denis Howell, the campaign did pursue anti-racist moral education through the medium of football.

Several problematic historical developments nonetheless emerged from this anti-racist expansion to football's sanitation. Though not always intentionally, the movement's founders established continuities with earlier anti-violence promotions and the anti-fascist movement. The anti-racist canvass entailed two interwoven approaches. The first approach, advocated by the CRE, the Professional Footballers' Association (PFA) and regional anti-racist initiatives, endorsed football as the public location for anti-racist education. In this arena, football's representation of the nation, as in earlier campaigns, must not be tarnished by the presence of racial abuse and discrimination in an increasingly multicultural Britain. The second approach, carried out by local supporters and fanzines, promoted aggressive intimidation against bigoted supporters and a community policing atmosphere, where spectators regulated each other's conduct, maintained by local fans. These spectator associations were often affiliated with Anti-Fascist Action (AFA), the predominant anti-fascist group remaining at the end of the century. Both approaches drew on the need for public order and the elimination of a disruptive element in Britain's national sport. However, each group upheld their vision of the football environment in different ways. While institutional anti-racist programmes engaged in a publicity campaign that once again aimed to sanitize football culture, grass-roots supporters contributed by violently challenging racist activity on matchdays.

The anti-racist debate in football, despite its relative successes, produced a number of unfavourable consequences. First, the adoption of aggression and violence again discouraged women from participating in both the consumption of football and in supporter-based anti-racist campaigns. While women already faced challenges in becoming welcome spectators, the masculine tone of football terraces was emphasized by the promotion of belligerence within stadiums. While concerns about racial difference escalated, anti-racist movements failed to recognize the construction of gender exclusions and the creation of hypermasculine environments in football. Second, the focus on anti-racism concealed larger debates about class unity and Britishness which proceeded from the conflicts between neo-fascists and anti-fascists in the 1970s. Inasmuch as debates about football's purpose shifted to the 'racial problem', they commensurately obscured ongoing fractures in class politics. Moreover, the anti-racist programme used sport to bolster the emblematic image of the nation and a fictively peaceful multiculturalism. Third, anti-racists imagined a separate sphere of relations, where football could be extracted from its historical and political context and treated for its ignominious ills. This approach to racism neglected the origins of discontent within British society and failed to address the ongoing anxieties about multicultural integration which troubled young working-class men. Though they often worked in the short-term to suppress racist behaviours, these methods encouraged oversimplifications in addressing both the origins of racisms and means to address them. Finally, with an early emphasis on continuing the fight against fascism, anti-racist initiatives defined specific roles for 'racist' and 'anti-racist', defined by specific behaviours and codes of conduct. Certain practices became codified and reified within these roles, which were meant to be learned within the sport and taught outside of it. The blatant demonstrations of racial abuse perpetrated earlier by fascist movements – most often chanting, verbal abuse and banana-throwing – became defined as 'racist' while aggressively challenging such behaviours became the work of 'anti-racist' supporters. Such behaviours lost much of their political significance in this era, while racism remained as virulent as ever. As a result, the anti-racist movement often manifested as a vacuous, behavioural-based approach to combating racism which removed racist activity from its local and national contexts. All of these oversimplifications mystified the historical and social significance of racism and the deleterious effects of experiences of racism for black players.

Reasserting the continuities between football fan cultures of the 1960s and 1970s and the emergence of racisms within football spectating transgresses several trends within other studies of football and racism. In sociological circles, a recent trend has emerged which attempts to disconnect football 'hooliganism' from football racism, and, in particular, political fascist movements, largely in an effort to understand how racisms have become more subtle and less distinguishable within contemporary football.[2] These academic investigations often double as examinations of the effects of local policy and attempt to create more immediate directives for football anti-racist organizations. I am sympathetic to these approaches, especially where they succeed in discovering the nuanced manifestations of racial discrimination within spectating cultures, ownership and management, and their contextual connections to British society at large.[3] The historical roots of contemporary racisms, however, still need to be studied in their contexts of emergence, where historicization and contextualization can reveal their connections to other constructs of power and forms of social disruption. This chapter departs from previous studies on football and racism by engaging written sources and images rather than ethnographic or survey-based research. This allows for a historical approach which analyses change over time and looks for larger and broader continuities, contextual change in football culture and the articulations of racial difference in post-war British society.

My goal is not to reassert the authority of the so-called 'racist/hooligan couplet', but to question the assumptions behind it in efforts to imagine new approaches to the complex of racism, exclusion and violence which pervaded football from the 1970s to the mid-1990s. I do not simply wish to reduce football racism to a form of antisocial behaviour, but to understand how environments where antisocial behaviour reigned created spaces where racial abuse and racial violence could be perpetuated, as well as how fans responded to these new forms of racist conduct. These demonstrations and attitudes often included specific racial and political content as young working-class men reasserted their position within the contested social landscape of post-colonial Britain. Further, several moral arguments and political discourses, along with several anti-racist organizations, did reduce racism to nothing more than a set form of antisocial behaviour, ignoring the racial specificities of these discourses. Interrogating this conflation and the moral enemies anti-racist organizations created through this approach will show how moral arguments and anti-racist education have been deployed through sport in Britain. Examining continuities between state and popular responses to racism and their associations with earlier forms of football disorder reveals how the moral repertoire of Britishness expanded as well. Several agencies of the state, football clubs and sectors of the public constituted new anti-racist messages in football which developed upon the prescriptions for social order and the maintenance for control developed in anti-violence messages of the 1960s and 1970s. These new prescriptions also perpetuated the violent nature of football environments, but attempted to repackage and sanitize anti-racist discourses by ridding them of their extreme left-wing connotations. Such messages proposed anti-racism, itself a complex of contradictory and simplified messages, as a necessary form of middle-class propriety and respectable behaviour in the new multicultural, commercial football industry.

The first section of this chapter addresses the development of the joint anti-racist campaign created by the CRE and the PFA. Much like previous neo-nationalist, anti-fascist and Home Office manoeuvres which centralized football in broader political discourses, this state-sponsored project utilized football to attempt a broader anti-racist message. Football functioned as a resource for the agency's increasingly public approach to combating racism in well-known sections of British society. An emphasis on preventing youth from learning racist behaviour featured, while a contextual understanding of racism only existed inasmuch as the programme imagined football to be a microcosm of society. Their failure to interrogate the broader origins of racist conduct, rooted in social conflict and economic inequalities in Margaret Thatcher's Britain, limited the usefulness and impact of the programme to within stadium walls. The second section addresses the emergence of anti-racist fanzines. These fanzines espoused a blatantly violent approach to address racist spectators, and preferred supporters to police their own football environments rather than have the state or the police involved. Several highly publicized incidents of racism in football in the 1990s provided fodder for debates about racism in football and how it should be tackled. The persistence of anti-fascist attitudes within the grass-roots anti-racist movement is the subject of the third section. Several fanzines adopted anti-fascist affiliations with AFA and continued to imbue football with class politics. The conundrum of racial difference troubled anti-fascists, who exacerbated antagonisms within stadiums and feared that the debate over race would prevent working-class unity. They also promoted the fanzine as a political resource, much like the newspaper in previous decades, and used it to disseminate their own vision of what football should look like in the post-colonial era. In the end, though popular anti-racist messages worked to minimize overt racisms, they also established a discursive and structural framework in which race became the key topic and most respected division of power. Other axes of discrimination and division, such as gender, sexuality, religion and class, were sufficiently marginalized in an effort to simplify the public uses of sport in Britain. Anti-racist politics obscured more subtle exclusions within stadium environments, where women and specific groups of men could not participate in either football spectating or anti-racist movements without difficulty.

The State's Response: The CRE and the Labour Task Force

The state's anti-racist involvement in football piggybacked on an increasingly large grass-roots movement instigated by anti-fascists and anti-racists on the local level, and did not become institutional until 1993 under the CRE's Campaign Unit. Nonetheless, the CRE-PFA campaign gave the football anti-racist movement government legitimacy and better resources than any of the local or regional associations. The programme, originally named Let's Kick Racism Out of Football, received funding from the Football Trust, which earlier financed changes to stadiums and the implementation of CCTV. With its initial funds, the campaign sought to gain publicity and club support. All but one of the English professional clubs and nearly half of the Scottish clubs signed on by early 1994, and therefore adorned their stadiums with posters, stickers, advertisements and public address announcements.[4] The campaign used these resources to gain media publicity and raise awareness that clubs would not tolerate overt racist conduct, two goals that an initial CRE review thought the campaign had achieved.[5] The group also released a fanzine entitled *Kick It!* which harnessed the popularity of alternative publications to broadcast its own institutional anti-racist messages. The campaign received several facelifts from the CRE's various coordinating councils in its first few years and its initiatives changed based on their recommendations.[6] Several relaunches, most importantly as Kick It Out in 1997, capitalized on the growing media concern with racism in football and the movement's elevation to a cause célèbre in English society.[7]

This national programme provided leadership for willing clubs and examples of how to implement low-level campaigning tactics and, in the long run, largely contributed to the successful decrease in explicit forms of racist conduct at matches. The CRE needed a boost of brief success to stem its mounting irrelevance in British politics and government administration. In its brief history from 1976, the CRE had been unable to register a large political triumph after initially pursuing discrimination cases in education, employment and housing. Many of their difficulties stemmed from thin support from Conservative administrations (1979–97) and Home Office leaders who displayed inconsistent commitment to remedying social inequalities of any sort. Their original priorities established the CRE as a protective government agency, with varying success in changing social practices, and very little public recognition.[8] Though the agency boasted a series of publications that disseminated its research findings – including books, journals, occasional papers and pamphlets – the organization lacked a strong public profile and increasingly invoked criticism from several different angles. The Policy Studies Institute, a politically unaffiliated think tank on social policy, independently investigated the CRE and its legal initiatives, and in 1991 released their detrimental findings. The PSI found the CRE negligent in many of its duties, especially regarding employment discrimination and legal representation for the poor, and recommended that the Race Relations Act and the CRE be completely overhauled.[9] The report tarnished the image of the group and its overseeing body, the Home Office, and encouraged institutional changes in ensuing years.

The football campaign provided a well-publicized and broadly popular initiative that helped re-establish the relevancy of the CRE. Sir Herman Ouseley, who served as the executive chairman of the CRE from 1993–2001, oversaw changes in the agency's public performance and emphasized the need for public acceptance. Let's Kick Racism Out of Football not only served as a key programme under Ouseley's new leadership, but provided a limited and approachable public target to reduce racism. Unlike the amorphous and ever-changing discriminations in larger areas like education and housing, football presented what seemed like a bounded environment. By targeting fascist and racist instigators, as well as the football clubs which had too long ignored this growing problem, the CRE could be seen as successful in a popular arena. An anti-racist programme in football afforded the opportunity to demonstrate some tangible success in fighting popular racisms. Success in a single social site could be marketed as evidence of achievement, in contrast to ongoing legal battles, social research and pushes for legislative changes that pursued long-term goals with little public appeal. Furthermore, the programme capitalized on the popularity of the sport itself: by allying with clubs and the PFA, if one supported football one should also support anti-racism in football.

In a metaphorical sense, the CRE's choice of football revealed how they imagined football as a microcosm of British society. If sport operated as a representation of the nation, then eliminating racism within football would translate to battling racism in larger social and cultural contexts. If the CRE succeeded in purging the sport of its racist elements, then it enhanced its own efficacy and fulfilled its broader social purpose. In reconstructing the sport as a harmonious sphere of social relations, they hoped that they could mimic their efforts in the macrocosm. Challenging racial discrimination in sport also overlapped with employment concerns, as black players could be regarded both as public icons and as black labourers in a discriminatory industry. In many ways, the campaigners represented themselves as a bridge between society and sport, especially with its emphasis on youth education. The CRE's Campaign Unit commented:

> The first campaign we did was a football campaign ... because we looked at the whole area of young people and how to get to them, what medium we could use which would hold a message against racism and for equal opportunity and would also speak very clearly and directly to all people.[10]

By attacking racism in football, the CRE capitalized on the opportunity to present concrete, substantial advancements in the battle against racism in the nation's most popular sport and booming leisure industry. In doing so, they repaired their public image and benefited from football's popularity and exposure. Much like neo-fascist and anti-fascist organizations, the CRE capitalized on debates about race in football to build their organization's prominence.

Let's Kick Racism Out of Football also fitted with new initiatives spawned by the CRE in 1994 to educate the public using large-market advertising campaigns to expand the image and scope of the agency. Conservative Home Secretary Michael Howard launched the Public Education Campaign by hiring advertising powerhouse Saatchi & Saatchi to develop a series of ads that made the public aware of both the extent of racial discrimination in British society and the measures the CRE took to combat it.[11] The CRE took ads in cinemas, billboards and television commercials, using new media and increased funding to attend to their civic profile. The football campaign mimicked these moves by capitalizing on football's popularity, beginning their canvass with media-based materials and activities such as distributing messages in club programmes and fanzines. The initial launch and preliminary activities of the CRE-PFA project garnered the desired widespread media attention, and also piqued the interest of other anti-racist organizations. The Runnymede Trust, an independent policy research organization on racism and multiculturalism, followed closely the developments of the football campaign. Despite having paid attention to fascism in football in the 1970s, the Trust's only other large collections on football racism appeared with the CRE's launch in 1993.[12] Even regional and local papers took notice of how their clubs adopted the campaign, and lent their support to activities as well.[13]

Despite widespread public support, the programme's messages and publications actually promoted very limited understanding of racisms and means to combat them, especially when its materials targeted a younger audience. Several testimonial accounts of racial abuse at football matches lamented that children learned such acts through attending matches. Journalist Amanda Kendal wrote that during a 1994 FA Cup match 'Latics' striker Darren Beckford was abused from the terraces – most disturbingly by a young child who called him a "nigger". The child's father, standing next to him, did nothing.'[14] After discussing the abuse he received as a player in the late 1970s, Garth Crooks commented, 'But it's sad because the younger ones are learning it', presumably through attending matches.[15] Such testimonials encouraged an emphasis on edifying youthful spectators on the deleterious effects of racist behaviour. The articles in *Kick It!* aimed at changing adolescent racist behaviour in two main ways: by promoting successful black footballers and issuing calls for further proactive measures by young fans. In the short term, these goals often succeeded in controlling unwanted racist activities. But as a result of the emphasis on immediate outcomes, hardly any of the content of the fanzines addressed the contextual complexities of racism, but instead discouraged specific forms of racial abuse that black players recalled as disturbing and humiliating. The audience and format of the fanzine itself precluded racial understandings or discussions about contributing factors in the creation of racial attitudes.

The magazine also promoted football as a mythic bastion where the sporting experience could be perfected by eliminating racism. In the first issue, Ouseley said, 'Football is a beautiful sport. Thousands of people play it regularly; millions watch the game every week. Football belongs to us all. Racist abuse and chanting and loutish behaviour should not be allowed to spoil our enjoyment.'[16] The CRE stressed that an uninhibited, ideal sporting experience should be the goal. For many of football's anti-racist initiatives, the removal of racism became a project incorporated into the larger goal of sanitizing the entire sport. The contextual causes and social origins of racism in Britain faded into the background, as the CRE extracted the football experience from its broader setting. By imagining the football arena as a separate and dislocated sphere of relations, the CRE not only protected the interests of British football but also disconnected racist conduct in the sport from the broader debates about racial difference and discrimination within British society. As such, football racism could be treated, exposed and challenged without considering more extensive social fractures outside the sport, much less their amelioration.

Though it often encouraged preventing racist behaviours in the short term, this subtle separation contradicted the CRE's stated goal of bridging the gap between sport and society. The stated purpose of the CRE-PFA fanzine, *Kick It!*, 'includes advice on what supporters can do to help stop the divisive and destructive force of racism, and to help promote good relations between people of different racial groups.' Ouseley added, 'It will also be targeted to young people in schools, youth clubs and colleges as part of the wider aim of creating more tolerant, and less racist, attitudes in our society.'[17] The emphasis on simplifying the message for youth resulted in banal understandings of the political uses of racism and instead reified behaviours as the target of political action.[18] Though they imagined that the programme could be educative of larger issues of racial discrimination in society, especially for younger audiences, CRE's pursuits within football usually failed to connect racisms and the construction of racial difference with the social and structural genesis of racial attitudes outside the football stadiums.

The emphasis on behaviour can be most prominently detected in the multiple articles, editorials and interviews that focused on the abuse of black players. By exposing the behaviours black players despised – namely racial chanting, banana throwing and verbal abuse – the fanzine championed the idea that eliminating behavioural traits of the crowd would lead to the end of football racisms. Consider the following editorial comments from the first issue of *Kick It!*: 'We've all seen it, or heard it: bananas (and worse) thrown at black players; the constant chants of coon, nigger, black b*****d; the gobbing; the monkey chants and hoots of derision when black players get possession; and the taunts on the pitch itself ... We simply cannot afford to sit back and think it's all history now.'[19] The emphasis on eliminating specific behaviours can also be seen in an article depicting changes to policing racism. *Kick It!* editors encouraged police to monitor racist abuse in the stands, even though the experiences of the 1970s showed police that pushing to make interventions could cause further violent behaviour. One article read: 'Police forces take their responsibilities in this area seriously, but some of them are still afraid of arresting people for chanting, lest this should incite worse incidents such as fighting between the two teams' supporters'. The author supported using newly installed CCTV systems to aid in prosecuting behaviour, as 'this dilemma can be avoided by making arrests after the match, in the knowledge that the evidence against the offenders will be on film'.[20]

Policing racism predictably focused on removing fans who exhibited racist behaviour, especially as legislation generated to tackle racial abuse specifically focused on chanting and throwing objects onto the field. The Football Offences Act of 1991 passed with the intent of allowing prosecutable charges for racist conduct in football. However, the original stipulations allowed for arrest of spectators when chanting in concert with one or more others, not on an individual basis. As a result, the original legislation was relatively toothless and, as others have noted, superfluous in light of other public order legislation. The law also applied only to England and Wales. After some small adjustments in subsequent years, spectators could be charged for individual acts, but the arrest and prosecution numbers remained very low. As in the 1970s, many overtures at football legislation aimed to ease public anxieties about football violence, and only mildly addressed decreasing the incidence of unwanted conduct.[21]

Despite anti-racists' relative success in decreasing the incidence of offensive behaviours, their larger goals of educating football spectators on the broader cultural ramifications and origins of such behaviour failed. The conceptualization of the make-up of contemporary racisms, as defined by behaviour, ignored the attitudes and social relationships which buttressed them and made them possible. The CRE-PFA campaign perpetuated this focus on conduct by repeatedly making supporters aware of the 1991 Football Offences Act, which targeted 'indecent or racialist chanting'. Printed campaign materials nearly always included segments which instructed fans on the details of the Act and how it could deter racist behaviour when fans relayed problems to police and stewards.[22] Envisaging racism as a closed repertoire of behaviours denied the relational and political content of racial abuse in wider social settings, confining racial attitudes to spectators within the limited boundaries of the football milieu. Concentrating sanitizing efforts on racist behaviours also treated such behaviours as universal in their intent, rather than recognizing the multiple variations in motivations for such conduct, especially in light of local football partisan conflicts and the political contexts of specific post-colonial cities. Racist behaviour was often perceived as a tactic within the small arena of player/spectator interaction: spectators engaged in racial abuse to set players off their game. The racial content of such remarks were often ignored by official anti-racist campaigns, despite the CRE-PFA desire to make 'racism in society' evident. In the end, the programme's activities attempted a functional use of football as a popular sport to spread anti-racist messages to British society. Overt behaviours were challenged and minimized while broader social divisions and racialized understandings of spectator interaction were obscured.

The CRE-PFA campaign nonetheless established the perception and expectation that racism and anti-racism in football could condition and inform larger social ills, and vice versa. Shortly after achieving its long-awaited victory, the Labour Party in 1997 instituted the Football Task Force (FTF) in response to campaign promises to better regulate and promote sport in England. The executive summary of the FTF's final report clearly articulated the influential connections between sport and society:

> Football's power to unite surpasses that of any other sport – but so does its power to divide. The game commands the hearts and minds of millions. There is no more powerful vehicle to take to young people a positive message of tolerance and respect. But football can also be a focal point for racism and xenophobia. Racism is not a problem of football's making. It is society's problem. Yet it is an issue the game cannot afford to sideline. It presents it with responsibilities – and new opportunities. The game's ruling bodies – and clubs and players as its ambassadors – have a responsibility to protect and promote its image as the game that unites the world. They must act wherever necessary to ensure people can watch and play free from prejudice and abuse. They also have an opportunity to make a positive contribution to creating a better society ... For a game often accused of taking more than it gives, the value of work by football to 'put something back into society' cannot be overstated.[23]

Clearly, the functional uses of sport for tackling racism within British society featured in the FTF's approach to anti-racism in football, with special emphasis on football's growing commercial popularity. In addition, the FTF also intimated that the role of British football in generating a protective and idealistic role for sport within society would improve Britain's international relations. In the FTF perspective, football provided not only a way of combating racism, but also of improving Britain's global image.

For the FTF, anti-racism also became a function of other desirable commercial and national incentives, cheapening not only the potential of legitimate anti-racist messages but also mystifying the racist experiences of black players, spectators and British citizens. Eliminating racial abuse at matches and racial discrimination in managerial decisions would increase the number of talented players available for selection for international duty. According to the FTF, the proposed elimination of racism in football 'is about the quality of English football – country and clubs need to draw on the talents of the whole community; the more players the national team manager can choose from, the stronger England's chances of success'. Making the national side more representative of Britain's growing black population would not only serve to appease calls for inclusion but also to bolster the ambitions of the public for England's international footballing prowess. The FTF bent the relationship between sport and society towards fulfilling broader national sporting objectives in addition to anti-racism. The anti-racist impulse in football could also be utilized to further the financial profitability of football as a commercial enterprise. In other recommendations, the report stated that 'there are sound commercial and footballing reasons why everybody should have an interest in its [anti-racism's] success'. The FTF continued, 'Football clubs with support spread through all sections of the community can boost crowds and maintain stable finances. The game's current popularity may not last indefinitely.' Supporting a welcoming environment towards spectators of all ethnic backgrounds determined the financial health of the football industry. Creating an atmosphere of acceptance and tolerance encouraged profitability, and anti-racism's popularity could be useful towards those ends. The imagined connections between society and sport usually worked to serve ends beyond removing racism, and therefore undermined the state's capability to effect lasting social and cultural transformations.

As in previous decades, the state's involvement in regulating antisocial behaviour within British football reflected larger goals of maintaining idealized forms of British propriety, national commitment, and appropriate public behaviour. In fact, the anti-racist movement in football did not gain public approval and state legitimacy until concerns about multiculturalism in an increasingly diverse Britain became prevalent political issues. Both the CRE and the Labour Party limited the efficacy of institutionalized anti-racism by endorsing a narrow focus on specific forms of behaviour and decontextualizing social relationships within sport. In contrast, the challenge against racism from spectators pursued an entirely different direction.

The Supporters' Response: Fanzines and Anti-Racism in Football

The fanzine, as both a genre and a political outlet, emerged from the subcultural politics of style and criticism within the football world. Descendant of musical magazines which addressed the disjuncture and disassociation of a generation of punk provocateurs, football fanzines allowed fans to express their own alternative views and opinions.[24] Fanzines evolved into a collection of unconventional supporter perspectives on the goings-on in the football industry, usually with specific focus on a single club.[25] Written with gritty language and infused with humour, fanzines operated to channel fans opposition to clubs' decisions and the growing commercialization of the sport in the 1980s and 1990s. In many ways, they served as a grass-roots instrument against the decreasing accessibility and accountability of football clubs, allowing supporters to apply public pressure and express unorthodox attitudes. Most often, they included comics, editorials, letters and reports of clubs' activities. In the late 1980s, a few supporter-based fanzines adopted the express purpose of promoting anti-racism within their football clubs.

As evidenced by early anti-racist fanzines, spectators adopted a community policing policy to prevent racist abuse and behaviour within their closely guarded football environments. Inasmuch as this trend reflected earlier promotion of community policing by the British government and police officials, it also indicated supporters' desire to maintain control over the football experience which was constantly changing and shifting. As the communal familiarity of spectating football diminished with its commercialization, spectators fought to retain the ability to monitor the crowds on the terraces. In attempting to control terrace environments, as well as the newly mandated seated areas, spectators sought to minimize the role of the clubs and police in dictating the shape of the supporters' experiences.[26] As racism posed a growing challenge to British football, spectators adopted community policing practices against racial abuse as a mechanism for imposing social order within stadiums. Echoing anti-fascist predecessors, anti-racist approaches in the late 1980s and 1990s involved creating environments which proved threatening and intimidating to spectators participating in racial abuse. Anti-racist fanzines often incorporated aggression and violence against racism into their informal statements of purpose, encouraging loyal male spectators to oppose the scourge of racism in football with force.

Establishing that the spectators of local clubs deplored racial abuse became the task of fanzine writers. Building such reputations discouraged both home and away fans from participating in racial abuse, but also allowed spectators' collectives to establish their own moral superiority. Foxes Against Racism (FAR), a small collective of anti-racist supporters of Leicester City FC, discussed their intentions in their fanzine, *Filbo Fever*:

> All the individuals within Foxes Against Racism have had enough of so-called football fans using football as a soapbox to continually – and without retribution – spout this filth. We aim to achieve this by: 1) becoming a catalyst for changing attitudes on the terraces and within LCFC and in the surrounding communities. This entails becoming a visible and audible presence among City fans as a whole challenging racist attitudes on and off the terraces by any means necessary, and helping other non-racist football fans to gain in confidence and help them to speak out too ... 2) Constantly monitoring racism among City fans, and at grounds we visit, and (as appropriate) will provide information to LCFC itself; and press them to adopt further reactive and preventative measures which will enable us ordinary Leicester City fans to kick racism out of football for good.[27]

Other anti-racist fanzines carried similar statements, which not only clearly advocated the use of aggressive community policing 'by any means necessary', but also perceived racist and anti-racist roles as definable and mutually exclusive. As evidenced, fanzines and proactive anti-racists pressured clubs to help them create unwelcoming environments for those participating in racial abuse. Several letters to editors at fanzines helped to build pressure on clubs as well. A letter to *Flashing Blade*, a fanzine for Sheffield United, stated, 'It is only when fans like you reading this complain to the club every time you hear racist abuse at the Lane that they will take it seriously'. After discussing the problematic and unreliable interventions of club-appointed stewards, the letter's author demanded that other supporters pressure the club's chairman: 'We must remain vigilant and Charles Green will get the stewards to act if we keep protesting'. Maintaining a racism-free environment, through community policing and exerting pressure on local clubs, became the primary goal of many fanzine editors and committed anti-racist activists in British football. In doing so, they created a mutually exclusive division between racist and anti-racist roles in the football environment, maintained by shared antipathies and a sense of moral privilege.

Anti-racist fanzines promoted different ways of identifying racists and challenging their activities. Like the police, anti-racists often had trouble identifying individuals within a crowd in order to pursue them by 'any means necessary'. Leeds Fans United Against Racism and Fascism began eliminating the presence of racial abuse and fascist demonstrations at their club in the mid-1980s.[28] Their fanzine, *Marching Altogether*, intermittently ran a section that aimed at identifying particularly evasive offenders. 'Who Is the Dickhead in the Lowfield Seats?' displayed a map of the stadium and an X in the approximate area of the origin of racial abuse at recent matches. The article recalled that during a recent match with Tottenham FC, a club known for its large Jewish following, a Leeds fan had participated in racial abuse and needed to be brought forward. 'Who was the dickhead at the Spurs match who started singing "Spurs are on their way to Belsen ..." you know, all that anti-Jewish, gas chamber-Hitler shit?' asked the article. 'If you know him or if you are that dickhead, the message is Fuck Off and Die!'[29] The article promoted community policing not only through direct confrontation, but by asking other fanzine readers to aid in the identification process. Anti-racist supporters used the fanzine publication not only to spread messages, but also to aid in community policing methods. Local government administrations followed supporters' lead in proactively creating community policing techniques. The Reading Council for Racial Equality recommended to Labour's Football Task Force 'that season ticket holders could be issued with a "red card" so that they can show their offence at others' comments which can be caught on video'.[30] In this proposal, not only would fans be involved in pressuring offenders to desist from racial abuse, but also actively pursuing police justice. The Council insinuated that with video footage, fans given the red card could be identified and prosecuted upon review of CCTV recordings. Anti-racist activists thus generated community policing practices that adapted to the changing physical environments of football stadiums.

The motivations for fighting racism within football varied, and often betrayed goals beyond moral opposition to racial abuse. Most prominently, many fans expressed anxiety about the reputation of British football and their local clubs as racism became a publicly recognized problem. *You Wot!*, the anti-racist alternative fanzine for Torquay United, addressed the decline of the nation's game in the opening editorial of its first issue: 'YOU WOT! is opposed to fascism and racism. If these evils are allowed to triumph, then our game will die a slow death. Black players will be reluctant to join clubs, our league and teams will suffer and attendances will drop.' The editor expressed concerns about the waning popularity of football when damaged by racisms within the sport, which would lead to weakening commercial returns and the overall regression of British football. Apprehension about the viability of the industry and its embodied image of propriety motivated supporters to stem the proliferation of ugly racial incidents. After chairman Ron Noades stated on a BBC television programme that he preferred 'hard white men' to 'artistic black players', who could not tolerate a cold British winter, Crystal Palace fans chastised Noades not only for universalizing black players as weak and effeminately artsy, but also for bringing disrepute to the cherished club and halting the team's momentum.

> All the woes this season began with the pathetic remarks of our chairman. Whether taken in context or not, they were quite simply rank stupidity of the highest order ... The whole affair has brought shame on Crystal Palace and put the club on the back pages for the wrong reasons.

Anti-racists brooded over the adverse publicity engendered by racial abuse, and worried that their club's reputation would suffer. Beyond ideological resistance to racial discrimination, supporters anxiously protected the sport and its local clubs.

Anti-racists in football also defended their clubs' managerial and selection decisions regarding black players, though they often interpreted their social meanings differently. In 1996, *Flashing Blade* printed a telling conversation between one black supporter writing to the editor and the editor's response. The exchange revealed how loyalty to club and hostility to racist fans could be intertwined and complicated. Ramon Mohamed wrote in, 'I thought we were living in the multi-cultural "rainbow" nineties and not the bigoted days of the seventies and eighties.' In response to racial chanting Mohamed:

> shouted back at the morons challenging their racism. Another 'white' Blade also verbally attacked the racists and I applaud his bravery and would like to thank him ... Is it just coincidental that, at the time of writing, Sheffield United don't have a single black player in the first team squad?

The editor replied, 'It is a sorry tale you relate ... Well done to the True Blade who had the courage to stand up and challenge them.' Yet, despite the editor's initial agreement and advocacy for policing racist conduct, he quickly defended the club for not having black representation in the squad: 'It is unfortunate that United had no black players in the squad until the arrival of Paul Parker, but I'm positive this was by accident rather than design'.[31] The editor continued by noting other successful teams without black players, whose managers were apparently blameless.[32] While the black supporter risked testifying not only against overt racist conduct in the terraces, but also the perceptible discrimination in team selection, the editor chose to protect the club and manager's reputation instead of considering the possibility of institutional prejudice. A third party, Sean O'Brien of Leeds, wrote in the following month defending Mohamed's position. He added that 'it should not be about whether we have any black players at all. Everyone should be treated as equal; race should not come into it.'[33] This egalitarian comment subverted both other parties by shaming their position as overly cognizant of racial difference, and concluded the dialogue on the matter. However, O'Brien's comments also denied the specificity of race in exclusionary practice, and therefore inadvertently undermined the charges of bigotry against the club. The discussion revealed how particular incidents could spur forthright discussions about the construction of racial difference in football. It also illuminated how loyalties to club challenged supporters' steadfast opposition to racism in the sport.

In many cases, supporters demanded that their clubs sign a black player to remove any suspicion of racial discrimination among the management and boardrooms. With the recent increase in racial abuse at Barnsley Football Club, some supporters insisted that the club take action. Keith Latham wrote in *South Riding*:

> Some other league clubs in our area ie. Sheffield Wednesday and United, and Leeds, have all had their problems with idiots chanting monkey noises from their terraces. The clubs concerned have taken on coloured players and what happens? Normal football support reigns again. Gone are the racist slurs and the support doesn't fade, if anything, it steadily improves. I'm not asking Mr. Machin [club chairman] to use a token coloured player to ward off the problem, but to seriously consider the worth of an investment to help kill two birds with one stone on his next venture into the transfer market.[34]

Latham's comments repudiated the common fear that signing black players would deter supporters who preferred a homogenous white team. On the contrary, Latham intimated that signing black players would improve the team and thus increase ticket sales. Wary of perceiving adding a black player as a substitute for practically opposing racial abuse in the terraces, Latham did recognize that such a player would improve the team and show the club's supporters that black players were accepted. Signing a black player, Latham hinted, would also distinguish Barnsley from other clubs in the midlands burdened with racist supporters.

In response, John Wray seconded the motion:

> Whether these people acknowledge it or not the future of British football is multiracial ... Sometime in the future Barnsley F.C. will buy black players but how much do we have to suffer in the meantime?, and what a way to ruin our national sport and what is potentially the town's best asset.

Wray supported the idea that failing to sign black players affected the quality of the product. In addition, Wray betrayed that his opposition to racism in the game depended on his desire to uphold the vulnerable reputation of club and country. As in other debates in fanzines, additional parties chimed in with atypical viewpoints. One anonymous writer challenged utilizing black players for political purposes.

> After reading the letters in the last two issues of S.R. aimed at the signing of a black player ... I would ask cannot we go further than this. Could we not, as a club, sign a player who would rid the terraces of all prejudices, E.G. a female, black, lesbian, one parent family, who had blood ties to George Courtney and Saddam Hussein.

With tongue firmly in cheek, the writer suggested that no player should be denied opportunity because of skin colour, but that the club should seek to improve its fortunes without regard for political opportunities to express multicultural solidarity.[35] The author also suggested the club introduce a 'token' minority player into a hostile environment, thus intimating that black players carry the burden of eradicating football racisms. Though meant as humorous sarcasm, the intimation of sexism and homophobia in supporting collectives was rare, and ultimately not pursued or discussed further. Again, the willingness of fanzines to facilitate outspoken arguments about the construction of racial difference and opposition to racial exclusion is striking. Furthermore, supporters expressed various levels of comfort with using their local club and the national sport as a stage for political expressions of multiracial harmony, not to mention anti-sexism or other battles for political correctness, in Britain.

Regardless of their level of ease with political activism, some supporters defended their right and responsibility to police their own terraces and assume the burden of keeping racism outside the game, especially when it kept other parties at bay. Foxes Against Racism decried the club's decision to bring in a consulting firm to strategize the creation of a formal anti-racist campaign, separate from their own grass-roots movement, at Leicester City. FAR criticized the National Coalition Building Institute for their lack of existing involvement and knowledge of British football: 'The NCBI is an American-based organization who are completely unconnected with football, and whose ideas and philosophies (!!) are light years away from the lives and experiences of us "simple" Blue Army folk!' Protesting the condescending tone of institutional campaigns, the editorial concluded, '"All for One and One for All" is the slogan for the LCFC/NCBI initiatives. FAR's version might well be "Shut up or piss off, racist arseholes!!"'[36] Given most Americans' unfamiliarity with British football, the club's invitation to NCBI irked FAR supporters and challenged their authority as anti-racist activists. In defence of their legitimacy, FAR claimed to have special knowledge of the specificities of LCFC terrace culture. 'It is only other fans who can effectively target racists amongst us; let club officials sort out those amongst their number who "need attention"!'[37] FAR preserved their status as legitimate, exclusive regulators of racist conduct at their club, who needed no help from external organizations, especially those who failed to be self-reflective about their own managerial and institutional racisms.

Leicester supporters also ridiculed the launch of the CRE-PFA national campaign, criticizing the government for their delayed response. FAR resisted national coordination as much as they did the club's externally imposed anti-racist organization. In the second year of CRE's investment in football anti-racism, they held a campaign rally in London on the same day as several fan groups and the Football Supporters' Association (FSA) held theirs in Manchester. FAR took offense at the mutual timing: 'The CRE knew it ... and decided to scupper it completely, anyway!! That's the trouble with "do-gooding" outsiders – they always want something in return i.e. all the credit.' Supporters hated being displaced in their position as anti-racist football regulators. The editor concluded, 'Us footy fans are sick of being treated like dispensible pawns for a "greater purpose". As members of the Blue Army we have no time for manipulators and con-artists ... piss off to obscurity where you came from.'[38] While the CRE selected football as a place to battle racism in the cultural realm, and gain some political capital, everyday supporters found their efforts intrusive and moralizing. Unlike the CRE, they found it reprehensible to use sport for political ends. The supporters' brand of anti-racism protected football, the club and black players by aggressively removing racist conduct from the terraces. Very often, they ignored or disdained the political overtones of their own activism.

Other supporters' campaigns came under criticism from local fans for lacking toughness and better organization, despite the fact that fans often deplored formal political intervention in football. Though they often shunned national coordinating efforts, many found their local fan-based organizations weak and derivative. At Everton, local anti-racists borrowed an Italian slogan, 'No al Razzismo', after an editor saw anti-racist efforts at a match on the continent. The fanzine, *When Skies Are Grey*, reprinted a letter from a displeased local fan:

> It's good to see the WSAG campaign, but its got to be said its pretty crap. 'No al razzismo' what the fuck is that? Why not try something like 'I go in the Street End, but I'm not a racist twat like the 200 dickhead fuckwits in the middle'. Arsehole racists with no brains are not going to be swayed by a middle class anti racist slogan written in Italian.[39]

Again, the supporter's disdain for moralizing and patronizing anti-racist messages was evident. Some fans found supporter-based campaigns sloppy, ill-planned, and lacking motivation. In this case, the supporter clearly preferred an antagonistic community policing policy. He further criticized the club for lacking masculine bravado in taking on racist supporters:

> Its obvious Everton FC will do nothing to control/stop this when all they have to do is pay a couple of bruisers a tenner each to sit at the game and when racist chants are started to get them to shout them down with things like 'Fuck off you racist twats' very loudly and very aggressively.

As opposed to politically correct activities and media-based advertisement campaigns, this supporter represented a large body of spectators who craved both forceful policies against racists and immediate ground-level responses to racial abuse.

In this particular case, pressure from fans to stifle anti-racist slogans and national media involvement succeeded. A few months after the initial criticisms, *When Skies Are Grey* changed tactics: 'We have become aware that whilst we are running such a visible anti-racism campaign we may be contributing to the problem ... WSAG is constantly being asked by the local and national media to discuss racism at Everton, and we're sick of it.' The fanzine decided to 'give our no al razzismo campaign a lower profile for the time being. It is hoped that when we do it will contribute towards starving the few racists there are of the "oxygen of publicity".'[40] Apparently, the movement attracted both national media and political extremists from neo-fascist parties and the Socialist Workers' Party, all of whom Everton anti-racists detested. Instead of promoting football as a social space for political debate, the fanzine responded to requests from fans to temper the political connotations of their anti-racism. Being forced into the national spotlight created other problems, such as drawing neo-fascists and unwanted publicity, which supporters found distracting when attempting to combat racism aggressively on the social level.

Though community policing constituted the major component of spectator campaigns, not all supporters adopted the policy uncritically. Many wondered whether physical confrontation in the stadiums would lead to more violence outside of it. Some supporters feared vengeance in other venues, especially in small communities. One acute journalist interviewed supporters who came to the consensus 'that it is best to keep quiet, or perhaps point out the ringleaders to stewards'. The article told the story of young Charlton fans: 'One pupil was worried about the consequences "if you shop [report] someone and they see you on the street the next day". The others nodded agreement.'[41] Despite the constant pressure to report or confront racial abuses, some spectators, especially younger ones, feared retribution in other social settings. Community policing worked for men who had the physical character and masculine disposition to carry out aggressive altercations, but not for all men.

In addition to unaggressive men, community policing policies also worked to further exclude women from the football environment. The promotion of aggressive conduct, though interconnected to anti-racist purposes, heightened the belligerent tensions and encouraged the escalation of machoism within football settings. The continuation of masculine codes of conduct proved unwelcoming to women, excluding them in two ways. First, women could be uncomfortable in tough settings where hostile behaviour and violent exchanges proliferated. The sanitization of violence in the 1970s and 1980s gave way in the anti-racist era to the reassertion of violence as the means of settling conflict. Women's consumption of football and involvement with other hardcore supporters was minimal. Second, women could not participate in the anti-racist campaign without adopting community-policing aggression as the informal policy code of their activism. Such policies encouraged women to be violent, and like many non-violent men, women could be unwelcome in terraces where aggressive anti-racism ruled. The available evidence which discussed women's participation in community policing or anti-racist campaigns is minimal. No women appeared in the lists of editors of anti-racist fanzines, and very few, if any, women wrote into fanzines to express their opinions. This absence is telling. Anti-racism in football, as both a grassroots political expression and attention-grabbing national campaign, involved almost no women. The dominance of masculine antagonisms structured the consumption of football and the pathways for women's participation in political anti-racisms on the local level in British football.

The promotion of community policing tactics also operated as an extension of the reclamation and imposition of public order in football. Whereas removing violence from the football realm became the purpose of the government's sanitization campaign in the 1970s and mid-1980s, violent hostility became fundamental in the removal of overt racisms. In addition, by emphasizing their antipathies towards specific forms of racist expression and racial abuse, supporters' groups reified racism as a body of conduct, not the imposition of racial difference for the purposes of power in social and structural relationships. They defined supporters as either racist or anti-racist, creating mutually opposing roles defined by specific forms of conduct. Such an emphasis disallowed the possibility of various forms of unrecognized racisms, including less overt managerial discrimination and social pressures on black players. By creating forums for the public discussion of racism within sport, however, fanzine editors and supporters produced forthright debates that questioned how to protect one of Britain's cherished cultural traditions. The defence of public order in this cultural site generated plainspoken and practical discussions about how to combat racism in British sport, and infrequently, in British society. Much like their response to earlier anti-violence measures, however, supporters often ignored the British government's involvement in football affairs, defending their campaigns against racism as locally specific, legitimate and pragmatic.

Anti-Fascist Influence and Fanzines in the Anti-Racist Era

Despite the proliferation of national and local anti-racist agendas, anti-fascist political groups maintained their political position and continued their unconventional forms of political practice. The creation of many anti-racist fanzines was underwritten, both ideologically and financially, by anti-fascists who still perceived football as a contested political site. Though relatively ignored by national media campaigns, and subsequently by academics, the persistence of anti-fascism into the era dominated by supporter-based movements and the CRE-PFA campaigns shaped how other supporters articulated their anti-racist messages. Anti-fascists influenced the anti-racist campaign by heartening the community policing impulse, but they also worked to establish connections between anti-racist groups at different clubs. Not all anti-racist efforts adopted an anti-fascist message, allowing for complicated and overlapping messages with intermittent conflicts about the politics of racism in football.

By the late 1980s the Anti-Nazi League's authority faded and Anti-Fascist Action (AFA) carried more influence with football supporters. Though *Searchlight* continued to investigate neo-fascist activities, their emphasis lay with international matches and neo-fascist demonstrations at English national team matches. AFA renewed its interest in local football politics as grass-roots supporters' campaigns gained influence in 1987 and 1988 in Leeds and other northern industrial cities. In fact, many of the early anti-racist campaigners had affiliations with AFA. In 1988, at the dawn of anti-racist movements in football, the AFA called on the sport's governing bodies and supporters to help them fight fascism in the nation's sport. Responding to a surge in recent police inquiries into football gang activity and their neo-fascist connections, AFA requested that the Football League and the Football Association take drastic action against ongoing neo-fascist involvement in football.[42] The request emphasized clubs' 'inability to come to terms with racism and fascism on the football terraces' and stated that 'it is an outrage ... that in order to succeed in the sport, black players have also to overcome the added obstacle of learning to tolerate filth and abuse from terrace racists every time they touch the ball.'[43] Of course, football governors ignored the statement, but it allowed AFA to mark their continuing displeasure at the industry's failure to respond to renewed neo-fascism in football.

Anti-fascist publications began monitoring the anti-racism movement in football, recognizing football as a politicized cultural institution. *Fighting Talk*, the main outlet of the AFA, scrutinized football-related campaigns and noted highly publicized incidents of discrimination and abuse in football. Still committed to the same aggressive political principles, AFA continued stressing the solidarity of working-class men and the challenges racism posed to that imagined unity.[44] The magazine published a running column containing stories of violent football conflict, as well as prominent columns from anti-racist fanzines. They also became a clearing house for stickers and t-shirts from anti-fascist groups organized around local clubs like West Ham AFA or Chelsea AFA (see Figures 7.1 and 7.2).[45]

Other anti-fascist splinter groups followed British football as well, attempting to understand how football became a site of political negotiation. In 1991, the Campaign Against Racism and Fascism (CARF), a group of anti-fascists who split from the ANL and the *Searchlight* organization, established their own publication which also produced a bimonthly section updating its readers on football-related activities. CARF regularly reprinted articles from fans involved with LFUARF and the Football Supporters' Association, columns from Crystal Palace's *Eagle Eye* and other fanzines, and reports of the worst incidents of racial abuse. In the issue which introduced 'Football Update', the ongoing column, CARF attacked Sunderland FC's administration for apparent hypocrisy. A day after receiving the Football Association's 'Top Family Club' award, CARF reported several incidents of black and Pakistani schoolchildren being abused outside the stadium. Fifteen-year old Asma Bibi and his classmates wrote the club's manager, Malcolm Crosby, describing the actions of spectators who 'shouted out unkind and abominable words because of our colour, like "Black Bastards", "Paki" and "Black Niggers". They wound down their car windows and spat at people going by.' After receiving little sympathy from the club, the kids contacted CARF, who printed their story.[46] Like AFA, CARF sought to publicize incidents ignored by national media, and encouraged their members to participate in football alongside committed anti-racists.

In 1994, editors of *Fighting Talk* published a special issue on football fascism which attempted to inform AFA members, with broad strokes, of the growing importance of both neo-fascism and anti-fascism in football. Like other football supporters, AFA members challenged the legitimacy and efficacy of the CRE-PFA media blitz. They emphasized their knowledge of local specificities and lack of confidence in movements backed by government agencies. 'It is ultimately those who go regularly to football who will be the ones who have real respect and influence at games, and we would call on all anti-fascists to support these

Figure 6.2: West Ham Anti-Fascists logo.   Figure 6.3: Chelsea Anti-Fascists logo.

anti-fascist supporter initiatives'. The writer clarified, 'Support meaning physical, financial and vocal, getting involved if your club has an anti-fascist element, and setting up one if it doesn't'.[47] AFA emphasized that only an aggressive approach, and not a media campaign, would be effective. They also asserted that community policing was better suited to the new all-seated spaces in the larger British stadiums. 'One article in a programme hardly makes a "campaign"', claimed one editor. 'Clubs say people shouting racist abuse will be thrown out, but at many clubs the police and stewards say they can't get to people in the new all-seaters ... Clearly only an AFA-style approach can really deal with the problem on the ground.' Fundamentally, AFA recognized the significance of debates about racism and fascism within football. However, they also challenged the CRE's efforts to coordinate the campaign and create an uncontroversial anti-racist message.

The AFA levelled its most scathing attacks at the national campaign's latest fanzine, *United Colours of Football*. Created by Kick It Out, the Football Supporters' Association, football's governing bodies, and the regional organization Football Unites, Racism Divides in Sheffield, the fanzine became the voice of the nationally coordinated anti-racist campaign in 1996. In many ways, *United Colours of Football* displayed the convergence of a single nationally coordinated anti-racist programme. With the institutional support of the major football organizations, and the allegiance of several fanzines, the publication became the primary voice of anti-racism in football. It represented a mainstream organizational approach to removing racism from the game.

AFA maintained that fans should have the right to organize their anti-racist and anti-fascist efforts apart from this coordinated campaign. 'United Colours is so concerned not to offend the football/political establishment that it ends up looking to that establishment for the solutions – clubs should, police should, etc.' Not only did the national campaign rely too heavily on governmental authority, but the AFA also thought it generated a decontextualized message that focused too heavily on black players. *United Colours* certainly promoted black role models and accentuated how they navigated through the challenges of racism in football. AFA editors found their messages thin:

> It's good that football grounds are being seen as an arena for anti-racist struggle like any other – but if the starting point is that racism/fascism is caused by 'social issues' outside the ground – unemployment, poor housing etc. etc. – then just telling people to support black players won't change anything.

The commentator concluded, 'All it means is they've put their prejudices aside for 90 minutes'.[48] AFA's trenchant criticisms addressed how the national campaign failed to bridge the gap between sport and society. Because anti-fascists and many local anti-racists felt that their work in the terraces translated to political success by directly challenging the ideologies and practices of neo-fascism, they found the national campaign's efforts insubstantial and impractical. Local anti-racists thought they could legitimately change minds through direct, and sometimes aggressive, physical and vocal confrontations. They also believed that connecting anti-racism to the larger contextual issues neo-fascists brought into debates about football – such as increased job competition, concerns about immigration controls and poor council housing – would expose wider and broader maladies within British society that transgressed the boundaries of the sport.

However, the AFA usually conceptualized these societal ills within the framework of class conflict, limiting their ability to perceive other divisions of power, and understand the complex social relationships and racisms in football. As evidenced by the Anti-Fascist Football Fans Congress (BAFF), held in Dusseldorf, the AFA experienced limits to their efforts at contextualizing football racisms, much like the original endeavours of the CRE-PFA campaign discussed above. In 1994, the AFA attended the international conference of anarchists, anti-fascists and football supporters to discuss the direction of anti-fascism in European football. Twenty-six German clubs attended the congress, and St Pauli FC of Hamburg organized the festivities. St Pauli had been influential in creating anti-racist momentum in Germany during the early 1990s, and became a role model for British supporter-based movements, many of whom published updates on the German club's activities within British fanzines. Visitors from Italy, the Netherlands, Scotland and Britain attended, with the AFA represented by anti-fascist editors of *Red Attitude* from Manchester. *Fighting Talk* reported the proceedings at length, offering a window onto the attitudes and practices of anti-fascists in an era dominated by the national anti-racist campaign.

The congress's initial charter agreement reiterated their commitment to preventing neo-fascism from dividing working class unity through the medium of football. Though they agreed to issue a liberal agenda for clubs to support, they added, 'The problem also has to be tackled at [the] source – on the terraces amongst the young working class people, at whom the fascists aim their propaganda'. The representatives also agreed that programmes generated by clubs and national football and anti-racist bodies lacked concrete applications and failed to effect real change. Like local clubs, anti-fascists perceived their challenges to racism as locally specific, practical and highly effective.

Disruptive participants, however, challenged the insistence on class unity above all else. Feminist fans from St Pauli attempted to expand class-based politics to create a forum where supporters deliberated the overlapping divisions of sexism and fascism. Many feminist supporters served as local social workers or in club-based community schemes, which allowed extreme anti-fascists to rebuke them as part of 'middle class lefty elements ... obsessed with political correctness'. AFA and the British anti-fascist contingent abhorred the interruption. They reported:

'The main arguments of such people were about the attitudes to women and sexism
on the terraces. Obviously sexism is a problem but to hijack a conference which was
specifically about fighting racism and fascism is a diversion and the motives of such
people have to be questioned.

Clearly, gender discrimination ranked a distant third behind the AFA's concern
for class unity and racial difference, in that order. Though granting that football
suffered from gender exclusion, anti-fascists marginalized these concerns while
attempting to recentre the importance of fighting fascism. British anti-fascists
also objected to how the discussions over gender occupied time at the conference. 'A workshop which was originally designed to come up with practical
ideas about fighting organized fascist groups at football grounds was sidelined
into abstract arguments about whether sexism is a form of fascism and whether
it should be treated with the same priority', they complained. They found the
debate 'bereft of any economic analysis and completely ignorant of class based
politics'. Attempts to broach key questions about the relationship between fascism and feminism found little traction with other anti-fascists, who ignored
sophisticated conversations about divisive social relationships outside of class.
Reports of the conference in AFA's publication betray extreme derision of feminist politics, with no attention to feminist attitudes or arguments. Importantly,
Fighting Talk did report that since the conference, offices at St Pauli had been
bombed, with the club concluding that feminists had been responsible for the
attacks. Whether or not the accusations were justified, it is clear that anti-fascists
demonized and ostracized the feminist element at the congress. British anti-fascists remained limited in their vision of social and cultural politics, venerating
working-class harmony while only marginally recognizing the detriment of
racial exclusion. Feminist activists, women and discussions of gendered exclusions were not only rejected, but also obfuscated by the constant attention to
class politics and the reproduction of aggressive masculinities in football.[49]

Outside of international conferences, anti-fascists adapted to changing
methods within politicized football. Whereas fifteen years earlier the newspaper
formed a central site of political negotiation and debate, the fanzine took its place
in anti-fascist football campaigns. While newspapers still proved marginally
important, anti-fascists often opted to disseminate messages through alternative
and humorous fanzines. The AFA established formal alliances with *Red Attitude*
(supporting Manchester United), *Tiochfaid Ar La* (written by another association, Celtic Fans Against Fascists), *Our Day Will Come* (supporting Celtic and
Manchester United) and *Celtic Fans Against Racism*, among others.[50] Other fanzines, especially *Marching Altogether* (LFUARF) and *You Wot!* (Torquay United
FC, Gulls Against Racism and Fascism), maintained an emphasis on fighting
fascism without official factional alliances. In the late 1980s, despite challenges
from some fans to depoliticize their fanzines, or at least downplay anti-fascist

rhetoric, many of the editors defended their position. 'There have been criticisms of *Marching Altogether* in the past that we concentrate too closely on the fascists but their effect cannot be underestimated', explained one Leeds supporter.[51] With increased media attention to neo-fascist activity in football during this period, many anti-fascist supporters perceived that threatening political elements had made their return to football. While the press sensationalized the neo-fascist presence, and nearly everyone overestimated the level of neo-fascist involvement, anti-fascists considered eliminating neo-fascism central to the battle against racism in football. Establishing the fanzine as the new political outlet proved fundamental to this battle. When asked about the importance of the fanzine on the football front, one *Red Attitude* editor commented, 'The original objective in any project like this is to secure first base or occupy the territory in which you want to operate. In this respect the fanzine was a major success.'[52]

Red Attitude and *Our Day Will Come* became the two dominant anti-fascist fanzines supported by the AFA. Each promoted violent community policing, the primacy of working-class indivisibility and the unabashed politicization of British football. Each endorsed violence in a staggering manner. In a question and answer interview with *Red Attitude* editors years later, one responded to a query on the success of removing racial abuse at Old Trafford by stating, 'Quite simply because year after year we have out-violenced them'.[53] The Manchester fanzine also took on the Football Supporters' Association for promoting a patronizing moral campaign that lacked political content and the practical benefits of physical intimidation. They turned their pens toward mocking and threatening FSA members who 'do little beyond providing the odd clever quote for the media'.[54] One satirical article compared the FSA's approach to racists in the terraces with that of *Red Attitude* readers. Five comparisons emphasized the necessity of violence when confronting racist spectators. Where the FSA member would report him to the nearest steward or policeman, *Red Attitude* readers 'report him to the nearest Shining Path death squad for whom racism is an offence punishable by summary execution'. Instead of pouring Bovril down his neck 'intentionally pour petrol down his neck and set fire to the bastard'.[55] Another suggestion entailed disguising a meat pie as an explosive, shoving it into the racist's mouth: 'The resulting explosion will hopefully start a trend to rival the firecrackers seen at etc. etc.'. Finally, while an FSA member would demand firm action from the club through a letter, the fanzine suggested RA readers 'follow the racist home, smash all his windows, burn down his house, kill him and all family and dance on their graves'.[56] While such an article stressed satirical contrast, the violent rhetoric still educated the reader on conduct during aggressive confrontations, even if overstated. Though intended to be humorous, the article revealed the violent imagination of anti-fascists and their high regard for intimidating community policing which worked to prevent unwanted conduct in the short term.

Marching Altogether, whose founding organization LFUARF had some ties with AFA, also exhibited extremely violent language and illustrations. National campaigns, other fanzines and anti-fascists widely lauded LFUARF for being the earliest and most successful anti-racist group in the north of England. Their language and illustrated comics proved extremely violent as well. One comic, '101 Things to Do with a Nazi Skin', facetiously advocated setting fire to one racist fan, hanging him from the top of the stands on a meathook and bashing him in the head with a hammer.[57] Another comic, Eric the Football Hooligan, typically satirized the stereotypical football supporter as over-excitable, stupid and unnecessarily violent. However, when Eric confronted a man throwing a banana on the pitch, he punched his face. Eric's violent engagement was lauded here as bravery and courage, and the final frame narrated, 'If you have a racist friend, now is the time for your friendship to end'.[58] Certainly, the writers intended the high level of violent imagery as whimsical folly, but it also indicated a preference for creating a threatening environment, monitored and regulated by anti-racist fans.

Not all readers of the fanzine found the penchant for violence acceptable. Rex wrote in to tell how he found himself standing next to neo-fascist sympathizers who racially abused players on the pitch. Describing himself as 'completely powerless to do anything' as a minority voice in the terraces, he confessed, 'I know violence is a terrible thing but I feel VERY violent towards them, I am beginning to lose my temper now so I'd better sign off'. Rex's ambivalence towards violence was rare in the pages of the fanzine, but showed that the pressures of non-violent propriety and the push for physical confrontation could often be at odds. His consideration of violence as a course of action revealed that masculine aggression contradicted the wider goals of sanitizing football. Rex's expressions exhibit how many spectators faced juxtaposing messages about how to make the sport respectable and enjoyable for all.

Other fanzines, especially those not directly affiliated with AFA, adopted a more tempered anti-fascist approach. An exchange in the fanzine *You Wot!* illustrated a beneficial and non-violent impulse in Torquay. The fanzine reprinted a letter from a BNP member who protested anti-racist activities at the club. His submission derided 'scrounging immigrants' and 'loony lefties' for invading the nation and not supporting native Britons. The editor responded, 'I can understand you feeling that black people are taking jobs and houses away from the average white person. Many people do when they don't know the facts.' He continued:

> But remember, black people are not to blame for lack of investment in British industry which has caused so much unemployment. Neither are they to blame for the government freezing local council's funds for building affordable accommodation for rental or purchase.

He finished his critique of British capitalism in the Thatcher era by emphasizing that black and migrant labourers faced the same challenges as white Britons. Class solidarity was the only way forward: 'We need to work together as a united front and not a divided one if we are to get investment to create jobs and funding to create housing for black and white as equals'.[59] The response addressed each grievance individually, attempting to provide an explanatory and informative discussion for readers. As the quote revealed, anti-racists seeking to protect black players represented broader political issues debated by neo-fascists and anti-fascists. While *Our Day Will Come* certainly encouraged violent confrontation, they also exhibited, albeit infrequently, a penchant for educative debate rather than violence. One article proclaimed:

> The 'easily swayed' racially prejudiced fans need to be talked to, argued with and confronted in a clear class-conscious manner which demolishes racist myths (they're taking our housing and jobs, Africa as the source of AIDS, etc.) and shown that racism must be tackled both because it is oppressive and because it divides and weakens the working class.[60]

Clearly, anti-racist activism in football became productive of larger debates, allowing supporters to enact political discussions which addressed issues outside of the stadium. In this case, anti-fascists in football chose to create a platform to counter the origins of popular racisms, even if they assumed racial divisions to be derivative of the partition of working-class men.

Such expressions of restraint and cognizance of contextual politics were rare in the hotly contested environment of British football during this era. Whereas the CRE attempted to continue football's reformation through media and education, anti-fascists, and many anti-racist associations which followed their lead, established violent confrontations and aggressive community policing as the primary means of eliminating overt racisms. While they succeeded in diminishing the occurrence of specific anti-racist behaviours, such an emphasis often neglected the contextual and social origins of racial discrimination. With few exceptions, anti-fascists and anti-racists chose to combat racial discrimination with the threat of violence, limiting anti-racist politics to the confrontation of a moral enemy, the epitomized racist football supporter, who participated in a bounded repertoire of behaviours.

Conclusions

As the evidence shows, several interested parties – including government agencies, anti-racist associations, supporters' groups and anti-fascist political factions – capitalized on the opportunity racism in football provided to politicize the football environment. Though all tackled racial abuse in football as a problem plaguing the sport and the industry, they did so with different motivations. By eliminating racial abuse from British football, many realized they could protect the sport, local clubs, spectator experiences and the commercial business of British football. Therefore, British football became a cultural institution which generated discussions and debates about racial difference, racist conduct and anti-racist initiatives. These discussions created racist and anti-racist roles and produced open conversations about race and British society by establishing what behaviours belonged to each position. Problematically, these discussions rarely provided a contextualized or historicized understanding of the constitution of racial difference, were often limited to discussing racist behaviour against black players and failed to recognize the problems of post-colonial integration in a purportedly harmonious multicultural Britain. They also neglected to tackle other divisions of power which overlapped with the construction of racial difference, namely gendered exclusion and the lack of involvement of women in football anti-racist organizing. As British football became a site for education and dialogue about racisms and anti-racism in Britain, the forms anti-racism took adopted the legacy of using violence to promote social order. Just as the government promoted the use of violence, aggression and coercion to rid British football of its violent participants, spectators implemented similar community policing and violent initiatives to sanitize British football. In the end, both aimed to protect the sport and its representational image rather than the people involved in the sport.

8 'A DIFFERENT SET OF RULES': BLACK FOOTBALLERS, ANTI-RACISM AND WHITENESS

While the previous two chapters analysed the conflicts between racists and anti-racists, and neo-fascists and anti-fascists, this chapter pays close attention to the responses of black players in the milieu of violence, racism and football. As black footballers began to appear regularly for clubs in the late 1970s and early 1980s, they primarily struggled with questions of professionalism and respect within a publicly visible labour market that emphasized loyalty, club pride and respectability. In the face of ongoing racial abuse and discrimination, black players were often criticized for 'acting out' when responding to taunts or ill-treatment. As representatives of clubs, and more broadly of British football, black players consistently came under pressure to defer to the best interests of the sport and to damper their personal emotions. As anti-racist organizations began to recruit and campaign with black footballers, however, these men came under the concomitant pressures of allegiance and resistance. When faced with situations or questions involving racial abuse, black players endeavoured to maintain proper professional conduct, but were also often asked to express tempered derision towards racial abuse. More visceral, aggressive responses by these men to racial abuse had no place. Instead, black players often responded to racial abuse with cleverness, humour and undermining rejoinders that defused the volatility of specific situations without surrendering their reliability as representatives of the national sport. This chapter will elucidate the historical and transformational experiences of black players, their participation in a highly contested and politically charged social arena and the ways in which their lives have been appropriated by anti-racist organizations in an effort to stop football racisms. In doing so, it reveals how racial and classed divides in society were not only reflected in black players' experiences, but also challenged notions of a harmonious, multicultural Britain during this period.

The voices of black players and the spectators who abused them are difficult to contextualize. Most come from published collections of interviews and oral histories, early works tracing the development of black sportsmen and players' recollections. Thus, the responses of black players to racism have been mediated by time and editorial decisions. In addition, black players often self-censored their comments in order to avoid criticism. Nonetheless, when read with prudence, the sources reveal a rich array of responses by black players, as well as several different articulations of their often frustrating position as anti-racist actors. Supporters' publications and fanzines also provide a wealth of spectator perspectives on racism and anti-racism and help to contextualize both abusers' and anti-racists' efforts to make black players, and the ambiguities of their position, emblematic of larger social and cultural contests within Britain. Documentation from anti-racist organizations, especially those specific to local clubs, reveal how agencies advocated black players to negate football racism at both the local and national levels. Using these sources, this chapter will explore how black players responded to racial abuse, their participation in anti-racist campaigns and the problematic messages deployed by British anti-racist organizations that chose football as their primary arena of communication. As with some other anti-racist campaigns across Europe in the post-war period, anti-racist agencies in football suffered from oversimplification and a failure to understand the complex politics and continually changing terrains of racism and anti-racism in modern Britain.

The constant demand to act professionally, to ignore their own personal or political sentiments and to respond within the limits of acceptable boundaries defined by others in sporting environments can be described as 'whiteness'. I suggest that the challenges black players faced existed within decidedly normative boundaries established by club owners, coaches, fans and other players, nearly all of whom were white. In sport, whiteness often acted as a normative force which enacted racial exclusions through the creation of acceptable and unacceptable behaviours in different sporting environments. These norms worked to suppress participation and resistance by racial minorities who did not conform to particular sporting values maintained by predominantly white men. Whiteness, in its broadest definitions, has been described as a set of social relations and perceptions that shape patterns of dominance and support white privilege.[1] Historians must, however, be specific about what they mean by 'whiteness' in different historical contexts, lest it become an unhelpful and indiscriminate tool with limited analytical dexterity for a wide variety of dominating principles, power relationships and exclusions.[2] The racial signifier implied in the term connotes the presence of racial exclusions and/or racially exclusive environments imagined within boundaries of conduct and behaviour by white historical actors. In this case, the signifiers 'white' and 'black' were discursively employed by racists and anti-racists alike with the intention of recognizing and identifying characteristics of race, nationality and ethnicity, often with unintended epiphenomenal outcomes.

Studies of whiteness have often traced the development of supremacist and white working-class movements within North America and Europe in efforts to understand the characteristics of groups that championed their white heritage and used it to set themselves apart in social hierarchies.[3] Special attention has been paid to the American South and American immigration, where different groups of white people created and delineated distinct white identities in relation to black Americans.[4] Studies of twentieth-century sport, and especially British football, have also considered whiteness's role in ordering and structuring antipathies towards non-whites. These have been exceedingly helpful in understanding the contextually dependent and dynamic systems of logic that lead to racial violence and racial abuse.[5] Other contemporary sociological studies have utilized the analytical power of whiteness studies by exploring racial discrimination and the construction of exclusive environments in coaching ranks, whether white footballers and coaches are cognizant of doing so or not. While overt racism persists, both black and white football authorities often fail to see the familiar narratives and performances that constitute racialized environments and prevent black and Asian fluency in technical and social conversations.[6]

Using these previous studies as background, I argue that within post-colonial societies, whiteness can operate as a normative set of behaviours, pressures and expectations that non-white social actors are strongly encouraged to accommodate and only occasionally resist. Whiteness is indeed a normative force that subtly hierarchicalizes difference by underwriting environments where 'black' and 'white' identities and the expectations surrounding them are naturalized and often obscured. White men and women create racial assumptions in different historical contexts that not only engender whiteness as white ethnicity but also build expectations for others attempting to work, live and produce in environments white people control. These expectations not only reflect common-sense behaviours deemed 'white' but also assumptions about class-, gender- and sex-specific conduct that overlap with and intersect racial performance. The pressures of whiteness create environments where non-white men and women must experience the burdensome prescriptions for acceptable behaviour, political expression and personal identity. Though these pressures are never totalizing, they can be overwhelming, working to challenge black expression and black identities. The dominant attitudes of whiteness are not ubiquitous and fixed, but rather contingent and contextually variable. In post-war British football, constructions of whiteness depend greatly on the assumptions of both racist attitudes and anti-racist responses. They are not merely socially constructed, but culturally dependent and rooted in expectations of the national image and peaceful society British football represented, and how its players purportedly epitomized socially acceptable political attitudes in post-colonial British popular culture.

In studying articulations of race in football, as elsewhere, whiteness must be used as a descriptive and analytical tool, rather than as a divisive term that promotes the reification and persistence of 'race' itself.[7] In using whiteness, one runs the risk of giving form to the imaginary binary white/black and thereby excluding the multiple identities, nationalities and ethnicities present in post-war Britain. For example, one glaring omission in early anti-racist efforts was the absence of recognition of Asian footballers who began to play profession-ally in the mid-1990s, a problem that several football anti-racist organizations recently aimed to rectify. People who do not fit neatly into an oversimplified black/white binary certainly disrupt it, challenging the ontology of racial cat-egories in the process. Nonetheless, cultural analysts are still left with the need to discover why several different football-related bodies – clubs, supporters, players and coaches – used these terms nearly exclusively, and how these cul-tural disruptions reflected broader political and ideological deployments of race. Interrogating these football discourses can reveal the ways in which the separa-tion of socially constructed and universalized black and white identities came to be within post-war British popular culture. In exploring their construction through British football, these discussions will reveal the presence of homog-enizing and essentialized cultural identities both reflected in and produced by sporting, leisure and commercial contexts. An analysis of black players' conflicts will make clear and plain the contradictions and problems of deeply racialized cultural markers used in football during this period. Examining the significance of whiteness in these particular cultural dialogues, not only for its racial saliency, but also as it colluded with and expressed other social exclusions (class, gender, sexuality, etc.), will reveal the multiple nodes of power that support white privi-lege and codes of conduct in Britain's beloved sport.

Racial Abuse in Football

Though some forms of racial abuse have been discussed in earlier chapters, exam-ining the forms of abuse experienced by black players further demonstrates the pressures on black footballers. As soon as successful black players succeeded at top levels in the 1960s, they faced racialized expressions of opposition. As early as 1965 Everton fans at Goodison Park chanted their version of Zulu chants at South African Albert Johanneson throughout the game, along with several vile shouts.[8] Bermudian Clyde Best, West Ham's prolific fullback, recalled con-stantly receiving abusive and violent threats from spectators from his first season in 1969 onwards.[9] As their integration continued apace, black players came to expect verbal abuse and racist invective on a regular basis. By the 1970s, spec-tators directed constant verbal abuse at the various emerging black footballers. Black players' heightened exposure increased the opportunities to bring racist spite to the terraces and to practise abuse, and coincided with outbreaks of football violence throughout Britain. Racial abuse took many forms, of which verbal abuse was the most common, but also included chanting, songs, throwing objects and spitting.

Verbal abuse proved popular because of the proximity of the players to spectators in the terraces, providing a space for interaction between them near the sidelines. Cyrille Regis remembered frequently being labelled a 'black bastard' by opposing fans. He replied, 'I hear it from the terraces a lot, even now, but it's nothing new to me; I've been hearing it from my school days.'[10] Danny Thomas, while playing for Coventry, also recalled an incident that disturbed him: 'The ball went into the crowd and, as one guy went to throw it back, he said "Here you are, nigger!" Then threw it hard at me. I went for him, but fortunately, the linesman stopped me.'[11] Regis's and Thompson's responses typify many of the reactions by black players. Temperance and persistence mark many of their comments, as they looked to reply to abuse within acceptable boundaries determined by sportsmanship and humility. Regis clearly denies the significance of the event, failing to victimize himself through the situation. Their failure to actively resist can be described as a strategy of security. Instead of working to change the behaviour of supporters, both responded with temperance and a humble riposte that avoided criticism.[12] Thompson remembered showing a willingness to proactively confront the spectator in this situation, and described his encounter as though he did not passively accept such abuse. The tension in both responses reveal that black players faced a tight range of moderate reactions that effectively avoided direct confrontation.

Of course, verbal abuse and fan antipathies towards black players often depended on a variety of factors: the social and political environment of British home cities, the perceived relationship the player had with the supporters, their professed loyalties and their allegiance to the club. Black players were accepted and 'belonged' within supporters' and players' circles when they displayed acceptable attitudes outlined by working-class and sporting values articulated in British football. While these values were situationally dependent on the club and city, white football men respected black players who exhibited physical strength, football aptitude, unquestioned allegiance, honesty, effectiveness, masculine respectability and a tempered but passionate and unpretentious demeanour. Black players generated cultural capital within supporters' and players' cultures when they adopted these values and they reflected in their on-field conduct, especially their responses to racial taunting.[13] Thus, many black players presented themselves accordingly in efforts to control their working environment and the presence they conveyed to spectators.

This conditional acceptance of black players not only rested on the enactment of culturally coded values, but also the players' apparent allegiance to the supporters' club. One anonymous fan recalled that regular racial insults existed 'just to get at the other away fans and their black players. If we had one he would be all right.'[14] The response was notable not only for the establishment of a double standard based on club allegiance, but also because the fan supposedly participated in racist abuse to aggravate rivalries between supporters. In this case, black players became the subject of derision not only in efforts to abuse them and perhaps affect their on-field performance, but also as a bit-part in the ongoing chatter, mockery and violence occurring between rival groups of fans in the terraces. Racist abuse, though, went above and beyond poking at visiting players, who challenged home supporters' community allegiances and territorial control of football stadiums. Studies in grounds across England confirmed that black players were more frequently targeted for abuse, both with and without racialized content, in fans' taunts. This abuse often extends to black people, both supporters and bystanders, in communities surrounding stadiums.[15]

Racist abuse was never only a way to deride players from the away squad, no matter their ethnic or cultural background. In these fraught environments racial divisiveness superseded concerns about the proper expression of sporting values and football prowess. Regis related a story on the contradictions of spectator racism: 'At Tottenham, Chris Hughton and I were running for a ball and he's black as well ... I heard somebody in the crowd shout "you black bastard!" I thought I must be mistaken cause he's black too and they're supposed to be his supporters.'[16] In another instance, Chris Kamara, an early black player recalled, 'When I was at Portsmouth I was booed the whole time by a section of our own supporters.'[17] Both examples illustrated how racialized discourse was not always dependent on club allegiance, but often structured around the perceived threat of black players within a homogenous white environment. Rather than being part and parcel of the antipathies of the game, spectators apparently racialized their comments because of broader concerns about black players in British sport.

The distinct recognition of phenotypes of black players, and the racial abuse directed toward them, cannot be assimilated widely into the general derision aimed at disliked or unwelcome players in any environment. The racial signifier attached to racist abuse indicated spectators' eagerness to distinguish and prioritize racial discourse within broader patterns of scorn and contempt. Nick Hornby, whose best-selling, self-reflective memoirs reveal plenty about the phenomena of racism and football violence, relayed a quote-worthy passage: 'When an opposing black player commits a foul, or misses a good chance, or doesn't miss a good chance, or argues with the referee, you sit quivering in a panic of liberal foreboding. "Please don't say anything, anybody"'. Then a fellow fan rises 'and he calls him a cunt, or a wanker, or something else obscene, and you are filled with an absurd sense of metropolitan sophisticate pride, because the adjectival epithet is missing'. Hornby concluded, 'It's not much to be grateful for, really, the fact that a man calls another man a cunt but not a black cunt'.[18] Hornby's memoirs are indeed exceptional for their expressive quality. They illustrated the blurred lines between routine abuse at opposing players and attacks that involved racial and sexual distinctions. Surely, general disparagement could easily take on a racial adjective, and in this case a sexed and gendered value, to further debase the player. But the addition of these specific distinctions cannot be ignored, as Hornby subtly acknowledged. They indicate that fans noticed outward markers of supposed racial difference and were willing to read those differences into systems of meaning where white dominance inside and outside football precluded the acceptance of negatively feminized and sexualized black men. The use of a racial epithet established alterity for blacks within the football world that was already well-established in post-colonial Britain, declaring a seamless, white Britishness for the sport.[19] Such abuse reimagined a frame of reference where black men – immigrant or British-born, player or spectator – were outlined as peripheral, womanly and invasive.[20] Racist fans were not only displeased with black players invading this particular homogenous white arena of popular culture but also drew on racial values created outside of football but reinforced within it.

Two other common forms of abuse, throwing bananas onto the pitch and monkey-grunting, used colonial symbols to recreate racial subordination and recall supposedly animalistic traits of black players. In the early 1980s, Garry Thompson and Danny Thomas, two black players for Coventry, commented that the banana throwing and verbal abuse had become almost mandatory when they visited certain clubs.[21] Grunting and mimicking ape noises usually accompanied the bananas, no matter the venue.[22] After witnessing fellow fans throw bananas at one particular opponent, Hornby explained, 'The bananas were designed to announce, for the benefit of those unversed in codified terrace abuse, that there was a monkey on the pitch ... one can only presume that John Barnes was the monkey to whom they were referring'.[23] As discussed in Chapter 6, these actions placed the emergence of black players like Barnes firmly in a post-colonial frame, positioning them as subordinate, savage and exotic.[24] They were also meant to dehumanize, marking them as inferior to white players and supporters in British football, and separating them as bestial in a supposedly civilized setting. The actions reveal how fans overlapped the sporting world and broader frames of British imperial history and politics.

It must be emphasized that these articulations not only reflected racialized cultural symbols salient in British society, but also revealed spectators' concerns about actual social relations in Britain. Richard Turner, a self-reflective fan steeped in football culture during the 1980s, commented, 'I would argue that British society is a racist society and, although racist chanting at football grounds is particularly blatant and aggressive, the racism present in many fans is a reflection of racist attitudes inherent in the world outside soccer grounds'.[25] Certainly, some argued the mere presence of immigrant players formed the basis of increased racial tensions. Stuart Pane, a postal messenger, replied to a question regarding racial violence in football:

> I dunno how it started. There was just growing violence, you know. Really it all started when the coloureds come over here. I mean to me I don't care about 'em ... A lot of 'em, they're all mouth and they try kung fu and all this. They're bleedin' useless to me, like. But once they started to come over and you started going Paki bashin', nigger bashin' and all this sort of thing, that's what brought the violence up in this country ... But when they started comin' over a lot, people started thinking that the white people was going homeless and poor ... A bloke who's poor has only gotta see a coloured geezer in a big flash car and he thinks ...[26]

In Pane's view, the double threat of the immigrants' presence and their menace to white jobs created concern. Immigrants – Asian, West African or Afro-Caribbean – constitute a singular threatening group to non-immigrant job security. Pane essentialized a wide range of immigrant identities into a singular, monolithic menace, as the success of a 'coloured geezer' also immediately translated into an opportunity for 'white' success stolen by an immigrant. Furthermore, Pane clearly adopted a violent attitude towards blacks, and justified his violence by declaring immigrants aggressive and steeped in martial traditions. In an era of steeply frightening economic decline, immigrant competition for jobs and housing clearly comprised an incentive for racial tensions in football.

The most telling suggestion, however, derived from these spectators' comments on the social context, is that they all volunteered this information in discussions and interviews regarding their attitudes towards supporting football. Not only did football constitute a substantial portion of their perceptions of identity, but they implicated their experiences as spectators with their attitudes towards contemporary political debates. As discussed in Chapter 1, Britain swirled with controversies about post-colonial migration throughout the post-war period, especially after the influx of formerly colonized peoples from the Caribbean and India after 1948. Race riots in Notting Hill in 1958 and Brixton and Toxteth in 1981 exacerbated racial conflict and polarized political approaches to law and order in black communities. In addition, Parliament addressed racial discrimination through the Race Relations Acts of 1965, which was later amended in 1968 and 1976 to eliminate inequities in housing, employment, education and public services for blacks in Britain. The Acts instigated divisive discourses about the racial and cultural constitution of Britain, and caused a backlash of neo-nationalist and nativist political canvassing. Finally, the financial depression of the early 1970s limited the availability of housing and elevated competition for jobs, ensuring that conversations about racial integration and cultural assimilation remained both frequent and volatile. Fans drew on the language and terms of the debates going on around them and responded by linking their own material circumstances to their positions on racism in football. Thus, while immigrants served as a focus for angst regarding employment and 'white' identity, the public discourse outside the sport helped to determine the language in which fans framed and discussed their own lives. A mutually reinforcing environment of tension had been created, and professional football provided an arena for negotiation.

The Pressures of Whiteness

Black players' responses reflected the limits placed on their personal and political articulations as employees of clubs and representatives of the sport, but also how they managed, subverted and reappropriated derogatory abuse in unique ways. Their reactions often reflected their incentive to maintain amenable relationships with clubs and spectators, but also included a wide range of other responses that revealed the pressures of British whiteness in football. Most prominently, players always struggled not only to live within the limits of loyalty and fans' approval, but also wrestled with questions of professionalism and respect. These concerns reflected the normative pressures of whiteness within football cultures, where dominant football authorities prescribed respectable behaviours and closely scrutinized questionable conduct.

Black players' reflections and recollections of the football environment reveal the apparent contradictions between a two-part measure for professional success. First, black players were expected to display courage, assertiveness and strength in their playing style. A frequent and subtly racist complaint about black players was that they lacked 'bottle', or the courage to get 'stuck in' to the British game. Coventry City coach Ron Wily criticized Garry Thompson for not being as aggressive as his non-black teammates. Thompson remembered, 'He used to say to me, "I don't think you're aggressive enough." One day, he called me over and said: "I think you're a coward. All you people are".'[27] Such attitudes remapped undifferentiated physiological and psychological characteristics on black men who did not grow up in the British football system and therefore supposedly had not been assimilated into the more masculine, aggressive British style.[28] Second, supporters and clubs compelled black players to defer to football authorities and the 'best interests' of the sport with temperance and reverence. Because sport reflected the nation, and because it embodied the nation's cherished values, black players were to act respectably, embracing their privileged position in professional football with hard work and little objection to working conditions. Black players risked transgressing the bonds of the relationship between players, supporters and clubs by disregarding the call to sportsmanship, which elevated the club and its success above personal or individual complaints, sufferings or accomplishments. These expectations created a paradox for some players, who sometimes felt that these two sets of masculine values contradicted one another. Many found a mindset of both aggression and deference inconsistent. Several examples reveal the pressures of this contradiction and how black players responded to such demands.

John Colquhoun, who played at Millwall in London and extensively in Scotland, remembered that the pressures of operating within the football environment evoked mixed emotions among both black and white players. 'We were playing [Glasgow] Rangers and Mark Walters was having a great game against us. Then all of a sudden all of these bananas and monkey shouts came on the pitch. It was really shocking', wrote Colquhoun. 'I was disappointed in the [Midlothian] Hearts supporters ... I was also disappointed in my own performance. Not for what I did on the park but because I let this go on. I didn't do anything.' Colquhoun's disappointment in his home supporters, but more importantly himself, illuminated not only the professional expectations which conditioned his response, but also his desire to express personal condemnation of the acts of racism at the match. He continued:

> I felt that, if I was in a small circle of friends and somebody had done something like this or told a racist joke, I would pride myself in confronting the issue. I would say something to make them feel uncomfortable. I had to ask myself why I didn't do anything, just because there was a different set of rules.[29]

Colquhoun's recognition of a public and a private world were central to his response. What he expected of himself within an intimate private setting could not be replicated in the public arena of sport, where his professionalism and livelihood would have been threatened by a more assertive reaction. The football environment was governed by 'a different set of rules', a pervading sense of whiteness characterized by the values of diligence, allegiance and subordination to a majority group of white supporters and club officials. While he was expected to be self-assured and forceful in his playing style, the social and professional expectations of the white governors of his workplace conditioned his personal response to racial abuse.

Colquhoun, speaking later as a representative of the Scottish Football Players' Association, recalled that fans and other players 'make remarks openly to young, black players. And when you challenge them they say "Ask him, he doesn't mind. He doesn't mind being called so and so"'. As evidenced by white players' comments, black players not only came to anticipate abuse but their counterparts expected them to absorb it. The jovial attitudes between players obscured the expectation that black players show deference to the codes of conduct created within football circles by white men. No player, black or otherwise, was to dispute the supposedly humorous racial taunts that hierarchicalized players within the sporting environment. Colquhoun added that supporters and other players levelled taunts at the youngest black players, those under the age of twenty. Taking advantage of rank and status, he asked rhetorically, 'What are they going to do? Confront an older, senior professional and cause trouble against the establishment, as it were? I don't know if I would do that.' Colquhoun's language is important for understanding how intense the pressures of professionalism could be. Allusion to the 'establishment' indicated that he perceived a broad set of burdens and difficulties that went beyond challenging an individual white player. A more aggressive or assertive response to racial abuse by other players or supporters amounted not only to transgressing loyalty and allegiance, but also a political challenge to the authority and sanctity of the football club. Colquhoun noted that before anti-racist politics in football were championed in the mid-1980s 'to be openly political was not the done thing'. Young black players who made such racial abuse into a political issue could expect to be outcast. They 'would be seen to be making trouble if they challenged racism'. Clearly, ignoring or perpetuating racial abuse posed a challenge to black players. Moreover, the way in which white men created a complex and shifting masculine code of conduct imposed the more subtle yoke of whiteness on black players.

Other players imagined responding to racism on the field within the bounds of acceptable respectability, but did so by challenging the social meaning of professionalism. Mark Bright, a player at Crystal Palace in London, commented in a local fanzine:

> I think that if ever one of my teammates says something to an opposing player, if they had a challenge, and he got up and said something [racist], I'd be quick to say to him at half-time, or at the end of the game: 'I heard what you said, I don't like it. You should show a bit more respect for your fellow professionals and the people in your team.'[30]

Bright turned the expectations of professionalism within his club's culture on its head. To Bright, professionalism meant a thoughtful but assertive confrontation with another player where he expressed his displeasure and registered his complaint on the spot. His response challenged the construction of professionalism and respect by white players, reworking these concepts to include proper 'professional' treatment to non-white participants. The comment also revealed that Bright affirmed the status of black players as apposite 'professionals' who helped to constitute the professional environment. Such articulations of black professionalism were rare in the sources consulted here, but since Bright expressed these thoughts in an interview with a fanzine editor, one can assume that he meant them for public consumption, especially for supporters and close members of the football club.

With concerns about professionalism and respectability looming large, black players often used humour as a deflective and undermining device within social conversations about football and racism. Since their success as labourers depended on their relationships with supporters, fellow players and coaches, warding off potentially damaging situations proved critical. Of course, as seen above, humour was often the mechanism by which racist invective was levelled. Chris Kamara recalled, 'It was hard to keep playing in those conditions, but to be honest what hurt most of all was when you'd walk into a room and your own team-mates would go quiet because they'd been telling jokes that would offend you.'[31] In contrast, several black players used humour as a mechanism to avert racialized criticism, which pre-empted more opportunities for harassment. In some cases, humorous anecdotes revealed that black players preferred to be quoted for their wit rather than marked as victims of racial abuse. John Barnes's first practice at Liverpool exemplified this trend. Sitting next to two non-black teammates, 'Cups of tea were put before the two established [white] players. Barnes looked up at the woman who brought them. He said: "What am I, black or something?" Everyone fell about.'[32] The story disclosed several key dynamics of the relationship between black players, their teammates and the media. First, Barnes cleverly avoided making an overtly political statement about his experience of discrimination, but still challenged the circumstances of his abuse. By intimating that his skin colour prevented him from being served, his humour worked in his favour, helping him to avoid a public discussion of racism while still noting that discrimination had occurred. Second, the joke also reinforced his position within the team, acting within masculine behavioural boundaries that rewarded self-deprecation and witty banter. Critically, Barnes played with his own 'blackness', insinuating that it did not exist, if only for the joke, in order to achieve belonging within his environment. Perhaps his peers found it humorous because his rejoinder inscribed him with a temporary, fictive whiteness that granted him acceptance within the immediate circumstances. Third, Barnes volunteered the anecdote in an interview with journalist Dave Hill years later, and in his telling doubled the avoidance of a blatant anti-racist statement, again showing his preference for being known for humour rather than his victimization. In sum, the joke, though deployed as a strategy to avoid volatility, affirmed that Barnes not only understood the expectations of a sporting environment dominated by white-centred codes of conduct, but also could only assimilate through mimicry.[33]

Black players' willingness to undermine static reckonings of race also emerged in comments by Coventry's Garry Thompson, who said of Jamaican-born teammate Danny Thomas, 'I don't know why they call both of us black. Danny's more of a mahogany colour.' Thompson's sarcasm again satisfied the interviewer, sociologist Ellis Cashmore, who recast the premise of the joke in his own terms: 'In their way, they offered another version of two-tone to the city!'[34]

However, Thompson's rejection of an undifferentiated 'black' categorization is important. It not only provided humour for the interview, but also suggested the diversity of skin colour and identities within a supposedly fixed black classification. Like Barnes's quip, undermining the universalization of black players made both jokes amusing and suggested the inherent instability of racial groupings.

While many players were willing to absorb racial abuse or create subtle challenges to what constituted blackness and whiteness, others chose not to conceal their contempt for discrimination and abuse within football. While at Sheffield United in the late 1980s, Bromley-born Tony Agana 'was subjected to derisive "monkey" noises and reacted with "keep you happy" ape-like gestures himself'. Agana reversed the intended effect of the racist act by mimicking the supporters' gesticulations, emphasizing their preposterousness. According to one fanzine writer, Agana's actions had their intended effect: 'Strangely, there was no comeback'.[35] Other black players tried more aggressive tactics. Londoner Richie Moran, in a piece reflecting on his experiences in British football in the 1980s, recalled that while at Birmingham City an opposing manager racially abused him. 'I decided that a discussion about racism was not on the agenda, so I punched him. One can debate the rights and wrongs of my actions, and I do not advocate violence as the solution to the problem, but it certainly felt good at the time'. Moran added that the incident encouraged him to leave football, especially after his own management told him he should learn to tolerate such abuse. Struggling with how to respond, he added:

> All my life I have wanted someone to explain to me the reasoning behind the notion that I should 'rise above' racism ... Yet, surely, facing up to racism is the best way to counter it, rather than doing nothing by subscribing to an ill-defined and vague notion of 'rising above' it.[36]

Moran faced pressure to endure abuse, supposedly to protect the club from unwanted scrutiny and to maintain a hierarchy of black and white players in the sport. Moran's ambivalence about his response disclosed his deep resentment for such an order, but his aggression proved unacceptable within the white codes of conduct established in the football setting. Aggression betrayed the fickle balance between tempered respectability and strong-minded defiance expected of footballers, exemplified by the indistinct and elastic prescription to 'rise above it'.

Aggressive responses to racial abuse also had consequences. After an incident in 1992, Stoke City striker Mark Stein faced legal charges after assaulting Stockport County's Jim Gannon, after Gannon repeatedly called him a 'monkey' and a 'short, ugly black wanker'. The court ordered Stein to pay £500 in fees, a relatively major fine but still a paltry sum for a professional footballer. The judge commented, 'You suffered from extreme provocation and will probably suffer more during your career'.[37] Certainly such responses were not favoured by fans and clubs. Practically, aggression could result in suspensions which denied the club the player and any contribution they might have towards success. Symbolically, aggression transgressed the respectable expectations created for black players' conduct. Constructed almost entirely by white players, club management and owners and media, these inscriptions of whiteness narrowly limited the acceptable range of responses by black players, and excluded them when more open, political or aggressive responses to racial abuse emerged.

One particularly telling example involved one of England's most successful national footballers, Paul Ince. Recalling a confrontation Ince had with another player on the England squad, one particularly perceptive fanzine editor commented, 'There is a perverse kind of logic at work in certain sections of the media which states that when a black person complains about racial abuse, they somehow deserve it because they are whingers and moaners, or have a chip on their shoulder'.[38] That black players had a 'chip on their shoulder' emerged as a common response to black indignation. Former player and sociologist Colin King recognized that throughout the 1980s the notion was 'continually applied to black players by white coaches creating an inherent and ongoing question mark about their ability to succeed'. These judgments imposed inflexible notions of black players who were only allowed to behave in relation to the demands of white coaches and managers. In contrast, white players frequently expressed their anger at a variety of situations, 'which [was] seen as a quality white men demonstrate to succeed'.[39] Therefore, when Ince was called a 'black cunt' by ex-England captain Stuart Pearce and reported the incident, Ince's Manchester United supporters complained that 'it was portrayed in the media as Ince's fault because he is a mouthy, confrontational player'. In short, they objected to the idea that 'black football players should be seen and not heard'.[40] A double standard, subtly communicated in the charge of unprovoked and superfluous aggression, undermined Ince's ability to defend himself from racial abuse. The expectations of players to live within complex and often contradictory codes of behaviour determined by white football authorities limited black players' choices and helped to control any conduct deemed rebellious.

Ince has also made light of being both the first black captain of England's national squad in 1993 and becoming the first black coach in the Premier League at Blackburn in 2008. When Ince claimed the captaincy again for a match in 1997, he said, 'When I was first given the armband, a lot was made of the fact that I was the first black skipper. I'd have preferred it if it had been said I was just the new skipper'.[41] Ince's comment revealed some displeasure at becoming a groundbreaking role model for black athletes in Britain, perhaps because it partially obscured his leadership and playing capabilities. In this case, he specifically denied that his blackness should be considered. bell hooks has commented that such denials of black identity often betray larger systems of domination that actively encourage blacks to internalize negative perceptions of blackness even as they distrust white environments. 'Yet, blacks who imitate whites (adopting their values, speech, habits of being, etc.)', she noted, 'continue to regard whiteness with suspicion, fear, and even hatred'.[42] While many blacks may remain rather silent about their own perceptions of whiteness, they later express their discomfort at operating within white environments and remember 'the representation of whiteness as terrorizing'.[43] She concluded that many black people 'do not know themselves separate from whiteness'.[44] Thus, Ince's carefully couched statement revealed an unwillingness to be a general representative for black communities in a sporting environment dominated by other white men. Even when he became the first black manager fifteen years later, he simply said, 'I definitely can open the door for black managers', and left the Equality and Human Rights Commission to exalt him in the public eye: 'This will elevate him to role model status. For young black men across Britain this is certainly a good thing.'[45]

The normative encumbrances of whiteness were also recognizable to supporters, especially those attentive to the growing call for anti-racist initiatives by the 1980s. An early fanzine devoted to anti-racism at Barnsley printed a fake advertisement for humour, a common genre in fanzine literature. Aimed to spite club management that rarely and reluctantly signed black players, the following message appeared:

> If you're black you're going to look a bit daft walking round with a Barnsley FC shirt on. I mean the club just doesn't sign black players, does it? Therefore the club is pleased to announce its latest product – the Oakwell skin-whitener. Impress your friends as you switch cultures ... After a few weeks see the results.

To accentuate the effect of the 'skin-whitener' identical pictures of a man with black and white skin emblazoned the page. The bottom of the advert was tagged as a 'we're-going-nowhere-cause-we're-so-racist-product'.[46] At first glance, the advert ridiculed the club's homogeneity and chastised club management for ignoring the role black players could play. But the entire advert also assumed that racism marred the club's success, with little regard for the individuality, talent or expression of black players. As declared in the tagline, the opposition and negation of racism was expected to stimulate progress by welcoming black players. The advert also clearly articulated that black players were the ones expected to change, and in this case manipulate their physical bodies, in order to achieve belonging and accomplishment at Barnsley. The product here, the 'skin-whitener', clearly displayed the racial specificity of whiteness in creating an exclusionary culture that could be inscribed on the body. In this case, these particularly astute supporters intimate that Barnsley ignored these players not because they were black, but because they were not white.

Other supporters similarly concerned with the relationship between black players and football clubs imagined the possibility of Asian players participating at the professional level, something which occurred very infrequently before the mid-1990s. Fanzine contributor Abid Rahim asked, 'Alright, so it's not happened yet, but in reality what would the first Asian star be up against? How much of his identity, culture or religion would he need to compromise to fit in?'[47] Rahim noted that not only would the first Asian football celebrity be forced to carry the burden of 'standard bearer' for Indian and Asian communities, but he would also be limited in his political capacity as 'clubs prefer people who fit in'. Rahim noted:

> Football is like most other industries. The 'shop floor' is the changing room and training ground, with banter and behaviour set deep in white working class culture. The use of offensive language and innuendo continues to be central to the way many players, coaches, managers and supporters express themselves.

He added that 'within this environment the challenges any Asian player faces would be immense and the questions asked of him many'. Rahim's emphasis on the normative boundaries of football environments revealed that Asian players might face further barriers to social and political acceptance. Not only were they not white, they were often not British. Alternatively, Rahim thought that this Indian pioneer 'may decide to be "Jack the lad". Made in Britain. Just wants to play football, loves drinking, fast cars, flash labels. If he can make it, why can't other Asians? There's no racism in football, it's just about ability and fitting in.' The sarcasm of Rahim's closing sentence underscores the immense pressures non-white footballers faced in environments where individual expression and politicized behaviour were not allowed.

The experience of supporting football was also marked by the behavioural codes of whiteness. In another anti-racist fanzine, black Mancunian 'Mikey' remembered the burdensome experience of watching football in an exclusionary white enclave.

> Every Saturday I have to make the transition from my black environment to the white one ... I look at the fixture list and brace myself for the abuse if we are playing a team with a 'dirty black bastard' in defence or a 'flash nigger' up front ... I don't want to fight 28,000 people.

This fan not only recognized the extreme frequency of verbal abuse, but how racist invective contributed to the broader production of an exclusionary assembly of supporters. The transition to the football world forced Mikey to recognize the stadium as a chaotic but segregated milieu, where the common environment of whiteness was supported by the constant cruelties of fans against black players. His comments not only bear witness to the small number of non-white supporters at matches, but also to the aggregate of conditions and influences that generated exclusionary supporting cultures. Mikey concluded, 'Football has always been an aggressive, working class, mainly male sport. I accept that. What I can't accept is that it is still a mainly white sport.'[48] Like most fans, Mikey recognized the gendered and class-specific composition of British football, but here challenged the racial exclusions that supported the persistence of whiteness within the sport.

Overall, his comments clearly indicate the burdens black men faced when they attempted to find a niche within the football world and how these men attributed those burdens to a generalized whiteness that shaped their experiences.

The Use and Abuse of Black Players

The challenge that black players and supporters faced required navigating a minefield of potentially explosive situations, especially when they purposefully failed to conform to prescribed behaviours. They received little sympathy or support from clubs, football associations or the government. Though the Home Office was extremely concerned about football violence between fans throughout the 1970s, they were nearly oblivious to the persistent racial abuse that emerged.[49] The toothless Football Offences Act, which outlawed racist chanting and abuse at matches, both came late and failed to result in many convictions, as most stewards and police were unwilling to use its provisions for arrest.[50] Almost all clubs denied the problem, ignoring belated calls from the Football League's Graham Kelly in 1981, to 'nip it in the bud'.[51] David Polkinghorne, Chief Superintendent of New Scotland Yard, dismissed those concerns as 'a little sensitive', describing the terraces as 'a ground for racial harmony, where working class blacks and whites stand side by side. I don't see it as a problem.' Clearly, Polkinghorne had failed to attend any matches. A letter to the *Times* editorial staff, in contrast, charged football authorities with stalling: 'The bodies most directly involved in any confrontation with racial violence on the football terraces, the Football Association and the clubs themselves, have by their very inactivity allowed random hooliganism to assume its current political dimension'. Furthermore, 'they disassociate themselves from the racist elements among their supporters'.[52] Much like black players, football clubs avoided discussing racisms in football in an attempt to prevent politicization of the sport.

But by the late 1980s, a wide range of anti-racist initiatives, both private and public, promised to at least contest the growing frequency of direct racial abuses, albeit failing to challenge more subtle forms of exclusion promoted within white football cultures or recognize the distinct experiences of black players. Fuelled by fans' discontent and growing sympathy for black players, regional organizations like Show Racism the Red Card and Football Unites Racism Divides, along with the Commission for Racial Equality's Kick It Out programme, emerged in the 1980s and early 1990s as explicit racial abuses in public settings escalated. These organizations were preceded and later supported by clubs' and supporters' initiatives as well, whose fanzines and newsletters documented the development of several threads of anti-racist discourse and delineated a wide range of initiatives to prevent overt racial abuse. Most prominently, these organizations committed to publicizing the problem by canvassing in club programmes and matchday activities, initiating development work with clubs and launching several grass-roots educational initiatives. While the national programme, Kick It Out, eventually developed a comprehensive strategy that aimed at building awareness, regional and local agendas concentrated on working with police, partnering with local race equality councils and promoting participation by black and Asian athletes.[53]

Another key strategy advocated by nearly all organizations, and of particular interest to quantifying whiteness in British football, was the use of black players in several different capacities as ambassadors of anti-racist platforms. The use of black players proved highly problematic in several respects, and displayed the ways in which black players' personal expressions were precluded, their personalities limited and their experiences ignored. The most prominent black historical figure has been Arthur Wharton, discovered as the first black footballer in England by writer Phil Vasili. Wharton joined Rotherham Town in 1889, but was only marginally successful as a sportsman.[54] But contemporary anti-racist organizations have lauded his importance as a black athlete, making him a consistent fixture in today's campaigns against racism in football. Anti-racist organizations reifying Wharton's achievements, most prominently in a travelling exhibition supported by the most prominent anti-racist organizations in football, were responding to ongoing racial abuse and racial discrimination within British football by attempting to dignify the earliest black athletes.[55] As Wharton's biographer, Vasili provided the information necessary for the exhibition on the History of Black Footballers in Britain, which became a staple of several anti-racist organizations' community educational efforts for youth. In the exhibit, Wharton was lauded as a supremely talented Sheffield athlete and forgotten contributor to breaking colour boundaries in the late nineteenth century. The anti-racist narrative is familiar: Wharton faced constant discrimination and challenges because of his ethnicity, but managed difficult circumstances through displays of valour and humility.[56] Promoted by Football Unites Racism Divides, the exhibition travelled across Britain and did more than any other anti-racist initiative in football to raise awareness of the history and legacy of black football players. Nonetheless, the reductivism of Wharton's life betrayed some abuses perpetuated by anti-racist discourses.

Most pertinent to the study of whiteness, and the use and abuse of black footballers in anti-racist strategies, is the reconstruction of Wharton's personality and style in Vasili's retelling of the footballer's life. In two different books, Vasili recounted Wharton's life with a liberal journalist's flair.[57] Throughout the accounts, Vasili portrayed Wharton as hyper-physical, combative and even violent. In doing so, Vasili fixed Wharton as a black Briton with typically working-class experiences and characteristics. Vasili described that as a goalkeeper, Wharton typically aimed for opponents' heads when attempting to punch the ball clear, noting that 'goalkeepers could handle the ball anywhere in their own half and could be shoulder-charged with or without the ball. This physicality appealed to Arthur ... His combative nature could also be seen in his off-pitch dealings with the clubs who employed him'.[58] Vasili intimated that alcohol was often involved in Wharton's dust-ups, especially off the field. He also recalled that Wharton never backed off a challenge to fight those who called him a 'nigger'.[59] Whereas the pressures of whiteness in the 1970s often limited aggressive responses to racial abuses and discrimination, Vasili's reconstruction of Wharton's personality firmly established the athlete as reflective of working-class values: hardworking, aggressive, rough, ready to drink and defiantly responsive to others' affronts. Vasili constituted Wharton's life to reflect white working-class attributes, which in itself created a delineated personality and experience for Wharton as a black sportsman. Though not exactly like the pressures of whiteness in the 1970s, Vasili's account of Wharton three decades later still demanded a fixed behavioural code for black expression, based primarily on epitomized British, white working-class, masculine values. Such accounts certainly appealed to rowdy working-class football supporters, who often championed aggression and rebelliousness as aspects of working-class life in urban settings, and therefore made Wharton an acceptable stronghold of football's anti-racist interests.

Vasili also emphasized Wharton's lax sexual license, recounting his adultery at length. The author attributed Wharton's personal misfortune to a wide range of factors, but concluded that 'as influential, however, and possibly more so, was Arthur's inability to keep his dick inside his long johns in the presence of his wife's sister'.[60] Before moving on to recount other black footballers' contributions, Vasili investigated at length the extent of Vasili's relationship with his sister-in-law. The crassness of his tone and the emphasis on Wharton's physical member rather than his own personality betray Vasili's intention of re-creating Wharton as a philanderer, a working-class black man committed to exploring his sexual options. Vasili also used the notion that Wharton might have died of syphilis to ask: 'Further proof that he'd been putting it about as a young man?'[61] Eroticizing Wharton confirmed stereotypical associations of the hypersexualization of supposedly threatening black men. Furthermore, the manner in which Vasili recounted these fiascos was not condemning, but rather somewhat congratulatory of a sexual life well-lived. In Vasili's narrative, he was respected as much for his willingness to challenge racism in British sport as he was for his supposedly typical working-class lifestyle. Whether Wharton actually embodied such characteristics, which can be doubted as he was born into a wealthy Ghanaian family, is of little significance. Vasili played up Wharton's supposedly working-class demeanour, replete with aggressive encounters, sexual freedom and youthful insolence. Wharton's sexual life has little to do with the history of black footballers, but it helped Vasili to package the historical legacy of anti-racism in football as an acceptable centrepiece in working-class football culture.

Outside of Arthur Wharton, several other clubs and organizations lauded the early history of black players, especially those associated directly with their football club or local alliance. In most cases, they attempted to appeal universally to the tragedy of black experiences, though often emphasizing the positive outcomes black players experienced in local communities specific to the clubs. In the opening issue of *Tiocaidh Ar La!: For Celtic and Ireland*, a fanzine meant to support both Celtic FC and the Republic, an article on the history of black players at the Scottish club appeared. Beginning with early footballer Abdul Salim and concluding with contemporary player Paul Elliot, the article traced several lesser-known black influences in Scottish football. The article was meant to raise awareness and serve as a call to action for contemporary anti-racist efforts at the club. 'Next time a black player plays at Parkhead, whether for Celtic or our opponents, let us hear none of the silly noises and racist chants', the editors warned. 'Let's keep the Little Hitler's and the Alf Garnet's off our terraces. Our history and traditions are bigger and more important than the few mugs who want to indulge in that.'[62] Here black players were noted for their football accomplishments and lauded for their associations with the club. Both tests of worth ignored the individuality of the players and precluded their own political expressions. Within an attempt to universalize the plight of black players, the subjects were noted for their contributions as players, not as black men. No spaces existed for the players to speak for themselves. They were used by well-meaning anti-racist supporters to promote a growing legacy of black participation that primarily promoted the tradition and heritage of the club's democratic values.

Black players were also used as role models, a common derivative in several sporting contexts. Role models typically are lauded for their behaviour both within and outside of their sport, and often come to represent the national, ethnic and gendered values of dominant groups of supporters. They are in turn promoted as paragons of sporting culture, worthy to be emulated by younger generations. The Reading Council for Racial Equality, which created the Partnership to Keep Racism Out of Football, noted that 'there is encouraging evidence to suggest that young black fans see black players as positive role models, and tend to follow the players rather than the clubs'. As a key recommendation to football authorities, they added that 'the position of black players as role models for youths of all ethnic backgrounds creates a responsibility on players for actively supporting the anti-racism message'.[63] The CRE's national Kick It Out campaign explicitly recognized adopting such tactics with successful black players such as John Fashanu, Paul Elliot, Erik Thorsvedt and others from the early 1990s on.[64] Early distributions of the campaign's nine point action plan and media posters were emblazoned with player sponsors. On a national level, the Labour Party's Football Task Force's report on football racism also recommended advocating role models for Britain's youth, blacks and others alike. 'Young footballers need positive role models in all areas of the game', noted the report. 'Professional players are of course the most influential role models for young players. It is a fact as old as the game itself that children imitate what they see on the pitch – good or bad.'[65]

Of course, rendering black players as role models proved problematic for several reasons, obscuring contradictions within anti-racist ideas. First, many players, regardless of ethnic background, resisted adopting idealized personas, as it limited their lifestyles and senses of personal expression.[66] Second, acting as a role model in British football delimited behavioural choices, and often minimized opportunities for forthright political and vocal challenges to racism. In essence, categorizing black footballers as role models controlled their behaviours, limited unwanted outbursts and sanitized their conduct on and off the field. As exemplified above, living within the boundaries of whiteness without transgressing complicated and sometimes contradictory codes of behaviour proved difficult, especially when black players' conduct was expected to be apolitical. Third, black players were subtly encouraged to adopt national sporting values, which often reflected the white working-class constituencies of local clubs, in order to maintain their positions as role models and club representatives. Doing so not only subjected these role models to the pressures of living within white environments, but also encouraged successive generations of young black men to duplicate the sanitized performances of their black heroes. Role models presented young blacks with an athletic protagonist, but one who was forced to avoid radicalism and politicized challenges to the status quo. Fourth, employing black players to proactively demonstrate positive behaviour often neglected challenges to the negative abuse and discrimination in a case-by-case manner. Utilizing black players as role models served a public purpose, promoting an educational message of inclusion and respect. However, in choosing this tactic, the Commission for Racial Equality and others failed to recognize the abuses the players themselves were often subject to on a weekly basis. Black players' actual experiences of racism became marginalized while projecting a positive campaign for racial harmony.

In addition, when placed in positions of representation, role models are often subject to intense scrutiny. Mike Marqusee discussed how black athletes are actually afforded little space for the articulation of their own values and identities. Marqusee noted that role model status was 'that incubus on the back of so many sporting champions ... born out of a need to tame the democracy of sport', which often produces unwanted behaviours and characters.[67] Its origins lie with Victorian moralizers and amateur ideologies that championed gentility as much as performance. Marqusee astutely argued, however, that very few black athletes can achieve success as representatives for black communities within the framework of professional sports. 'By the very fact of becoming a high-profile (and well-rewarded) "symbolic representative" of an oppressed and excluded group, an individual is likely to share less and less in common with that group. And, in a further irony, the more black sports stars remind people of the oppressive realities of black life, the less they are accepted as role models for it.'[68] Once black athletes donned the cap of 'representative', they occupy a stifling, liminal space between the black communities from which they emerged and the sporting environments in which they operated.

A final strategy advocated by anti-racist initiatives was the biracial football couplet – an image of a black and white player arm in arm – which constituted the most explicit symbol of racial harmony in anti-racist campaigns. In 1993, when *Kick It Out* debuted its national anti-racist fanzine as a tool for mass publicity, two couplets graced its pages.[69] First, an insert poster showed two newly installed characters from *Roy of the Rovers*, Britain's most famous football comic. On the left was Rocky Race, son of the longstanding main character Roy Race, who had won numerous accolades in the pages of the comic since 1954. The fictive Rocky served as the epitome of the English sporting spirit, the inheritor of his father's football tradition: handsome, physically aggressive, conscientious, agreeable and loyal to his club, the imaginary Melchester Rovers. On the right was Rocky's sidekick, Paul 'Delroy' Ntende, a British-born striker of Nigerian descent. In the poster image, the two players are arm-in-arm, covered in sweat and grime, as if celebrating a goal. They are united with their fists in the air, under the caption, 'Delroy and Rocky Say: Let's Kick Racism Out of Football'. Both characters would be easily recognizable to nearly all football fans, and their union certainly conveyed a simple message of a black and white player working together for benefit of themselves, their fictitious squad and British football. But despite their idealistic pose, the projection of racial harmony proved thin when contextualized within the comic's broader cultural messages. Added as a regular in 1993, Ntende's character exemplified several stereotypes of black immigrants. Ntende was often referred to as 'Ragamuffin of the Rovers', as he appears in his first cover of the comic (See Figure 8.1). While praised for his on-field prowess, he created problems off the pitch and frequently appeared dishevelled. He lived in Brixton and recorded reggae music in the off-season. Writer and creator Stuart Green told the press that Ntende's inclusion marked a shift in the cultural meaning of the comic: 'The old Roy of the Rovers was born in the 1950s when Britain still had an empire and all the heroes were blond, blue-eyed and square-jawed. Roy Race had nothing in common with modern teenagers'. The addition of a black player offered a new direction in a post-colonial world: 'Delroy is more realistic. He is not comfortable with being a role model and likes nothing better than getting drunk and chasing women.' Green added that the inspiration for Ntende was a series of contemporary black players.[70] As a fictive representation of black footballers, Ntende compared unfavourably to both the classically handsome and chimerical Roy and to the daring and aggressive Rocky. The contrast between them emphasized Ntende's secondary status and accentuated his more 'realistic' sexual exploits and debauched personality. Green fixed Ntende's alterity, as he was evaluated against the established standard of ideal behaviour promoted by his white counterpart. Though the three characters got along, the wide gap between their personalities not only reflected the gap between late imperial Britain and a post-colonial, multicultural era, but also the divide between universalized and hierarchicalized racial groups epitomized by Roy and Rocky Race and Paul Ntende. In sum, the comic's cultural messages about black footballers and immigrants generally undermined the archetypal symbolism of harmonious racial interaction and projected equality envisaged by the poster insert.

Figure 8.1: Paul 'Delroy' Ntende on cover of Roy of the *Rovers Monthly*, 2 (October 1993) © Egmont UK, Ltd.

Figure 8.2: Photograph of Pelé and Bobby Moore, 7 June 1970 © Trinity Mirror Group.

A second image of a biracial couplet published in the national fanzine also reproduced racial divisions rather than mitigating them. The first picture in the programme's debut publication showed a post-match embrace between Bobby Moore, England's 1966 World Cup hero, and Pelé, Brazil's most famous footballer (See Figure 8.2). The photo, taken after a 1970 World Cup match, showed the two men smiling and looking one another in the eye. The caption under the photograph read, 'The picture that says it all – Pelé and Bobby Moore exchanging shirts'.[71] The intended message was clear: mutual respect leads to racial harmony. The image also drew on the historical legacy of two powerful football personalities, attempting to convey that racial harmony in football was timeless. However, the nationalistic overtones of the image destabilize the implication of peaceful coexistence. Moore, as a successful white footballer, represented England, while the image affirmed Pelé as an exoticized outsider. Pelé was projected as a likeable counterpart to Moore only because he is Brazilian, an outsider and visitor, and therefore not required to assimilate to the demands of British football. The image did not create a situation where the white homogeneity of British football was challenged by a successful black player. In fact, the first black player to make the English national squad was Viv Anderson, who did not debut for the national side until 1978. As evidenced in the above section, players in the 1970s experienced consistent abuse and discrimination. Again, while communicating supposedly straightforward anti-racist ideas, images of biracial couplets fixed racial difference and connoted the substandard performance and incongruity of black and white footballers. Both images also detached the anti-racist agenda from the central problems of abuse and discrimination, instead promoting an overly idealistic symbolism of racial harmony through black assimilation.

Lastly, anti-racist initiatives also created huge expectations for successful black footballers, responsibilities which many did not seek out. Everton, a Merseyside club renowned for its reluctance to field black players, signed its first black player in the modern era in 1994. Even before adding Nigerian Daniel Amokachi, supporters engaged in an intense debate in the local anti-racist fanzine, *When Skies Are Grey* (WSAG) on the consequences of an imminent addition. After noting the incessant racist chants by both fascist and non-fascist elements in home crowds, one fan suggested, 'how about WSAG issuing a petition in the next issue, which people can sign and send to support any decent black player if/when Everton try to sign one'.[72] Although the editors ignored the suggestion, clearly supporters hoped that signing a black player would directly or indirectly challenge the amount of racial abuse at home matches, therefore helping anti-racists in their ongoing battle against racism at the club. When Amokachi signed, expectations for his impact on the social and cultural battles waged among supporters were high. Immediately the editor of WSAG claimed that 'hopefully this signing will be one of the final nails in the coffin of racism at our club', especially since Amokachi succeeded at the club without delay.[73] Black players faced the daunting task not only of succeeding within abusive working conditions, but also bearing large symbolic burdens. Amokachi's move to Everton signalled to other clubs, and to their own anti-racist supporters, that Everton indeed welcomed black players, helping to break their reputation as a discriminatory institution.

Other fanzines across Britain echoed the sentiment that black players were the most effective at communicating anti-racist messages to large groups of supporters at local clubs. Torquay United's anti-racist alternative fanzine, *You Wot!*, published an article called 'Black Stars Give Racism the Boot', in which the editors argued that

> any United supporters that still feel black players shouldn't be allowed to play a part in our game should look at Darren Moore, Gregory Goodridge and Chima Okorie. *You Wot!* could print 2 million words of antiracism, but all the while these lads are doing the business we've no need to.[74]

Yet some anti-fascist associations, often deemed as overly radical and insincere in their loyalties to football anti-racism, protested black players' involvement in combating racism on the terraces. 'The fact that major names like Ian Wright, Vinnie Jones and Howard Wilkinson are prepared to speak out ... is a good thing, but, at the end of the day, the only people well-placed to challenge the racists are football fans themselves', wrote an Anti-Fascist Action member in a special issue of *Fighting Talk* devoted to fascism and football.[75] Preferring direct, aggressive action, anti-fascist supporters of football anti-racism preferred to police and control their own subcultural environments. From their perspective, black players could do little to change the conflicts within segments of the white working-class population and were therefore relieved of the duty of breaking racial barriers.[76]

Regardless of their involvement, black players both willingly and unwillingly adopted symbolic and strategic positions within anti-racist movements in football. Attempts to make black players emblematic of broader social and cultural contests for the racial landscape of post-colonial Britain proved thin, and often cast oversimplified messages that reinforced rather than mitigated racial difference. The pressures of whiteness, from codes of acceptability in work environments to behavioural expectations from clubs, players and supporters, created unnecessary burdens that hampered personal livelihoods and limited forthright political expressions by black players.

Conclusions

The success of black footballers threatened the white homogeneity of the football world and was met with racial abuse that attempted to locate them as representatives of essentialized racial groups in broader frameworks of negotiation about immigration, job competition and struggles for employment. Black players' responses to discrimination and abuse in football settings not only revealed their ability to manoeuvre within harsh circumstances and adopt a variety of social positions but also often subtly challenged the expectations of whiteness. In a strategy Stuart Hall termed the 'subaltern proliferation of difference', black players constantly fashioned new spaces for themselves within limited behavioural boundaries. Though often deferent to authority, black players created new possibilities merely by differing from the homogeneous white makeup of their environments.[77] However, white football men recoded exclusion as tolerance to black involvement, inasmuch as it conformed to acceptable apolitical and non-disruptive conduct, in efforts to avoid the charge of overt racism. Such practices often led blacks to self-correction, voluntary assimilation and the further marginalization of their free expression and interests.[78] These pressures were often exacerbated by anti-racist movements, which created role models out of black footballers and increased their responsibilities, with or without their consent. Such politicking appealed to many whites looking to solve racial discord, but further limited self-determination for black players and other black youths who emulated them.[79]

In the future, anti-racist strategies could not only focus on discrimination and racism, which should necessarily be quantified and opposed, but also allow black footballers spaces to project their own voices, create their own political messages and cast their own identities that challenge authoritative white hegemonic constructs. In doing so, they might pay closer attention to the actual experiences of racism as well, acknowledging the burdens black outsiders face in environments not of their own making. In addition to deconstructing and objecting to racial antagonisms, neo-fascist or otherwise, anti-racist strategies need to account for the broader impositions of whiteness that surround and enable racist discourses and activities. Accomplishing these objectives would help to break the constitution of uniform black identities, allowing for the expression of multiple cultural spaces occupied by various black political viewpoints. Breaking the expectations of whiteness marked by propriety, silent deference, a skewed sense of professionalism and loyalty to white working-class constituencies of supporters might empower black players to determine their own place in post-colonial popular culture.

CONCLUSION: LEGACIES OF VIOLENCE IN BRITISH FOOTBALL

Though I originally began this project seeking to better understand the social relationships which produced social outcasts in 1960s and 1970s Britain, the archival material revealed that a fundamental set of relationships lay outside interaction between groups of football supporters. The relationships between the state and working-class spectators conditioned the entire environment of football and its disorderly scourges of violence and racism. I realized that the history of football disorder demanded a comprehensive analysis of the state's violence against its own citizens in the social space of the football ground. The scholarly literature on the topic delved deep into questions of identity formation and the uses of feigned and actual aggression, but only rarely discussed the complex and contradictory governmental theatre of operations. While many speculated on the multiple motivations for individual and collective violence in football, the political uses of the 'football question' and how government agencies responded to this aspect of social disruption remained ignored. This evidence revealed that the state unequivocally encouraged the construction of violent, confrontational and aggressive environments through long and haphazard bureaucratic processes. Analysing the entire web of social relationships defied any Manichaean polarity between supporters and the state, and exposed how sport in post-war Britain represented broader conflicts about working-class instability, polarized dialogues about race and nation and the imposition of social order through various mechanisms of authority.

Examining this particular social arena also exposed how several groups of social actors politicized British sport and infused football with cultural significance. While many associate the re-emergence of law-and-order government with Thatcherism in the 1980s, the evidence here revealed that earlier Labour and Conservative administrations adopted the discursive power of law-and-order to attempt to institute discipline for young working-class men and generate political capital for themselves. Tories and Labour could agree that football disorder and those committing offenses should be purged from the sport to protect the profitability of the industry and the image of the nation. Government agencies under both parties attempted to achieve this through architectural, institutional and legal measures. The evidence revealed that despite promises for social provision and the reconstruction of working-class life in post-war Britain, Labour ministers in particular chose instead to institute law-and-order initiatives against football supporters who failed to exhibit proper forms of leisure consumption. Denis Howell and other Labour leaders displaced anxieties about their inability to redress material inequalities to the cultural realm. The language of failed morality among young working-class men, the future of Britain and the Labour Party, figured heavily in discourses about football and provided continuities with later Thatcherite agendas.

The salience of race in football also revealed problems with integration in post-colonial Britain. Football, like other sites of race dialogue in post-war Britain – immigration and citizenship conflicts, the Salman Rushdie affair and urban riots – encouraged discourses about the viability of integration and multicultural societies. Successful black players came to represent broader social fissures outside the sport: competition for jobs and housing, racial violence and immigration debates. Both neo-fascists and anti-racists attempted to utilize football to convey political messages about these issues to a broader audience. In many ways, both groups succeeded. Neo-fascists demonstrated and recruited at football matches in the 1970s, and again in the early 1990s, infusing sport with political purpose. They also effectively created their own publicity through football activities and exploited existing social networks among supporters to find new recruits. Anti-racists, on the other hand, developed initiatives which reduced the incidence of overt racial abuse, but obscured the persistence of racism and neglected other forms of social exclusion.

Together, these political factions developed a venue for the discussion of race in post-colonial Britain that became popularized and accessible to many citizens. In doing so, they narrowed social divisions about race to functions of class. Football provided a forum for discussions of race, immigration and racism which could alienate some working-class men, but provided others opportunities for political mobilization. Discussions of race and racism in football invited working-class men to debate topics which affected their livelihoods through the venue of sport, using black players as proxies for black and migrant labourers in post-war Britain. Cultural and social dialogues about race in football transcended the boundaries of the sport and blurred the lines between sport as microcosm and society as macrocosm, becoming productive of race debates as much as they reflected them. These discourses proceeded because they were limited to a finite social space, without posing challenges to unequal social distribution and problems with racial integration in British society.

Of course, the creation of two opposite and antithetical terms – racist and anti-racist – did not solely emerge in sporting environments. But the public and popular messages about racism and anti-racism in football have helped to create the myth of two distinctly discrete categories. These categories were determined by specific acts and codes of behaviour, which purportedly reflected one's ideological and perhaps political position. Football has provided a platform for the creation of racist and anti-racist identities in Britain, even as it sets the parameters and connotations for each role. The creation of these positions has been a crucial by-product of the contest over black footballers and presence of racism within the game. Both terms have been oversimplified and reflected the reductive usage of race language within the game. Contemporary analysts and football activists justifiably feared that definitions of the 'racist' role encapsulated too narrow a collection of behaviours, focusing primarily on fascist 'folk devils' and ignoring the more complex racial antipathies generated by local football conflicts.[1] Outside of becoming a member of neo-fascist political factions, football supporters and clubs perpetuated a sporting ethos where less overt racisms could be ignored. For instance, contemporary racisms within the game often concentrate on the influence of foreigners on the British style. Since some of these foreign players are not black, anti-foreign protests, such as the proposed rule to limit the number of foreign players on British league teams, are not recognized as racial in content.[2] The 'anti-racist' role also proved minimal: a supporter wore an anti-racist T-shirt or sticker and refrained from racial chanting or abuse. Both roles deny understandings of the broader social conflicts reflected within race dialogues in sport, and fail to recognize the post-colonial significance of debates about race in football. Cultural and economic limitations on foreign players, and the treatment they receive from the press, players, coaches and the public might prove fruitful in understanding other racial antipathies and how they reflect anxieties about migration in Europe. Anti-racists also polarized the spectating population, where many supporters failed to comprehend or knowingly participate in either role. Further, black players – their voices and their experiences – have been removed from the racist/anti-racist battle. They became merely referents each role used to further its goals. As such, their silence and general lack of political involvement reflected their unwillingness to politicize sport and the more immediate demands of surviving within institutional football culture.[3] The creation of racist and anti-racist white roles in football reflected the divergence of political attitudes, but also contributed to the obfuscation of racial and gendered exclusions within football and British society.

Recently, football anti-racist organizations have responded to calls for expanded social programmes with proficiency. The inclusion of Asians became a primary form of challenging the black/white dichotomy among players and developed into a primary initiative within anti-racist organizations like Football

Unites, Racism Divides (FURD) in Sheffield and Kick It Out (KIO), the national programme now supported by the Professional Footballers Association (PFA), the FA Premier League, the Football Foundation and The Football Association.[4] This initiative has been somewhat successful in challenging Asian exclusion on the grass-roots level, though astute arguments against privileging Asians note that doing so categorizes individuals according to race and nationality, thus perpetuating the myth of universal difference.[5] More successful initiatives approach building new social relationships between young children of different cultural, ethnic and religious backgrounds. Responding to new challenges in the twenty-first century, football anti-racist organizations have refined their programmes. FURD does an excellent job of caring for children within their community and infusing sports programmes with more expansive anti-racist education, which seeks not only to limit racism in sport, but also to provide pathways for cultural interaction and appreciation. KIO coordinates national and local programmes and responds to all accusations of racism within the game. Both organizations have formed international reputations, allying with organizations in continental countries to build Europe-wide alliances that promote awareness and exercise oversight of educational programmes. These organizations, however, maintain their focus on behavioural forms of racism, only occasionally exhibiting broader considerations of the problems and challenges of post-colonial life and multiculturalism in Britain, much less broadening structural and institutional inequalities. This, in part, can be explained by their desire to remain politically neutral and continue to promote sport as an avenue for socialization.

Football environments, on the other hand, have changed very little since the imposition of CCTV and all-seated stadiums in the late 1980s. Several sports analysts have argued that these two innovations, which work together to promote easier regimentation of football supporters, also increase commercial benefits. Under the threat of continued surveillance and separated from one another, supporters now watch football in highly individualized and policed settings. These new environments have changed the ways in which working-class people experience football spectating. First, with the increase in ticket prices and bond schemes that accompanied all-seated stadiums, many lifelong supporters could no longer afford to go to as many matches as they did in the 1970s and 1980s. In general, throughout the 1990s, football became a sport consumed more often by middle-class men and women who could afford the higher ticket costs.[6] Second, they continue to promote strict regulations and discipline in spectating. Seats limit fans' mobility to a designated space, whether they sit or not, and encourage them to avoid physical contact with other spectators. They also direct attention forward. As many supporters have noticed, the experience of spectating has become much more individual and restrained. After a match in 2007 at Old Trafford in Manchester, United manager Alex Ferguson criticized the team's supporters for failing to create 'atmosphere' at the home stadium. Colin Hendrie, Independent Manchester United Supporters Association spokesman, took offense: 'It's almost like a police state in a football ground now and if you do stand up, people will take your arm, put it behind the back of your neck and throw you out of the ground. Under those circumstances, what atmosphere does he want?'[7] Supporters recognize that contemporary football consumption occurs in disciplined environments under surveillance and the threat of personal prosecution.

Nonetheless, politicians and media commentators look to the British experience with football violence, and in particular the state's supposedly 'successful' management of the phenomenon, when considering how to institute security elsewhere. The increasing incidence of football violence throughout Europe and the world has not only piqued the interest of researchers but also induced many to seek British expertise in stamping out unwanted violence.[8] After a 2010 World Cup qualifying match between Serbia and Italy had to be abandoned because of extreme violence in the stadium, FIFA president Sepp Blatter praised England for giving the world 'an important legacy' of organization, discipline and respect among fans: 'You have given to the world security in the stadiums. You have built all your stadia, there are no fences and everyone is sitting.' He added that 'if only all the national associations in the world, and their leagues had stadiums like this, we would have more fair play in our game'.[9] Both the persistence of football violence in Britain and the violent and divisive imposition of this much-esteemed order have been ignored in these demands to follow the British example in sanitizing football.

All of these contemporary experiences are informed by the legacies of state intervention into British professional football. Violence and racism have been challenged as moral evils, but continue to be structured by the consumption and regulation of the sport. In the future, the ability to utilize sport's popularity to disseminate effective anti-racist and non-violent messages will depend on supporters' willingness to imagine richer and more contextualized understandings and remedies for exclusionary social relationships outside the sport. Effective anti-racist politics must balance both short- and long-term approaches to avoid oversimplification and aggression, considering research into the cultural, social and material origins of racial and gendered exclusions, as well as outbreaks of social violence. In addition, politicians and historians must recognize the allure of sports and how citizens participate in sports consumption to exercise political choices and generate discussions of nationhood and belonging, in addition to creating communal and personal identities. Interrogating the imagined division between sports and society will lead to better understandings of how social exclusion and social violence come to occur in local settings, as well as their origins in broader social fissures and historical, post-colonial relationships.

NOTES

Introduction

1. For examples of recent scholarship see P. McDevitt, *'May the Best Man Win': Sport, Masculinity and Nationalism in Great Britain and the Empire, 1880–1935* (London: Palgrave, 2004): N. Garnham, 'Patronage, Politics and Modernization of Leisure in Northern England: The Case of Alnwick's Shrove Tuesday Football Match', *English Historical Review*, 117:474 (2002), pp. 1228–46; J. A. Mangan (ed.), *Making European Masculinities: Sport, Europe, Gender* (London: Frank Cass, 2000) and J. Hargreaves, *Sport, Power and Culture: A Social and Historical Analysis of Popular Sports in Britain* (Cambridge: Polity Press, 1986).

2. C. Elkins, *Imperial Reckoning: The Untold Story of Britain's Gulag in Kenya* (New York: Henry Holt, 2005).

3. S. Cohen, *Folk Devils and Moral Panics: The Creation of the Mods and the Rockers* (London: MacGibbon and Lee, 1972); S. Hall, C. Critcher, T. Jefferson, J. Clarke and B. Roberts, *Policing the Crisis: Mugging, the State, and Law and Order* (London: MacMillan, 1978); B. Bowling, 'The Emergence of Violent Racism as a Public Issue in Britain, 1945–81', in P. Panayi (ed.), *Racial Violence in Britain in the Nineteenth and Twentieth Centuries* (Leicester: Leicester University Press, 1993); R. Witte, *Racist Violence and the State* (New York: Longman, 1996).

4. See the thorough review of academic literature in A. Tsoukala, *Football Hooliganism in Europe: Security and Civil Liberties in the Balance* (London: Palgrave, 2009).

5. The body of literature by sociologists and anthropologists is expansive, and only the work on issues related to this project can be reviewed in this introduction. For a more complete review of the literature, see S. Frosdick and P. Marsh, *Football Hooliganism* (Cullompton: Willan, 2005).

6. J. Williams, E. Dunning and P. Murphy, *Hooligans Abroad: The Behaviour and Control of English Fans in Continental Europe* (London: Routledge, 1984); E. Dunning, P. Murphy and J. Williams, *The Roots of Football Hooliganism: An Historical and Sociological Study* (London: Routledge, 1988); P. Murphy, J. Williams and E. Dunning, *Football on Trial: Spectator Violence and Development in the Football World* (London: Routledge, 1990).

7. See the collected essays in E. Dunning and N. Elias, *Quest for Excitement: Sport and Leisure in the Civilizing Process* (Oxford: Blackwell, 1986).

8. J. H. Kerr, *Understanding Football Hooliganism* (Buckingham: Open University Press, 1994).

9. For the earliest anthropological work on football violence see P. Marsh, *Aggro: The Illusion of Violence* (London: Dent, 1978).

10. See G. Armstrong and R. Harris, 'Football Hooligans: Theory and Evidence', *Sociological Review*, 39:3 (1991), pp. 427–58; G. Armstrong, *Football Hooligans: Knowing the Score* (Oxford: Berg, 1998); R. Giulianotti, *Football: A Sociology of the Global Game* (Cambridge: Polity Press, 1999).

11. Tsoukala, *Football Hooliganism in Europe*; M. Taylor, *The Association Game: A History of British Football* (London: Longman, 2007), pp. 310–17.

12. Taylor, *The Association Game*, p. 318.

13. Tsoukala made a striking case for studying the history of regulation and state involvement in response to football violence. See *Football Hooliganism in Europe*, Introduction.

14. S. Greenfield and G. Osborn, 'When the Writ Hits the Fan: Panic Law and Football Fandom', in A. Brown (ed.), *Fanatics: Power, Identity and Fandom in Football* (London: Routledge, 1998); J. M. Lewis and A. Scarisbrick-Hauser, 'An Analysis of Football Crowd Safety Reports Using the McPhail Categories', in R. Giulianotti, N. Bonney and M. Hepworth (eds), *Football, Violence and Social Identity* (London: Routledge, 1994), pp. 153–68.

15. I. Taylor, 'Soccer Consciousness and Soccer Hooliganism', in S. Cohen (ed.), *Images of Deviance* (Harmondsworth: Penguin, 1971), pp. 134–64.

16. I. Taylor, 'On the Sports Violence Question: Soccer Hooliganism Revisited'. in J. Hargreaves (ed.), *Sport, Culture and Ideology* (London: Routledge, 1982), pp. 152–97.

17. See J. Clarke, 'Football and Working Class Fans: Tradition and Change', in R. Ingham (ed.), *Football Hooliganism: The Wider Context* (London: Inter-Action Imprint, 1978), pp. 37–60; S. Hall and T. Jefferson (eds), *Resistance Through Rituals: Youth Subcultures in Post-War Britain* (London: Hutchinson, 1976).

18. A. Portelli, 'The Rich and the Poor in the Culture of Football', in S. Redhead, *The Passion and the Fashion: Football Fandom in the New Europe* (Aldershot: Avebury, 1993).

19. For a review of the literature on class composition, see Frosdick and Marsh, *Football Hooliganism*, pp. 84–5.

20. E. Trivizas, 'Disturbances Associated with Football Matches', *British Journal of Criminology*, 21 (1980), pp. 276–88.

21. Dunning et al., *The Roots of Football Hooliganism*, pp. 186–9.

22. See the arguments on class in many articles in the special issue on hooliganism in *Sociological Review*, 39:3 (1991).

23. In many ways, this work responds to Steve Redhead's call for renewed studies of the historical background to football violence, rather than a narrow focus on the immediate and local policy concerns. See S. Redhead, 'Some Reflections on Discourses on Football Hooliganism', *Sociological Review*, 39:3 (1991), pp. 479–86. It also furthers the project of understanding the intersections of politics and sport history. See J. Hill, '"What Shall We Do with Them When They're Not Working?": Leisure and British Historiography', in B. Bebber (ed.), *Leisure and Cultural Conflict in Twentieth-Century Britain* (Manchester University Press, 2012).

24. I borrow the language to discuss this conceptual conundrum from Eric Weitz, who explained the reflexive and productive nature of political debates over gender in European communism. See E. D. Weitz, 'The Heroic Man and the Ever-Changing Woman: Gender and Politics in European Communism, 1917–1950', in L. L. Frader and S. O. Rose (eds), *Gender and Class in Modern Europe* (Ithaca, NY: Cornell University Press, 1996), pp. 311–52.

25. On the social function of government inquiries into football, see Taylor, 'Soccer Consciousness and Soccer Hooliganism', p. 161. David Canter and his research group have

also discussed the problems with 'legislation by crisis' in their book *Football in Its Place* (London: Routledge, 1989).

26. D. Elliot and D. Smith, 'Football Stadia Disasters in the United Kingdom: Learning from Tragedy?', *Organization and Environment*, 7:3 (1993), pp. 205–29; I. Taylor, 'English Football in the 1990s: Taking Hillsborough Seriously?' in J. Williams and S. Wagg (eds), *British Football and Social Change: Getting Into Europe* (Leicester: Leicester University Press, 1991), pp. 3–24.

27. The body of literature on post-1945 racism(s) in Britain is substantial and growing. For an entrée into the wide range of themes, theoretical debates, and empirical studies during this period see J. Solomos, *Race and Racism in Britain*, 3rd edn (New York: Routledge, 2003); L. Back and J. Solomos (eds), *Theories of Race and Racism: A Reader* (London: Routledge, 2000); M. Bulmer and J. Solomos (eds), *Ethnic and Racial Studies Today* (London: Routledge, 1999); H. Goulbourne, *Race Relations in Britain Since 1945* (London: Palgrave Macmillan, 1998); M. Bulmer and J. Solomos (eds), *Racism* (Oxford: Oxford University Press, 1999); J. Solomos and L. Back, *Racism and Society* (London: Palgrave Macmillan, 1996); R. Skellington, *'Race' in Britain Today*, 2nd edn (London: Sage Publications, 1996).

28. For example, see M. Banton, *Race Relations* (London: Tavistock, 1967); S. Patterson, *Dark Strangers* (Harmondsworth: Penguin, 1968); E. J. B. Rose and N. Deakin (eds), *Colour and Citizenship* (London: Institute for Race Relations, 1969); N. Deakin, *Colour, Citizenship and British Society* (London: Panther, 1970). For a comprehensive yet measured critique of the development of 'race relations science' see C. Waters, '"Dark Strangers" in Our Midst: Discourses of Race and Nation in Britain, 1947–1963', *Journal of British Studies*, 36:2 (April 1997), pp. 207–38.

29. See L. Tabili, 'A Homogenous Society?: Britain's Internal "Others", 1800–Present', in C. Hall and S. Rose (eds), *At Home with the Empire: Metropolitan Culture and the Imperial World* (Cambridge: Cambridge University Press, 2006), pp. 53–76. See also J. Rex, *Race, Colonialism and the City* (London: Routledge, 1973); R. Miles and A. Phizacklea (eds), *Racism and Political Action in Britain* (London: Routledge, 1979); A. Sivanandan, *A Different Hunger: Writings on Black Resistance* (London: Pluto, 1982).

30. The most salient debate in sociological circles has been that between John Rex, a self-proclaimed 'radical Weberian', and Robert Miles. See J. Rex, *Race Relations in Sociological Theory*, 2nd edn (London: Routledge, 1983); R. Miles, *Racism and Migrant Labour* (London: Routledge, 1982); R. Miles, *Racism* (London: Routledge, 1989).

31. CCCS, *The Empire Strikes Back: Race and Racism in 70s Britain* (London: Hutchinson, 1982); P. Gilroy, *'There Ain't No Black in the Union Jack': The Cultural Politics of Race and Nation* (London: Hutchinson, 1987); J. Solomos, *Black Youth, Racism and the State* (Cambridge: Cambridge University Press, 1988); S. Hall, 'Ethnicity: Identity and Difference', *Radical America*, 24 (1990) pp. 9–20, ; D. Morley and K. Chen (eds), *Stuart Hall: Critical Dialogues in Cultural Studies* (London: Routledge, 1996).

32. B. Carter, M. Green and R. Halpern, 'Immigration Policy and the Racialization of Migrant Labour: The Construction of National Identities in the USA and Britain', *Ethnic and Racial Studies*, 19:1 (January 1996), pp. 135–57; K. Paul, *Whitewashing Britain: Race and Citizenship in the Post-War Era* (Ithaca, NY: Cornell University Press, 1997); I. Spencer, *British Immigration Policy Since 1939: The Making of Multi-Racial Britain* (London: Routledge, 1997); R. Hansen, *Citizenship and Immigration in Post-War Britain: The Institutional Origins of a Multicultural Nation* (Oxford: Oxford University

Press, 2000); A. M. Hussain, *British Immigration Policy Under the Conservative Government* (Aldershot: Ashgate, 2001).

33. See Hall and Rose, *At Home with the Empire*, especially the introduction.

34. L. Tabili, 'The Construction of Racial Difference in Twentieth-Century Britain: The Special Restriction (Coloured Alien Seamen) Order, 1925', *Journal of British Studies*, 33 (January 1994), pp. 54–98; Paul, *Whitewashing Britain*.

35. W. Webster, *Imagining Home: 'Race', Gender and National Identity 1945–64* (London: University College London Press, 1998).

36. D. McCrone, 'Unmasking Britannia: The Rise and Fall of British National Identity', *Nations and Nationalism*, 3:4 (1997), pp. 579–96.

37. B. Murray, *The Old Firm: Sectarianism, Sport and Society in Scotland* (Cork: Collins Press, 2001).

38. G. MacPhee and P. Poddar (eds), *Empire and After: Englishness in Postcolonial Perspective* (Oxford: Berghahn, 2007), pp. 1–9; R. Weight, *Patriots: National Identity in Britain, 1940–2000* (London: Macmillan, 2002), pp. 1–16.

39. The key sociological studies on racism in football focus on identity politics and problems with multiculturalism, and only marginally recognize the intersections of racism and violence in football. See J. Garland and M. Rowe, *Racism and Anti-Racism in Football* (London, Palgrave Macmillan, 2001); L. Back, T. Crabbe and J. Solomos, *The Changing Face of Football: Racism, Identity and Multiculture in the English Game* (Oxford: Berg, 2001). See also L. Back, T. Crabbe and J. Solomos, 'Beyond the Racist/Hooligan Couplet: Race, Social Theory and Football Culture', *British Journal of Sociology*, 50:3 (September 1999), pp. 419–42.

40. It should be noted that 'self-policing' is a term frequently associated with Michel Foucault's conceptualization of self-discipline, where an individual, through various implements of correction imposed from without, learns to avert certain behaviours before they are enacted, thus 'policing' one's own conduct. The term was used by several British authorities and football spectators in documents read for this study, with no connection to Foucault's ideas. Rather than self-discipline, they used the term to mean the policing of a community, collective, or social group by one or more of its own members. See M. Foucault, *Discipline and Punish: The Birth of the Prison* (London: Vintage, 1977).

41. For an organized summary of the intricate relationship between sports and politics in the post-war period, see M. Polley, *Moving the Goalposts: A History of Sport and Society Since 1945* (London: Routledge, 1998).

42. For a popular sociological investigation of the intimacies of group violence in football, see B. Buford, *Among the Thugs* (New York: Norton, 1991).

43. For a discussion of civil liberties and the promotion of security, see Tsoukala, *Football Hooliganism in Europe*, pp. 6–10.

44. See, for example, the work of the sports sociologists at the University of Leicester, who became the primary research centre supported by the Football Trust. Dunning et al., *The Roots of Football Hooliganism*; Williams et al., *Hooligans Abroad*.

45. Rogan Taylor, a onetime Chair of the Football Supporters' Association, became a major academic voice on contemporary football with his book on the National Federation of Football Supporters' Clubs. See R. Taylor, *Football and Its Fans: Supporters and their Relations with the Game, 1885–1985* (Leicester: Leicester University Press, 1992). Several key voices in the academic literature on football anti-racism are also involved in fan- and club-based initiatives, further blurring the lines between 'primary' and 'second-

ary' in this particular arena of social research. See the Preface to Back et al., *The Changing Face of Football*.

46. L. Tabili, 'Race is a Relationship and Not a Thing', *Journal of Social History*, 37:1 (Fall 2003), pp. 125–30.

47. See S. Rose and H. Rose, 'Less Than Human Nature: Biology and the New Right', *Race & Class*, 27:3 (1986), pp. 47–66.

48. For a wonderfully enlightening discussion of the problems surrounding the perpetuation of race, as well as the foundation of the attending terminology, see B. J. Fields, 'Slavery, Race and Ideology in the United States of America', *New Left Review*, 181:3 (May/June 1990), pp. 95–118.

49. See Introduction to Solomos, *Race and Racism in Britain*, quote from p. 2. On race as a 'nodal point' as opposed to an individualized and non-universal political 'issue', see Introduction to A. M. Smith, *New Right Discourse on Race and Sexuality: Britain, 1968–1990* (Cambridge: Cambridge University Press, 1994).

50. P. Gilroy, 'The End of Anti-Racism', *New Community*, 17:1 (1990), pp. 71–83.

51. After a short debate about these imprecise labels, most football analysts outside of the press have attempted to move beyond 'hooligan' language, or at least to qualify how they use the term. For example, see J. Williams, 'Who Are You Calling a Hooligan', in M. Perryman (ed.), *Hooligan Wars: Causes and Effects of Football Violence* (Edinburgh: Mainstream, 2001), p. 45; Frosdick and Marsh, *Football Hooliganism*, pp. 25–45.

52. For the best examples of this area of study, see A. King, *The End of the Terraces: The Transformation of English Football* (Leicester: Leicester University Press, 1998); S. Wagg (ed.), *British Football and Social Exclusion* (London: Routledge, 2004).

53. The distinction is most clearly articulated in Garland and Rowe, *Racism and Anti-Racism in Football*. On fascism in football as a readily identifiable 'folk devil', see Back et al., 'Beyond the Racist/Hooligan Couplet'.

1 An Introduction to Football Violence

1. J. Walvin, *Football and the Decline of Britain* (London: Macmillan, 1986).

2. R. Holt and T. Mason, *Sport in Britain, 1945–2000* (Oxford: Blackwell, 2000), pp. 146–7.

3. B. Bebber, '"A Misuse of Leisure": Football Violence, Politics and Family Values in 1970s Britain', in Bebber (ed.), *Leisure and Cultural Conflict in Twentieth-Century Britain*.

4. Taylor, *The Association Game*, p. 274.

5. Ibid., 129.

6. Holt and Mason, *Sport in Britain*, p. 165.

7. Phil Vasili's characterization of the 1966 World Cup team as working-class heroes is fairly accurate. See P. Vasili, *Colouring over the White Line: The History of Black Footballers in Britain* (London: Mainstream, 2000), pp. 127–8. Contemporary analysis of the symbolic constructions of playing 'style' are analysed in C. Critcher, 'Putting on the Style: Aspects of Recent English Football', in Williams and Wagg (eds) *British Football and Social Change*.

8. R. Wakeman, 'The Golden Age of Prosperity, 1953–73', in Wakeman (ed.) *Themes in European History Since 1945* (London: Routledge, 2003), pp. 59–85.

9. W. Meeusen, 'European Economic Integration: From Business Cycle to Business Cycle', in Wakeman (ed.), *Themes in European History since 1945*, pp. 234–62.

10. Wakeman, 'The Golden Age of Prosperity', p. 64.

11. Meeusen, 'European Economic Integration', p. 241.

12. A. Havighurst, *Britain in Transition*, 4th edn (Chicago, IL: University of Chicago Press, 1985), p. 529.

13. K. O. Morgan, *The People's Peace* (Oxford: Oxford University Press, 1990), pp. 277–80.

14. Paul, *Whitewashing Britain*.

15. Gilroy, *'There Ain't No Black in the Union Jack'*, pp. 85–94.

16. A. Whipple, 'Revisiting the "Rivers of Blood" Controversy: Letters to Enoch Powell', *Journal of British Studies*, 48:3 (July 2009), pp. 717–35.

17. A. Bonnett, 'How the British Working Class Became White: The Symbolic (Re)formation of Racialized Capitalism', *Journal of Historical Sociology*, 11:3 (September 1998), pp. 316–40.

18. B. Schwarz, '"The Only White Man in There": The Re-Racialization of England, 1956–1968', *Race & Class*, 38:1 (1996), pp. 65–78.

19. C. Peach, 'Empire, the Economy, and Immigration: Britain 1850–2000', in P. Slack and R. Ward (eds), *The Peopling of Britain: The Shaping of a Human Landscape* (Oxford: Oxford University Press, 2002), pp. 255–80.

20. Morgan, *The People's Peace*, pp. 292–3.

21. Cohen, *Folk Devils and Moral Panics*.

22. K. Thompson, *Moral Panics* (London: Routledge, 1998), p. 46.

23. For a measured analysis of the 'permissive society', see D. Sandbrook, *White Heat: A History of Britain in the Swinging Sixties* (London: Abacus, 2006), esp. ch. 27.

24. P. Cohen, 'Sub-Cultural Conflict and Working-Class Community', Occasional Paper No. 2 (Birmingham: Birmingham Centre for Contemporary Cultural Studies, 1972).

25. For early analyses of youth subcultures, and the media responses to them, see Hall and Jefferson (eds), *Resistance Through Rituals*; D. Hebdidge, *Subculture: The Meaning of Style* (London: Routledge, 1979).

26. Hall et al., *Policing the Crisis*, pp. 240–2.

27. Ibid., pp. 273–93.

28. Ibid., p. 247.

29. Havighurst, *Britain in Transition*, p. 551.

30. S. Hall and M. Jacques (eds), *The Politics of Thatcherism* (London: Lawrence and Wishart, 1983).

31. For more detailed commentary on Thatcherism see S. Hall, *The Hard Road to Renewal: Thatcherism and the Crisis of the Left* (London: Verso, 1988); B. Jessop, K. Bonnett, S. Bromley and T. Ling, *Thatcherism: A Tale of Two Nations* (Cambridge: Polity, 1989).

32. Smith, *New Right Discourse*, quote on p. 5.

33. The more thoughtful investigations into British football violence and football professionalization by sociologists have attempted to provide as much contextual information as possible. See Ingham (ed.) *Football Hooliganism*, especially the Introduction by Ingham and chapter by J. Clarke, 'Football and Working Class Fans: Tradition and Change', pp. 37–60; Taylor, 'Soccer Consciousness and Soccer Hooliganism'; I. Taylor, 'Class, Violence and Sport: The Case of Soccer Hooliganism in Britain', in H. Cantelon and R. Gruneau (eds) *Sport, Culture and the Modern State* (Toronto: University of Toronto Press, 1982), pp. 39–97; S. Redhead, *Post-Fandom and the Millennial Blues: The Transformation of Soccer Culture* (London: Routledge, 1997); King, *The End of the Terraces*.

34. Taylor, 'Soccer Consciousness and Soccer Hooliganism'; J. Clarke, 'Football and Working Class Fans'.

35. G. P. T. Finn, 'Football Violence: A Societal Psychological Perspective', in Giulianotti et al. (eds), *Football, Violence and Social Identity*, pp. 87–122.
36. Armstrong, *Football Hooligans*, p. 233.
37. Giulianotti, *Football: A Sociology*; G. Armstrong and R. Giulianotti, 'Constructing Social Identities: Exploring the Structured Relations of Football Rivalries', in G. Armstrong and R. Giulianotti (eds), *Fear and Loathing in World Football* (Oxford: Berg, 2001), pp. 267–79.
38. R. Holt, *Sport and the British: A Modern History* (Oxford: Oxford University Press, 1990), pp. 341–3.
39. See, for example, National Archives, Kew, Surrey, Public Record Office, Metropolitan Police files (hereafter MEPO) 2/7992, police records regarding Chelsea Football Club and Stamford Bridge, 1947–1962. For the uninitiated, terraces are open areas without seats for viewing the match.
40. See witness statements of match between Newcastle and Millwall at Cold Blow Lane on 26 January 1957, MEPO 2/7991, police records from Millwall Football Club; Metropolitan Police report, East Ham Station, 20 June 1958, MEPO 2/8245, police records from West Ham United Football Club.
41. For example, see Metropolitan Police Special Duty document, East Ham Station, 27 June 1958, MEPO 2/8245.
42. For an example of records indicating adult and female involvement see the following reports as a representative example. Durham Constabulary Report, 7 March 1973, in Public Record Office, Home Office files (hereafter HO), 287/2051; Greater Manchester Police Statement of Witness, 1 May 1975, HO 287/2053.
43. In T. Watt (ed.), *The End: 80 Years of Life on Arsenal's North Bank* (Edinburgh: Mainstream, 1993), pp. 112 and 130–1.
44. Undated comment in R. Taylor, A. Ward and J. Williams (eds), *Three Sides of the Mersey* (London: Robson Books, 1998), p. 154.
45. J. Lang, *Report of the Working Party on Crowd Behaviour at Football Matches* (London: HMSO, 1969), p. 8.
46. See Working Party on Crowd Behaviour at Football Matches, Report of a Meeting at St James Park, Newcastle, 2 June 1969, p. 2, HO 287/1500. This also happened later at Newcastle, in 1974. See R. Taylor and A. Ward (eds), *Kicking and Screaming: An Oral History of Football in England* (London: Robson, 1998), p. 256.
47. Bedfordshire Police Report, 3 September 1975, HO 287/2053.
48. Leeds Police report, 20 April 1971, HO 287/2051.
49. See Frosdick and Marsh, *Football Hooliganism*, pp. 27–8 for a good discussion of the problems with defining the term.
50. Taylor et al. (eds), *Three Sides of the Mersey*, p. 66.
51. Taylor and Ward (eds), *Kicking and Screaming*, p. 259.
52. *The End*, p. 152.
53. The subject of supporter segregation is covered in Chapter 3.
54. Taylor and Ward (eds), *Kicking and Screaming*, p. 259.
55. Bristol Constabulary report, 3 May 1973, HO 287/2051.
56. Marsh, *Aggro*.
57. I am not the first to raise this criticism, nor to explore the detriments of ritualized violence in the terraces. See, for example, Williams et al., *Hooligans Abroad*; Murphy et al., *Football on Trial*; Murphy et al., *Football on Trial*; Giulianotti et al. (eds), *Football, Violence and Social Identity*; Armstrong, *Football Hooligans*.

58. Liverpool and Bootle Constabulary report, 1 March 1972, HO 287/2051.

59. Ibid., p. 2.

60. See, for example, the various arrest files from West Midlands Constabulary and Liverpool and Bootle Constabulary in HO 287/2051.

61. D. Robins and P. Cohen, *Knuckle Sandwich: Growing up in a Working-Class City* (Harmondworth: Penguin, 1978), p. 137; D. Hobbs and D. Robins, 'The Boy Done Good: Football Violence, Changes and Continuities', *Sociological Review*, 39:3 (1991), pp. 569–71.

62. City of Oxford Police Headquarters, submission to Harrington Inquiry, 18 October 1967, National Archives, Public Record Office, Ministry of Housing and Local Government (hereafter HLG) 120/1465.

63. See the other submissions to the Harrington Inquiry in the above folder.

64. Nottinghamshire Combined Constabulary, General Report, 29 April 1975, HO 287/2053.

65. Newcastle Upon Tyne City Police submission to Harrington Inquiry, 17 October 1967, HLG 120/1465.

66. Wiltshire Constabulary Report, Station D, Swindon Town FC vs Northampton Town FC, 3 September 1976, HO 287/2053.

67. Working Party on Crowd Behaviour at Football Matches, Report of Meeting at Ibrox Park, 16 June 1969, HO 287/1500.

68. Taylor and Ward (eds), *Kicking and Screaming*, p. 255.

69. Hampshire Constabulary Report, 21 March 1977, HO 287/2053.

70. Taylor and Ward (eds), *Kicking and Screaming*, p. 260.

71. Dumfries and Galloway Constabulary, submission to Harrington Inquiry, 16 October 1967, HLG 120/1465.

72. Stoke-On-Trent City Police submission to Harrington Inquiry, 17 October 1967, HLG 120/1465.

73. Hobbs and Robins, 'The Boy Done Good', pp. 564–5.

74. See D. Robins, *We Hate Humans* (Harmondsworth: Penguin, 1984), p. 47.

75. Letter to Home Office from Liverpool and Bootle Constabulary, 21 November 1970, HO 287/2051.

76. Greater Manchester Police, Statement of Witness, 1 May 1975, HO 287/2053.

77. See West Midlands Constabulary Report, 26 September 1971, HO 287/2051.

78. J. Williams, 'Having an Away Day: English Football Spectators and the Hooligan Debate', in Williams and Wagg (eds), *British Football and Social Change*, pp. 160–84, especially pp. 166–8.

79. For example, see report from Liverpool and Bootle Constabulary, 4 September 1970, HO 287/2051.

80. Williams, 'Having an Away Day', pp. 173–5.

81. For astute work on Casuals, see Redhead (ed.), *The Passion and the Fashion*.

82. S. Frith, 'Frankie Said: But What Did They Mean?', in A. Tomlinson (ed.) *Consumption, Identity and Style* (New York: Comedia, 1990), pp. 172–85.

2 Moral Anxieties, National Mythologies and Football Violence

1. Cohen, *Folk Devils and Moral Panics*; S. Hall, 'The Treatment of "Football Hooliganism" in the Press', in R. Ingham (ed.), *'Football Hooliganism': The Wider Context* (London, Inter-Action Inprint, 1978), pp. 15–36; G. Whannel, 'Football Crowd Behaviour and

the Press', *Media, Culture & Society*, 1 (1979), pp. 327–42; P. Murphy, J. Williams and E. Dunning, 'Soccer Crowd Disorder and the Press: Processes of Amplification and De-amplification in Historical Perspective', in *Football on Trial*, pp. 96–128; S. Frosdick, 'Beyond Football Hooliganism', in S. Frosdick and L. Walley (eds), *Sport and Safety Management* (Oxford: Butterworth-Heinemann, 1999), pp. 3–10.

2. Specifically, see Hall, 'The Treatment of "Football Hooliganism" in the Press'; Armstrong, *Football Hooligans*, ch. 4.

3. See Murphy et al., 'Soccer Crowd Disorder and the Press', pp. 117–26.

4. King, *The End of the Terraces*, especially ch. 7; G. Armstrong and D. Hobbs, 'High Tackles and Professional Fouls: The Policing of Soccer Hooliganism', in G. T. Marx and C. Fijnaut (eds), *Undercover Police Surveillance in Comparative Perspective* (Amsterdam: Kluwer Law International Press, 1995), pp. 175–93.

5. An excellent entrée to this literature is found in Thompson, *Moral Panics*.

6. G. Pearson, *Hooligan: A History of Respectable Fears* (London: Macmillan, 1983).

7. Cohen, *Folk Devils and Moral Panics*. Cohen's study developed on the initial idea of a 'moral panic' by his colleague, Jock Young. See J. Young, 'The Role of Police as Amplifiers of Deviance: Negotiators of Drug Control as Seen in Notting Hill', in S. Cohen (ed.), *Images of Deviance* (Harmondsworth: Penguin, 1971), pp. 27–61.

8. Hall and Jefferson (eds), *Resistance Through Rituals*.

9. Hall, 'The Treatment of "Football Hooliganism" in the Press', p. 16.

10. Ibid., pp. 17–20 and 24–6.

11. Walvin, *Football and the Decline of Britain*, p. 51.

12. See P. A. J. Waddington, 'Mugging as a Moral Panic: A Question of Proportion', *British Journal of Sociology*, 37:2 (1986), pp. 245–59. Waddington wrote, in part, as a response to the arguments by Stuart Hall et al. on the moral panic over muggings in Britain.

13. Thompson, *Moral Panics*, pp. 11–12.

14. J. Clarke et al., 'Subcultures, Cultures, and Class', in Hall, *Resistance Through Rituals*, pp. 71–3.

15. S. O. Rose, 'Cultural Analysis and Moral Discourses: Episodes, Continuities, and Transformations', in V. E. Bonnell and L. Hunt (eds), *Beyond the Cultural Turn: New Directions in the Study of Society and Culture* (Berkeley, CA: University of California Press, 1999), pp. 217–38. Quote on p. 223.

16. Ibid., pp. 223–4. See also Pearson, *'Hooligan'*.

17. Rose, 'Cultural Analysis and Moral Discourses', p. 229.

18. Murphy et al., 'Soccer Crowd Disorder and the Press'. Murphy et al. examined the *Leicester Mercury* to discuss long-term trends.

19. *Daily Mail*, 16 December 1964.

20. Hall et al., *Policing the Crisis*, ch. 3, especially pp. 53–6.

21. *Times*, 3 September 1969.

22. See Home Office Press Summary, 26 September 1969, National Archives, Public Record Office, Home Office files (hereafter HO) 287/1500.

23. Suggestions from Public to Home Office, undated, HO 300/112, file 27.

24. *Celtic View*, 12 August 1970, HO 287/2052.

25. *Daily Telegraph*, 26 August 1974.

26. Thompson, *Moral Panics*, p. 7.

27. P. Jenkins, *Intimate Enemies: Moral Panics in Contemporary Great Britain* (Berlin: Aldine de Gruyter, 1992).

28. E. Goode and N. Ben-Yehuda, *Moral Panics: The Social Construction of Deviance* (Oxford: Blackwell, 1994).
29. Charles Drago, Association Internationale Contre La Violence Dans Le Sport, 'A Reason To Hope', English translation sent to Denis Howell, April 1976, HO 300/113.
30. 'Why Waste Words on the Weirdies', *Police: The Monthly Magazine of the Police Federation*, 2:2 (October 1969), pp. 12–13.
31. 'Close the Ground', in ibid., pp. 16–17.
32. The Harrington Report, conducted by a group of social psychologists led by J. A. Harrington, was sanctioned by the Home Office during the 1966–7 football season. The commission sent a questionnaire sent to all British constabularies, and the answers provide an excellent cache of evidence on police attitudes and perceptions of football disorder.
33. Letter from Chief Constable's Office, Law Courts, York to Harrington Commission, 18 October 1967, National Archives, Public Record Office, Office of Housing and Local Government (hereafter HLG) 120/1465.
34. For a further discussion of the Safety at Sports Ground Bill and its implications for physical space division, see Chapter 3.
35. *Parliamentary Debates, House of Commons*, vol. 745, col. 1803 (27 April 1967).
36. Ibid., vol. 751, col. 1864 (26 October 1967).
37. Ibid., vol. 929, col. 1353 (6 April 1977).
38. Ibid., vol. 931, col. 751 (5 May 1977).
39. Ibid., vol. 745, col. 1802–3 (27 April 1967).
40. Ibid., vol. 751, col. 1864 (26 October 1967).
41. Thompson, *Moral Panics*, pp. 12–13 and 36–9.
42. For the fluctuating history of the position of Minister of Sport, see Polley, *Moving the Goalposts*, pp. 23–4.
43. See *Parliamentary Debates, House of Commons*, Written Answers, vol. 759, col. 398 (29 February 1968).
44. For example, see R. Samuel, *Theatres of Memory, Volume I: Past and Present in Contemporary Culture* (London: Verso, 1994).
45. P. Wright, *On Living in an Old Country: The National Past* (London: Verso, 1985); D. Lowenthal, *The Past Is a Foreign Country* (Cambridge: Cambridge University Press, 1985); D. Lowenthal, *The Heritage Crusade and the Spoils of History* (Harmondsworth: Penguin, 1997); R. Samuel, *Theatres of Memory, Volume II: Island Stories: Unravelling Britain* (London: Verso, 1998).
46. Preface and ch. 1 of R. Colls and P. Dodd (eds), *Englishness: Politics and Culture, 1880–1920* (London: Croom Helm, 1986).
47. E. Hobsbawm and T. Ranger (eds), *The Invention of Tradition* (Cambridge: Cambridge University Press, 1983).
48. J. Mali, *Mythistory: The Making of a Modern Historiography* (Chicago, IL: University of Chicago Press, 2003), especially ch. 1.
49. See J. Gillis (ed.), *Commemorations: The Politics of National Identity* (Princeton, NJ: Princeton University Press, 1994).
50. R. Giulianotti, 'Social Identity and Public Order: Political and Academic Discourses on Football Violence', in Giulianotti et al. (eds), *Football, Violence and Social Identity*, pp. 10–36.
51. The final recommendations of the Lang Report were published as Lang, *Report of the Working Party on Crowd Behaviour at Football Matches*.

52. *Parliamentary Debates, House of Commons,* vol. 751, col. 1864 (26 October 1967).
53. Ibid., vol. 931, col. 725 (5 May 1977).
54. See 'North and South', in Samuel, *Island Stories.*
55. Letter from Football Association to Home Office, 25 October 1965, National Archives, Public Record Office, Metropolitan Police files (hereafter MEPO) 2/9483.
56. *Parliamentary Debates, House of Commons,* vol. 931, col. 727 (5 May 1977).
57. Letter from Alan Hardaker, Football League, to J. D. Addison at Home Office, 1 October 1969, HO 287/1500.
58. Report of a Meeting of the Working Party on Crowd Behavior at Football Matches, held at St James' Park, Newcastle, 2 June 1969, HO 287/1500.
59. *Parliamentary Debates, House of Commons,* vol. 931, col. 725 (5 May 1977).
60. Sheffield and Rotherham Constabulary submission to Harrington Commission, 17 October 1967, HLG 120/1465.
61. Draft Letter from Harrington Commission to Selected Police Chiefs, undated, HLG 120/1465.
62. Letter to D. J. Trevelyan at Home Office from Deputy Chief Constable at Liverpool and Bootle Constabulary, 24 April 1972, HO 287/2051.
63. Cheshire Constabulary submission to Harrington Commission, 7 November 1967, HLG 120/1465.
64. See S. Gilman, *Difference and Pathology: Stereotypes of Sexuality, Race and Madness* (Ithaca, NY: University of Ithaca Press, 1985); L. Davidoff, *Worlds Between: Historical Perspectives on Gender and Class* (London: Routledge, 1995).
65. See Morgan, *The People's Peace,* pp. 298–316.
66. *Parliamentary Debates, House of Commons,* vol. 931, col. 740 (5 May 1977).
67. Home Office Meeting Minutes, chaired by D. J. Trevelyan, 2 October 1969, HO 287/1500.
68. Home Office Meeting Minutes, chaired by the Home Secretary, 13 August 1970, HO 287/1630.
69. *Parliamentary Debates, House of Commons,* vol. 788, col. 566 (15 October 1969).
70. 'Howell Puts Thugs on Penalty Spot', *Guardian,* 2 September 1975.
71. *Parliamentary Debates, House of Commons,* vol. 893, col. 1781 (19 June 1975).
72. Ibid., vol. 929, col. 1342 (6 April 1977).
73. See Confidential British Embassy in Mexico Memo, 'Football: Mexican Attitudes to the England Team', prepared by Eric Vines, First Secretary (Information), dated 24 June 1970, National Archives, Public Record Office, Foreign and Commonwealth Office (hereafter FCO) 7/1649.
74. Letter from Mr Brinson, Foreign and Commonwealth Office to C. P. P. Baldwin, 18 May 1970, FCO 7/1649, file 7.
75. Letter from B. P. Austin, American Department, to Mr Baldwin, Information Policy Department, 21 May 1970, FCO 7/1649, file 8.
76. Confidential Memo, The World Cup 1970: The Politics of Football, sent from British Embassy in Mexico to Foreign Commonwealth Office, 24 June 1970, FCO 7/1649.
77. Telegram from British Embassy in Mexico to Foreign Commonwealth Office and Denis Howell, dated 11 June 1978, FCO 7/1649.
78. 'The World Cup 1970: The Politics of Football', FCO 7/1649.
79. J. A. Robson, American Department to C. P. Hope, British Embassy in Mexico, 8 July 1970, FCO 7/1649.
80. For example, see *Daily Telegraph,* 6 June 1970.

81. Many European competitions play two 'legs' in a single round of the tournament, a full match in each club's home stadium.
82. British Consulate-General in Rotterdam, W. F. B. Price, Report on Incidents at Rotterdam on the Occasion of the Football Match Between Feyenoord and Tottenham Hotspur on May 29ᵗʰ 1974, 4 June 1974, FCO 47/683.
83. Ibid., p. 6–7.
84. Letter from British Consulate-General, W. F. B. Price to R. V. Juchau, Consular Department, Foreign Commonwealth Office, 4 June 1974, FCO 47/683.
85. Price, Report on Incidents at Rotterdam, p. 7, FCO 47/683.
86. *Times*, 31 May 1974.
87. *Guardian*, 31 May 1974.
88. Both quoted in the *Guardian*, 31 May 1974.
89. W. F. B. Price to R. V. Juchau, Foreign and Commonwealth Office, 4 June 1974, FCO 47/683.
90. Harold A. Stein to the Netherlands Ambassador, London, 30 May 1974, FCO 47/683.
91. Larry Ross to Margaret Thatcher, MP, 30 May 1974, FCO 47/683.
92. Margaret Thatcher, MP to Roy Hattersley, Minister of State, 3 June 1974, FCO 47/683, file 5. A formal apology was given by Price to both the Dutch police authorities and the Dutch government. Tottenham Football Supporters' Club and the Mayor of Haringey also issued apologies the following week. See letter from Foreign and Commonwealth Office to Margaret Thatcher, 10 June 1974, FCO 47/683, file 6.
93. Telegraph from Barnes at Consular's Office, The Hague to Foreign and Commonwealth Office, 30 May 1974, FCO 47/683.
94. W. H. B. Price to R. V. Juchau, FCO, 4 June 1974, FCO 47/683, file 4.
95. Report on Incidents at Rotterdam, p. 5, FCO 47/683.
96. W. H. B. Price to Foreign and Commonwealth Office, 30 May 1974, FCO 47/683, file 2.
97. Letter from Ted Graham, MP to Roy Jenkins, Home Secretary, 5 June 1974, FCO 47/683, file 7.
98. *Guardian*, 31 May 1974.
99. Letter from Roy Hattersley to Ted Graham, 21 June 1974, FCO 47/683.
100. Quoted in *Daily Mirror*, 5 August 1974.
101. *Parliamentary Debates, House of Commons*, vol. 893, col. 1800 (19 June 1975).

3 Violent Environments

1. The body of work on the Taylor report and post-Hillsborough stadium changes is increasingly large. See Taylor, 'English Football in the 1990s'; King, *The End of the Terraces*.
2. J. Bale, *Sport, Space and the City* (London: Routledge, 1992); J. Bale, 'The Spatial Development of the Modern Stadium', *International Review for the Sociology of Sport*, 28:2 (1993), pp. 122–33.
3. J. Bale, *Landscapes of Modern Sport* (Leicester: Leicester University Press, 1994).
4. G. Armstrong and M. Young, 'Legislators and Interpreters: The Law and "Football Hooligans"', in G. Armstrong and R. Giulianotti (eds), *Entering the Field: New Perspectives on World Football* (Oxford: Berg, 1997), pp. 175–92. Foucault's various work on prisons, clinics, and social discipline informs a wide body of social research into power and power relationships in the modern world. See M. Foucault, *Madness and Civilization: A History of Insanity in the Age of Reason* (London: Vintage, 1965); *The Birth of the Clinic: An Archaeology of Medical Perception* (London: Vintage, 1973); *Discipline and Punish*.

5. See Bale, *Landscapes of Modern Sport*, pp. 83–4.

6. Tsoukala, *Football Hooliganism in Europe*, pp. 66–70.

7. P. Borsay, *A History of Leisure: The British Experience since 1500* (London: Palgrave, 2006), pp. 64–72.

8. Richard Lane, Home Office to Mr Skuffrey, 4 September 1974, National Archives, Public Record Office, Home Office files (hereafter HO) 300/113, file 3.

9. For records on Howell's involvement in this process, see National Archives, Public Record Office, Department of the Environment files (hereafter AT) 60/2 and AT 60/37.

10. *Parliamentary Debates, House of Commons*, vol. 867, col. 1090–1 (19 June 1975). Second Reading of Safety at Sports Grounds Bill, presented by Denis Howell, Minister of Sport.

11. Appendix C to the Winterbottom Report, p. 2. The Winterbottom Report, never published by HMSO like other government publications, was kept for consultation by the subsequent Wheatley Commission. The report was submitted to the Home Office in June 1971 but kept within the agency so as to further facilitate Wheatley's investigation. It can be found in National Archives, Public Record Office, Housing and Local Government files (hereafter HLG) 120/1618. Appendix C was the 'Memorandum on the Policing of Football Grounds in Scotland', prepared by Ratcliffe.

12. The Harrington investigation was carried out by J. A. Harrington, Research Director of the Birmingham Research Group. Its final recommendations were published as *Soccer Hooliganism: A Preliminary Report* (Bristol: John Wright and Sons, Ltd., 1968).

13. Submission to Harrington Commission from Cyril T. G. Carter, Chief Constable's Office at York, 18 October 1967, HLG 120/1465.

14. Submission to Harrington Commission by City of Glasgow Police Headquarters, J. A. Robertson, Chief Constable, 1 November 1967, HLG 120/1465.

15. For works on fan violence in other parts of Europe and Latin America, see E. Dunning, P. Murphy, I. Waddington and A. E. Astrinakis, *Fighting Fans: Football Hooliganism as a World Phenomenon* (Dublin: University College Press, 2002).

16. Harrington Report, final recommendations, p. 33.

17. Ibid., p. 34.

18. The final recommendations of the Lang Report were published as Lang, *Report of the Working Party on Crowd Behaviour at Football Matches*.

19. Notes of Meeting held at St James Park, Newcastle, 2 June 1969, Working Party notes, HO 287/1500.

20. Working Party on Crowd Behaviour at Football Matches, Modifications to Final Report proposed by the Chairman, HO 287/1500.

21. Working Party on Crowd Behaviour at Football Matches, Wording of Report, Incorporating the Modifications proposed by the Chairman (and Others), p. 2, HO 300/83.

22. Ibid., p. 4.

23. Winterbottom's Report can be found in HLG 120/1618. There was some Home Office conflict over whether or not to publish the report. Of course, Winterbottom, as a staunch advocate against football violence and something of a moral crusader himself, wanted to publish his findings. The Home Office and Eldon Griffiths, Secretary of the Department of the Environment, wanted Wheatley to have as many resources as possible. Further, they wanted to maintain that the government had proposed the licensing scheme and first report under the Conservatives, rather than the representatives for the Football League or the Sports Council. See the correspondence between Griffiths, Wheatley and Winterbottom in HLG 120/1618.

24. C. J. Stephens, Chief Scientist of the Home Office, A Brief Analysis of Some Scientific Aspects of Football Crowd Safety, submitted for Cabinet consideration, 29 March 1971, p.3, National Archives, Public Record Office, Cabinet Office files, CAB 130/508.

25. Ibid., 2.

26. Ibid., 3.

27. Winterbottom's figures here may also reflect knowledge of the SCICON report, an independently researched technical report on terrace spacing, crush barriers, gangways, and ingress and egress. The SCICON report can be found in HO 300/85, file 5. It eventually was published as Appendix A in the final Wheatley report as well.

28. Final Winterbottom Report submitted to Eldon Griffiths at the Department of the Environment, officially titled, 'Report of the Team Appointed to Consult Football Clubs on Safety of Grounds', June 1971, HLG 120/1618.

29. Ibid., 9.

30. Winterbottom Report, Technical Appendix II: Existing Information and Sources, p. 2, HLG 120/1618.

31. See 1976/77 Home Office Circular, which included the recommendations issued in July 1975 after the first round of foreign incidents, HO 300/113, file 22A.

32. D. A. S. Sharp, Home Office to Sir Robert Marshall (Conservative, Arundel), undated (July 1975?), AT 60/39.

33. Deputy Assistant Commissioner for Operations, New Scotland Yard, prepared notes for meeting with Home Office on 13 August 1970. Enclosed in letter to D. J. Trevelyan, Home Office, 7 September 1970, HO 287/2052 (Part Two).

34. The argument for the displacement of fan violence has been made effectively by tracking the spatial orientations of Sheffield fans. See Armstrong, *Football Hooligans*, ch. 8.

35. See, for example, Mr Gerrard's comments in Note of a Meeting with Representatives of the Football Interests at the Home Office, 13 August, 1970, HO 287/1630.

36. Editorial by Howell in the *Daily Mail*, 20 March 1974.

37. In Taylor and Ward (eds), *Kicking and Screaming*, p. 263.

38. In Watt (ed.), *The End*, p. 161.

39. Cleveland Constabulary Report on Fifth Round FA Cup Match, Middlesbrough vs Arsenal, Ayresome Park, Middlesbrough, 24 March 1977, HO 287/2053.

40. Watt (ed.), *The End*, p. 162.

41. See the Harrington Report, p. 36; Lang Report, p. 9.

42. Football/Ministerial Working Party on Crowd Problems, Visit to Birmingham City, 1 April 1974, HO 300/112. The Party's visits to most first division grounds generally reveal the same physical divisions in place: sunken terraces, police pathways, divided terraces, advertising barriers, and some combination of sectioning or penning, especially during derby matches.

43. See letter from Denis Howell to R. H. Jennings Esq., Managing Director, QED Engineering Limited, 11 July 1974, HO 300/112, file 43. Howell forwarded a commercial reference for collapsible fencing from one of his constituents in Birmingham onto other clubs. In the attached notes, he adamantly maintained the need for gateways in perimeter fences.

44. *Parliamentary Debates, House of Commons*, vol. 893, col. 1800 (19 June 1975).

45. Letter from QED Engineering Limited to Denis Howell, 17 June 1974, HO 300/112.

46. McDonnell and Hughes Architects, Plan for Pitch Invasion Deterrent, sent to Liverpool City Police, 15 May 1974. The plan was immediately forwarded to Denis Howell on 28 May 1974, in HO 300/112, file 40.

47. Letter from Deputy Chief Constable at Merseyside Police to Denis Howell, 28 May 1974, HO 300/112, file 40.
48. 'Wembley to Put "Cage" Around Fans', *Evening Standard*, 5 February 1975. The Working Party collected this and other press articles in HO 300/113.
49. *Evening Standard*, 29 April 1974.
50. *Daily Express*, 24 May 1974.
51. See the following cartoons, respectively: Stanley Franklin in *Daily Mirror*, 29 January 1968, Arthur Horner in *Sun*, 1 June 1974, Raymond Jackson in *Evening Standard*, 14 September 1968.
52. This image can be found in AT 25/246. It is not numbered but the pages are collated within Howell's other briefs, notes, correspondence and press clippings in the file.
53. City of Glasgow Police submission to Harrington Commission, 1 November 1967, HLG 120/1465.
54. Nottinghamshire Combined Constabulary report on Notts County vs Manchester United, 29 April 1975, p.8, HO 287/2053.
55. Ibid., 7.
56. Liverpool and Bootle Constabulary Report on Everton vs Liverpool, 24 February 1971, HO 287/2051.
57. Watt (ed.), *The End*, pp. 130–1.
58. South Yorkshire Police, Witness Statement of Heidi Gleissner, 22 October 1975, HO 287/2053.
59. Letter from Heidi Gleissner, Sue Isherwood, Carole Parkhouse, Linda Crosby and Violet Wright to The Chief Constable, West Yorkshire Police. The letter was copied to all the national newspapers, Ted Croker at the Football Association, Denis Howell and Leeds United's manager Jimmy Armfield. Dated 3 September 1975. In HO 287/2053.
60. Letter from C. D. Smith, Chairman of Manchester United Supporters' Club to Denis Howell, Department of the Environment, 2 May 1974, AT 25/246.
61. The Winterbottom Report, p. 10, HLG 120/1618.
62. Attachment on Financial Considerations, Press Release by Notts. County Football Club, 11 March 1975, HO 287/2053.
63. Though Howell couldn't enforce statutory changes to football grounds in the Sports Grounds Bill, he did exert political pressure against several clubs, and used football's governing bodies to encourage clubs to make the changes as well. See the multiple discussions surrounding preparations for Notts County vs Manchester United, 19 April 1975, in HO 287/2053.
64. Football/Ministerial Working Party on Crowd Problems, Visit to Middlesbrough, 24 April 1974, HO 300/112.
65. Metropolitan Police report of West Ham United vs Manchester United, 30 October 1975, HO 287/2053.
66. The Winterbottom Report, p. 22, HLG 120/1618.

4 Police and the State

1. Taylor, 'Soccer Consciousness and Soccer Hooliganism'.
2. C. Stott, 'Police Expectations and the Control of English Soccer Fans at "Euro 2000"', *Policing: An International Journal of Police Strategies and Management*, 26 (2003), pp. 640–55.

3. C. Stott, 'How Conflict Escalates: The Inter-Group Dynamics of Collective Football Crowd "Violence"', *Sociology*, 32 (1998), pp. 353–77; M. O'Neill, *Policing Football: Social Intervention and Negotiated Disorder* (Oxford: Berg, 2005).

4. See Part II of Williams et al., *Hooligans Abroad*; Armstrong, *Football Hooligans*, chs 4–5.

5. For the argument about police building their own public image through football in the late 1980s and 1990s, see Armstrong, *Football Hooligans*, pp. 38 and 107.

6. See G. Armstrong and D. Hobbs, 'Tackled from Behind', in Giulianotti et al. (eds), *Football, Violence and Social Identity*; Armstrong and Hobbs, 'High Tackles and Professional Fouls'.

7. For one example among many, see Football/Ministerial Working Party on Crowd Problems Visit to Birmingham City, 1 April 1974, National Archives, Public Record Office, Home Office files (hereafter HO) 300/112.

8. On responses to the media, see Metropolitan Police report, Shepherd's Bush Station, Branch Note, Queen's Park Rangers Versus Millwall Football Match Report, 28 March 1966, National Archives, Public Record Office, Metropolitan Police files (hereafter MEPO) 2/9483. See also the files in National Archives, Public Record Office, Office of Housing and Local Governement (hereafter HLG) 120/1465.

9. See, for example, Chief Superintendent J. D. B. Chester, Northumberland Constabulary report on incidents at St James' Park, 9 March 1974, National Archives, Public Record Office, Department of Environment files (hereafter AT) 25/246, file 11.

10. See Notes of Deputy Assistant Commissioner 'A' (Operations), New Scotland Yard, 2 September 1970. Sent to D. J. Trevelyan, Home Office, 7 September 1970, HO 287/2052.

11. Metropolitan Police, Catford Station, Millwall Football Club – Police Arrangements, 17 October 1967, MEPO 2/7991.

12. Metropolitan Police, Southwark Station, Millwall Cup Tie, 28 January 1957, MEPO 2/7991, file 17A. For one Millwall FA Cup tie at Cold Blow Lane the club paid for roughly 90 officers for 45,646 spectators, a ratio of 1:507. This ratio is representative of other police registers during this era. See match reports in MEPO 2/7991, MEPO 2/8245, MEPO 2/9483, MEPO 2/11286.

13. Metropolitan Police Report, Southwark station, 26 January 1957, Millwall vs Newcastle Cup Tie, MEPO 2/7991.

14. For example, see Leicestershire Constabulary report on Leicester City vs Liverpool, 8 September 1975, HO 287/2053. Police schedules indicate an Assistant Chief Constable, one Chief Superintendent of Police, one Superintendent of Police, nine Inspectors, 21 Sergeants, 220 Constables, ten Special Constables, and two Police Dogs all serviced the match.

15. For example, Leeds United employed 450 police for an estimated attendance of 44,500 fans. See report of Assistant Chief Constable W. A. J. Goulding, Area Headquarters in Leeds, 18 October, 1976, HO 287/2053.

16. See Minute Sheet of Halifax Subdivision, 17 November 1970, HO 287/2051.

17. See Operational Order and police register for Notts County vs Manchester United, 25 March 1975, PRO HO 287/2053. 596 total police personnel were employed for the match.

18. See chart of Police and Steward Employment at Association Football Grounds in England and Scotland, 1973/74, HO 300/108, file 18. Quote from Arsenal FC description of steward responsibilities.

19. Watt (ed.), *The End*, p. 157.

20. Ibid., pp. 124–5.
21. See, for example, Hampshire Constabulary Report, Southampton FC vs Manchester United, 26 February 1977, HO 287/2053.
22. Statement of Witness, William Kay, taken by Greater Manchester Police, 21 April 1975, HO 287/2053.
23. J. D. Marron in unaddressed letter (to Halifax Police Branch?), 23 March 1976. Received in Home Office police report files, 24 March 1976, HO 287/2053.
24. Schedule of Police Injured, Metropolitan Police Office, A8 Branch, 29 April 1975, HO 287/2053.
25. Leeds City Police Report, Superintendent Fieldhouse, Leeds United vs West Bromwich Albion, 20 April 1971, HO 287/2053.
26. J. M. Lewis, 'Crowd Control at English Football Matches', *Sociological Focus*, 15:4 (October 1982), pp. 417–23.
27. Working Party on Crowd Behaviour at Football Matches, Report of a Meeting, Ibrox Park, 16 June 1969, HO 287/1500.
28. Frank Williamson, Her Majesty's Chief Inspector of Crime, to D. J. Trevelyan, Home Office, 17 October 1969, HO 287/1500.
29. Williamson, quoted by J. H. Waddell, Home Office, in letter to Roy Jenkins, 12 August 1970, HO 287/2052.
30. See Football/Ministerial Working Party on Crowd Problems, Visit to Stoke City, 25 July 1974, HO 300/112.
31. Williamson's suggestion noted in 'Report of Visit to Bristol', 22 August 1974, AT 25/247.
32. Harrington Report, p. 35.
33. Ibid., p. 40.
34. From National Federation of Football Supporters' Clubs Conference Report, May 1975, p. 48. In Taylor, *Football and Its Fans*, p. 164–5.
35. Mrs. J. McKay to Denis Howell, 2 May 1974, AT 60/12.
36. For example of use of mounted police for escorts, see Football/Ministerial Working Party on Crowd Problems, Visit to Stoke City, 25 July 1974, HO 300/112, file 44.
37. See Part II of Appendix B to Winterbottom Report, Commander H. Mitchell, Metropolitan Police, p.7, HLG 120/1618. Mitchell indicated that 27 of 40 total grounds employed roughly ten horses, while four unnamed, major clubs used twenty horses per match.
38. See Chief Constable, Liverpool and Bootle Constabulary to D. J. Trevelyan, 24 November 1970, HO 287/2051, file 15.
39. Gary Armstrong has described how police forces in Sheffield used mounted police indiscriminately to charge crowds in streets as well, in order to move them along or force them to flee an area. See *Football Hooligans*, pp. 107–8.
40. Honorary Secretary of Association of Chief Police Officers of England and Wales, to Chief Constabularies at the London Metropolis, Birmingham, Liverpool, Manchester, Middlesbrough, Sheffield, and Sunderland, 28 April 1965, MEPO 2/9483.
41. Chief Superintendent John B. Smith, Catford Station, Metropolitan Police, Report on Millwall Football Club, Police Arrangements, 17 October 1967, MEPO 2/7991, file 39A.
42. T. E. Mahir, Assistant Commissioner, Commissioner's Office D9 Branch, Confidential Instruction on Police Dogs Use in Connection with Rowdyism and Crowds, 8 April 1965, MEPO 2/9483.

43. C. G. Burrows, Honorary Secretary, Association of Chief Police Officers of England and Wales and Chief Constable's Office, Oxford, document 11/52/17, MEPO 2/9483. I speculate that the ACPO were concerned about the use of police dogs in this capacity after publicized accounts of dog violence in the policing of the American civil rights movement in the early 1960s.

44. *Parliamentary Debates, House of Commons*, vol. 882, col. 1533–5 (4 December 1974).

45. Northumberland Constabulary Report, Football Match at St James Park, 12 March 1974, AT 25/246.

46. R. M. M. Campbell, Assistant Chief Constable, City of Edinburgh Police, to Harrington Commission, 23 October 1967, HLG 120/1465.

47. William Smith, Chief Constable, City of Aberdeen Police, to Harrington Commission, 16 October 1967, HLG 120/1465.

48. Derby County and Borough Constabulary to Harrington Commission, 21 October 1967, HLG 120/1465.

49. Working Party on Crowd Behaviour at Football Matches, Report of a Meeting Held at Ibrox Park, Glasgow, 16 June 1969, HO 287/1500.

50. Note from 'OSCAR', *Arsenal Football Club Programme*, 1 April 1950. In *The End*, pp. 74–5.

51. A. Leese, Chief Fire Officer, Coventry, 'Public Risks at Sports Grounds', *The Municipal and Public Services Journal*, 19 January 1968. Collected by the Home Office in HO 300/83.

52. Notes of Meeting with Representatives of the Football Interests at the Home Office, 13 August 1970, HO 287/1630.

53. Operational Order, Superintendent, Metropolitan Police Office, A8 Branch, 12 September 1968, MEPO 2/11286, file 2A.

54. Wheatley commission, Note of a Meeting with Representatives of the Federation of Scottish Football Supporters' Clubs, Edinburgh, 9 September 1971, HO 287/1631, file 16.

55. W. A. Ratcliffe, Assistant Chief Constable, Glasgow, Memorandum on Policing of Football Grounds in Scotland, Appendix C to the Winterbottom Report, PRO HLG 120/1618.

56. Operational order, Superintendent, Metropolitan Police Office, A8 Branch, 12 September 1968, MEPO 2/11286.

57. Extract from the Minutes of 101st Central Conference of Chief Constables held on 6 November 1969, PRO HO 287/1500.

58. D. J. Trevelyan, Home Office to J. F. Claxton, Department of the Director of Public Prosecutions, 26 September 1969, HO 287/1500.

59. D. J. Trevelyan, Home Office to J. F. Claxton, Department of the Director of Public Prosecutions, 24 October 1969, HO 287/1500.

60. Letter from F2 Division to D. J. Trevelyan, Home Office, 4 October 1969, HO 287/1500.

61. J. F. Claxton, Department of the Director of Public Prosecutions to D. J. Trevelyan, Home Office, 20 October 1969, HO 287/1500.

62. Chief Constable, Liverpool and Bootle Constabulary to F. W. C. Pennington, General Secretary, Association of Chief Police Officers, 8 September 1972, HO 287/2051.

63. Liverpool and Bootle Constabulary, Brief on Football Hooliganism and Associated Violent Behaviour, 8 September 1972, HO 287/2051.

64. Notes of a Meeting with Representatives of Football Interests at the Home Office, 13 August 1970, HO 287/1630.
65. Assistant Chief Constable of Operations, Hampshire Constabulary, Report on Southampton FC vs Manchester United FC, 21 March 1977, HO 287/2053.
66. Northumberland Constabulary report on incidents at St James Park, 12 March 1974, AT 25/246.
67. City of Glasgow Police submission to Harrington commission, 1 November 1967, HLG 120/1465.
68. Police Operational Order, Notts. County vs Manchester United, 25 March 1975, HO 287/2053.
69. Briefing by Supervisory Officer, Notts. County vs Manchester United, 25 March 1975, HO 287/2053.
70. For example, see the Harrington Report, pp. 32–3, and suggestions from constables in HLG 120/1465.
71. Such was the case in Leeds: see Football/Ministerial Working Party on Crowd Problems, Visit to Leeds United, 25 April 1974, HO 300/112.
72. Williamson's position noted in J. H. Waddell, Home Office to Secretary of State, 12 August 1970, HO 287/2052.
73. Greater Manchester Police, Statement of Witness, 15 April 1975, HO 287/2053.
74. Greater Manchester Police, Statement of Witness, 21 April 1975, HO 287/2053.
75. Greater Manchester Police, Statement of Witness, 3 May 1975, PRO HO 287/2053.
76. Heidi Gleissner, Susan Isherwood, Carole Parkhouse, Linda Crosby, and Violet Wright to Denis Howell, 3 September 1975, HO 287/2053.
77. Carole Parkhouse to Chief Superintendent Tunnicliffe, South Yorkshire Police, 27 October 1975, HO 287/2053.
78. South Yorkshire Police Investigation into Complaint, Chief Superintendent Tunnicliffe to Deputy Chief Constable, 25 November 1975, HO 287/2053.
79. South Yorkshire Police Investigation into Complaint, Inspector Phillips to Chief Superintendent Isherwood, 19 December 1975, HO 287/2053.
80. Laird Budge, Arsenal fan, in *The End*, p. 159.
81. A. Green, *Arsenal Football Club Programme*, 12 April 1969. In *The End*, p. 105.
82. *Parliamentary Debates, House of Commons*, vol. 893, col. 1790 (19 June 1975).
83. Ibid., vol. 791, col. 1486 (20 November 1969).
84. Armstrong, *Football Hooligans*; Armstrong and Hobbs, 'Tackled From Behind', and 'High Tackles and Professional Fouls'.
85. See the essays in D. Lyon (ed.), *Theorizing Surveillance: The Panopticon and Beyond* (Devon: Willan, 2006); C. Norris and G. Armstrong, *The Maximum Surveillance Society: The Rise of CCTV* (Oxford: Berg, 1999). For original conceptualizations of the Panopticon, see Foucault's interpretation of Jeremy Bentham's prison in *Discipline and Punish*.
86. For example, see Home Office Circular, Hooliganism by Football Supporters, 1969, HO 287/1500.
87. Note of a Meeting on Soccer Hooliganism, held at Home Office, 2 October 1969, HO 287/1500, file 11.
88. Frank Williamson, Her Majesty's Inspector of Crime, to D. J. Trevelyan, Home Office, 17 October 1969, HO 287/1500.
89. Commander H. Mitchell, Metropolitan Police, Appendix B to Winterbottom Report, 27 May 1971, HLG 120/1618.

90. 'City's Early Warning to Beat the "Hoolies"', *Birmingham Evening Mail*, 5 September 1975.

91. Operational Order, Notts County vs Manchester United, 25 March 1975, HO 287/2053. The order notes that only ten radios were used by supervisors of several hundred police.

92. The Winterbottom Report, p. 22, HLG 120/1618.

93. Bedfordshire Police report, Luton vs Chelsea, 3 September 1975, HO 287/1630.

94. Notes of a Meeting at the Home Office, 13 August 1970, HO 287/1630.

95. Note of a Meeting between police representatives and Home Office officials, 2 October 1969, HO 287/1500.

96. Note of a Meeting on Hooliganism by Football Supporters, 2 October 1969, HO 287/1500.

97. See Football/Ministerial Working Party on Crowd Problems, Visit to Chelsea, 28 March 1974, AT 60/39.

98. Ibid.

99. In addition to the citations below, see files on Working Party visits to Middlesbrough, Newcastle and Coventry in HO 300/112 for evidence of the use of photography in these areas.

100. *Daily Telegraph*, 28 October 1975. Scotland Yard could only photograph arrestees if they convicted a crime which necessitated fingerprinting in the first place.

101. Football/Ministerial Working Party on Crowd Problems, Visit to Stoke City, 25 July 1974, HO 300/112.

102. Note of a Meeting at Greater Manchester Police Headquarters with Home Secretary Merlyn Rees, 30 October 1976, HO 287/2056.

103. See Armstrong and Hobbs, 'Tackled From Behind', and 'High Tackles and Professional Fouls'.

104. For an excellent account of this process, in the context of the addition of seated stadiums, see King, *The End of the Terraces*.

105. See, for example, letter from Ned Boulting to Denis Howell, 21 August 1974, HO 300/114.

106. See Proposal for Identicard System, McCrudden, Newton and Partners Systems Consultants, sent to Home Office, 4 September 1974, HO 300/114. See also Shop and Commerce Ltd. to Denis Howell, 11 May 1974, AT 60/12.

107. See Background Note on Identity Card Schemes, Department of the Environment, undated (1974), HO 300/114, file 4.

108. Everton, in particular, developed a complicated 'Travel Club' scheme for European matches in 1975. See letter from Everton Football Club to R. D. Compton, Department of the Environment, 28 July 1975, AT 60/39, file 2.

109. See, for example, Notes by D. V. Ellison, Chief Passenger Marketing Manager for British Rail, Meeting with Denis Howell, 10 September 1974, National Archives, Public Record Office, British Transport Commission and British Railway files (hereafter AN) 156/469.

110. A. Johnson, National Union of Football Supporters, to Denis Howell, 6 August 1974, AT 25/247.

111. Mrs. J. McKay to Denis Howell, 2 May 1974, AT 60/12.

112. Football/Ministerial Working Party on Crowd Problems, Visit to Stoke City, 25 July 1974, HO 300/112.

113. Richard Lane to Miss R. J. Cox, Sports Division, Department of the Environment, 13 September 1974, HO 300/114.
114. Hampshire Constabulary to the Harrington Commission, 19 October 1967, HLG 120/1465.
115. Football/Ministerial Working Party on Crowd Problems, Visit to Leeds United, 25 April 1974, HO 300/112.
116. Harrington Report, p. 39.
117. Lang, *Report of the Working Party on Crowd Behaviour at Football Matches*, p. 9. Lang's group mentioned an individual trial at a West Ham United vs Manchester United match at Upton Park in East London on 29 March 1969. The results must have been underwhelming, because the report gave no specific details, but concluded that it would be of benefit only in the future.
118. Note of a Meeting between Home Office and police representatives, 2 October 1969, HO 287/1500.
119. *Parliamentary Debates, House of Commons*, vol. 893, col. 1785 (19 June 1975).
120. Safety at Sports Grounds Bill, Points Raised During the Debate on Second Reading in the House Of Commons, 19 June 1975, Notes prepared by Denis Howell, AT 60/37, file 45.
121. The details of this process are recounted in G. Armstrong and R. Giulianotti, 'From Another Angle: Police Surveillance and Football Supporters', in C. Norris, J. Moran and G. Armstrong (eds), *Surveillance, Closed Circuit Television and Social Control* (London: Ashgate, 1999), pp. 113–35.
122. Frosdick and Marsh, *Football Hooliganism*, Part IV.

5 Stretching Punishment

1. S. Greenfield and G. Osborn, *Regulating Football: Commodification, Consumption and the Law* (London: Pluto, 2001).
2. E. Trivizas, 'Offences and Offenders in Football Crowd Disorders', *British Journal of Criminology*, 20:3 (July 1980), pp. 276–88; E. Trivizas, 'Sentencing the Football Hooligan', *British Journal of Criminology*, 21:4 (October 1981), pp. 342–9.
3. Armstrong and Hobbs, 'Tackled From Behind'.
4. Armstrong and Young, 'Legislators and Interpreters'.
5. Working Party on Crowd Behaviour, Report of Visit to Bristol, 22 August 1974, National Archives, Public Record Office, Department of the Environment files (hereafter AT), 25/247.
6. Ibid.
7. Home Secretary Reginald Maudling to Denis Follows, Football Association, 27 August 1970, National Archives, Public Record Office, Home Office files (hereafter HO), 287/1630.
8. Trivizas, 'Offences and Offenders in Football Crowd Disorders', pp. 278–9.
9. Trivizas, 'Disturbances Associated with Football Matches'.
10. Trivizas, 'Sentencing the Football Hooligan', pp. 344–6. Though the records consulted for this chapter do not include the entire record of arrests for any one district over the entire period, I reviewed all records which were periodically sent on to either office. In particular, the Home Office wanted statistics from high-profile derbies or annual arrest statistics from troublesome areas.

11. Tottenham and St Anns Road district Schedules of Prisoners Charged, in letter from Commander E. F. Maybanks, New Scotland Yard to Miss Green, Home Office, Police Department, 3 March 1977, HO 287/2053.

12. Theft could be charged under Section 1 of the Theft Act 1968 if magistrates and/or police requested serious sentencing. The Criminal Damage Act of 1971 could also be used in certain cases, as could the Prevention of Crime Act 1953, especially in weapons charges. Police were given discretion in which charges, above or beyond the Public Order Act 1936, to bring against spectators.

13. See, for example, the arrest schedules from Chelsea v. Fulham, 15 February 1977, HO 287/2053.

14. West Midlands Constabulary report to D. J. Trevelyan, Home Office, 2 March 1972, HO 287/2051.

15. J. Williams, 'Football Hooliganism: Offences, Arrests and Violence – A Critical Note', *British Journal of Law and Society*, 7:1 (1980), pp. 104–11.

16. Armstrong and Hobbs, 'Tackled From Behind'. The Wolverhampton case predates their estimation of the first use of Crown Court charges in London in November 1973 by eighteen months.

17. See the review of previous studies in Frosdick and Marsh, *Football Hooliganism*, pp. 84–5.

18. Schedule of Prisoners Charged at Tottenham & St Anns Rd. (YT and YA) in Report of Metropolitan Police, 21 February, 1977, HO 287/2053.

19. See, for example, the various arrest files from West Midlands Constabulary and Liverpool and Bootle Constabulary in HO 287/2051.

20. Frank Williamson to D. J. Trevelyan, Home Office, 17 October 1969, HO 287/1500.

21. Comments by Superintendent Ralphs from Stoke, in Football/Ministerial Working Party on Crowd Problems, Visit to Stoke City, 25 July 1974, HO 300/112, file 44.

22. Notes for reply to Newcastle Football Club, Denis Howell, 5 November 1975, AT 60/41.

23. Working Party on Crowd Behaviour, Report of Visit to Bristol, 22 August 1974, AT 25/247.

24. *Parliamentary Debates, House of Commons*, vol. 751, col. 1864 (26 October 1967).

25. Ibid., vol. 775, col. 31 (9 December 1968).

26. For example, see Teddy Taylor's comments in *Parliamentary Debates, House of Commons*, vol. 751, col. 1864 (26 October 1967), and Sir Greville Janner (Labour: Leicester) in vol. 782, col. 1597 (1 May 1969).

27. See Note of a Meeting between Home Secretary and Denis Howell, 10 September 1974, HO 300/113, file 7.

28. *Parliamentary Debates, House of Commons*, vol. 929, col. 1353 (6 April 1977). There is no record that the Home Office acted on the suggestion.

29. Ibid., vol. 931, col. 728 (5 May 1977).

30. Ibid., vol. 893, col. 1783 (19 June 1975).

31. Hall and Jefferson (eds), *Resistance Through Rituals*.

32. Football/Ministerial Working Party on Crowd Problems, Visit to Newcastle, 25 April 1974, HO 300/112, file 32. See also Visit to Sunderland, 24 May 1974, file 31.

33. *Parliamentary Debates, House of Commons*, vol. 931, col. 789 (6 April 1977).

34. See Hall, 'The Treatment of "Football Hooliganism" in the Press', pp. 15–36.

35. See Taylor, *Football and Its Fans*, pp. 163–9.

36. Letter from Dorothy M. Woolley, Secretary of Manchester United Fan Club to Denis Howell, 30 April 1974, AT 60/12.

37. Working Party on Crowd Behaviour At Football Matches, Report of a Meeting at Ibrox Park, Glasgow, 16 June 1969, HO 287/1500.

38. Letter from Alan Hardaker, Football League Secretary, to Working Party/Home Office officials, 1 October 1969, HO 287/1500.

39. Memorandum by Chairman J. G. Lang to Working Party on Crowd Behaviour at Football Matches, undated (summer/early fall 1969), HO 287/1500.

40. See *Report of the Working Party on Crowd Behaviour at Football Matches* (London: HMSO, 1969), paragraph 30. The debated paragraph, initially marked 29A, was reworked several times to achieve the desired tone. See Working Party on Crowd Behaviour at Football Matches, Modifications to Final Report Proposed by Chairman, undated (summer/early fall 1969). In HO 287/1500.

41. On Taverne, see *Parliamentary Debates, House of Commons*, vol. 751, col. 1864 (26 October 1967). On Callaghan, see vol. 782, col. 1597 (1 May 1969).

42. Note of a Meeting with Representatives of the Football Interests at the Home Office, 13 August 1970, HO 287/1630.

43. Home Secretary Reginald Maudling to Denis Follows, Football Association, 27 August 1970, HO 287/1630.

44. Football/Ministerial Working Party on Crowd Problems, Visit to Newcastle United, 25 April 1974, HO 300/112.

45. Letter from the Magistrates' Association to Roy Jenkins, Minister of State for the Home Department, 20 November 1975, AT 60/41.

46. On the Tottenham incident, see Chapter 2. In August of 1974, a young man fatally stabbed another at Blackpool, and many newspapers falsely reported it as the first murder among football spectators. See *Daily Telegraph*, 26 August 1974. On earlier incidents of fatal violence see Dunning et al., *The Roots of Football Hooliganism*.

47. *Guardian*, 30 July 1975.

48. Letter from T. J. Higgs, Chairman of South West London Commission Area, Petty Sessional Division of Wallington, to Denis Howell, Department of Environment, 30 July 1975, AT 60/39, file E1.

49. Letter from J. A. Chilcott, Legal Department of Home Office to D. A. S. Sharp, Department of Environment, 30 July 1975. In AT 60/40. Two 'senior detention centres' existed, but between 1974–6 the Home Office Advisory Council on the Penal System continuously considered discontinuing their use, AT 60/41, file E5.

50. Home Office brief prepared for Home Secretary Roy Jenkins by Police Department at Home Office, 6 September 1974, HO 300/113.

51. Letter from Private Secretary S. G. Norris, Home Office to Mr Chilcott, Legal Department, and other Home Office officials, 21 August 1974, HO 300/113.

52. See, for example, The National Council of Women for Great Britain Memorandum on the Working of the Children and Young Persons Act 1969 prepared for the House of Commons Expenditure Committee, July 1974, AT 25/247. The committee consisted of several juvenile judges, magistrates and social workers, and supported Howell in his fight for more attendance and detention centres.

53. D. Downes and R. Morgan, 'Dumping the "Hostages to Fortune"?: The Politics of Law and Order in Post-War Britain', in M. Maguire, R. Morgan and R. Reiner (eds), *The Oxford Handbook of Criminology* (Oxford: Oxford University Press, 1994), pp. 87–9.

54. See A. Newbury, 'Youth Crime: Whose Responsibility?', *Journal of Law and Society*, 35 (2008), p. 131–49, see p. 133.

55. D. B. Cornish and R. V. G. Clarke, *Home Office Research Study: Residential Treatment and its Effects on Delinquency*, 32 (London: HMSO, 1975).
56. R. Smith, *Children and the Courts* (London: Sweet and Maxwell, 1979), p. 99.
57. See Newbury, 'Youth Crime: Whose Responsibility?' p. 137.
58. Letter from D. A. S. Sharp, Home Office to Private Secretary for Denis Howell, 17 September 1974, AT 25/247.
59. For the meeting notes and prepared briefs for the meeting between Howell and Jenkins, see Note of a Meeting Between the Home Secretary and Mr Denis Howell, 10 September 1974. In HO 300/113, files 5–7. The quotes in the previous two paragraphs are drawn from the meeting minutes.
60. The CYPA would not be reviewed until the 1975–6 session, under Cmd. 6494.
61. Letter from R. M. Whalley, Home Office to T. H. Williams, Legal Advisers Branch, and Mr Richard Lane, 15 January 1975, HO 300/113, file 10.
62. Note from T. H. Williams, Legal Adviser's Branch to R. M. Whalley, Home Office, 17 January 1975, HO 300/113, file 11B.
63. Note of a Meeting with Mr Howell, 12 May 1975, HO 300/122, file 75.
64. See Howell and other MPs comments in the *Guardian*, 2 September 1975.
65. Brief on Sentencing Policy: Meeting with Home Secretary, 16 September 1975, prepared by Department of Environment, AT 60/39.
66. Appendix 3, The Scope for New Penalties, attached to Brief for Home Secretary's Meeting with Denis Howell, 11 October 1976, HO 287/2055.

6 The Football Front

1. For various aspects of the commercialization of football, see King, *The End of the Terraces*.
2. See Back et al., 'Beyond the Racist/Hooligan Couplet'.
3. Back et al., *The Changing Face of Football*; Garland and Rowe, *Racism and Anti-Racism in Football*.
4. C. Husbands, *Racial Exclusionism and the City: The Urban Support of the National Front* (London: Unwin Hyman, 1983); H. Fielding, *The National Front* (London: Routledge, Keegan & Paul, 1980); S. Taylor, *The National Front in English Politics* (London: Palgrave Macmillan, 1982).
5. M. H. Williams, *The Impact of Radical Right-Wing Parties in West European Democracies* (London: Palgrave Macmillan, 2006).
6. Ibid., ch. 8 on the impact of peripheral politics.
7. P. Vasili, *The First Black Footballer: Arthur Wharton, 1865–1930* (London: Frank Cass, 1998).
8. C. Harris, 'Post-war Migration and the Industrial Reserve Army', in W. James and C. Harris (eds), *Inside Babylon: The Caribbean Diaspora in Britain* (London: Verso, 1993), pp. 9–54; G. Lewis, 'Black Women's Employment and the British Economy', in *Inside Babylon*, pp. 73–96; Peach, 'Empire, the Economy, and Immigration'.
9. See Vasili, *Colouring over the White Line*.
10. For example, see B. Woolnough, *Black Magic: England's Black Footballers* (London: Pelham, 1983).
11. *Bulldog*, 37 (January or February 1984?), p. 8. *Bulldog* was released intermittently due to constraints on publication and funding. Therefore, while all of the issues are numbered, they are not always dated.

12. See also C. King, *Offside Racism: Playing the White Man* (Oxford: Berg, 2004), p. 19.
13. In E. Cashmore, *Black Sportsmen* (London: Routledge, 1982), p. 194.
14. R. Turner, *In Your Blood: Football Culture in the Late 1980s and Early 1990s* (London: Working Press, 1990), p. 31.
15. Supporter quoted in Hill, *'Out of His Skin': The John Barnes Phenomenon* (London: Faber and Faber, 1989), p. 71.
16. *Bulldog*, 38 (November/December 1983?), p. 8.
17. *Bulldog*, 36 (October 1983?), p. 6.
18. *Bulldog*, 2 (October 1977), p. 5.
19. *Bulldog*, 17 (February/March 1980), p. 6.
20. For example, see account of violence at Tottenham in *Bulldog*, 24 (September 1981), p. 6.
21. *Bulldog*, 25 (November/December 1981), p. 6.
22. In Robins, *We Hate Humans*, p. 112.
23. Hill, *'Out of His Skin'*, pp. 134–7.
24. Back et al., 'Beyond the Racism/Hooligan Couplet', p. 420.
25. Turner, *In Your Blood*, p. 31.
26. *Bulldog*, 14 (August 1979?), p. 6.
27. Ibid.
28. *Bulldog*, 15 (September 1979?), p. 6.
29. See *Bulldog*, 20 (January/February 1981?); *Bulldog*, 28 (June/July 1982).
30. *Bulldog*, 28 (June/July 1982?), p. 6.
31. *Bulldog*, 8 (October 1978?), p. 2.
32. See, for example, *Bulldog*, 31 (January 1983), p. 6.
33. *Bulldog*, 24 (September 1981), p. 3.
34. *Bulldog*, 18 (March/April 1980), p. 6.
35. *Bulldog*, 18 (March/April 1980), p. 6.
36. Quoted in Robins, *We Hate Humans*, p. 101.
37. Ibid., 109.
38. *Fortune's Always Hiding*, 4 (October/November 1989), pp. 8–9.
39. Quoted in N. Lowles, 'Far Out with the Far Right', in Perryman, *Hooligan Wars*, p. 118.
40. Hill, *'Out of His Skin'*, p. 102.
41. See D. Canter, M. Comber, and D. Uzell, *Football in its Place: An Environmental Psychology of Football Grounds* (London: Routledge, 1989); Lowles, 'Far Out with the Far Right', pp. 111–4.
42. See comments from police in J. Garland and M. Rowe, 'Racism and Anti-Racism in English Football', in U. Merkel and W. Tokorski (eds), *Racism and Xenophobia in European Football* (Oxford: Meyer and Meyer, 1996).
43. On the conspiratorial frameworks of fascism against other parties and the state, see M. Billig, *Fascists: A Social Psychological View of the National Front* (New York: Harcourt, Brace, Jovanovich, 1978).
44. See *Camerawork* (Fall 1977), special issue on Lewisham marches. See also John Tyndall's comments in the *Daily Mail*, 17 August 1977.
45. *Western Daily Press* (Bristol), no date (early 1978?) in Runnymede Collection (hereafter RC), Sub-fonds 6, Box 55, subsection 2.
46. *Daily Star*, 8 December 1980.
47. See accounts in the *Daily Mail*, 23 and 24 March 1981.
48. Taylor, *The National Front in English Politics*, p. 131.

49. *National Front News*, Editorial Bulletin, no. 86 (undated), RC MDRXT/6/02/B, Box 55, Folder 4.
50. *Bulldog*, 16 (November/December 1979), p. 6.
51. For example, see letters to the editor in *Bulldog*, 39 (January/February 1984?), p. 8.
52. See *Bulldog*, 21 (March/April 1981?), p. 5. The *Daily Mail's* 'league' may be derivative of earlier fictive contests focused on hooliganism and football violence rather than racism. In 1974, the *Daily Mirror* established the 'League of Shame' to report on arrest records at different stadiums. See Frosdick and Marsh, *Football Hooliganism*, p. 117.
53. *Bulldog*, 40 (March/April 1984?), p. 8.
54. Ibid., p. 7.
55. See *Bulldog*, 8 (June 1978), p. 4.
56. *Bulldog*, 11 (February/March 1979?), p. 2.
57. *Bulldog*, 19 (May/June 1980?), p. 6.
58. *Bulldog*, 16 (November/December 1979), p. 6.
59. *Bulldog*, 14 (August 1979?), p. 6.
60. See Chapter 2, and Williams et al., *Hooligans Abroad*.
61. For example, see *Bulldog*, 19 (May/June 1980?), p. 18.
62. The Press Council, Press Release No. W12483/1913, RC Subfonds 6, Box 55, Folder 1.
63. See 'Complaint by National Front: Summary of Adjudication', RC Subfonds 6, Box 55, Folder 1.
64. See Lowles, 'Far Out with the Far Right', pp. 112–3.
65. *Spearhead*, 201 (July 1985), pp. 4–6.
66. *Vanguard*, 40 (Autumn 1993), pp. 12.
67. Lowles, 'Far Out with the Far Right', p. 120.
68. *Searchlight* special issue, 'Terror on Our Terraces' (Autumn 1985).
69. For example, *The Anti-Nazi League: A Critical Examination*, a resistance pamphlet produced by the Colin Roach Centre (1995). In British Library, Main Collection (hereafter BL): YD.2006a.8935.
70. *Red Action*, 1 (February 1982), p. 1.
71. *Red Action*, 3 (May 1982), article entitled 'Grounds for Rebellion'.
72. *Red Action*, 1 (February 1982), p. 1.
73. K. Bullstreet, *Bash the Fash: Anti-Fascist Recollections, 1984–93* (London: Kate Sharpley Library, 2001), pp. 1–2, BL: YD.2005.b.1768. Obviously, the name "Bullstreet" is most likely a fabricated surname meant to protect the author's confidentiality and subtly promote his street credentials.
74. *The Anti-Nazi League: A Critical Examination*, p. 13.
75. *Bash the Fash*, ch. 3.
76. *The Anti-Nazi League: A Critical Examination*, p. 4–5.
77. *Bash the Fash*, p. 4.
78. In *Morning Star*, 29 December 1977.
79. Special issue, 'Terror on Our Terraces', p. 6.
80. Ibid., p. 3.
81. 'Putting the Boot In', *Labour Weekly*, 8 May 1981.

7 'Ten Years behind the Times'

1. Article entitled 'Ten Years Too Late', from the fanzine *Two Sevens*, reprinted in *Our Day Will Come: Celtic and Manchester United Fanzine*, 13 (Summer 1994?).

2. See Back et al., *The Changing Face of Football*; Garland and Rowe, *Racism and Anti-Racism in Football*.

3. See, for example, the beneficial evaluations of anti-racist organizations in football: C. Kassimeris (ed.), *Anti-Racism in European Football: Fair Play for All* (Plymouth: Lexington, 2009).

4. Garland and Rowe, *Racism and Anti-Racism in Football*, pp. 54–6.

5. Commission for Racial Equality, *Lets Kick Racism Out of Football: Campaign Evaluation Stage One – Supporters* (CRE Research and Information, May 1994).

6. In 1995, the campaign was taken over by the Advisory Group Against Racism and Intimidation (AGARI), a steering group which sought to broaden the CRE's initiatives in the campaign. Later the campaign received autonomy under the CRE as it evolved into *Kick it Out*, an even broader project that emphasized its new ties with other footballing organizations. See Garland and Rowe, *Racism and Anti-Racism in Football*, pp. 55–6.

7. See Back et al., *The Changing Face of Football*, pp. 192–3.

8. See R. Honeyford, *The Commission for Racial Equality: British Bureaucracy and the Multiethnic Society* (New Brunswick, NJ: Transaction Publishers, 1998). Despite Honeyford's conservative conclusions and questionable analysis, his background work on the CRE established a good history of the CRE's initiatives.

9. Press Release and Summary of the Policy Studies Institute, 7 June 1991, Runnymede Collection (hereafter RC), Subfonds 6, Box 61, Folder 3.

10. Interview with CRE Campaigns Unit, quoted in J. Carver, J. Garland and M. Rowe, *Racism, Xenophobia and Football: A Preliminary Investigation*, Research Paper 3 (University of Leicester: Centre for the Study of Public Order, 1995), p. 19.

11. Commission for Racial Equality News Release no. 539, 6 September 1994, RC Subfonds 6, Box 61, Folder 5.

12. See RC Subfonds 6, Box 140, Folder 3 for the large collection of press clippings and releases assembled by the Runnymede Foundation between 1993 and 1995.

13. See, for example, the report on Gillingham Football Club in *The Chatham Standard*, 13 August 1993.

14. *Morning Star*, 13 May 1994.

15. *Independent*, 27 October 1993.

16. *Kick It!*, 1 (1994), introductory comments.

17. Sir Herman Ouseley in Commission for Racial Equality News Release No. 537, 18 August 1994, RC Subfonds 6, Box 140, Folder 3.

18. See Back et al., *The Changing Face of Football*, ch. 7.

19. *Kick It!*, 1 (1994), editorial comments.

20. Ibid., p. 4.

21. For details, see Osborn and Greenfield, *Regulating Football*.

22. *Kick It!*, 1 (1994), p. 3.

23. *Eliminating Racism from Football: A Report by the Football Task Force*, submitted to the Minister for Sport (Tony Banks) by David Mellor on 30 March 1998, British Library (hereafter BL), m02/10680.

24. For the excellent work on the genealogy and purpose of football fanzines, see Redhead, *The Passion and the Fashion*; and R. Haynes, *The Football Imagination: The Rise of Football Fanzine Culture* (London: Arena, 1995).

25. The main exception is *When Saturday Comes*, a popular national fanzine on English and European football.

26. The Taylor Report (1989) recommended that all stadiums should be converted to seating accommodations only. The FA followed the recommendations and mandated changes to all stadiums in the five years after the report's publication. The transition to all-seated stadiums has been widely championed, along with the implementation of CCTV, as responsible for the massive decline in football violence in the 1990s. All-seated stadiums have also been criticized, usually by spectators, as diminishing the communal aspects of football spectating.
27. *Filbo Fever*, 7 (August/September 1995), p. 23.
28. For a history of LFUARF activities, see B. Holland, L. Jackson, G. Jarvie and M. Smith, 'Sport and Racism in Yorkshire: A Case Study', in J. Hill and J. Williams (eds), *Sport and Identity in the North of England* (Keele: Keele University Press, 1996), pp. 165–86; J. Thomas, 'Kicking Racism Out of Football: A Supporter's View', *Race & Class*, 36 (January 1995), pp. 95–101.
29. *Marching Altogether*, 13 (April 1992), p. 11.
30. *Partnerships to Keep Racism Out of Football*, Conference Proceedings, 4 November 1997 (Reading: Public Impact Communications 1998). Conference sponsored by the Reading Council for Racial Equality. BL: YK.1998.b.4950.
31. Parker was signed between the time Mohamed submitted his letter and the editor published it, along with his response.
32. *Flashing Blade*, 51 (December 1996), Flashing Back – letters to editor section.
33. *Flashing Blade*, 52 (January 1997), Flashing Back.
34. *South Riding*, 7 (During 1990/91 Season?), p. 37.
35. *South Riding*, 9 (During 1991/92 Season?).
36. *Filbo Fever*, 4 (October/November 1994), p. 2.
37. *Filbo Fever*, 7 (August/September 1995), p. 3.
38. *Filbo Fever*, 4 (October/November 1994), pp. 2–3.
39. *When Skies Are Grey*, 33 (February 1994), letter to editor.
40. *When Skies Are Grey*, 35 (May/June 1994), editorial section.
41. *Times Educational Supplement*, 15 October 1993.
42. For analysis of undercover police operations in the late 1980s, see Armstrong and Hobbs, 'Tackled From Behind'.
43. Anti-Fascist Action statement to Football League and Football Association, 22 April 1988, RC Subfonds 6, Box 140, Folder 3.
44. See editorial statement, which appeared at the end of every issue, in *Fighting Talk*, 8 (undated, early 1994?).
45. Nearly all the items for sale in *Fighting Talk* bear evidence to the ways in which AFA organized local branches around football clubs, especially stickers, which were disseminated to combat BNP Party stickers and graffiti.
46. See *Campaign Against Racism and Fascism*, 8 (May/June 1992).
47. *Fighting Talk*, Football Special Issue, 9 (August 1994), p. 3.
48. Ibid., p. 11.
49. References and citations in this paragraph and the previous can be found in *Fighting Talk*, Football Special Issue, 9 (August 1994).
50. *Our Day Will Come* was one of the few fanzines that supported multiple clubs, in large part due to the number of Irish migrants living in Manchester.
51. *Marching Altogether*, 5 (November 1989).
52. Quoted in *Fighting Talk*, 10 (undated, fall 1994?).
53. *Red Attitude*, 12 (Spring 1997).
54. *Red Attitude*, 2 (October 1994).

55. Bovril is a yeasty, beef broth often thinned and warmed, and taken to matches when the weather is poor.

56. *Red Attitude*, 2 (October 1994).

57. The comic ran in several issues between 1990 and 1993. See *Marching Altogether*, 9 (undated, fall 1990) for the first comic, originally titled '101 Things to Do with a Ku Klux Klansman'.

58. *Marching Altogether*, 5 (November 1989).

59. *You Wot!*, 2 (September/October 1994).

60. *Our Day Will Come*, 10 (undated, fall 1991?).

8 'A Different Set of Rules'

1. G. Lipsitz, *The Possessive Investment in Whiteness: How White People Profit from Identity Politics* (Philadelphia, PA: Temple University Press, 1998); Bonnett, 'How the Working-Class Became White'.

2. P. Kolchin, 'Whiteness Studies: The New History of Race in America', *The Journal of American History*, 89:1 (June 2002), pp. 154–73.

3. For example, see T. Allen, *The Invention of the White Race: The Origin of Racial Oppression in Anglo-America* (London: Verso, 1997); A. Ferber, 'Constructing Whiteness: The Intersections of Race and Gender in US White Supremacist Discourse', *Ethnic and Racial Studies*, 21:1 (January 1998), pp. 48–63.

4. D. R. Roediger, *The Wages of Whiteness: Race and the Making of the American Working Class* (London: Verso, 1991); N. Ignatiev, *How the Irish Became White*, 2nd edn (London: Routledge, 2007); M. F. Jacobsen, *Whiteness of a Different Color: European Immigrants and the Alchemy of Race* (Cambridge, MA: Harvard University Press, 1999); G. E. Hale, *Making Whiteness: The Culture of Segregation in the South, 1890–1940* (London: Vintage, 1999).

5. Back et al., *The Changing Face of Football*.

6. King, *Offside Racism*.

7. V. Ware and L. Back, *Out of Whiteness: Color, Politics, and Culture* (Chicago, IL: University of Chicago Press, 2002), pp. 6–8.

8. Hill, 'Out of His Skin', p. 71. A movie depicting the Zulus as savages in battle with British troops had been released less than a year earlier. The chants mimicking *Zulu* (1964) were meant to deride the player.

9. Ibid., pp. 71–2.

10. In Cashmore, *Black Sportsmen*, p. 151.

11. Ibid., p. 194.

12. King, *Offside Racism*, p. 19.

13. Back et al., *Changing Face of Football*, pp. 93–5 and 130–1.

14. Robins, *We Hate Humans*, p. 112.

15. B. Holland, '"Kicking Racism Out of Football": an Assessment of Racial Harrassment in and around Football Grounds', *New Community*, 21:4 (October 1995), pp. 567–86.

16. Cashmore, *Black Sportsmen*, p. 154.

17. In S. Orakwue, *Pitch Invaders: The Modern Black Football Revolution* (London; Vista, 1998), p. 120. Orakwue's title provides some evidence of the threatening way in which many saw black footballer's encroachment into professional football.

18. N. Hornby, *Fever Pitch* (New York: Riverhead, 1992), pp. 189–90.

19. S. Hall, 'The Multi-cultural Question' in B. Hesse (ed.), *Un/Settled Multiculturalisms: Diasporas, Entanglements, 'Transruptions'* (London: Zed Books, 2000), pp. 217–8.
20. Smith, *New Right Discourse*, pp. 71–4.
21. Cashmore, *Black Sportsmen*, p. 194.
22. See Turner, *In Your Blood*, p. 31.
23. Hornby, *Fever Pitch*, pp. 188–9.
24. King, *Offside Racism*, p. 19.
25. Turner, *In Your Blood*, p. 31.
26. Robins, *We Hate Humans*, p. 51.
27. Cashmore, *Black Sportsmen*, p. 193.
28. On 'styles' of football, see C. Critcher, 'Putting on the Style: Aspects of Recent English Football', in Williams and Wagg (eds), *British Football and Social Change*, pp. 67–84.
29. 'Tackling Back: Combating Racism in Scottish Football', Report of a Conference organized by Stirling District Council. British Library (hereafter BL) 98/09500. Colquhoun became the Chairman of the Scottish Professional Footballers' Association and was brought to the conference to testify to acts of racism in Scottish football by recounting his own playing experiences in the 1980s.
30. *Eagle Eye*, 19 (November 1991).
31. Orakwue, *Pitch Invaders*, p. 120.
32. In Hill, *'Out of His Skin'*, p. 129.
33. H. Bhabha, 'Of Mimicry and Man: The Ambivalence of Colonial Discourse', *October*, 28 (Spring 1984), pp. 125–33.
34. Cashmore, *Black Sportsmen*, p. 194.
35. *Flashing Blade*, 52 (January 1997).
36. R. Moran, 'Racism in Football: A Victim's Perspective', *Soccer and Society*, 1 (2000), p. 192–3.
37. *Morning Star*, 13 May 1994.
38. *Red Attitude*, 4 (March 1995).
39. King, *Offside Racism*, pp. 24–5.
40. *Red Attitude*, 4 (March 1995).
41. In Jon Carter, 'Rewind: Ince Breaks Down Barriers', ESPNSoccernet, 9 June 2011.
42. bell hooks, *Black Looks: Race and Representation* (Boston, MA: South End Press, 1992), p. 166.
43. Ibid., p. 169.
44. Ibid., p. 166.
45. *Guardian*, 23 June 2008.
46. *South Riding: The Alternative Look at Barnsley Football Club*, 15 (April/May 1992), p. 27.
47. A. Rahim, 'The Standard Bearer', *United Colours of Football*, 2 (2001).
48. 'Black & a Blue' in *Bert Trautmann's Helmet*, a Manchester City fanzine, reprinted in *United Colours of Football*, 2 (2001).
49. In all of the documents reviewed for Chapters Three, Four and Five on the 'total policy of containment', none mentioned racism as a problem in the 1970s.
50. Garland and Rowe, *Racism and Anti-Racism in Football*, pp. 103–4.
51. *Times*, 3 March, 1981.
52. *Times*, 23 February, 1981.
53. For more details on individual programmes and initiatives, see Garland and Rowe, *Racism and Anti-Racism in Football*, ch. 3.

54. Vasili, *The First Black Footballer.*
55. Football Unites Racism Divides (FURD), 'History of Black Footballers Exhibition', exhibition documentation available at FURD. The exhibition has been sponsored (and co-sponsored) by different organizations in the UK at different times, including the Institute of Race Relations and Kick It Out.
56. For dominant anti-racist teleologies present in many anti-racist narratives, see P. Cohen, '"It's Racism What Dunnit": Hidden Narratives in Theories of Racism', in J. Donald and A. Rattansi (eds), *'Race', Culture and Difference* (London: Sage, 1992), pp. 62–103.
57. Vasili, *The First Black Footballer*; Vasili, *Colouring over the White Line.*
58. Vasili, *Colouring over the White Line*, pp. 19–20.
59. Ibid., p. 21.
60. Ibid., p. 24.
61. Ibid., p. 25.
62. *Tiocaidh Ar La!: For Celtic and Ireland*, 1 (Spring 1992). Alf Garnett was a fictional character on a series of British sitcoms, the most popular of which was *Till Death Us Do Part*, who frequently expressed his conservative, racist and nativist views of British politics and society.
63. Conference Proceedings, Partnerships to Keep Racism Out of Football, 4 November 1997, pp. 10–11, BL: YK.1998.b.4950.
64. *Kick It!*, published by the Commission for Racial Equality and Let's Kick Racism Out of Football (later renamed Kick It Out) Campaign, no. 1 (1993), BL: ZK.9.b.8661.
65. Eliminating Racism from Football: A Report by the Football Task Force, submitted to the Minister for Sport on 30 March 1998, BL: m02/10680.
66. For example, Ian Wright frequently resisted the responsibility. See I. Wright, *Mr. Wright: The Explosive Autobiography of Ian Wright* (London: Collins Willow, 1996).
67. M. Marqusee, *Redemption Song: Muhammad Ali and the Spirit of the Sixties*, 2nd edn (London: Verso, 1999), p. 13.
68. Ibid., p. 20.
69. *Kick It!*, 1 (1993).
70. *Daily Telegraph*, 16 October 1993, p. 3.
71. *Kick It!*, 1 (1994).
72. *When Skies Are Grey*, 33 (February 1994).
73. *When Skies Are Grey*, 37 (Fall 1994).
74. *You Wot!: The Anti-Racist Alternative Torquay United Mag*, 2 (September/October 1994).
75. *Fighting Talk*, 9 (undated, early 1994?).
76. See debates in *Fighting Talk* nos. 7–9 (undated, early 1990s).
77. Hall, 'The Multicultural Question', pp. 216 and 225–7.
78. Smith, *New Right Discourse*, pp. 18–20.
79. See Gilroy, *'There Ain't No Black in the Union Jack'*, pp. 116–7.

Conclusion

1. Back et al., *The Changing Face of Football.*
2. See, for example, *Guardian*, 27 May 2008. Sepp Blatter, a Football League official, has attempted to institute limits on the number of foreign players on each British team.
3. King, *Offside Racism.*
4. See Kassimeris (ed.), *Anti-Racism in European Football.*

5. See Ibid., ch. 6.
6. See, for example, T. Crabbe and A. Brown, '"You're Not Welcome Anymore": The Football Crowd, Class and Social Exclusion', in Wagg (ed.), *British Football and Social Exclusion*.
7. *Guardian*, 2 January 2008.
8. Dunning et al. (eds), *Fighting Fans*; Armstrong and Giulianotti (eds), *Fear and Loathing in World Football*.
9. *Guardian*, 13 October 2010.

BIBLIOGRAPHY

Allan, J., *Bloody Casuals: Diary of a Football Hooligan* (Ellon: Famedram, 1989).

Allen, T., *The Invention of the White Race: The Origin of Racial Oppression in Anglo-America* (London: Verso, 1997).

Armstrong, G., *Football Hooligans: Knowing the Score* (Oxford: Berg, 1998).

Armstrong, G., and D. Hobbs., 'Tackled from Behind', in R. Giulianotti, N. Bonney and M. Hepworth (eds) *Football, Violence, and Social Identity* (London: Routledge, 1994).

Armstrong, G., and R. Giulianotti, 'From Another Angle: Police Surveillance and Football Supporters', in C. Norris, J. Moran and G. Armstrong (eds), *Surveillance, Closed Circuit Television and Social Control* (Aldershot: Ashgate, 1998), pp. 113–35.

—, 'Constructing Social Identities: Exploring the Structured Relations of Football Rivalries', in G. Armstrong and R. Giulianotti (eds), *Fear and Loathing in World Football* (Oxford: Berg, 2001).

— (eds), *Entering the Field: New Perspectives on World Football* (Oxford: Berg, 1997).

— (eds), *Fear and Loathing in World Football* (Oxford: Berg, 2001).

Armstrong, G., and R. Harris, 'Football Hooligans: Theory and Evidence', *Sociological Review*, 39:3 (1991), pp. 427–58.

Armstrong, G., and D. Hobbs, 'High Tackles and Professional Fouls: The Policing of Soccer Hooliganism', in C. Fijnaut and G. T. Marx (eds), *Undercover Police Surveillance in Comparative Perspective* (London: Kluwer Law International, 1995), pp. 175–93.

Armstrong, G., and M. Young, 'Legislators and Interpreters: The Law and "Football Hooligans"', in G. Armstrong and Richard Giulianotti (eds), *Entering the Field: New Perspectives on World Football* (Oxford: Berg, 1997), pp. 175–92.

Back, L., and J. Solomos (eds), *Theories of Race and Racism: A Reader* (London: Routledge, 2000).

Back, L., T. Crabbe and J. Solomos, 'Beyond the Racist/Hooligan Couplet: Race, Social Theory and Football Culture', *British Journal of Sociology*, 50:3 (1999), pp. 419–42.

—, *The Changing Face of Football: Racism, Identity, and Multiculture in the English Game* (Oxford: Berg, 2002).

Bale, J., 'The Spatial Development of the Modern Stadium', *International Review for the Sociology of Sport*, 28:2 (1993), pp. 122–33.

—, *Landscapes of Modern Sport* (Leicester: Leicester University Press, 1994).

—, and O. Moen (eds), *The Stadium and the City* (Keele: Keele University Press, 1995).

—, *Sports, Space and the City* (London: Blackburn Press, 2001).

Banton, M., *Race Relations* (London: Tavistock, 1967).

Bebber, B., '"A Misuse of Leisure": Football Violence, Politics and Family Values in 1970s Britain', in B. Bebber (ed.), *Leisure and Cultural Conflict in Twentieth-Century Britain* (Manchester: Manchester University Press, forthcoming 2012).

Bhabha, 'Of Mimicry and Man: The Ambivalence of Colonial Discourse', *October*, 28 (Spring 1984), pp. 125–33.

Billig, M., *Fascists: A Social Psychological View of the National Front* (New York: Harcourt, Brace, Jovanovich, 1978).

Bonnett, A., 'How the British Working Class Became White: The Symbolic (Re)formation of Racialized Capitalism', *Journal of Historical Sociology*, 11:3 (September 1998), pp. 316–40.

Borsay, P., *A History of Leisure: The British Experience since 1500* (London: Palgrave, 2006).

Bowling, B., 'The Emergence of Violent Racism as a Public Issue in Britain, 1945–81', in P. Panayi (ed.), *Racial Violence in Britain in the Nineteenth and Twentieth Centuries* (Leicester: Leicester University Press, 1993).

Brown, A. (ed.), *Fanatics: Power, Identity and Fandom in Football* (London: Routledge, 1998).

Buford, B., *Among the Thugs* (New York: W.W. Norton, 1991).

Bulmer, M., and J. Solomos (eds), *Ethnic and Racial Studies Today* (London: Routledge, 1999).

— (eds), *Racism* (Oxford: Oxford University Press, 1999).

Canter, D., M. Comber, D. Uzzell and O. Popplewell, *Football in Its Place: An Environmental Psychology of Football Grounds* (London: Routledge, 1989).

Carrington, B., and I. McDonald (eds), '*Race*', *Sport and British Society* (London: Routledge, 2001).

Carver, J., J. Garland and M. Rowe, 'Racism, Xenophobia and Football', *Research Paper on Crime, Order and Policing* (Leicester: Centre for the Study of Public Order, 1995).

Cashmore, E., *Black Sportsmen* (London: Routledge, 1982).

Centre for Contemporary Cultural Studies, *The Empire Strikes Back: Race and Racism in 70s Britain* (London: Hutchinson, 1982).

Clarke, J., 'Football and Working Class Fans: Tradition and Change', in R. Ingham, *Football Hooliganism: The Wider Context* (London: Inter-Action Inprint, 1978), pp. 37–60.

Cohen, P., 'Sub-Cultural Conflict and Working-Class Community', Occasional Paper No. 2 (Birmingham: Birmingham Centre for Contemporary Cultural Studies, 1972).

—, '"It's Racism What Dunnit": Hidden Narratives in Theories of Racism', in J. Donald and A. Rattansi (eds), '*Race*', *Culture and Difference* (London: Sage, 1992), pp. 62–103.

Cohen, S., *Folk Devils and Moral Panics: The Creation of the Mods and the Rockers* (London: MacGibbon & Lee, 1972).

Colls, R., and P. Dodd (eds), *Englishness: Politics and Culture, 1880–1920* (London: Croom Helm, 1986).

Cornish, D. B., and R. V. G. Clarke, *Residential Treatment and Its Effects on Delinquency: Home Office Research Study No. 32* (London, HMSO, 1975).

Crabbe, T., and A. Brown, '"You're Not Welcome Anymore": The Football Crowd, Class and Social Exclusion', in S. Wagg (ed.), *British Football and Social Exclusion* (London: Routledge, 2004).

Critcher, C., 'Putting on the Style: Aspects of Recent English Football', in J. Williams and S. Wagg (eds), *British Football and Social Change: Getting into Europe* (Leicester: Leicester University Press, 1991), pp. 67–84.

Davidoff, L., *Worlds Between: Historical Perspectives on Gender and Class* (London: Routledge, 1995).

Deakin, N., *Colour, Citizenship and British Society* (London: Panther, 1970).

Downes, D., and R. Morgan, 'Dumping the "Hostages to Fortune"?: The Politics of Law and Orderin Post-War Britain', in M. Maguire, R. Morgan and R. Reiner (eds), *The Oxford Handbook of Criminology* (Oxford: Oxford University Press, 1994), pp. 87–134.

Dunning, E., and N. Elias, *Quest for Excitement: Sport and Leisure in the Civilizing Process* (Oxford: Blackwell, 1986).

Dunning, E., P. Murphy and I. Waddington, 'Towards a Sociological Understanding of Football as a World Phenomenon', in E. Dunning, P. Murphy, I. Waddington and A. E. Astrinakis (eds), *Fighting Fans: Football Hooliganism as a World Phenomenon* (Dublin: University College Dublin Press, 2002).

Dunning, E., P. Murphy, I. Waddington and A. E. Astrinakis (eds), *Fighting Fans: Football Hooliganism as a World Phenomenon* (Dublin: University College Dublin Press, 2002).

Dunning, E., P. Murphy and J. Williams, *The Roots of Football Hooliganism: An Historical and Sociological Study* (London: Routledge, 1988).

Elkins, C., *Imperial Reckoning: The Untold Story of Britain's Gulag in Kenya* (New York: Henry Holt, 2005).

Elliot, D., and D. Smith, 'Football Stadia Disorders in the United Kingdom: Learning From Tragedy?' *Organization and Environment*, 7:3 (1993).

Ferber, A., 'Constructing Whiteness: The Intersections of Race and Gender in US White Supremacist Discourse', *Ethnic and Racial Studies*, 21:1 (January 1998), pp. 48–63.

Fielding, H., *The National Front* (London: Routledge, 1981).

Fields, B.J., 'Slavery, Race and Ideology in the United States of America', *New Left Review*, 181:3 (1990), pp. 95–118.

Finn, Gerry P.T., 'Football Violence: A Societal Psychological Perspective', in R.Giulianotti, N. Bonney and M. Hepworth (eds), *Football, Violence and Social Identity* (London: Routledge, 1994).

Foucault, M., *Madness and Civilization: A History of Insanity in the Age of Reason* (London: Vintage, 1965).

—, *The Order of Things: An Archaeology of the Human Sciences* (London: Vintage, 1970).

—, *The Archaeology of Knowledge and the Discourse on Language* (London: Vintage, 1972).

—, *The Birth of the Clinic: An Archaeology of Medical Perception* (London: Vintage, 1973).

—, *Discipline and Punish: The Birth of the Prison* (London: Vintage, 1978).

Frith, S., 'Frankie Said: But What Did They Mean?' in A. Tomlinson (ed.), *Consumption, Identity and Style* (London: Comedia, 1990).

Frosdick, S., 'Beyond Football Hooliganism', in S. Frosdick and L. Walley (eds), *Sport and Safety Management* (Oxford: Butterworth-Heinemann, 1999).

Frosdick, S., and P. Marsh, *Football Hooliganism* (Devon: Willan, 2005).

Frosdick, S., and L. Walley (eds), *Sport and Safety Management* (Oxford: Butterworth-Heinemann, 1999).

Garland, J., and M. Rowe, 'Racism and Anti-Racism in English Football', in U. Merkel and W. Tokorski (eds), *Racism and Xenophobia in European Football* (Berlin: Meyer and Meyer, 1996).

—, 'Field of Dreams? An Assessment of Antiracism in British Football', *Journal of Ethnic and Migration Studies*, 25:2 (1999), pp. 335–44.

—, *Racism and Anti-Racism in Football* (London: Palgrave Macmillan, 2001).

Garnham, N., 'Patronage, Politics and the Modernization of Leisure in Northern England: the Case of Alnwick's Shrove Tuesday Football Match', *English Historical Review*, 117:474 (2002), pp. 1228–46.

Gillis, J., *Commemorations: The Politics of National Identity* (Princeton, NJ: Princeton University Press, 1994).

Gilman, S., *Difference and Pathology: Stereotypes of Sexuality, Race and Madness* (Ithaca, NY: Cornell University Press, 1985).

Gilroy, P., *'There Ain't No Black in the Union Jack': The Cultural Politics of Race and Nation* (Chicago, IL: University of Chicago Press, 1987).

—, 'The End of Anti-Racism', *New Community*, 17:1 (1990), pp. 71–83.

Giulianotti, R., 'Social Identity and Public Order: Political and Academic Discourses on Football Violence', in R. Giulianotti, N. Bonney, and M. Hepworth (eds), *Football, Violence, and Social Identity* (London: Routledge, 1994), pp. 10–36.

—, *Football: A Sociology of The Global Game* (Cambridge: Polity, 1999).

Giulianotti, R., N. Bonney, and M. Hepworth (eds), *Football, Violence, and Social Identity* (London: Routledge, 1994).

Goode, E., and N. Ben-Yehuda, *Moral Panics: The Social Construction of Deviance* (Oxford: Blackwell, 1994).

Goulbourne, H., *Race Relations in Britain Since 1945* (London: Palgrave Macmillan, 1998).

Greenfield, S., and G. Osborn, 'When the Writ Hits the Fan: Panic Law and Football Fandom', in A. Brown (ed.), *Fanatics!: Power, Identity and Fandom in Football* (London: Routledge, 1998).

—, *Regulating Football: Commodification, Consumption and the Law* (London: Pluto, 2001).

Hale, G. E., *Making Whiteness: The Culture of Segregation in the South, 1890–1940* (London: Vintage, 1999).

Hall, C., and S. Rose (eds), *At Home With the Empire: Metropolitan Culture and the Imperial World* (Cambridge: Cambridge University Press, 2006).

Hall, S., *The Hard Road to Renewal: Thatcherism and the Crisis of the Left* (London: Verso, 1988).

—, 'Ethnicity: Identity and Difference', *Radical America*, 24 (1990), pp. 9–20.

—, 'The Multicultural Question', in B. Hesse (ed.), *Un/Settled Multiculturalisms: Diasporas, Entanglements, Transruptions* (London: Zed Books, 2000), pp. 209–41.

Hall, S., 'The Treatment of 'Football Hooliganism' in the Press', in R. Ingham, *Football Hooliganism: The Wider Context* (London: Inter-Action Inprint, 1978), pp. 15–36.

Hall, S., C. Critcher, T. Jefferson, and J. Clarke, *Policing the Crisis: Mugging, the State and Law and Order* (London: Palgrave Macmillan, 1978).

Hall, S., and M. Jacques, *The Politics of Thatcherism* (London: Lawrence and Wishart, 1983).

Hall, S., and T. Jefferson (eds), *Resistance through Rituals: Youth Subcultures in Post-War Britain* (London: Hutchinson, 1976).

Hansen, R., *Citizenship and Immigration in Post-War Britain: The Institutional Origins of a Multicultural Nation* (Oxford: Oxford University Press, 2000).

Hargreaves, J. *Sport, Power and Culture: A Social and Historical Analysis of Popular Sports in Britain* (New York: St Martin's, 1986).

Harrington, J. A., *Soccer Hooliganism: A Preliminary Report* (Bristol: John Wright and Sons, Ltd, 1968).

Harris, C., 'Post-War Migration and the Industrial Reserve Army', in W. James and C. Harris (eds), *Inside Babylon: The Caribbean Diaspora in Britain* (London: Verso, 1993), pp. 9–54.

Havighurst, A., *Britain in Transition*, 4th edn (Chicago, IL: University of Chicago Press, 1985).

Haynes, R., *The Football Imagination: The Rise of Football Fanzine Culture* (London: Arena, 1995).

Haynes, R., and S. Redhead, *The Passion and the Fashion: Football Fandom in the New Europe* (Aldershot: Avebury, 1994).

Hebdidge, D., *Subculture: The Meaning of Style* (London: Routledge, 1979).

Hill, D., '*Out of His Skin': The John Barnes Phenomenon* (London: Faber and Faber, 1989).

Hill, J., '"What Shall We Do with Them When They're Not Working": Leisure and British Historiography', in B. Bebber (ed.), *Leisure and Cultural Conflict in Twentieth-Century Britain* (Manchester: Manchester University Press, forthcoming in 2012).

Hobbs, D., and D. Robins, 'The Boy Done Good: Football Violence, Changes and Continuities', *Sociological Review*, 39:3 (1991), pp. 551–79.

Hobsbawm, E., and T. Ranger (eds), *The Invention of Tradition* (Cambridge: Cambridge University Press, 1983).

Holland, B., '"Kicking Racism Out of Football": An Assessment of Racial Harassment in and Around Football Grounds', *New Community*, 21:4 (1995), pp. 567–86.

Holland, B., L. Jackson, G. Jarvie and M. Smith, 'Sport and Racism in Yorkshire: A Case Study', in J. Hill and J. Williams (eds), *Sport and Identity in the North of England* (Keele: Keele University Press, 1996), pp. 165–86.

Holt, R., *Sport and the British: A Modern History* (Oxford: Oxford University Press, 1988).

Holt, R., and T. Mason, *Sport in Britain, 1945–2000* (Oxford: Blackwell, 2000).

Honeyford, R., *The Commission For Racial Equality: British Bureaucracy and the Multiethnic Society* (London: Transaction Publishers, 1998).

Hornby, N., *Fever Pitch* (New York: Riverhead Books, 1992).

Husbands, C., *Racial Exclusionism and the City: The Urban Support of the National Front* (London: George Allen and Unwin, 1983).

Hussain, A. M., *British Immigration Policy under the Conservative Government* (Aldershot: Ashgate, 2001).

Ignatiev, N., *How the Irish Became White*, 2nd edn (London: Routledge, 2007).

Ingham, R. (ed.), *Football Hooliganism: The Wider Context* (London: Inter-Action Inprint, 1978).

Ismond, P., *Black and Asian Athletes in British Sport and Society: A Sporting Chance?* (London: Palgrave Macmillan, 2003).

Jacobsen, M. F., *Whiteness of a Different Color: European Immigrants and the Alchemy of Race* (Cambridge, MA: Harvard University Press, 1999).

Jarvie, G. (ed.), *Sport, Racism and Ethnicity* (London: Falmer Press, 1991).

Jenkins, P., *Intimate Enemies: Moral Panics in Contemporary Great Britain* (Berlin: Aldine de Gruyter, 1992).

Jessop, B., K. Bonnett, S. Bromley and T. Ling, *Thatcherism: A Tale of Two Nations* (Cambridge: Polity, 1989).

Kerr, J., *Understanding Soccer Hooliganism* (London: Open University Press, 1994).

King, A., *The End of the Terraces: The Transformation of English Football in the 1990s* (Leicester: Leicester University Press, 1998).

King, C., *Offside Racism: Playing the White Man* (Oxford: Berg, 2004).

Kolchin, P., 'Whiteness Studies: The New History of Race in America', *The Journal of American History*, 89:1 (June 2002), pp. 154–73.

Lang, J., *Report of the Working Party on Crowd Behaviour at Football Matches* (London: HMSO, 1969).

Lewis, G., 'Black Women's Employment and the British Economy', in W. James and C. Harris (eds), *Inside Babylon: The Caribbean Diaspora in Britain* (London: Verso, 1993), pp. 73–96.

Lewis, J. M., 'Crowd Control at English Football Matches', *Sociological Focus*, 15:4 (1982), pp. 417–23.

Lewis, J. M., and A. Scarisbrick-Hauser, 'An Analysis of Crowd Safety Reports Using the McPhail Categories', in R.Giulianotti, N. Bonney and M. Hepworth (eds), *Football, Violence and Social Identity* (London: Routledge, 1994), pp. 153–68.

Lipsitz, G. *The Possessive Investment in Whiteness: How White People Profit from Identity Politics* (Philadelphia, PA: Temple University Press, 1998).

Lowenthal, D., *The Past Is a Foreign Country* (Cambridge: Cambridge University Press, 1985).

—, *The Heritage Crusade and the Spoils of History* (Harmondsworth: Penguin, 1997).

Lowles, N., 'Far out with the Far Right', in M. Perryman (ed.), *Hooligan Wars: Causes and Effects of Football Violence* (Edinburgh: Mainstream, 2001).

Lyon, D. (ed.), *Theorizing Surveillence: The Panopticon and Beyond* (Devon: Willan, 2006).

MacPhee, G., and P. Poddar (eds), *Empire and After: Englishness in Postcolonial Perspective* (Oxford: Berghahn, 2007).

Mali, J., *Mythistory: The Making of a Modern Historiography* (Chicago, IL: University of Chicago Press, 2003).

Mangan, J. A. (ed.), *Making European Masculinities: Sport, Europe, Gender* (London: Frank Cass, 2000).

Mangan, J. A., and A. Ritchie (eds), *Ethnicity, Sport, Identities: Struggles for Status* (London: Frank Cass, 2004).

Marsh, P., *Aggro: The Illusion of Violence* (Toronto: J. M. Dent & Sons Ltd, 1978).

Mason, T., and R. Holt, *Sport in Britain, 1945–2000* (Oxford: Blackwell, 1998).

McCrone, D., 'Unmasking Brittania: The Rise and Fall of British National Identity', *Nations and Nationalism*, 3:4 (1997), pp. 579–96.

McDevitt, P. F., *'May the Best Man Win': Sport, Masculinity and Nationalism in Great Britain and the Empire, 1880–1935* (London: Palgrave Macmillian, 2004).

Meeusen, W., 'European Economic Integration: From Business Cycle to Business Cycle', in R. Wakeman (ed.), *Themes in European History since 1945* (London: Routledge, 2003), pp. 234–62.

Miles, R., *Racism and Migrant Labour* (London: Routledge, 1982).

—, *Racism* (London: Routledge, 1989).

Miles, R., and A. Phizacklea (eds), *Racism and Political Action in Britain* (London: Routledge, 1979).

Moran, R., 'Racism in Football: A Victim's Perspective', *Soccer and Society*, 1:1 (2000), pp. 190–200.

Morgan, K. O., *The People's Peace* (Oxford: Oxford University Press, 1990).

Morley, D., and K. Chen (eds), *Stuart Hall: Critical Dialogues in Cultural Studies* (London: Routledge, 1996).

Murphy, P., J.Williams and E. Dunning (eds), *Football on Trial: Spectator Violence and Development in the Football World* (London: Routledge, 1990).

Murray, B., *The World's Game: A History of Soccer* (Urbana, IL: University of Illinois Press, 1996).

—, *The Old Firm: Sectarianism, Sport and Society in Scotland* (Cork: Collins Press, 2001).

Newbury, A., 'Youth Crime: Whose Responsibility?', *Journal of Law and Society*, 35 (2008), p. 131–49.

Norris, C., and G. Armstrong, *The Maximum Surveillance Society* (Oxford: Berg, 1999).

O'Neill, M., *Policing Football: Social Interaction and Negotiated Disorder* (London: Palgrave Macmillan, 2005).

Orakwue, S., *Pitch Invaders: The Modern Black Football Revolution* (London: Vista, 1998).

Patterson, S., *Dark Strangers* (Harmondsworth: Penguin, 1968).

Paul, K., *Whitewashing Britain: Race and Citizenship in the Postwar Era* (Ithaca, NY: Cornell University Press, 1997).

Peach, C., 'Empire, the Economy and Immigration: Britain 1850–2000', in P. Slack and R. Ward (eds), *The Peopling of Britain: The Shaping of a Human Landscape* (Oxford: Oxford University Press, 2002), pp. 255–80.

Pearson, G., *Hooligan: A History of Respectable Fears* (London: Macmillan, 1983).

Perryman, M. (ed.), *Hooligan Wars: Causes and Effects of Football Violence* (Edinburgh: Mainstream, 2001).

Phillips, M. (ed.), *Deconstructing Sports History: A Postmodern Analysis* (Albany, NY: State University of New York Press, 2006).

Polley, M., *Moving the Goalposts: A History of Sport and Society since 1945* (London: Routledge, 1998).

Portelli, A., 'The Rich and the Poor in the Culture of Football', in R. Haynes and S. Redhead (eds), *The Passion and the Fashion: Football Fandom in the New Europe* (Aldershot: Avebury, 1994).

Preston, I., and S. Szymanski, 'Racial Discrimination in English Football', *Scottish Journal of Political Economy*, 47:4 (September 2000), pp. 342–63.

Redhead, S., 'Some Reflections on Discourses on Football Hooliganism', *Sociological Review*, 39:3 (1991), pp. 479–86.

—, *Post-Fandom and the Millennial Blues: The Transformation of Soccer Culture* (London: Routledge, 1997).

Rex, J., *Race, Colonialism and the City* (London: Routledge, 1973).

—, *Race Relations in Sociological Theory*, 2nd edn (London: Routledge, 1983).

Robins, D., *We Hate Humans* (Harmondsworth: Penguin, 1984).

Robins, D., and P. Cohen, *Knuckle Sandwich: Growing up in a Working-Class City* (Harmondsworth: Penguin, 1978).

Roediger, D., *The Wages of Whiteness: Race and the Making of the American Working Class* (London: Verso, 1991).

Rose, E. J. B., and N. Deakin (eds), *Colour, Citizenship and British Society* (London: Panther, 1970).

Rose, S. O., 'Cultural Analysis and Moral Discourses: Episodes, Continuities, and Transformations', in V. E. Bonnell and L. Hunt (eds), *Beyond the Cultural Turn: New Directions in the Study of Society and Culture* (Berkeley, CA: California University Press, 1999).

Rose, S., and H. Rose, 'Less Than Human Nature: Biology and the New Right', *Race & Class*, 27:3 (1986), pp. 47–66.

Samuel, R., *Theatres of Memory, Volume I: Past and Present in Contemporary Culture* (London: Verso, 1994).

—, *Theatres of Memory, Volume II: Island Stories: Unravelling Britain* (London: Verso, 1998).

Sandbrook, D., *White Heat: A History of Britain in the Swinging Sixties* (London: Abacus, 2006).

Schwarz, B., '"The Only White Man in There": the Re-Racialization of England, 1956–1968', *Race & Class*, 38:1 (1996), pp. 65–78.

Sivanandan, A., *A Different Hunger: Writings on Black Resistance* (London: Pluto,1982).

Skellington, R., 'Race', in *Britain Today*, 2nd edn (London: Sage, 1996).

Smith, A. M., *New Right Discourse on Race and Sexuality: Britain, 1968–1990* (Cambridge: Cambridge University Press, 1994).

Smith, R., *Children and the Courts* (London: Sweet and Maxwell, 1979).

Solomos, J., *Black Youth, Racism and the State* (Cambridge: Cambridge University Press, 1988).

—, *Race and Racism in Britain*, 3rd edn (London: Routledge, 2003).

Solomos, J., and L. Back, *Racism and Society* (London: Palgrave Macmillan, 1996).

Spencer, I., *British Immigration Policy since 1939: The Making of Multi-Racial Britain* (London: Routledge, 1997).

Stott, C., 'How Conflict Escalates: The Inter-Group Dynamics of Collective Football Crowd "Violence"', *Sociology*, 32 (1998), pp. 353–77.

—, 'Police Expectations and the Control of English Soccer Fans at 'Euro 2000', *Policing: An International Journal of Police Strategies and Management*, 26 (2003), pp. 640–55.

Tabili, L., 'The Construction of Racial Difference in Twentieth-Century Britain: The Special Restriction (Coloured Alien Seamen) Order, 1925', *Journal of British Studies*, 33 (January 1994), pp. 54–98.

—, *'We Ask for British Justice': Workers and Racial Difference in Late Imperial Britain* (Ithaca, NY: Cornell University Press, 1994).

—, 'Race is a Relationship and Not a Thing', *Journal of Social History*, 37:1 (Fall 2003), pp. 125–30.

—, 'A Homogenous society? Britain's Internal "Others", 1800–Present', in C. Hall and S. Rose (eds), *At Home with the Empire: Metropolitan Culture and the Imperial World* (Cambridge: Cambridge University Press, 2006), pp. 53–76.

Taylor, I., 'Soccer Consciosness and Soccer Hooliganism', in S. Cohen (ed.), *Images of Deviance* (Harmondsworth: Penguin, 1976), pp. 134–64.

—, 'Class, Violence and Sport: The Case of Soccer Hooliganism in Britain', in H. Cantelon and R. Gruneau (eds), *Sport, Culture and the Modern State* (Toronto: University of Toronto Press, 1982), pp. 39–97.

—, 'On the Sports Violence Question: Soccer Hooliganism Revisited', in J. Hargreaves (ed.), *Sport, Culture and Ideology* (London: Routledge, 1982), pp. 152–97.

—, 'English Football in the 1990s: Taking Hillsborough Seriously?', in J. Williams and S. Wagg (eds), *British Football and Social Change: Getting into Europe* (Leicester: Leicester University Press, 1991), pp. 3–24.

Taylor, M., *The Association Game: A History of British Football* (London: Longman, 2007).

Taylor, R., *Football and Its Fans: Supporters and Their Relations with the Game, 1885–1985* (Leicester: Leicester University Press, 1992).

Taylor, R., and A. Ward (eds), *Kicking and Screaming: An Oral History of Football in England* (London: Robson, 1995).

Taylor, R., A. Ward and J. Williams (eds), *Three Sides of the Mersey: An Oral History of Everton, Liverpool and Tranmere Rovers* (London: Robson, 1998).

Taylor, S., *The National Front in English Politics* (London: Macmillan, 1982).

Thomas, P., 'Kicking Racism out of Football: A Supporter's View', *Race & Class*, 36:4 (January 1995), pp. 95–101.

Thompson, K., *Moral Panics* (London: Routledge, 1998).

Trivizas, E., 'Offences and Offenders in Football Crowd Disorders', *British Journal of Criminology*, 20:3 (1980), pp. 276–88.

—, 'Sentencing the "Football Hooligan"', *British Journal of Criminology*, 21:4 (1981), pp. 342–9.

—, 'Disturbances Associated with Football Matches', *British Journal of Criminology*, 24:4 (1984), pp. 361–83.

Tsoukala, A., *Football Hooliganism in Europe: Security and Civil Liberties in the Balance* (London: Palgrave, 2009).

Turner, R., *In Your Blood: Football Culture in the Late 1980s and Early 1990s* (London: Working Press, 1990).

Vasili, P., *The First Black Footballer: Arthur Wharton, 1865–1930* (London: Frank Cass, 1998).

—, *Colouring over the White Line: The History of Black Footballers in Britain* (Edinburgh: Mainstream, 2000).

Waddington, P. A. J., 'Mugging as a Moral Panic: A Question of Proportion', *British Journal of Sociology*, 37:2 (1986), pp. 245–59.

Wagg, S. (ed.), *British Football and Social Exclusion* (London: Routledge, 2004).

Wakeman, R., 'The Golden Age of Prosperity, 1953–73', in R. Wakeman (ed.), *Themes in European History Since 1945* (London: Routledge, 2003), pp. 59–85.

Walvin, J., *Football and the Decline of Britain* (London: Macmillan, 1986).

—, *The People's Game: The History of Football Revisited* (Edinburgh: Mainstream, 1994).

Ware, V., and L. Back, *Out of Whiteness: Color, Politics, and Culture* (Chicago, IL: University of Chicago Press, 2002).

Waters, C., '"Dark Strangers" in Our Midst: Discourses of Race and Nation in Britain, 1947–1963', *Journal of British Studies*, 36:2 (April 1997), pp. 207–38.

Watt, T. (ed.), *The End: 80 Years of Life on Arsenal's North Bank* (Edinburgh: Mainstream, 1993).

Webster, W., *Imagining Home: Gender, 'Race' and National Identity, 1945–64* (London: University College London Press, 1998).

Weight, R., *Patriots: National Identity in Britain, 1940–2000* (London: Macmillan, 2002).

Weitz, E., 'The Heroic Man and the Ever-Changing Woman: Gender and Politics in European Communism, 1917–1950', in L. L. Frader and S. O. Rose (eds), *Gender and Class in Modern Europe* (Ithaca, NY: Cornell University Press, 1996), pp. 311–52.

Whannel, G., 'Football Crowd Behavior and the Press.' *Media, Culture & Society*, 1 (1979), pp. 327–42.

Whipple, A., 'Revisiting the "Rivers of Blood" Controversy: Letters to Enoch Powell', *Journal of British Studies*, 48:3 (July 2009), pp. 717–35.

Williams, J., 'Football Hooliganism: Offences, Arrests and Violence – A Critical Note', *British Journal of Law and Society*, 7:1 (1980), pp. 104–11.

—, 'Having an Away Day: English Football Spectators and the Hooligan Debate', in J. Williams and S. Wagg (eds), *British Football and Social Change: Getting into Europe* (Leicester: Leicester University Press, 1991), pp. 160–84.

—, *Lick My Boots: Racism in English Football* (Leicester: University of Leicester, 1992).

Williams, J.,'Rangers is a Black Club: Race, Identity and Local Football in England', in J. Williams and R. Giulianotti (eds), *Game Without Frontiers: Football, Identity and Modernity* (Aldershot: Ashgate, 1994), pp. 153–83.

—, 'Who You Calling a Hooligan?', in M. Perryman (ed.), *Hooligan Wars: Causes and Effects of Football Violence* (Edinburgh: Mainstream, 2001), pp. 37–53.

Williams, J., E. Dunning and P. Murphy (eds), *Hooligans Abroad* (London: Routledge, 1984).

Williams, J., and S. Wagg (eds), *British Football and Social Change: Getting into Europe* (Leicester: Leicester University Press, 1991).

Williams, M. H., *The Impact of Radical Right-Wing Parties in West European Democracies* (London: Palgrave Macmillan, 2006).

Witt, R., and B. Reilly, 'English League Transfer Prices: Is There a Racial Dimension?', *Applied Economics Letters*, 2:7 (July 1995), pp. 220–2.

Witte, R., *Racist Violence and the State* (London: Longman, 1996).

Woolnough, B., *Black Magic: England's Black Footballers* (London: Pelham, 1983).

Wright, I., *Mr. Wright: The Explosive Autobiography of Ian Wright* (London: Collins Willow, 1996).

Wright, P., *On Living in an Old Country: The National Past* (London: Verso, 1985).

Young, J., 'The Role of Police as Amplifiers of Deviance: Negotiators of Drug Control as Seen in Notting Hill', in S. Cohen (ed.), *Images of Deviance* (Harmondsworth: Penguin, 1971), pp. 27–61.

INDEX

Page numbers in italics denote illustrations and figures. Page numbers including an 'n' refer to notes.

Agana, Tony (player), 216
Amokachi, Daniel (player), 228–9
Anderson, Viv (player), 228
Anti-Fascist Action (AFA), 166, 176, 179, 195, 195–9, 200
Anti-Fascist Football Fans Congress, 198
anti-fascist groups, 16, 147–8, 150, 162–3, 166–72
  links with anti-racism, 179, 194–202
Anti-Nazi League (ANL), 166, 169–70, 195
anti-racism, 2, 9, 175–203
  campaigns, 179–81, 196–8
  education, 175, 178, 181–2, 184
  fanzines, 175, 176, 179, 180, 182, 183, 186–202
  Germany, 198
  image of, 178
  initiatives to counteract anti-racism, 221–9
  links with anti-fascism, 179, 194–202
  post-war era analysis, 6–10
  role of police, 183–4
  role of women, 176–7, 179, 193–4
  use of football environment, 177, 178–9, 180–2, 232
Armstrong, Gary, 253n39
Armstrong, Gary (ethnographer), 114
Asian footballers, 208, 219–20, 233–4
Association Contre La Violence Dans Le Sport, 47
Association of Chief Police Officers (ACPO), 99, 105, 106, 109

banana throwing, 153–4, 172, 177, 183, 211, 214
Barnes, John (player), 211, 216
BBC, 164
Beckford, Darren (player), 182
Best, Clyde (player), 208
biracial football couplets, 225–8, 227
black footballers, 8, 23, 147, 148, 150–1, 205–30, 232
  abuse of, 2, 152–4, 155–6, 171-2, 177, 182, 183, 208–13
  aggression, 217–18
  as ambassadors for anti-racism, 222–4
  biracial football couplets, 225–8, 227
  discrimination by football clubs, 2, 189–91, 219, 228–9
  History of Black Footballers in Britain (exhibition), 222
  professionalism, 214–16
  responses to racial abuse, 205–6, 209, 229–30
  as role models, 224–5, 230
  use of humour to avert racism, 216
  visiting players, 210
  'whiteness', pressure of, 17, 206–8, 213–21, 222–3, 225, 229, 230
black people, image of, 22–3, 159, 201, 212
Blake, Noel (Birmingham player), 154
Blatter, Sepp (FIFA president), 235
bourgeois values, 15, 17
Bright, Mark (player), 215

Britain
    economy, 21–3, 26, 27
    national mythologies, 40, 52–3
    national values, 59–60, 65
    role in international affairs, 20–1
    sporting image, 40, 61, 64–5
British National Party (BNP), 165
British Rail, 119
Britishness, culture of, 8–9, 10, 17, 52–3,
    151
Bulldog (NF newspaper), 152–7, 163, 164,
    165, 167, 170
Bullstreet, K (anti-fascist), 168–9

Callaghan, James (Home Secretary), 113,
    136, 137, 140
Campaign Against Racism and Fascism
    (CARF), 166, 195–6
Carter-Jones, Lewis (Labour MP), 58
Cashmore, Ellis (sociologist), 216
casuals, 16, 29, 36–7
CCTV, 16, 98, 114, 120–1, 183, 188, 234
Celtic Fans Against Racism (fanzine), 199
chanting, 155–6, 172, 177, 183, 184, 209
Charlton, Bobby (player), 62
Charlton, Jack (player), 170
Children and Young Persons Act (1969),
    124, 139–40
civil rights, 84, 109, 123
Clarke, John, 4
Claxton, J. F. (DPP), 108–9
Clemitson, Ivor (Labour MP), 60, 132
closed-circuit television *see* CCTV
Clough, Brian (manager), 170
Colquhoun, John (player), 214, 215
Commission for Racial Equality (CRE), 14,
    176, 178, 179–86, 225
Communist Party of England, 154
community self-policing, 9–10, 176, 186–8,
    193–5, 197, 200, 240n40
    Coventry, 115–16
    Leicester, 191, 192
conference of anarchists, anti-fascists and
    football supporters (1994), 198–9
Conservative Party, 25
    economic policies, 21–2, 26
    reactions to football violence, 49, 50
Cookson, Bernard (cartoonist), 86, *86f3.1*

Crooks, Garth (player), 182
crowd safety, 72–3
Crown Courts, 128, 142

Daily Express, *86*
Daily Mail, 43
Daily Star, 163
Daily Telegraph, 45
Deighton, Ted (Secretary, Leeds Joint
    Branch Board of Police), 48
Department of the Environment, 123, 125,
    135, 138, 142
Direct Action Movement (anarchist group),
    166, 169
disasters, 6, 69–70, 78–9, 80, 164, 165, 167,
    239n26
documentary sources, 11–12
Drago, Charles (Director, Association Con-
    tre La Violence Dans Le Sport), 47

Eagle Eye (fanzine), 196
Elkins, Caroline (writer), 2
Elliot, Paul (player), 224
Evening News, 86, *86*
Evening Standard, 86

FA Premier League, 234
fans *see* supporters
fanzines, 175, 176, 179, 180, 182, 183
    anti-fascist influences, 194–202
    and anti-racism, 186–94, 206, 221
    promotion of violence, 200–1
    and 'whiteness', 219–21
Fashanu, John (player), 224
Follows, Denis (Football Association), 78,
    105
Ferguson, Alex (manager, Manchester
    United), 234–5
Fighting Talk (AFA publication), 195, 196,
    198, 199, 229
Filbo Fever (fanzine), 187
Flashing Blade (fanzine), 187, 189–90
football
    anti-fascist groups, 147–8, 150, 166–72
    anti-racism, 10–11, 17, 175–203
    influence of Thatcherite policies, 27
    neo-fascist activities, 147–66
    protection of reputation, 53–60, 65

racial abuse, 208–13
racism, 14, 17, 147, 148–9, 175–203
rivalries, 8, 28, 32, 35
role in society, 10–11, 20, 27–8
Football Association, 54–5, 134, 195, 234
football authorities, reactions to football
    violence, 42, 46, 58–9
football clubs
    and anti-racist campaigns, 179–80
    Arsenal, 84, 91, 100, 107
    Aston Villa, 102
    Barnsley, 190–1, 219
    Birmingham City, 154, 216, 250n42
    black players, discrimination by clubs, 2,
        189–91, 219, 221, 228–9
    Blackburn, 119, 218
    Cardiff, 119
    Celtic, 46, 92–3, 223–4
    Charlton Athletic, 193
    Chelsea, *170*
    Coventry City, 118, 153, 213
    Crystal Palace, 189
    Everton, 119, 192, 193, 228–9
    Glasgow Rangers, 76, 78, 135
    Halifax Town, 100
    Huddersfield Town, 54
    Leeds United, 31, 66, 102, 112, 156, 188
    Leicester City, 187, 191–2
    Manchester United, 57, *58*, 66, 90, 92,
        100, 234–5
    Middlesbrough, 84, 93
    Millwall, 214
    Newcastle, 55, 76
    Nottingham County, 93
    Nottingham Forest, 170
    Queens Park Rangers, 117
    resistance to space divisions, 92–4
    Rotherham Town, 150, 222
    Sheffield United, 187, 189–90, 216
    Sheffield Wednesday, 69–70, 170, 190
    Spurs, 62–6, 188
    St Helen's, 54
    St Pauli (Hamburg), 198
    Stoke, 119
    Sunderland, 154, 196
    Torquay United, 188–9, 229
    West Ham, 153, *196*
    see also stadiums; supporters

Football Foundation, 234
Football League, 55, 118, 195
Football Offences Act (1991), 184, 221
Football Supporters' Association, 192, 196-
    7, 200
Football Task Force (FTF), 184–6, 188, 224
Football Trust, 121, 179
Football Unites, Racism Divides, 12, 197,
    221, 222, 233–4
football violence
    anti-fascist views on, 168–9
    challenge to national mythologies, 53
    explanations of, 28
    exploitation by politicians, 39, 40,
        49–51, 53–4, 73
    forms of, 29–36
    government response to, 15–16, 28
    historiography, 2–6
    links with racism, 9, 11, 175–203
    neo-fascist activities, 151–6
    police attitudes, 47–9
    sensationalization by media, 39, 41–2
    spatial divisions, use for prevention, 45,
        72–82
    see also disasters; moral panics
Foreign and Commonwealth Office, 61–2,
    65
Foucault, Michael, 70–1
Foxes Against Racism (FAR), 187, 191–2
Freud, Clement (Liberal MP), 55–6

Gannon, Jim (player), 217
Garden House Hotel trial (1970), 25
Garnett, Alf (TV character), 267n62
gender exclusion, 9, 10, 15, 176–7, 179,
    193–4, 198-9
Giles, Ronald Carl (cartoonist), 57, *58*
Gilroy, Paul, 14
Giulianotti, Richard, 53
Green, Stuart (writer), 226
Griffiths, Eldon (Conservative MP), 60, 79
Guardian, 44–5, 64, 65–6

Hain, Peter (ANL organizer), 169–70
Hall, Stuart, 4, 25, 41, 230
Hardaker, Alan (chairman of Football
    League), 135–6

Harrington commission, 48–9, 53, 56, 74–6, 103–4, 115, 120, 246n32, 249n12
Hattersley, Roy (government minister), 66
Hendrie, Colin (MUSA spokesman), 235
Heysel disaster (1985), 6, 164, 165, 167
Hillsborough disaster (1989), 6, 69–70
hippies, 47–8
History of Black Footballers in Britain (exhibition), 222, 267n55
Home Office, 29, 30, 49–51, 79, 98–9, 109, 110, 116
hooks, bell, 218–19
hooliganism, definition and use of, 14, 15, 31
Hornby, Nick (writer), 210–11
Howard, Michael (Home Secretary), 181
Howell, Denis (Sports Minister), 20, 40, 59–60, 73, 99, 106, 232
    attempts to circumvent legal restrictions, 135, 138–43
    and CCTV, 121
    comments on working-class families, 133–4
    and football violence abroad, 64, 66, 67
    identification policies, 118, 119
    lack of regard for spectators, 87–8
    moral entrepreneur, 51–2, 125
    policy of containment, 82–8
    in praise of police, 113

Ibrox Park disaster (1971), 6, 78–9, 80
ID cards, 98, 118–20
identification policies, 114, 116–21, 129
immigration, 7, 9, 22–3, 212
    government policies, 27
Immigration Act 1971, 25
Ince, Paul (player/manager), 218, 219
Indian Workers' Movement, 154
Industrial Relations Act 1971, 25

Jenkins, Roy (Chancellor of the Exchequer), 22, 49, 50, 51, 109, 139, 140–1, 142, 143
Johanneson, Albert (player), 208
Johnson, A. (Chairman, National Union of Football Supporters), 119
Johnson, James (Labour MP), 106
Johnson, Walter (Labour MP), 50, 131–2

Kamara, Chris (player), 210, 216
Kaye, Howard, 91
Kendal, Amanda (journalist), 182
Kick It! (fanzine), 180, 182, 183, 225–6
Kick It Out (anti-racist campaign) *see* Let's Kick Racism Out of Football
King, Colin (sociologist and former player), 218

Labour Party
    economic policies, 21–2, 26
    penal reform, 124, 140–1
    reactions to football violence, 49, 50, 51, 144
    role in anti-racism, 184–6
    sport promotion, 184–5
Laing inquiry *see* Working Party on Crowd Behaviour at Football Matches
Laing, Sir John, 76, 136
Latham, Keith (supporter), 190
leafleting, 161–2, 169–70, 173
League of Louts, 163, 167
Leeds Fans United Against Racism and Fascism (LFUARF), 188, 196, 199, 201
Let's Kick Racism Out of Football (anti-racist campaign), 12, 179–81, 192, 196, 221–2, 224, 234, 263n6
licensing schemes, stadiums, 72, 78
logos, 157–8, *158*, 170, 175, *196*
Lomas, Kenneth (Labour MP), 50

Macfarlane, Neil (Conservative MP), 121, 132
Magistrates Association, 137–8
magistrates courts, 109, 124, 125, 126–7
    pressure to impose stricter sentences, 135–43
    see also punishment
Manchester United Fan Club, 134
Marching Altogether (fanzine), 188, 199, 200–1
Marqusee, Mark, 225
Marsh, Peter (ethnographer), 32
masculinity, 3, 4, 8, 10, 28, 158, 165
Mau Mau (Kenya), 2
Maudling, Reginald (Home Secretary), 126, 136, 136–7
McDonnell and Hughes Architects, 85

Mexico, 61–2
mods and rockers, 23–4, 41
monkey noises, 183, 190, 211, 214, 216
Monro, Hector (Conservative MP), 60
Moore, Bobby (player), *227*, 228
moral panics, 29, 67
  analysis, 40–3
  influence of interest groups, 46–51
  social context, 43–6
Moran, Richie (player), 216
Mumford, Gary (NF supporter), 162
Munro, Henry (Minister for Sport), 79
mythologies *see* national mythologies

National Coalition Building Institute, 191
National Federation of Football Supporters, 119
National Football Intelligence Unit, 118
National Front News, 162
National Front (NF), 148, 149, 151–60
  and anti-fascist groups, 167–8, 170–2
  black players, abuse of, 152–4
  campaigning activities, 161–2
  dissociation from violent tactics, 165–6
  media attention, 163, 164–5
  newspapers, 152–7, 162–3, 164, 165, 167, 170–3
  opposition to multiculturalism, 158–9
  recruitment activities, 156–8, *157*, 161
  street violence, encouragement of, 161–2
  use of international matches, 155, 164
  youth participation, 163–4
national mythologies, 40, 52–3, 148–9
National Union of Football Supporters, 119
Neill, Terry (manager), 84
neo-fascism, 12, 14, 16, 147–73
  dissociation from violent tactics, 164–6
  newspapers, 162–3, 164, 165, 167, 170-3
  political impact, 150
  use of football to promote ideologies, 151–3, 155, 160–6, 232
newspapers
  and neo-fascism, 170-3
  exaggeration of football violence, 39, 41-2
  reactions to spatial discipline proposals, 86
  role in demonizing youth, 44

Noades, Ron (chairman, Crystal Palace FC), 189
Ntende, Paul 'Delroy' (comic character), 226, *227*

Ostend, 66
Our Day Will Come (fanzine), 199–200, 202
Ouseley, Sir Herman (executive chairman, CRE), 180, 182, 183

parental responsibility, 125–6, 133–4, 144
Partnership to Keep Racism Out of Football, 224
Pearce, Stuart (player), 218
Pelé (Brazilian player), *227*, 228
photography, 117–18
physical space divisions in stadiums, 72–82, 122
  admission controls, 74, 78, 93
  commercial barrier products, 85
  crush barriers, 80, 81, 90
  detention facilities, 84, 110–11
  ditches, 75, 89
  end-taking, 89–90
  funding, 73, 92–3
  gangways, 73–4, 75
  minimum personal space, 81
  penning, 74–5, 83
  perimeter fences, 75–7
  resistance to, 89–95
  role in promoting supporter confrontation, 84
  slope inclines, 80, 81
pitch invasions, 30–1, 32, 75, 76–7, *86*, 89
police authorities
  Birmingham, 117
  Cheshire, 56
  Coventry, 117, 118
  Derby, 105
  Dumfries and Galloway, 35
  Edinburgh, 107
  Glasgow, 74–5, 103, 135
  Leeds United, 48
  Liverpool, 56, 109
  Luton, 116
  Manchester, 118
  meetings with government agencies, 98–100

Metropolitan Police, 30, 105–6, 115, 120–1, 126
Middlesbrough, 118, 133
Newcastle, 33, 76–7, 118
Oxford, 33
Scotland Yard, 83, 100, 109, 118, 127
Sheffield, 56
Stoke-on-Trent, 35, 103, 115, 118
Sunderland, 133
Swindon, 33–4
West Midlands, 121
York, 48–9, 74
Police (magazine), 47–8
police records, 4, 29–30, 33–4, 127, 128
policing, 1, 2, 16, 97–121
    arrests, 104, 108–10, 111, 125–6, 129
    brutality, 65–6, 87, 90–1, 111–14, 122
    costs, 100
    crowd control tactics, 73–4, 104–6
    detention of spectators, 84, 110–11
    dogs, use of, 104, 105–6, 112
    horses, use of, 104–5, 112, 253n37, 253n39
    identification policies, 116–21, 129
    information sharing, 116–17
    photography, use of, 117–18
    racism, 183–4
    ratios, 100, 252n12
    refusal to protect citizens, 111–12
    relations with supporters, 33–4, 100–2, 104
    snatch squads, 104
    stewards, use of, 100, 107–8
    tactics and strategies, 102–11, 122
    verbal networks of communication, 114–16
    see also community self-policing
Policy Studies Institute (PSI), 180
political ideology, 150
Polkinghorne, David (New Scotland Yard), 221
Portelli, Alessandro, 4
Powell, Enoch (MP), 22–3
Powers of Criminal Courts Act 1973, 137
Price, W. F. B. (Consulate-General, Rotterdam), 63, 64, 65
Price, William (Labour MP), 50

Professional Footballers' Association (PFA), 176, 178, 179–86, 234
Public Education Campaign, 181–2
punishment, 122–45
    attendance centres, 131, 137–8, 139, 140
    avoidance of, 130
    charges, 126–7, 128, 129
    community service, 141
    corporal punishment, 134, 142–3, 144
    delays in court appearances, 125–6
    fines, 16, 130, 132–4, 135
    forms of punishment, 127, 129–35
    parliamentary discussions, 130–2
    reports of trials, 128
    sentencing policies, 2, 127, 135–43

Race Relations Act 1965, 212
race riots, 5, 14, 17, 27, 101, 155, 172, 212
Race, Rocky (comic character), 226
racial abuse, black footballers, 9
racism, 175–203
    campaigns against, 179–86
    development of conceptualizations, 13–14, 147
    links with fascism, 149
    post-war era analysis, 6–10
    public and political debate, 148
    see also whiteness
Racist League, 163
Reading Council for Racial Equality, 188, 224
Red Action (anti-fascist magazine), 167
Red Attitude (fanzine), 198, 199–200
Rees, Merlyn (Home Secretary), 118, 142–3
Regis, Cyrille (player), 209, 210
Rivers of Blood speech, 1968 (Powell), 22–3
Rotterdam, 61, 62–6
Roy of the Rovers (football comic), 226, *227*
Runnymede Trust, 182

Safety at Sports Ground Bill, 49, 72–3, 82, 121, 138, 142
Salim, Abdul (player), 223–4
Searchlight (anti-fascist magazine), 164, 166–7, 170–1, 195
self-identification, 28, 36–7
sentencing policies *see* punishment
Show Racism the Red Card, 221

skinheads, 23, 29, 35–6, 43, 44, 156
Smith, C. D. (Chairman, MUSU), 92
Smith, David (Chairman, National Federation of Football Supporters Clubs), 104
social exclusion, 27
Socialist Workers' Party (SWP), 166, 169, 193
South Riding (fanzine), 190–1
sport, promotion of, 20
Sports Council, 20, 52
spot the ball competitions, 73
Spriggs, Leslie (Labour MP), 54, 55, 132
stadiums
    Ayresome Park, 84
    containment policies, 82–8
    detention facilities, 84, 110–11
    disasters, 6, 69–70, 78–9, 164, 165, 167, 239n26
    Goodison Park, 208
    Hampden Park, 75
    Heysel, 6, 164, 165, 167
    Highbury, 84
    Hillsborough, 6, 69–70
    Ibrox Park, 34, 75, 78–9, 80
    Leeds, 31, 120
    licensing schemes, 72, 78
    Millwall, 105
    Old Trafford, 92, 118, 234–5
    pitch invasions, 30–1, 32, 75, 76–7, *86*, 89
    safety, 50
    seated areas, 90, 197, 234, 264n26
    spatial organization, 1, 6, 15–16, 45, 69–82
    St James Park, 76
    swaying among spectators, 31, 74, 77, 81, 104
    Tranmere, 30
    Upton Park, 93
    Wembley, 75, 157
    White Hart Lane, 101–2
state violence, historiography, 2–6
Stein, Mark (player), 217
Stephens, C. J. (Home Office Chief Scientist), 79–80
stewards, role in policing, 100, 107–8
Stormer (NF comic), 161
street violence, 161–2

student uprisings 1968, 24–5
subcultures, 23–4, 29, 35–6, 43, 156–7
    Chelsea, 156–7
Sunday Mirror, 164
supporters, 71
    arrests by police, 104, 108–10, 111, 125–6, 129
    Arsenal, 101
    Aston Villa, 102
    banana throwing, 153–4, 172, 177, 183, 211, 214
    Barnsley, 190–1
    behaviour, 14, 15, 29–36, 183, 184
    behaviour outside stadiums, 36, 63, 83, 154, 161–2, 196
    behaviour when abroad, 40, 53, 60–6, 82, 155
    Birmingham City, 154
    and black footballers, 153
    Bristol, 32, 125–6
    Cardiff City, 125–6
    Celtic, 199
    chanting, 155–6, 172, 177, 183, 184, 209
    Charlton Athletic, 193
    Chelsea, 30, 163
    class distinctions, 56
    Coventry City, 118
    Crystal Palace, 189
    demonizing of, 41–2, 55–7
    detention by police, 84, 110–11
    Everton, 192, 193, 208, 228
    group culture, 35–6
    Halifax Town, 101
    Hearts, 214
    ID cards, 98, 118–20
    identification policies, 114, 116–21, 129
    Leeds United, 31, 102, 112, 120, 156, 188, 196, 199, 200
    Leicester City, 187, 191–2
    Liverpool, 33, 69–70
    Manchester United, 34–5, 66, 90, 92, 101, 104, 118, 134, 199, 218, 235
    Middlesbrough, 101, 111
    monkey noises, 183, 190, 211, 214, 216
    National Front (NF) recruitment, 156–7
    Newcastle, 30
    non-violent supporters, 90–2, 104, 113
    Nottingham Forest, 128

partisanship, 21, 28, 35
Portsmouth, 210
relations with police, 33–4, 100–2, 104
resistance to space divisions, 89–95
responses to anti-racism, 186–94
segregation, 6, 71, 74–5, 82–8, 93–4
Sheffield United, 187, 189–90, 216
social background, 3–4, 4–5, 56
Spurs, 62–6, 101–2
swaying, 31, 74, 77, 81, 104
territorial conflicts between rival fans,
    32–3, 34, 36, 61, 84, 89–90
Torquay United, 188–9, 199, 201
West Ham, 208
Wolverhampton, 128

Taverne, Dick (Home Office Minister),
    50–1, 131, 136
Taylor, Ian, 4
Taylor Report (1989), 69–70, 94, 264n26
Taylor, Teddy (Conservative MP), 131
Teddy boys, 23, 43
telephone hotlines, 115–16
terminology, use of, 13, 14, 15, 241n48,
    241n51
territorial conflicts between rival fans, 32–3,
    34, 84, 89–90
Thatcher, Margaret, 26–7, 64–5, 118, 147
Thomas, Danny (Coventry player), 153, 209,
    211, 216
Thompson, Garry (Coventry player), 153,
    211, 213, 216–17
Thorsvedt, Erik (player), 224
Times, The, 44, 45, 64, 221
Tiochfaid Ar La! (fanzine), 199, 223–4
Torney, Tom (Labour MP), 64
Trevelyan, D. J. (Home Office administra-
    tor), 115
Tyndall, John (head of NF), 163–4, 165

Ullyett, Roy (cartoonist), 86, 86*f*3.2
United Colours of Football (fanzine), 197–8

Vasili, Phil (writer), 222–3, 260n7
voting patterns, 150

weapons, 32–3, *86*
welfare state, 26
Wharton, Arthur (first professional black
    player), 150, 222–3, 260n7
Wheatley commission, 78–9
When Skies Are Grey (fanzine), 192, 193,
    228
whiteness, 206–8, 213–21, 222–3, 225, 229,
    230
Williamson, Frank (Chief Inspector of
    Crime), 103, 110–11, 115, 117, 130
Wilson, Harold, 20–1, 49
Wily, Ron (Coventry City Coach), 213
Winterbottom, Walter (Sports Council
    director), 46, 77, 81–2, 87, 249n11,
    249n23
women, 30
    complaints of police treatment, 91, 112
    exclusion, 9, 10, 15, 176–7, 179, 193–4
    feminist activists, 198–9
    National Front advertising, 157–8, *157*
    as parents, 133–4, 144
working-class people
    alienation from society, 4, 171–2
    anxieties about immigrant workers, 151,
        159
    culture, 21
    and neo-fascism, 160–6
    parents, 125–6, 133–4, 144
    relations with middle-classes, 57
    Thatcherite policies, 26–7
    values, 209–10, 222–3
    white identity, 23, 212–13
Working Party on Crowd Behaviour at
    Football Matches, 53, 76–9, 82–3, 107,
    115, 120, 135–6, 138, 246n51
Working Party on Football Hooliganism
    (1973-7), 72
World Cup (1966), 20–1, 43, 53, 105–6,
    241n7
World Cup (1970), 61–2
World Cup (2010), 235
Wray, John (Barnsley FC), 190

You Wot! (fanzine), 188–9, 199, 201, 229
youth degeneration, 23–6, 29, 41, 54, 55–7,
    132, 168

For Product Safety Concerns and Information please contact our EU
representative GPSR@taylorandfrancis.com
Taylor & Francis Verlag GmbH, Kaufingerstraße 24, 80331 München, Germany

www.ingramcontent.com/pod-product-compliance
Ingram Content Group UK Ltd.
Pitfield, Milton Keynes, MK11 3LW, UK
UKHW021620240425
457818UK00018B/652